The Economic Diplomacy of Peace in the Middle East

Libby Lahar

The Economic Diplomacy of Peace in the Middle East

Paris Protocol to the Oslo Accords

palgrave
macmillan

Libby Lahar
International Institute of Social Studies (ISS)
The Hague, of Erasmus University
Rotterdam, The Netherlands

ISBN 978-3-031-93990-7 ISBN 978-3-031-93991-4 (eBook)
https://doi.org/10.1007/978-3-031-93991-4

This Palgrave Macmillan imprint is published by the registered company Springer Nature Switzerland AG.
The registered company address is: Gewerbestrasse 11, 6330 Cham, Switzerland

Contents

Acronyms

AHLC	Ad Hoc Liaison Committee
ACRS	Arms Control and Regional Security of the Madrid Process Multilateral Track
BCBS	Basel Committee on Bank Supervision
BDS	Boycott Divestment and Sanctions
BOI	Bank of Israel
CAI	Comprehensive Agreement on Investment
CETA	European Union-Canada Comprehensive Trade Agreement
COGAT	Coordinator of Government Activities in the Territories
DFLP	Democratic Front for the Liberation of Palestine
DOP	Declaration of Principles on Interim Self-Government Arrangements
EC	European Commission
ECF	Economic Cooperation Foundation
EEAS	European External Action Service
EEC	European Economic Community
EFTA	European Free Trade Area
EP	European Parliament
EPA	Economic Partnership Agreement
ERP	European Recovery Programme
EU	European Union
EWG	Environment Working Group of the Madrid Process Multilateral Track
FFPA	Freezing of Funds paid by the Palestinian Authority in Connection with Terrorism from Revenues Transferred by the Israeli Government Law
FTA	Free Trade Agreement

FTZ	Free Trade Zone
GAFTA	Greater Arab Free Trade Area
GATT	General Agreement on Tariffs and Trade
GDP	Gross Domestic Product
GNP	Gross National Product
GOI	Government of Israel
HAMAS	Islamic Resistance Movement (Harakat al-Muqawama al-Islamiya)
ICC	International Criminal Court
ICJ	International Court of Justice
IDF	Israel Defense Forces
IMF	International Monetary Fund
JEC	Joint Economic Committee of the Oslo I Accord
JWC	Joint Water Committee of the Oslo II Accord
LAS	League of Arab States
MAG	Military Advocate General unit of the Israeli Defence Force
ME	Middle East
MENA	Middle East North Africa
MEPP	Middle East Peace Process
MNE	Multinational Enterprise
MS	Member State
NAFTA	North American Free Trade Agreement
NATO	North Atlantic Treaty Organization
NGO	Non-Governmental Organization
NIR	International Council of Swedish Industry (Näringslivets Internationella Råd)
NIS	New Israeli Sheqel
NWO	New World Order
NTB	Non-Tariff Barrier
OAS	Organization of the American States
ODA	Official Development Assistance
OECD	Organization for Economic Co-operation and Development
OECD DAC	the Organization for Economic Co-operation and Development's Development Assistance Committee
OIC	Organization of Islamic Cooperation
OPT	Occupied Palestinian Territory
OQ	Office of the Quartet
OQR	Office of the Quarter Representative
PA	Palestinian Authority
PADICO	Palestine Development and Investment Ltd.
PALTRADE	Palestinian Trade Center
PCBS	Palestinian Central Bureau of Statistics

PECDAR	Palestinian Economic Council for Development and Reconstruction
PFLP	Popular Front for the Liberation of Palestine
PIBF	Palestinian International Business Forum
PLO	Palestine Liberation Organization
PMA	Palestine Monetary Authority
PNA	Palestinian National Authority
PNC	Palestinian National Council
POG	Pot of Gold
PRDP	Palestinian Reform and Development Plan
PSF	Palestinian Security Forces
OQR	Office of the Quartet Representative
REDWG	Regional Economic Development Working Group of the Madrid Process Multilateral Track
RWG	Refugees Working Group of the Madrid Process Multilateral Track
SADC	Southern Africa Development Community
SDG	Sustainable Development Goals
SS	Protection Squadron (Schutzstaffel) of Nazi Germany
SUPR	Special Unite on Palestinian Rights of the United Nations
TIPH	Temporary International Presence in the city of Hebron
TPP	Transpacific Partnership
TTIP	Transatlantic Trade and Investment Partnership
UDHR	Universal Declaration of Human Rights
UAE	United Arab Emirates
UN	United Nations
UN CEIRPP	Committee on the Exercise of the Inalienable Rights of the Palestinian People
UNCTAD	United Nations Conference on Trade and Development
UNCTAD APPU	Assistance to the Palestinian People Unit
UNDP	United Nations Development Programme
UN DPI	United Nations Department of Public Information
UN ECOSOC	Economic and Social Council
UNESCO	United Nations Education, Scientific, and Culture Organization
UNGA	United Nations General Assembly
UNHCR	United Nations Human Rights Council
UNRWA	United Nations Relief and Works Agency for the Palestine Refugees in the Near East
UNSC	United Nations Security Council
UNSCO	United Nations Special Coordinator Office for the Middle East Peace Process

UNSG	United Nations Secretary-General
US	United States
USAID	United States Agency for International Development
USSR	Union of Soviet Socialist Republics
VAT	Value Added Tax
WB	World Bank of the United Nations
WB MDTF	World Bank Multi Donor Trust Fund
WB RTF	World Bank Public Financial Reform Trust Fund
WBGS	West Bank Gaza Strip
WCO	World Customs Organization
WTO	World Trade Organization
WW	World War
WWG	Water Resources Working Group of the Madrid Process Multilateral Track

Key Documents[1]

The Israeli-Palestinian Conflict

Date	Document
29 November 1947	United Nations General Assembly Resolution 181, Plan of Partition, UN Doc. GA Res. 181
21 November 1967	United Nations Security Council Resolution 242, The Situation in the Middle East, UN Doc. S/RES/242
21 October 1973	United Nations Security Council Resolution 338, Ceasefire in the Middle East, UN Doc. S/RES/338
22 November 1974	United Nations General Assembly Resolution 3236 (XXIX), Recognizing the Inalienable Rights of the Palestinian People in Palestine, UN Doc. GA RES/ 3236(XXIX)
20 August 1980	United Nations Security Council Resolution 478 condemning Israel's annexation of East Jerusalem, UN Doc. S/RES/478
14 November 1988	Palestinian National Council Declaration of Independence, UN Doc. A/43/827, S/20278
13 September 1993	Oslo I Accord—Declaration of Principles on Interim-Self Government Arrangements (DOP)
29 April 1994	Protocol on Economic Relations between the Government of the State of Israel and the Palestinian Liberation Organization representing the Palestinian people (also known as Paris Protocol)
4 May 1994	The Gaza Strip Jericho Area Agreement (also known as The Cairo Agreement)

[1] All the Agreements, Memorandums, and Protocols are part of the Oslo Peace Process between Israel and the Palestinian Liberation Organization (unless otherwise specified).

29 August 1994	Agreement on Preparatory Transfer of Powers and Responsibilities
27 August 1995	Protocol on Further Transfer of Powers and Responsibilities
28 September 1995	Oslo II Accord—The Interim Agreement on the West Bank and the Gaza Strip (also known as The Taba Agreement)
6 May 1996	Israel-PLO Permanent Status Negotiations-Joint Communique
9 May 1996	Agreement on Temporary International Presence in the City of Hebron (TIPH)
17 January 1997	Protocol Concerning the Redeployment in Hebron (also known as The Hebron Protocol)
23 October 1998	The Wye River Memorandum (also known as Wye Agreement)
4 September 1999	Sharm el-Sheikh Memorandum on Implementation Timeline of Outstanding Commitments of Agreements Signed and the Resumption of Permanent Status Negotiations
5 October 1999	Protocol Concerning Safe Passage between the West Bank and the Gaza Strip (also known as Safe Passage Protocol)
25 July 2000	Trilateral Statement on the Middle East Peace Summit at Camp David (United States President William J. Clinton; Israeli Prime Minister Ehud Barak; Palestinian Authority Chairman Yasser Arafat)
23 December 2000	The Clinton Parameters, President Clinton's Proposal on Israeli-Palestinian Peace
28 March 2002	The Saudi (Arab) Peace Initiative presented by Crown Prince Abdullah
30 April 2003	A Performance-Based Roadmap to a Permanent Two-State Solution to the Israeli-Palestinian Conflict of the Middle East Quarter
1 December 2003	Geneva Initiative (also known as Geneva Accord) led by former Israeli Minister Yossi Beilin and former Palestinian Authority Minister Yasser Abed Rabbo
9 July 2004	Legal Consequences of the Construction of a Wall in the Occupied Palestinian Territory, Advisory Opinion of the International Court of Justice (Press release no. 2004/28)
27 November 2007	Annapolis Conference Joint Understanding on Negotiations (United States President George W. Bush; Israel Prime Minister Ehud Olmert; Palestinian Authority President Mahmoud Abbas)
29 November 2012	United Nations General Assembly Resolution 67/19, concerning the upgrade of the Status of Palestine in the General Assembly to an Observer State, UN Doc. A/RES/67/19
23 December 2016	United Nations Security Council Resolution 2334, concerning the Israeli Settlements in Palestinian Territory occupied since 1967, including East Jerusalem, UN Doc. S/RES/2334
28 December 2016	Secretary of State John Kerry Remarks on Middle East Peace (also known as Kerry Parameters)
January 2020	Peace To Prosperity—A Vision to Improve the Lives of the Palestinian and Israeli People of US President Trump

Key Players[2]

Palestinian

Name	Position
Mahmoud Abbas (Abu Mazen)	Chairman of the portfolio of the Occupied Territories of the PLO Executive Committee (1988–1996); Coordinator of Madrid negotiations process (1991–1993); the PLO representative to the Oslo I Accord signing (1993); Head, Negotiating Affairs Department, PLO (1994–1996); Secretary-General, Executive Committee of the PLO (1996–2004); President of the Palestinian Authority (2005–present)
#Mohammed Abu Kosh	Director, Department of Economic Development (throughout the 1980s–1993); Member of the Oslo I negotiations team (1993); Member of the economic negotiations team to the Paris Protocol (1994)
Attaf Alawi	Member of the economic negotiations team to the Paris Protocol (1994)
Yasser Arafat (Abu Ammar)	Chairman, PLO (1969–2004); President, PNA (1994–2004)
Hassan Asfour	Member of the Palestinian National Council (1984–2018); Secretary of the negotiation committee of the bilateral track negotiations of the Madrid peace process (1991–1993); member of the Oslo I negotiations team (1993)

[2] The key players' position addresses their official positions during the Oslo process, specifically the Oslo I Accord and Paris Protocol negotiations' context (and not a full bio). Those who are marked with a Hashtag (#) have parts of their interviews presented in the thesis (noting that not all of the interviews conducted in the framework of this thesis have been included in this study).

Hanan Ashrawi	Member of the Intifada Political Committee (1988–1993); Official Spokesperson of the delegation to the Madrid Peace Process (1991–1993); and a member of the Executive Committee of the delegation to the bilateral track negotiations of the Madrid Process (1993)
#Maher Elkurd	Director of Economic Affairs of the Occupied Territories of the PLO (late 1980s–1993); member of the Oslo I negotiations team (1993); Economic Advisor to Chairman Arafat (1994); Deputy Minister of National Economy (1996–2006)
Amin Haddad	Coordinator of the Multilateral Working Groups of the Madrid multilateral negotiation track (1992–1994); Technical Head of the economic negotiating team for the Paris Protocol (1994); Director of the Aid Coordination and Facilitation Department, PECDAR (1993–1994)
Akram Haniye	Press representative of the PLO leadership in Tunis (1986–1994); Coordinator and media liaison of the delegation to the Madrid bilateral negotiation process in Washington DC (1991–1993)
#Samir Hulileh	Member of the Economic Development Working Group of the multilateral track negotiations of the Madrid peace process (1991–1993); Member of the economic negotiations team to the Paris Protocol (1994); Assistant, Undersecretary Ministry of Economy and Trade (1994–1997)
Faisal Husseini	Chief representative in the disputed territories and Head of the Fatah faction in the West Bank (1980s–1993); Head of the delegation to the Madrid Peace Conference (1993)
Faruq al-Qaddumi (Abu al-Lutf)	Member of the PLO Political Department (throughout the 1990s)
#Ahmad Qurei (Abu Ala)	Director General, Economic Branch of the PLO (1970s–1993); Member of Fatah Central Committee (from 1989 onwards); Head of the negotiation team to the Oslo I Accord (1993); Head of the economic negotiations team to the Paris Protocol (1994); Founder and Director of the Palestinian Economic Council for Development and Reconstruction (PECDAR) (1993–1996); Prime Minister of the Palestinian National Authority (2003–2006)
Afif Safieh	Delegate to The Netherlands (1987–1990); Delegate to the United Kingdom (1990–2005)
#Nabil Shaath	Chief negotiator to the General Agreement part of the Oslo peace process (1993–1994); Minister of Planning and International Cooperation (1994–2003); Foreign Minister (2003–2005); Member of Cabinet of President Abu Mazen (2003–present)

#Mohammad Shtayyeh	Head of the delegation for multilateral talks with the Regional Economic Development Working Group (1991–1993); Finance Director, PECDAR (1993–1995); Minister of PECDAR (1996–2019); Head of the Economic Commission, and Head of the Political Mobilization Commission, PLO (2009–2019); Prime Minister (2019–present)
Nasser Tahboub	Accounting and Taxation Lecturer at the Birziet University (1991–1994); Member of the economic negotiations team to the Paris Protocol (1994); Director General of Value-Added Tax (VAT) and Excises, Ministry of Finance (1994–1997); Director General of Customs and Excise, Ministry of Finance (1997–2003)

Israeli

Name	Position
#Arie Arnon	Senior economist, Research Department, Bank of Israel (BOI) (throughout the 1980s–mid-1990s)
#Avi Ben Basat	Senior Director of the Research Department and Foreign Currency Department, Bank of Israel (1991–1996); Head of the Monetary Issues of the Paris Protocol negotiations team (1994)
Yossi Beilin	Deputy Minister of Foreign Affairs (1992–1995); Minister of Economy and Planning (1995–1996)
#David Brodet	Budget Director, Ministry of Finance (1991–1994); Chief Negotiator of the Paris Protocol negotiations team (1994); Director General, Ministry of Finance (1995–1997)
Oded Eran	Head, Economic Affairs Division, Ministry of Foreign Affairs (1992–1996); Ministry of Foreign Affairs Representative to the Paris Protocol negotiations (1994)
#Yoram Gabai	State Revenue Commissioner, Ministry of Finance (1989–1995); Chairman of the Taxation and Customs Committee (fiscal issues) of the Paris Protocol negotiations team (1994)
Avi Gil	Advisor to Foreign Affairs Minister, Peres (1988); Chief of Staff of Prime Minister, Peres (1995–1996)
Shlomo Gur	Political Advisor to the Deputy Foreign Affairs Minister, Beilin (1992–1996)
#Tamar Hacker	Legal Advisor of the Ministry of Finance (1988–1996); Member of the Paris Protocol negotiations team (1994)
#Yair Hirschfeld	Member of the Oslo I Accord negotiations team (1993)
#Ephraim Kleiman	Economic Advisor and member of the Paris Protocol negotiations team (1994)

#Israel Oz	Chief of Staff, Ministry of Finance (1992–1996); Coordinator of the Paris Protocol negotiations team (1994)
Shimon Peres	Foreign Minister (1992–1995); Prime Minister (1995–1996)
Ron Pundak	Member of the Oslo I Accord negotiations team (1993)
Yitzhak Rabin	Prime Minister (1992–1995)
#Daniel Rothschild	Coordinator of Government Activities in the Territories (COGAT) (1991–1995); Senior Member of the Paris Protocol negotiations team (1994)
Uri Savir	Director-General of the Ministry of Foreign Affairs (1993–1998); Chief Peace negotiator to the Oslo I Accord (1993)
Yitzhak Shamir	Prime Minister (1986–1992)
#Pnina Sharvit Baruch	International Law Department of the Military Advocate General (MAG) Unit, Israeli Defence Force (IDF) (1989–2009); Legal Advisor of the IDF to the Civil Affairs negotiations (1993); Legal Advisor of the IDF to the Paris Protocol negotiations (1994)
#Avraham (Baiga) Shochat	Minister of Finance (1992–1996); Head of the economic negotiations team to the delegation to the Paris Protocol (1994)
Yoel Singer	Member of delegation to the Director of the International Law Department, IDF (1980s); Legal Advisor, Ministry of Foreign Affairs (1993–1996); Member of the Oslo I Accord negotiations team (1993)
#Arie Zeif	Director of Customs and VAT Directorate of the Ministry of Finance (1991–1996); Head of Customs Issues of the Paris Protocol negotiations team (1994)

International

Name	Position
Sten Andersson	Minister of Foreign Affair (1985–1991), Sweden
Hafez el-Assad	President (1971–2000), Syria
James Baker	Secretary of State (1989–1992); White House Chief of Staff (1992–1993), United States
George H. W. Bush	President (1989–1993), United States
Bill Clinton	President (1993–2000), United States
Jan Egeland	State Secretary in the Ministry of Foreign Affairs (1990–1997), Norway
Mikhail Gorbachev	General Secretary of the Communist Party of the Union of the Soviet Socialist Republics (1985–1991); President (1990–1991), Russia
Johan Jørgen Holst	Foreign Affairs Minister (1993–1994), Norway

Saddam Hussein	President (1979–2003), Iraq
Mona Juul	Diplomat, Foreign Affairs Ministry; Facilitator of the Oslo back-channel negotiation track (early 1990s–1993), Norway
#Jan Pronk	Minister of Development Cooperation (1989–1998), Netherlands
Terje Rød-Larsen	Founder and director of the Research Institute for Applied Social Science, Fafo; Facilitator of the Oslo back-channel negotiation track (early 1990s–1993), Norway
Dennis Ross	Director, Policy Planning Office of the State Department (1989–1992); Middle East Envoy (1993–2000), United States
Maximilianus (Max)	Foreign Affairs Minister (1981–1982);
van der Stoel	Ambassador to the United Nations (1983–1986); Member of the Council of State (1987–1991), Netherlands
Thorvald Stoltenberg	Minister of Foreign Affairs (1990–1993), Norway
Hussein bin Talal	King (1952–1999), Jordan

List of Figures

CHAPTER 1

The Untapped Potential

1.1 Introduction

'Oslo was never about economics.'[1]

Economic incentives as motivation for achieving targets, other than in the economic sphere, have always been an integral part of foreign relations. Whether imposed as sanctions or used for encouragement, economic incentives are being applied in pursuit of political, military, and social goals, with the Middle East (ME) conflict being no exception.

The perception of the DOP, Oslo I,[2] was that there is a need to promote economic development in the West Bank and Gaza Strip (WBGS), as well as to encourage economic cooperation between Israel and the Palestinians. Both should be achieved through tools such as the Marshall Plan[3] for the region, the establishment of Free Trade Zones (FTZs), and

[1] Hirschfeld, Interview, 2 January 2017.

[2] DOP—*Declaration of Principles on Interim Self-Government Arrangements*—See list of acronyms, and full text in Appendix A (Declaration of Principles on Interim Self-Government Arrangements ISR-PA (13 September 1993), United Nations General Assembly (UNGA), United Nations Security Council (UNSC), A/48/486, S/26560 (11 October 1993).

[3] The Marshall Plan was an American initiative passed in 1948 for foreign aid to Western Europe, generating the European Recovery Programme (ERP) to stimulate the economic growth post-World War II.

L. Lahar, *The Economic Diplomacy of Peace in the Middle East*,
https://doi.org/10.1007/978-3-031-93991-4_1

international coordinating assistance mechanisms for the Occupied Palestinian Territory (OPT).

The agreement regulating the interim economic arrangement between Israel and Palestine was signed on 29 April 1994. This agreement, *The Protocol on Economic Relations to the Oslo Accords* (commonly known as *Paris Protocol*),[4] states in its preamble: 'The two parties view the economic domain as one of the cornerstones in their mutual relations with a view to enhance their interest in the achievement of a just, lasting and comprehensive peace.' Indeed, the vision of a thriving Palestinian economy served as a catalyst for the progress of the peace process towards a permanent agreement underpinned by the Paris Protocol agreement.

The 1993 Oslo Accord was a fundamental breakthrough in the Israeli-Palestinian conflict and ushered in new hope for the region's future. The vision of Oslo, as specifically expressed in the Paris Protocol, further reinforced the international community's approach towards supporting the economic development of Palestine, encouraging the endorsement of the Oslo guidelines in its future endeavours.

Oslo was not about economic cooperation, as the quote of Yair Hirschfeld, one of the '*Oslo architects*', clearly demonstrates. Neither are any other peace efforts and initiatives to resolve conflicts, let alone the Israeli-Palestinian one. Yet, ever since the conflict began, economic incentives, positive and negative, have played a role in the pursuit of peace and prosperity for both nations in the region.

In fact, this is evident from a series of events, that is, imposing sanctions on Israel through the Arab League boycott strategy in 1945, the 1973 Arab oil embargo targeting nations in support of Israel, and the ongoing *Boycott Divestment and Sanctions* (BDS) movement pressuring Israel to end the Palestinian oppression, among others. Additionally, while economic cooperation has been a core element in framing the Middle East Peace Process (MEPP) since the start of the 90s, it has also been associated with the Palestinian National Development Plan developed in the late 90s. Moreover, in 2013, the European Union (EU) also linked the MEPP

[4]The Paris Protocol—*The Protocol on Economic Relations between the Government of the State of Israel and the Palestinian Liberation Organization representing the Palestinian people*—See full text in Appendix B (The Protocol on Economic Relations between the Government of the States of Israel and the P.L.O., representing the Palestinian people (29 April 1994), UNGA, UNSC, A/49/180, S/1994/727 (4 May 1994).

progress with the upgrading of the Israel-EU Association Agreement, as well as the latest Abrahams Accords[5] signed in September 2020.

Paradoxically, despite numerous initiatives, roadmaps, plans, incentives, and development and aid assistance in the decades following the Oslo I Accord, greater economic (inter)dependency coincided with higher intensity in the Israeli-Palestinian conflict, while peace has become further beyond reach. This paradox contrasts with the finding that economic incentives in other (comparably) protracted conflicts have been successful in ending armed conflict and, moreover, enhanced resilience in the face of asymmetry and oppression. This paradox motivates the puzzle addressed in this book concerning the liberal peace theory outlining the path to achieving peace in the Middle East.

1.2 The Quest for the Pot of Gold

Decisions regarding whether to pursue peace agreements between Israel and Arab countries in the Middle East region have always been motivated by economic considerations. These played a central role in decision-making regarding past peace agreements, for both Israel and the Arab countries, that is, Egypt (1979) and Jordan (1994) (Hashkes, 2021: 43–44). The latest peace agreements signed between Israel, the UAE and Bahrain in September 2020, later joined by Morocco in December of that year and by Sudan in early 2021, were also highly motivated by economic considerations. Unofficial economic relations between Israel and these Arab states have been in place since the early 2000s. However, the signing of the accord normalized the economic relations, and this opened new paths and possibilities, beyond expectations, for both sides (Ravid, 2022: 119–124, 332). The Accords have been changing the political and economic arena of the region while opening the door to new economic initiatives and cooperation between the Arab world and Israel. Not only are these yet to be fully uncovered, but also, despite the turmoil the region has been facing since 7 October 2023, new economic initiatives and cooperations have been continuously established, only behind closed doors (Grossman, 2024).

[5] Abraham Accords are a joint statement between Israel, the United Arab Emirates (UAE), and the United States of America (US) signed on 13 August 2020. It is used in connection with the Israel-United Arab Emirates, and Israel-Bahrain normalization agreements.

Indeed, economic considerations played a significant role in both Israel and Palestine's pursuit of the peace agreement. Moreover, beyond the economic potential, the decision was also motivated by an aspiration for a wider change in the region that would lead to a new Middle East. The establishment of official economic, and, especially, trade relations, were perceived not only to enhance economic relations but also as a catalyst for achieving sustainable peace in the whole region.

Initially, during the negotiations on the Paris Protocol 1994, part of the Oslo I Accord, economics and trade were seen as pathways to establish peaceful coexistence and cooperation. Arguably, this philosophical basis of the liberal peace theory also guides other more successful projects, such as the EU or the Irish peace process, and less successful cases, such as the Cyprus conflict. The untapped trade potential, both with Palestine as well as with other Arab/Muslim countries, that this peace agreement would uncover was believed to fuel and support the peace process, culminating in the formation of two viable independent states, Israel and Palestine living side by side.

Following the 2000–2005 second Intifada,[6] the peace process stagnated alongside a growing economic dependency of the Palestinian economy on Israel. Yet, claims for an untapped trade potential, one that could be used as a motivation for the revival of the peace process, kept being championed, promoting the concept of economic peace in the region. In 2006, the West Bank and Gaza Strip were on the brink of a political split with Hamas (Islamic resistance movement) taking control over Gaza. On this front, a joint Israeli-Palestinian study led by the Peres Center for Peace and the Palestine Trade Center (PALTRADE), respectively, conducted a qualitative and quantitative analysis of historical trade performance and economic cooperation between Israel and Palestine. As part of this, over 150 in-depth interviews were conducted with Palestinian and Israeli businessmen, officials, and representatives of various trade and commerce organizations. The study claimed an economic, and, specifically, trade 'untapped potential' for both sides. For the year 2005, this potential amounted to approximately US$8 billion for the Palestinian gross domestic product (GDP) tripling the existing GDP at the time, and

[6] Intifada (Arabic intifāḍah انتفاضة)—Palestinian Uprising, either of two popular uprisings of Palestinians in the West Bank and Gaza Strip aimed at ending the Israeli occupation in the Palestinian Territory. The First Intifada was between 1987 and 1993, and the second was between 2000 and 2005.

approximately US$12 billion (in value-added terms), equivalent to approximately 10 per cent of Israeli GDP (Peres Center for Peace and Paltrade, 2006).

Despite the numerous turbulences in the region, local and regional political changes of governments and the Arab Spring, as well as new diplomatic and economic relations with third parties to be formed by both Israel and Palestine, the trade potential was claimed to exist also in more recent studies. In 2015, the Palestinian International Business Forum (PIBF), the Office of the Quartet Representative (OQR)[7] and the International Council of Swedish Industry (NIR) issued a report based on a methodology of two-level analysis: macroeconomic, and sectorial. With the focus on the main productive and exporting sectors of the Palestinian economy, it was argued that considering the economic data for the year 2015, a change in the current trade arrangement between Palestine and Israel could lead to the rise of the share of exports (goods and services) in the Palestinian GDP from 16 per cent to as much as 42 per cent within 15 years. As for Israel, the analysis shows that the shift could have been a major growth engine having the potential to generate cumulative export gains of 50 per cent of Israel's total present export, as well as to have the potential to raise Israeli GDP per capita to a level close to the top 15 richest countries in the world (Nashashibi et al., 2015).

In 2018, a study conducted by the Tony Blair Institute for Global Change on Israel-Palestine trade relations revealed a significant decline in Israeli exports to Palestine, and a corresponding decline in Israeli imports from Palestine as a share of Israel's total exports and imports. The lost net Israeli exports to Palestine (excluding low-value-added exports and re-exports) are estimated at more than $4 billion a year, while lost Palestinian exports to Israel stood at $2–2.5 billion a year. In addition to this insight,

[7] The Middle East Quartet was established in 2002 and consists of the United Nations, the European Union, the United States, and Russia. Its mandate is to help mediate Middle East peace negotiations and to support Palestinian economic development and institution building. The Office of the Quartet Representative (OQR) was established in 2007 to support the work of the then-Representative, Tony Blair, former Prime Minister of Great Britain and Northern Ireland. In May 2015, with the departure of former Prime Minister Blair as the Quartet Representative, the OQR transitioned to the Office of the Quartet (OQ), reporting directly to the Quartet Envoys. The mandate of the Office of the Quartet is to increase Palestinian economic and institutional development and empowerment, as a support towards achieving a two-state solution. In the event of a resumption of final status negotiations the OQ would support Quartet members in their efforts to realize a successful outcome (The Office of the Quartet, 2023).

the study offered tools to revitalize the trade between Israel and Palestine to mutually benefit both economies (Gal & Rock, 2018). It is this search for the *Pot of Gold* (POG) in the Israeli-Palestinian conflict—the promise of mutual economic prosperity and regional integration that peace entails—that has supported and encouraged the pursuit of economic peace as the way for moving away from conflict in the region, translating into numerous policy papers, roadmaps, peace plans and different shapes and forms of local and international initiatives.

1.3 The Economic Peace Puzzle

This book investigates whether economic benefits, especially trade, can help shape the course of the Israeli-Palestinian conflict towards peace, critically examining the premise of economic peace, directly derived from the liberal peace theory, as a way for achieving economic development in the Middle East region. The Liberal Peace paradigm has shaped perceptions regarding conflict resolution, positing that peace is not to be imposed, only naturally achieved between countries, with international trade and democracy serving as its basis. This concept was a theoretical and policy relevant building block of the twentieth-century global world order. However, conflicts are now on the rise and more protracted, violent, intractable, fragmented, and asymmetric in nature.

The theory of economic interdependence of international trade and capital flows as a means to move away from violent conflict situations, supported by the liberal peace paradigm, has not been living up to its expectations in the Middle East region. Indeed, contestations regarding the pursuit of economic peace for the region have been expressed by local voices. For some, the outbreak of the First Intifada, already back in 1987, has been argued to serve as proof that economic peace is not viable for the Israeli-Palestinian conflict. The Intifada followed 18 years of a real GDP growth rate of 5.5 per cent on average and a per capita GDP growth rate reaching 2.6 per cent a year in the WBGS (Dessus, 2004), a scale of economic prosperity the Palestinian economy never experienced before (Kleiman, 2000; The Peres Center for Peace, 2009). Bijaoui (2014), on the other hand, argues that the economic peace theory is based on economic relations between states and, hence simply does not apply to situations of asymmetric relations where the balance of power is uneven, as in this case study. This book, however, provides inspiration and lessons based on an earlier episode governed by conflict and despair. Important lessons can be learned from the role that economic ideas, particularly regarding bilateral trade, played in achieving the unprecedented breakthrough of the 1993 Oslo I Accord. It examines how the 'Economic Peace for the Middle East' has been leading the peace process in the region.

A peace built on mutual (economic) benefits recurs in all official and informal initiatives, including the 2020 *Abraham Accords*. The Oslo peace process emerged against all odds, against the backdrop of the First Intifada, the rise of Hamas, and Israel outlawing the Palestinian Liberation Organization (PLO) movement. Now, Hamas, Gaza, outlook is as hopeless as in the late 1980s, if not more, yet a potential normalization agreement between Israel and Saudi Arabia offers prospects and hope for the region. This book investigates what we can learn from both Oslo and the derangement of the peace process. How to structure a viable peace, and what has been the role of economic incentives, and particularly bilateral trade in promoting peace processes in the region.

The book covers more than 30 years of economic development and cooperation in the framework of the Israeli-Palestinian conflict. It begins with the United Nations Conference on Trade and Development's (UNCTAD) adoption of the unprecedented Resolution 109 (V) in 1979 that focuses solely on the economic development of Palestinian Territory, making UNCTAD the first international organization to systematically examine the multifaceted development predicament of the Palestinian economy. The research extends until the times in which economic deprivation and an ongoing de-development process supported Hamas' rise to power in the Gaza Strip, bringing about the official split in Palestinian leadership by the end of 2008.[8] Taking into consideration more recent developments in the region, the discussion shifts to examine the potential role of economic incentives in shaping what lies ahead.

1.4 Intractable Conflicts

Intractable conflicts are characterized as recalcitrant, intense, deadlocked, and extremely difficult to resolve. These conflicts are also labelled as deep-rooted conflicts, protracted social conflict, enduring rivalries, and moral

[8] Palestine in this research project is defined as West Bank and Gaza Strip (WBGS). East Jerusalem has been effectively annexed by Israel in 1980, leading to differences in economic policy and trade regulations applying to this territory, requiring other layers of analysis that are beyond the scope of this book.

conflict (Coleman, 2003). The intractable conflict is enhanced through cognitive, affective, and social-structural mechanisms. These mechanisms lead to the conflict transformation, effectively distancing the conflict from the perceived incompatibilities that launched it (Vallacher et al., 2011). Once the parties to the conflict have developed a stable way of thinking about and behaving towards each other, the problem no longer revolves around issues per se, but rather centres on the mental and behavioural patterns defining the relationships and institutions that form the context of the conflict. The relationships are defined through the dynamics in the environment comprising the conflict. These dynamics, according to the dynamic system approach, are psychological and social mechanisms, within and between individuals and groups, and all other components included in these spaces. Together, these three elements need to be analysed to understand the intractable conflicts' trajectory (Coleman et al., 2007). Conflicts based on identity strife can be over any fundamental concept of identity or sense of self of a community. These types of conflicts can take place when the community feels compelled to resort to violence in order to protect the identity perceived as being under threat (Harris & Reilly, 1998: 9–12). This occurs when the reality and/or legitimacy of one side in the conflict seems to be denied by the other conflicting side (Kriesberg, 2001), as is currently the case in the Russian War against Ukraine. As *identity-based conflicts* are motivated by deep-rooted human needs, they become intractable (Kriesberg, 2005).

For the *intractable identity-based conflict,* the definitions of identity evolve and expand over time (Crocker et al., 2005: 12–14). A collective identity is an ascribed status characteristic based on ethnic, religious, linguistic, or other communal characteristics. The collective identity is regarded as determined by parentage and, hence immutable. Thus, all members of the community are viewed as those sharing the characteristics. This also perpetuates the differences between the communal groups making combatants consider everyone, who is a part of the community, as engaged in the conflict. Consequently, such collective identities may lead to particularly destructive conflicts, including genocide. Moreover, the perception of holding specific characteristics is shared not only by members involved in the conflict but also by non-members (Kriesberg, 2001). In the globalized world of increasingly complex interdependence among states, there is a rapid diffusion of intractable identity-based/deep-rooted conflicts. These conflicts create a vast spillover effect as identity does not necessarily reside within state borders. Whether refugees, emigrants, or a section of the community that are cut off by partition, the diaspora population closely identifies with its respective side in the conflict. Thus, the conflict is not limited to the spatial boundaries of the concerned nation states but extends beyond to include all those persons identifying with the warring sides. Often, these conflicts also revolve around the distribution of resources, for example, territory, economic power, and employment prospects. Nevertheless, at the core of the conflicts are identity-based issues of fundamental rights and a sense of self that are emotionally charged. Consequently, these conflicts are considered to be more prevalent, pervasive, durable, and insoluble than other types of conflicts (Harris & Reilly, 1998: 9–12). As such, the intractable identity-based/deep-rooted conflict resists every attempt to be resolved constructively (Kriesberg, 2005).

Though each conflict is unique in its historical trajectory and societal circumstances, all intractable conflicts (identity-based or not)[9] share common characteristics of context, core issues, nature of relations evolving between the conflicting sides, and their effects on possible outcomes (Coleman, 2006). Moreover, the creation of intense emotions such as humiliation is a common feature in intractable conflicts. These emotions play a crucial role in perpetuating the conflict and need to be reconstructed to resolve these conflicts (Goldman & Coleman, 2022). Over time, intractable conflicts tend to attract the involvement of many parties, become increasingly complicated, and result in a threat to basic human needs or values. Typically, they are associated with cycles of high and low intensity and destructiveness, as often costly both in social and economic terms, and can become pervasive, negatively affecting all aspects of disputants' lives, ranging from mutual alienation and contempt to atrocities, such as murder, rape, and genocide (Coleman, 2003, 2006). Leaders of parties to intractable conflicts tend to defy settlement out of the belief that it would result in zero-sum, and either a continuation of the hot war or a cold stalemate is more of an interest than any known alternative state of being (Crocker et al., 2005: 5). As these conflicts are highly intense and protracted, their transformation from violence to agreement takes place through a peace process, including intermittent setbacks and progress until a final peace agreement is achieved (Darby & Ginty, 2000: 11).

[9] For a detailed analysis of the different types of intractable conflict see Crocker et al. (2005: 10–21).

1.5 The Peace Process

A peace process is one that is practised in highly complex conflicts, that is, protracted conflicts (Newman & Richmond, 2006). The use of 'peace process' instead of 'peace agreement' in these types of conflicts originated during the 1970s, with a 'procedural bias' of the American administration engaged in the Egypt-Israeli peace agreement. Over time, the discussions between the American presidents and their advisers shifted from focusing on the substance of an Arab-Israeli peace agreement to those about the process. This resulted from 'a belief that big plans do not work, that they are too controversial, that they become targets of opposition rather than frameworks for agreement' (Quandt, 2010: 427). Thus, as a political institute, a peace process relates to a phased process of negotiating and nurturing peace and addresses all the related activities dealing with the promotion of peace, including and until a final peace settlement is reached (Selby, 2008). Each peace process covers five themes, that is, preparing for peace, violence, negotiations, peace accords, and post-accord peacebuilding and reconstruction. All of these, however, do not necessarily take place in a linear consecutive manner (Darby & Ginty, 2008: 1–2). Indeed, all peace processes share common criteria, yet at the same time follow varied directions (Darby & Ginty, 2000: 8).

Two main political-economy rationales are perceived as shifting the conflict from violence to a peace process: firstly, the political considerations that seemingly guide economic decisions, leading to the use of economic tools according to political interests, and secondly, economic interdependency and mutual benefits guide political decisions, both at the domestic and international level. Through the political rationale, the peace process is led by those holding political power, in both the domestic and international arena (Press-Barnathan, 2009: 2–3). Even if motivated by an economic rationale, the forms and functioning of peace processes are deeply affected by the political-economy considerations of local stakeholders. The peace process includes a wide range of issues, from corporation tax to credit rating that are disparate and divergent in their economic and social impacts. These could potentially be issues that cause some stakeholders to be left behind. Thus, also for an economic-driven peace process analysis, it is the local dynamics, situated within the global context, that need to be the focus of attention (Selby, 2008). Whether driven through economic or political rationale, these motivations affect one another, with the two often being used simultaneously (Press-Barnathan, 2009: 2–3).

The course of development of all conflicts involves multiple stages, from emergence and escalation to de-escalation and settlement. It is the length of each phase, and whether there is a regression to a previous stage that varies between conflicts (Kriesberg, 2001). The peace process, in relation to other types of conflicts, also begins with the conflicting sides moving away from violence. This is followed by establishing a 'cold peace' often marked by the signing of a peace (or a form of friendly/collaborative) treaty. Only afterwards a 'warm' or stable peace will develop over time through the normalization of relations (Darby & Ginty, 2000: 228–229; Press-Barnathan, 2009: 2–3). Indeed, a peace process can be viewed as complete only after the achievement of an agreement on a political and constitutional framework. Completion, however, does not necessarily imply the success of the process. Moreover, the detailed and complex implementations present multiple challenges making all peace processes fragile (Darby & Ginty, 2008: 4). Even when peace is successfully accomplished, it can take years to move from the 'cold' peace phase to the 'warm' one. Thus, there could be phases of deterioration in the relations leading to extensive stalemates, or even a resurgence of violence at times (Darby & Ginty, 2000: 8).

Despite the initial shift from violence, where a peace process is already in place, the violence is not wholly eliminated following a ceasefire, but only takes on new forms as it evolves (Darby & Ginty, 2000: 230–231). The continuation of violence contributes to the distrust accompanying the already existing suspicions towards the conflicting side. These suspicions get enhanced when non-state actors are participating in the peace process (either in intra or interstate peace negotiations) (Darby & Ginty, 2000: 5). Besides, the peace process itself may become a catalyst of inhibition rather than a peace promotor, as demonstrated in the peace processes in the Middle East, Basque Country, Colombia, Sri Lanka, and Northern Ireland. This conditions the occurrence of one of the following scenarios:

1. Situations in which the actors participating in the process recognize the benefits derived from the sheer existence of the process (for example, a respite from violence, greater opportunities to attract external aid and considerable international support) but are not motivated to pursue the peace process to a conclusion, such as a comprehensive peace accord.
2. Situations in which an accord has been reached, but the participants of the post-peace accord societies adopt a tardy or selective attitude

to its implementation. These cases may result in a grudging coexistence between former antagonists rather than a comprehensive attempt to deal with grievances (Darby & Ginty, 2008: 6).

Domestic politics play a role in international relations processes, but more so in conflict resolution (Bachar & Weiner, 2014). Any peace process, whether it involves mediators or not, or is between states, state and non-state actors, or implemented in civil war cases, is first and foremost between the immediate parties to the conflict (Press-Barnathan, 2009: 2–3). Thus, the domestic level of intergroup competition, specifically domestic politics, has a crucial influence on peace processes, including determining the degree of intragroup conflicts (Jennings, 2011). These dynamics and/or processes of the domestic intragroup are also reflected in the intergroup dynamics throughout the process (Bachar & Weiner, 2014). For an agreement to be implemented, however, it is not only the political will of the conflicting parties themselves that plays a role but also that of the international political and economic actors. To some extent, all conflicts involve international and transnational characteristics. The same applies to peacemaking processes. Additionally, these processes hold significant effects on cross-border dimensions affecting at minimum the neighbouring countries, if not the (sub-) region (Darby & Ginty, 2008: 4).

In such cases, the signing of a peace agreement exposes the leaders pursuing it to further risks. For instance, adversaries may take advantage of the settlement, while disgruntled followers might perceive the settlement as a betrayal of key values. Moreover, excluded parties might seek to alter or even destroy the agreement. The implementation phase of the agreement not only continues to expose the peacemakers to all those opposing it, but heightens the risks, insecurity, and uncertainty of all the civilians the agreement aims to address (Stedman, 1997).

1.5.1 *Spoilers of Peace*

A spoiler is any actor that opposes achieving an agreement, whether from within or from without, for whatever reason there may be, and through any means that will prevent the progress of the process, including but not limited to violence. Inside spoilers, also known as 'devious objectives spoilers', are parties involved in the peace process that take advantage of the situation to gain recognition and legitimacy, time, or material benefits, or to avoid international sanctions (Newman & Richmond, 2006). This type of spoiler often uses non-violent aspects of spoiling behaviour (Nilsson & Söderberg Kovacs, 2011). The non-violent means enable the inside spoilers to keep their incentives hidden while progressing with signing the peace treaty, signalling their willingness to implement a settlement, and yet fail in fulfilling their obligations to the agreement (Stedman, 1997). Outside spoilers are parties excluded from the process, whether excluded voluntarily or involuntarily. This type of spoiler tends to use overt violence as a strategy for undermining peace (Pearlman, 2009; Stedman, 1997, 2003; Waage, 2012).

Another way of categorizing spoilers is according to their goals. Spoilers, thus, can be either limited, greedy, or total. While spoilers with either limited or greedy goals could be insiders, the total ones are outsiders (Stedman, 1997). Any person or group could be viewed as a potential spoiler under changing circumstances. However, those who may fulfil the potential are only those who have the means and capabilities (for example, sufficient numbers of supporters, political influence, financial backing, media access, or organizational ability) to indeed conduct the spoiling. Thus, in addition to the types of spoilers according to motivation, objective, position and role, the opportunity, timing, capabilities, and degree of commitment all are to be taken into consideration when assessing one's 'spoiling' potential (Golan & Sher, 2019: 3–4).

An international peace process of an identity-based conflict often involves state and non-state actors. In such cases, it is likely that at the domestic level, the legitimate representation of the non-state actor has not yet been defined or is under agreement. If so, the prospect of a peace process, let alone a process, heightens the internal contestation. The party that partakes in the peace process not only gains further legitimacy for its status as the leader from the domestic population but also from the international community. To prevent the de facto official recognition of the non-state actor by other states, other factions participating in the civil war that are not involved in the peace process will act to spoil it. For such cases, in which one side is internally engaged in a civil war, Pearlman's (2009) '*internal contestation model*' outlines three factors that influence the non-state actors' decision-making on whether to support or spoil the peace process:

1. The position a group occupies in the internal balance of power;
2. The expected improvement in access to resources the group could have as a result of participating in the process; and

3. In what way negotiations or spoiling will affect the access to these resources.

A variety of factors determine the vulnerability of peace processes to spoilers. These factors are divided between the structural environment of the peace process and the character of actors involved, for example, the number of parties involved, issues at stake, economic interdependence, strategies of elites and/or rulers in the face of violence, and the attitudes and support for peace among followers (Stedman, 2003: 147; Nilsson & Söderberg Kovacs, 2011). The physical location also plays a part in determining the vulnerability to spoilers. A high-profile location for the negotiations increases awareness of the process. This can lead to visible opposition in the form of protests and or media attention outside the venue. These have a psychological effect on the negotiators, which in turn change the dynamics around the negotiation table. A negotiation location that is perceived to be partial, will increase the likelihood of the parties engaging in spoiling behaviour (Golan & Sher, 2019: 11–12).

Being conscious of the detrimental effects potential spoilers may have on a conflict resolution process enables leaders to react better to the adversaries' behaviour, aimed at sabotaging the process. Thus, in order to constrain the potential effect of spoilers, first and foremost, the awareness of the spoilers themselves should exist among leaders. This often results in limiting the public nature of the negotiations in order to avoid the unintended impact of the domestic constituents and adversaries on the negotiations process (Bachar & Weiner, 2014); and is usually undertaken through either keeping the process under complete confidentiality with no press interaction whatsoever; creating process legitimacy through a policy of a joint press outlet of both sides; or in the case of a third-party broker involvement, delegating press briefing to it (Golan & Sher, 2019: 11).

1.5.2 Back-Channel Negotiations

Back-channel negotiations are secret talks designed to foster the settlement of a conflict between the leadership of opposing groups, organizations, or nations. This communication contrasts with front-channel communication, which is publicly known to occur (Pruitt, 2008); and is either taking place in parallel to frontline diplomatic negotiations (Wanis-St, 2006); used both in pre-negotiation and negotiation phases as an adjunct to front-channel negotiation in sidebar talks (Pruitt, 2008); or as a pre-negotiation activity that can lead to substantive negotiations (Wanis-St, 2006).

Peacemaking is a process riddled with considerable uncertainties. Four categories of uncertainty require special attention as they pose dilemmas for potential peacemakers, with each of them serving as a motivation for using back-channels: (a) cost of entry into negotiations; (b) underlying interests and priorities; (c) the action of spoilers, either internal or external; and (d) outcome. In cases of intense conflicts where the concerned parties are fighting each other, militarily or otherwise, as communication with the other side implies recognition of it and may be associated with a sign of weakness or of readiness to sacrifice certain principles or interests, these categories separately, and even combined, are a strong motivation for choosing a secret back-channel negotiation track (Wanis-St, 2006).

In violent conflicts, seeing the other side as evil and thus not worthy of human contact and maintaining a firm boundary between the two groups is a psychological aspect that is used to strengthen intergroup solidarity. The secret back-channel contact provides political cover to leaders who want to explore the possibility of escaping the conflict by communicating with the enemy, while also using it to negotiate over recognition (Pruitt, 2008). Thus, in the context of international negotiations dealing with questions of war and peace, the back-channel negotiators tend to be individuals close to the decision-makers. This enables the negotiator to authoritatively explore a wider range of options, and to commit to a tentative agreement more readily than front-channel negotiators (Wanis-St, 2006). Besides, back-channel communication encourages informality and frank discussion of motives and concerns. Needs, goals, intentions, and fears about the opponents' proposals can be revealed more readily, along with information on firm demands and ones that can be modified. While in front-channel communication participants often spend a lot of time reshaping the past and accusing each other of earlier misbehaviour, it is less likely to be the case in back-channel communication, especially when an intermediary is involved in the form of a mediator. As a result, the parties are more likely to discover common ground and identify the points of real conflict beyond the apparent ones. Pruitt (2008) attributes this improved flexibility and future orientation to reduced audience effects, reduced number of people interacting, greater informality, and the non-binding nature of what is said.

As for mediators and external players, back-channel negotiations enable the involvement of international decision-makers in the negotiations without actually risking their prestige, popularity, or political office, reducing uncertainties regarding the costs they may pay for their involvement. While uncertainties are a part of any type of negotiation process, uncertainties associated with negotiations of violent conflicts create particular dangers because of the high stakes: political stability, peace, and political and physical survival. These make the back-channel process, more so the secret back-channel, attractive to decision-makers to help de-escalate a crisis or negotiate a more comprehensive agreement (Wanis-St, 2006).

Secrecy, by definition, implies exclusion and allows the negotiators to stay ahead of spoilers. Indeed, as for external spoilers, the dependence on secrecy may be the only way to reach an agreement in the short run, or in times of crisis. However, in the long run, it may cause spoilers to become more proactive about preventing the agreement from being implemented (Wanis-St, 2006). The slim participation in back-channel negotiations, prevents the comprehensive resolution of fundamental issues. The limited extent of solutions makes the agreement unsustainable. Nonetheless, problems resulting from narrow participation and secrecy can be diminished by insisting that the final agreement be reached in front-channel talks. This can be achieved through concerted efforts to bring representatives of as many groups as possible into the front-channel negotiation to create as broad a 'central coalition' as is feasible (Pruitt, 2008). Also, emphasis should be placed on the mechanisms that can deal with the different types of spoiling as they emerge throughout the talks between the negotiators themselves (Golan & Sher, 2019: 25–26). Indeed, getting to the negotiation table, and ways of negotiating, all have a crucial effect on the dynamics and outcomes of the negotiation process.

1.6 Outline of the Book

The more enhanced the intensity and intractability of a conflict, the more sources of conflict are involved (Fisher, 2000). Accordingly, in order to resolve the conflicts, multiple barriers will need to be overcome, including psychological, structural, strategic, and political (Ross, 2014). Intractable conflicts are considered to be resistant to resolution, being extremely detrimental, self-sustaining, and displaying marked resistance to intervention regardless of rational consideration to be addressed (Kriesberg, 2005). Intractable conflicts are often identity-based, deep-rooted conflicts. In their modern form, these conflicts take asymmetric shape, either in the form of guerrilla warfare, insurgency, civil war, or intrastate conflict, involving both territorial disputes and contested statehood, as in the Israeli-Palestinian conflict. Besides competition over scarce resources, and ideological, religious, or political rivalry, intergroup conflicts also exhibit a psychological dimension consisting of attitudes, emotions, biases, and beliefs. These psychological barriers render structural solutions insufficient as they reduce the motivation of the conflicting parties to consider solutions at all (Friend & Malhotra, 2019).

The intractable modern conflict—the identity-based, deep-rooted, asymmetric conflict, carries unique characteristics that affect its ways of negotiation and resolution. This book offers a political-economy comprehensive analysis of the economic relations between Israel and Palestine, as set in the 1994 Paris Protocol, part of the Oslo I Accord. The Protocol encapsulates the essence of complexities between economics and politics in the region as well as sets the framing of economic barriers and cooperation from 1967, when the Palestinian Territory was occupied, until today. The analysis of economic and trade relations, and trade policy considering the perspective of time, establishes the ways these have been used in the past to support the liberal economic peace in the region, and examines if these can be reshaped to provide a *Pot of Gold* that can support the quest for the way forward in the Israeli-Palestinian conflict once again. Thus, the structure of the book will be as follows:

1.6.1.1 Chapter 2—Asymmetric Conflicts and Their Resolution

- This chapter addresses international developments prior to the 1990s Oslo peace process and how the emerging liberal project of international order and the promotion of liberal economic peace through economic interdependence, especially trade, have been used as a motive to promote international peace agreements, including through economic development.

1.6.1.2 Chapter 3—Framing the Conflict through Economic Relations

- This chapter provides a political-economy overview of the course of events leading to the 1993 Oslo I Accord historical breakthrough and the signing of the Declaration of Principles (DOP).

1.6.1.3 Chapter 4—Oslo Through an Economic Lens—The Paris Protocol

- This chapter analyses the role and perceptions regarding the economic components of the Oslo I Accords in advancing the peace process and promoting the achievement of a viable peace agreement in the region. The centre of this analysis focuses on the 1994 Protocol on Economic Relations between Israel and Palestine, known as the Paris Protocol, as the overarching legal economic framework of the Oslo Accords and process in the years to follow.

1.6.1.4 Chapter 5—The Oslo Spirit

- This chapter addresses the role of a negotiation process in achieving mutual benefits in cases of asymmetric conflicts. Acknowledging that the negotiation process can be used to empower the weaker side and reduce asymmetricity and vice versa, and that these dynamics have the potential to affect power asymmetry in later stages, this chapter examines the negotiation process of the Protocol within the general negotiation framework of the Oslo process. The negotiation process here is explored through the prism of balance of power. The point is to explore whether and how they have contributed to the asymmetricity in the balance of power.

1.6.1.5 Chapter 6—Framing the Paris Protocol Through Political-Economic Relations

- This chapter provides an analysis of the politics of economics in regard to the Protocol's implementation to assess the role of the Protocol in the development trajectory throughout the years since signing. As the tension between politics and economics is that to determine the level of development, the chapter scrutinizes whether the economic sphere can overcome the political one in regard to the conflict.

1.6.1.6 Chapter 7—The Economic Diplomacy of Peace in the Middle East

- This chapter presents how, time and again, from the Oslo process to the (latest) 2023 war between Israel and Hamas, the alleviation of trade in the Middle East region has been used to boost the peace process between Israel and Palestine from a bilateral, regional, and international perspective. Examining the Economic Peace notion in time perspective, using the prism of asymmetry to symmetry, and considering the trade potential and the current trade performance, this chapter presents the political-development nexus framework, and accordingly sets the range of scale for the economic-diplomacy model of the liberal (economic) way for peace in asymmetric conflicts, bringing together the findings of this research, including an outlook on the recent 2023–2025 conflict.

References

Bachar, G., & Weiner, A. S. (2014). Governments, publics, and enemies: Intragroup dynamics as barriers to conflict resolution. *Dynamics of Asymmetric Conflict, 7*(2–3), 198–225.

Bijaoui, I. (2014). *The economic reconciliation process: Middle Eastern populations in conflict*. Springer.

Coleman, P. T. (2003). Characteristics of protracted, intractable conflict: Toward the development of a metaframework-I. *Peace and Conflict: Journal of Peace Psychology, 9*(1), 1–37.

Coleman, P. T. (2006). Intractable conflict. *The Handbook of Conflict Resolution: Theory and Practice, 2*, 533–559.

Coleman, P. T., Vallacher, R. R., Nowak, A., & Bui-Wrzosinska, L. (2007). Intractable conflict as an attractor: A dynamical systems approach to conflict escalation and intractability. *American Behavioral Scientist, 50*(1), 1454–1475.

Crocker, C. A., Hampson, F. O., & Aall, P. (2005). Introduction: Mapping the nettle field. Grasping the nettle: Analyzing cases of intractable conflict. In C. A. Crocker, F. O. Hampson, & P. Aall (Eds.), *Grasping the nettle: Analyzing cases of intractable conflict* (pp. 3–30). US Institute of Peace Press.

Darby, J., & Ginty, R. M. (2000). Introduction: Comparing peace processes. In J. Darby & R. M. Ginty (Eds.), *The management of peace processes*. Palgrave Macmillan UK, United States of America: St. Martin's Press LLC..

Darby, J., & Ginty, R. M. (2008). Introduction: What peace? What process? In J. Darby & R. M. Ginty (Eds.), *Contemporary peacemaking: Conflict, peace processes and post-war reconstruction*. Springer.

Dessus, S. (2004). A Palestinian growth history, 1968–2000. *Journal of Economic Integration, 19*(3), 447–469.

Fisher, R. (2000). Sources of conflict and methods of conflict resolution. *International Peace and Conflict Resolution, School of International Service*, The American University, 1–6.

Friend, W., & Malhotra, D. (2019). Psychological barriers to resolving intergroup conflict: An extensive review and consolidation of the literature. *Negotiation Journal, 35*(4), 407–442.

Gal, Y., & Rock, B. (2018, October 17). *Israeli Palestinian trade: In-depth analysis*, Middle East, Tony Blair Institute for Global Change.

Golan, G., & Sher, G. (2019). *Spoiling and coping with spoilers: Israeli-Arab negotiations*. Indiana University Press.

Goldman, J. S., & Coleman, P. T. (2022). A theoretical understanding of how emotions fuel intractable conflict: The case of humiliation. New York: Colombia University. http://www.humiliationstudies.org/documents/GoldmanNY05meetingRT2.Pdf.

Grossman, M. (2024). As the Israel-Hamas war continues, the Abraham Accords quietly turns four. Atlantic Council. Retrieved January 9, 2024, from https://www.atlanticcouncil.org/blogs/menasource/abraham-accords-anniversary-gaza/.

Harris, P., & Reilly, B. (1998). *Democracy and deep-rooted conflict: Options for negotiators*. International Institute for Democracy and Electoral Assistance.

Hashkes, E. (2021). *The economic bridges*. Matar.

Jennings, C. (2011). Intra-group competition and inter-group conflict: An application to Northern Ireland. *Defence and Peace Economics, 22*(1), 63–83.

Kleiman, E. (2000). Round table discussion. *The Economic Quarterly, 47*(1), 80–92.

Kriesberg, L. (2001). Mediation and the transformation of the Israeli-Palestinian conflict. *Journal of Peace Research, 38*(3), 373–392.

Kriesberg, L. (2005). Nature, dynamics, and phases of intractability. In C. A. Crocker, F. O. Hampson, & P. R. Aall (Eds.), *Grasping the nettle: Analyzing cases of intractable conflict* (pp. 63–89). Springer.

Nashashibi, K., Gal, Y., & Rock, B. (2015). *Palestinian–Israeli economic relations: Trade and economic regime*. Palestine International Business Forum, International Council of Swedish Industry (NIR) and Office of the Quartet Representative Tony Blair.

Newman, E., & Richmond, O. (2006). *The impact of spoilers on peace processes and peacebuilding*. United Nations University Press.

Nilsson, D., & Söderberg Kovacs, M. (2011). Revisiting an elusive concept: A review of the debate on spoilers in peace processes. *International Studies Review, 13*(4), 606–626.

Pearlman, W. (2009). Spoiling inside and out: Internal political contestation and the Middle East peace process. *International Security, 33*(3), 79–109.

Peres Center for Peace and Paltrade. (2006). *The untapped potential: Palestinian-Israeli economic relations: Policy options and recommendations.*

Press-Barnathan, G. (2009). *The political economy of transitions to peace*. University of Pittsburgh Press.

Pruitt, D. (2008). Back-channel communication in the settlement of conflict. *International Negotiations, 13*(1), 37–54.

Quandt, W. B. (2010). *Peace process: American diplomacy and the Arab-Israeli conflict since 1967*. Brookings Institution Press.

Ravid, B. (2022). *Trump's peace: The Abraham Accords and the reshaping of the Middle East*. Rishon LeZion, Israel, Miskal–Yedioth Ahronoth Books and Chemed Books.

Ross, L. (2014). Barriers to agreement in the asymmetric Israeli–Palestinian conflict. *Dynamics of Asymmetric Conflict, 7*(2–3), 120–136.
Selby, J. (2008). The political economy of peace processes. In M. Pugh, N. Cooper, & M. E. Turner (Eds.), *Whose peace? Critical perspectives on the political economy of peacebuilding* (pp. 11–29). Palgrave Macmillan UK.
Stedman, S. J. (1997). Spoiler problems in peace processes. *International Security, 22*(2), 5–53.
Stedman, S. J. (2003). Peace processes and the challenges of violence. In J. Darby (Ed.), *Contemporary peacemaking: Conflict, violence and peace processes* (pp. 103–113). Springer, Palgrave Macmillan.
The Office of the Quartet. (2023). *Office of the Quartet about us.* Retrieved July 15, 2023, from http://www.quartetoffice.org/page.php?id=4e3e7y320487Y4e3e7.
The Peres Center for Peace. (2009, July). *Economic peace? Political peace with economic prosperity*, Department of Economic and Business, Res 01-09/A07.
Vallacher, R. R., Coleman, P. T., Nowak, A., & Bui-Wrzosinska, L. (2011). Rethinking intractable conflict: The perspective of dynamical systems. In P. T. Coleman (Ed.), *Conflict, interdependence, and justice (The intellectual legacy of Morton Deutsch)* (pp. 65–94). Springer.
Waage, H. H. (2012). Proactive peace diplomacy: Jan Egeland. In M. Fixdal (Ed.), *Ways out of war* (pp. 91–116). Palgrave Macmillan US.
Wanis-St, J. A. (2006). Back-channel negotiation: International bargaining in the shadows. *Negotiation Journal, 22*(2), 119–144.

CHAPTER 2

Asymmetric Conflicts and their Resolution

The liberal peace paradigm (of trade interdependency as supportive of peace) has shaped the modern perception regarding conflict resolution. In an interdependent world of guns and butter, the importance of economics as both a punitive and incentive tool is more central than ever. However, international conflicts are now on the rise and becoming more protracted, violent, intractable, fragmented, and asymmetric in nature. Often, the deterioration occurs in conflicts between neighbouring countries. This chapter reviews the role of the liberal peace theory in the international order (Sect. 2.1), its strands, development of approaches (Sect. 2.2), and the emergence of the key sub-theory of economic diplomacy (Sect. 2.3). Considering the modern evolution of conflicts and its effects on the intractable, identity-based, deep-rooted conflict transformation into an asymmetric one, the last section addresses its resolution through trade (Sect. 2.4).

2.1 The Liberal Project of International Order

The liberal conception of order was brought into focus during the twentieth century, shaping the international world order of current times. The first phase of international system liberalism followed the end of World War I in 1919, with Woodrow Wilson's vision supporting a liberal world order, endorsed in the Versailles settlement with the establishment of the

L. Lahar, *The Economic Diplomacy of Peace in the Middle East*,
https://doi.org/10.1007/978-3-031-93991-4_2

League of Nations. The League of Nations, it was hoped, would usher in an entirely new system of interstate relations based on advanced liberal principles (Ikenberry, 2011: 17, 65). This framework, for the first time in history, presented a shared conviction of all Member States (MS) that the source of war is less important than the war itself, as war is the central problem in international relations (Holsti, 1991: 208).

The second phase came following World War II, with the liberal international framework being offered to challenge Soviet expansionism (Ikenberry, 2011: 17, 65). During the 1940s, US Presidents Franklin D. Roosevelt and Harry S. Truman based the new international system on Wilson's liberal principle but expanded the commitment to liberal multilateralism with a more direct role for the United States (US). Furthermore, in this new world order, the achievement of liberal multilateralism was through including the world economy stabilization (Ikenberry, 2014). The United Nations (UN), the successor to the League of Nations, was designed not only to help resolve international conflicts but also to have the capacity for both deterrence and military and economic coercion (Holsti, 1991: 245–7). Furthermore, it was also aimed at prevention by creating conditions of stability and well-being through international economic and social cooperation (Schrijver, 2006; UN, 1945: art. 55). The 1944 Bretton Woods conference laid the foundations for the international financial system, simultaneously promoting the advancement of liberal order in trade and finance (Helleiner, 2014: 1, 25).

The UN, together with the organizations launched at the Bretton Woods conference in 1944, were to take upon themselves an array of social and economic activities. These competencies were not aimed only to enable the expansion of US economic influence in the world, but more importantly, to build the basis of world peace (Holsti, 1991: 267). With the formation of the United Nations, the Bretton Woods, the General Agreement on Tariffs and Trade (GATT), the North Atlantic Treaty Organization (NATO, also known as the North Atlantic Alliance), and the 1957 European Economic Community (EEC), and the adoption of international charters, such as the Atlantic Charter, the UN Charter, and the Universal Declaration of Human Rights (UDHR), the years between 1944 and 1951 were the most intensive period for building international institutions, all based on liberal order (Ikenberry, 2011: 17, 159–160). In this system, relationships between MS became more hierarchical, institutionalized, and harnessed to an agenda of human rights and economic development. The Western liberal states, with the United States at the front, were occupied with the Cold War, modernizing their societies, rebuilding and expanding economic and security relations to promote the democratic capitalist world (Ikenberry, 2011: 17, 159–160). The perception of military security was dependent on general world prosperity, resulting in the establishment of the linkage between economic conditions and the origin of global conflicts at the international level (Holsti, 1991: 245–247).

The third phase of the international liberal order began with the end of the Cold War. This phase marked the end of an ideological hostility between East and West. It brought with it the acknowledgement of the supremacy of Western values, specifically those of economics, and even more of political freedoms. *The End of History* (Fukuyama, 2022) is much more than a philosophical allegory for the desired system to be created; it is the endpoint of the evolution of the political, and governmental system of mankind in the form of a Western liberal democracy (Russett, 1994: 4). States in all regions of the world transitioned towards democracy and pursued market strategies of economic development following the example of the US-led liberal principles, promoting the modernization forces (Ikenberry, 2011: 17, 159–160; Ikenberry, 2014). And with the liberal peace project becoming the model implemented in dozens of post-conflict and fragile states, the liberal and economic values of the international system were expanded all across the world (Paris, 2002: 638).

It has been argued that a fourth phase of the international liberal order marked by the war between Russia and Ukraine is emerging. Whether the turning point is defined by the Russian invasion of Ukraine in 2014 (Mearsheimer, 2014), or with the Russian attack on Ukraine in February 2022, the Russian aggression marks the end of *The End of History* (Fukuyama, 2022) with the liberal outcomes yet to be determined.[1]

[1] In February 2014 Russia annexed the Crimean Peninsula, part of Ukraine, followed by Russia supporting the paramilitary forces fighting Ukraine in Donbas until 24 February 2022. Then, the conflict escalated with the Russian invasion of Ukraine, which is the biggest attack on a European country since World War II. While some have referred to the events from 2014 to 2022 as a 'civil' or 'proxy' war (see, for example: Arel & Driscoll, 2023; Peterson & Kuck, 2014; D'Anieri, 2022; Hughes, 2014; Bandeira, 2019); others see in the 2022 escalation the continuation of the conflict that has been ongoing since 2014 (further to Mearsheimer, 2014, and Fukuyama, 2022 as aforementioned other examples include: Turan, 2023; Naz, 2023).

2.2 The Liberal Peace Paradigm

The origin of the liberal peace paradigm can be related to the three definitive articles in *Perpetual Peace* by Immanuel Kant—republic, pacific federation, and universal. These definitive articles represent the constitutional, international and cosmopolitan laws respectively (Doyle, 1986), and describe the lawful constitutions whose adoption is an essential precondition for a lasting international peace (Covell, 1998: 119–167). Constitutional law sets the moral foundation for liberal peace, international law emphasizes the importance of Kantian pacification, and cosmopolitan law adds material incentives to moral commitments. The cosmopolitan law leads to the spread of the 'Spirit of Commerce'. As this will sooner or later take hold of every nation, states will be impelled to promote peace and avert war (Doyle, 2005).

The theory of liberal peace has three simultaneous origins: first, commercial liberalism—the spread of capitalism and markets creates economic interdependence, mutual gains, shared interests, and incentives for international cooperation, dating back to Adam Smith; second, democratic peace—republican or democratic polities seek affiliation with each other and manifest pacific relations, traced to Kant; and lastly, liberal institutionalism—international law and institutions are the outgrowths of liberal societies that establish rule-based expectations and obligations between them, emerged from Lockean writings on rights and the rule of law (Doyle, 1997). Thus, there are three strands of thinking to comprise liberalism:

1. The political strand, which is divided into institutions and democracy,
2. The economic strand that heavily focuses on trade offers states a way to transform their position through economic growth rather than through military conquest, and
3. The social arguing strand states that developing personal relations leads to the reduction of conflict by promoting understanding. As personal contacts also occur at multiple transnational levels, they affect the foreign policy to be promoted (Nye, 1999: 44–46).

'Liberal peace is a discourse, framework and structure with a specific ontology and methodology, including the main components of democratisation, the rule of law, human rights, free and globalised markets, and neo-liberal development' (Richmond, 2006: 295). It offers a focus on the character of peace in the civil and societal, political-economic, and international spheres, coined as the combination of peace, democracy, and free markets (Richmond, 2009: 559). In regard to international relations, the liberal peace theory is a coherent family of ideational, commercial, and republican theories with common assumptions that not only explain cooperation among liberal states but pertain to liberal and non-liberal polities, conflictual and cooperative situations, security and political-economy issues, and both individual foreign policy and states' behaviour (Moravcsik, 2010).

The theoretical background for promoting free trade, as mutually beneficial to all engaged countries, leans on the principle of comparative advantage presented by David Ricardo in *On the Principles of Political Economy and Taxation*, 1817. John Stuart Mill (1840) proposed that intensified economic relations would lead to the reduction of conflicts among nations (Murshed, 2002; van Bergeijk, 2009: 25). In 1750, Baron de Montesquieu provided an economic approach to achieve mutual trust. He argued that as two nations who trade with each other become reciprocally dependent, 'peace is the natural effect of trade'. Mutual trading leads to the union between the nations 'founded on their mutual necessities' (de Montesquieu 1900: 316 in: Polachek & Seiglie, 2007: 1023). An extended argument advanced by liberalism regarding the trade-conflict relationship maintains that it is not merely the volume of trade but also the type of trade existing between partners that affects utility calculations for conflict (Barbieri, 2002: 23–27). At the international level, liberalism supports the establishment of a cooperative world order organized around principles of reciprocity and the rule of law. States can overcome the constraints of a competitive and decentralized international system and solve security dilemmas, pursue collective action, and create an open stable system. Powerful states will act with restraint while finding ways to credibly convey commitments to other states. Trade and exchange have a modernizing and civilizing effect on states, undercutting illiberal tendencies and strengthening the fabric of the international community (Ikenberry, 2011: 63). More than that, trade and exchange, have a similar effect, just like on the international community, on the forces of globalization, modernization, and economic development, and can transform the relation character between states by using material incentives to resolve political disputes peacefully (McDonald, 2007).

As liberal democracy spread across the world in the late 1970s and accelerated after the end of the Cold War, it brought democracies to global dominance (Ikenberry, 2014). Together with the growth in the wealth of democracies, the period following the end of the Cold War was one of 'increased ascendancy of liberal capitalist democracy' (Ikenberry, 2011: 2). Indeed, the belief that democracies should not fight each other was already integrated into the US foreign policy, with the 1918 fourteen points of President Woodrow Wilson. But democratic peace emerged as an axiom of US foreign policy only after it was invoked in speeches by former US President George Bush, and the then Secretary of State James Baker, and with democratization being defined as the third pillar of US foreign policy in 1994, during President Clinton's administration (Owen, 1994: 87).

Furthermore, in 1992 the issuing of *An Agenda for Peace* by the then Secretary-General (SG) of the UN Boutros Boutros-Ghali, with the support of the Security Council came out of the belief that 'the world now has the best chance of achieving international peace and security since the founding of the United Nations'. This was based upon the democratic peace paradigm as the way for embedding the liberal values among nation states worldwide (United Nations General Assembly (UNGA), 1992: 822). [2] In this agenda, democratization is the final stage of the Kantian tripod with peace leading to development and interdependency, then evolving into democratic governance (Russett, 2011: 129–132). The 1995 United Nations General-Secretary (UNSG) *An Agenda for Development* presented the vital problems facing the promotion of economic development, focusing on the malfunctioning of the international economic system in governing world economy (Boutros-Ghali, 1995).[3] This was then followed by the 1996, UNSG *An Agenda for Democratization*, emphasizing that democracy is not only perceived as the result of peace, but it is 'an ingredient for both sustainable development and lasting peace' as the culture of democracy helps in fostering a culture of development (Boutros-Ghali, 1996: 53).[4] Peace, development, and democracy were then inextricably linked, with the UN policy actively promoting national democratization through monitoring elections,

[2] UNGA (1992) Report 47/277, UNSC Report 24111, *An Agenda for Peace: Preventive diplomacy, Peacemaking and peace-keeping: Report of the Secretary-General pursuant to the statement adopted by the Summit Meeting of the Security Council on 31 January 1992*, A/47/277; S/24111 (31 January 1992).

[3] Boutros-Ghali (1995), *An agenda for development 1995: With related UN documents*, UN [ST/]DPI/1622/DEV.

[4] Boutros-Ghali (1996), UNGA Report 51/761, *An Agenda for Democratization*, [ST/]DPI/1867, A/51/761 (20 December 1996).

creating independent judicial systems, and strengthening of respect for human rights, and the rule of law (Lombardo, 2001).

Indeed, the international policy led by the liberalism-democratic nexus seems to support the democratic peace proposition. However, it is the same as the liberal order existing between the two World Wars. The same world order that failed to deliver the anticipated results. The difference between the two liberal systems—the one during the period between the two world wars, and the other after WWII—however, relies on the change in the international economic system. Embodied in the Bretton Woods institutions following WWII, the international economic system turned from a system of closed and rival imperial blocks during the period between the two world wars, to one based on an open trading system (Ikenberry, 2011: 19–20). This benefit of international exchange in the form of trade as an antidote against international conflicts, motivating the Bretton Woods institutions, is, in fact, the major lesson of liberal peace (van Bergeijk, 2019: 21). And unlike its interwar counterparts, the demise of the Bretton Woods system in the early 1970s did not lead to a phase of autarchy. On the contrary, it helped to unleash a period of even more intense economic globalization in which the reformed Bretton Woods institutions have continued to play a major role (Held & McGrew, 2000: 426).

The intensification of international integration in the post-Cold War world through regulatory regimes and institutions established governance standards across multiple domains of global politics, including the environment, trade, shipping, aviation, the internet, weapons of mass destruction, conventional weapons, human rights, and even criminal conduct. All helped in driving countries to become an actor in the liberal world order. These webs of alliances and open market regimes are all designed to enable the political project of liberal hegemons to continue to lead long after its relative power advantages has been eroded (Duncombe & Dunne, 2018). Indeed, it has been the most globally organized and deeply entrenched order the world has ever seen, one that is dominated by states that are liberal, capitalist, and democratic, with the prosperity of nearly every country, and the stability of its governments fundamentally depends on this order (Ikenberry, 2014). And the evidence for the dominance of the international economic system as the key influencer of the world order is provided through trade ties being the most important determinant of joint memberships between states in international organizations (Weede, 2011: 274).

2.2.1 *From Democratic Peace to Economic Peace*

The liberal peace hypothesis rests upon a variety of concepts, such as democratic peace, liberal international thought, liberal institutionalism, international law, capitalist peace, and free trade. Within the framework of liberal peace, the discourse on the factors promoting peace has been underway, with trade and democracy considered as the leading concepts. The democratic peace school of thought, on the one hand, supports the form of governance as being the cause of restraint of liberal states from using coercive threats against each other (Richmond, 2009: 559–560; Risse-Kappen, 1995; Russett, 1994: 4–5, 10–11). On the other hand, the economic school of thought supports trade through global markets and economic development as the restraining catalyst, also known as capital peace and commercial peace (Gartzke & Hewitt, 2010; Gleditsch, 2008; McDonald, 2010). Likewise, it has been argued that economic development can be the outcome either through trade or democracy (Mousseau et al., 2003). This is further reinforced by the perception that liberal peace is employed in order to explain the absence of conflict between democratic nations that are also economically interdependent (Murshed, 2011). Doyle (1986) reviewed these two strands as inseparably linked with the interaction of capitalism and democracy as the foundation of liberal pacifism. Doyle (2005) stated that alone, none of these constitutional, international, or cosmopolitan sources is sufficient. It is only when they are together that they plausibly connect the liberal polities characteristics and economies with a sustainable liberal peace. Once these conditions are met, only then can they be considered a sufficient explanation of liberal peace.

The democratic peace theory contends that it is the very nature of the democratic political system which explains why democracies do not fight or threaten other democracies (Oneal & Russet, 1997: 269–270). Other approaches see in it the closest thing to international relations empirical law, and the importance of democracy derived from democracy representing the nearest-perfect sufficient condition for peace (Chan, 1997).

Definitions of war, peace, and democracy play a key role in examining the existence of the democratic peace theory and as such, are instrumental in safeguarding the propositions themselves. On this front, the question of the mutual identity of democracies, as well as self-identity needs to be addressed (Williams, 2001). Although the definition is subjective, history shows that liberals have relatively stable conceptions of what counts as a democracy. Liberal states recognize one another according to relations of perception and belief (Owen, 1994: 128–129).

Whether it is due to established institutions, norms, or culture, the consensus in democratic peace theory is that conflict reduction depends more on both states being constrained by democratic norms and institutions than on the consequences of those constraints on each of the states individually (De Mesquita et al., 1999; Maoz & Russett, 1993; Russett, 1994: 4–5, 10–11). Other studies, although supportive of the argument that the pacifist benefits of democracy are much stronger when democracies interact, state that the monadic effect cannot be disclaimed entirely (Benoit, 1996; Bremer, 1992; Rousseau et al., 1996). Müller and Wolff (2004) show that the monadic treatment of both structure and norms in the literature is out of step with the dyadic form of the phenomenon. Risse-Kappen (1995: 58) states that the stability of the political system is as important as the type of regime, which implies that 'stable democratic systems constitute the main inhabitants of the "island of democratic peace"'. As such, a democracy may not be recognized as one if it is in the early stages of democratization. Historical records indicate that democracies have often failed to adopt their internal norms of conflict resolution in an international context (Rosato, 2003: 588).

Wars are a rare phenomenon. Thus, attributing the absence of war to democratic peace is as random as attributing it to other factors (Owen, 1994). Democracies were rare as well. Liberal democracies until the twentieth century were confined to the West and parts of Latin America. It was only after WWII that democracy began to reach beyond those realms, with the newly independent states establishing self-rule (Ikenberry, 2014). While the democratic peace phenomenon exists, only a correlation is demonstrated, not causation (Hayes, 2012). Thus, due to the insufficient evidence on democracy as the cause for peace among democracies led to the perception of economic institutions as the root cause (Mousseau, 2013). Democracy is what had been historically associated with a subset of countries who saw their global objectives coincide, negating the precondition for conflict to seldom arise. National preferences are rooted in the form of governance, as they are idiosyncratic relative to their governing structure or political cultures. Hence, not all democracies will necessarily have similar objectives on international issues, while the similar political preferences argument would be applicable to any type of regime, not only democracy. However, what all democracies do have in common is being a part of the Western Industrial system (Gartzke, 1998).

Both democratic peace and the zone of democratic cooperation are substantially limited to economically developed democracies. Indeed, the bilateral trade flows account for liberal values and democratic legitimacy, leading to the promotion of peace among democratic nations (Mousseau & Mousseau, 2008). This is supported by the findings that greater quantities of publicly held assets in democracies lead governments to pursue more aggressive foreign policies and increase the likelihood of their participation in military conflict. Thus, capitalism promotes peace (Gleditsch, 2008). Since the 1990s, economic freedom through domestic institutions associated with capitalism, competitive market structure, and measures supporting privatization and trade liberalization have played a larger role than democracy in the promotion of peace between states (McDonald, 2009, 2010). Advanced democracies differ from developing democracies in their wealth, integration into the global economy, and in their post-World War II preference for convergence (Gartzke, 2007).

Weede (2011: 275) claimed that democratic peace works most effectively among mature and prosperous market-oriented democracies, and the market-oriented economy is an outcome of capitalism. Indeed, it is capitalism and free trade that leads to economic development and prosperity, which then enables democracy. Furthermore, capitalism promotes peace irrespective of the economic institutional attributes of a dyadic partner while the capacity of democracy to promote peace is conditioned by the presence of democratic institutions in a dyadic partner. Thus, democracy heightens the risk of being targeted while capitalism reduces it (McDonald, 2010). Even then, while the capital peace notion of a market economy is necessary, it does not suffice for democracy (Gleditsch, 2008).

Since the establishment of the world trading system in 1945, the promotion of a multilateral order has become the dominant ideology setting the tone for the Western World. However, until the early 1990s, the relationship between trade and conflict received relatively little attention (Barbieri & Schneider, 1999: 388–390). The late awakening in dealing with the relations between trade and conflict, according to van Bergeijk (2009) resulted from the misperception of Ricardo's ([1820] 1962) and John Stuart Mill's ([1840] 1968) origin of thought. As most classical and neoclassical economists throughout time shared the belief that intensified economic ties could be the basis of peaceful relations between countries, cooperation and conflict analysis were unnecessary. 'If commerce can supersede war, specialisation probably pays. So analyse and stimulate free trade as pure economics and secure peace as a by-product' (van Bergeijk,

2009: 24–25). Use of the same models and methods for establishing the foundation for capitalist peace as those that established democratic peace relies on the same set of actors, resulting in both types of societies, democracies, and capitalists being better able to signal their resolve in an interstate crisis. Thus, differentiation between the foundation of these two strands of liberal scholarship became impossible (Schneider & Gleditsch, 2010).

The capitalist peace theory is not new. Scholars, as already demonstrated, often cite Kant or Montesquieu in tracing the roots of the cost-benefit tradition in the research on trade and conflict. Others like Paine, Bastiat, Mill, Cobden, and Angell, saw in market forces the power to end war (Barbieri & Schneider, 1999: 388–390). Rosecrance (1986) showed that trade is an increasingly more efficient means for acquiring products and markets than military conquest. States are deterred from initiating conflict against a trading partner out of fear of losing the welfare gains associated with trade (Polachek, 1980). Even if conflict does not lead to the cessation of trade, it will lead to inferior terms of trade conditions eventually resulting in welfare losses. As such, Polachek and McDonald (1992) explained that the more inelastic a country's import and export demand and supply are with a target country, the fewer conflicts between actors and the target. Hegre (2000) has argued that the relationship between trade and conflict is contingent upon development. With increasing economic development, the cost of seizing and holding a territory increases, and the expected utility of conquest decreases. Developed states are, therefore, more likely to be trading states.

International trade as a criterion to measure mutual economic dependencies allows peace to be grasped as needed. That is, peace is not one to be imposed but that which can be achieved naturally between countries, as endorsed according to the liberal peace proposition (Murshed, 2002). However, this is not limited to democracies as demonstrated in van Bergeijk's (2009: 25–27) analysis. Keynes (1919) emphasized the economic causes of war in the pressure of populations and the competitive struggle for markets, and saw demand management as the solution. In Hobson's *Imperialism* (1902), a permanent threat of war is dependent on clashes of commercial interests. Lenin stressed the importance of attracting foreign direct investments from the West; and Bernstein's Revisionism supported free trade, arguing that the international exchange of goods and services should be the basic for a network of mutual interest and interdependencies as an antidote against 'aggressive' imperialism. Weede

(2005) argues that economic freedom, of which free trade is an important component, promotes economic development, thus laying a foundation for democracy and peace; and Mousseau et al. (2003), and Hegre (2000), suggested that the impact of both democracy and trade may be conditional on both states having developed economies.

2.3 Economic Diplomacy

Economic Diplomacy refers to the process of international economic decision-making while looking into activities that lie at the interface between the two fields of Economics and International Relations: processes that examine how states conduct their international economic relations, how they negotiate with each other internationally, how they make decisions domestically, how these policies and the process of policymaking become more efficient, and how these processes interact to influence decisions about cross-border economic activities, such as export, import, investment, lending and aid that are being pursued by governments and non-state actors (Bayne & Woolcock, 2011; van Bergeijk, 2009).

In a broader sense, economic diplomacy can be seen as 'the narrow stem of a funnel through which all expressions of the interrelations between international political economy and diplomatic studies are channeled' (Okano-Heijmans, 2011: 15). Economic diplomacy is defined in terms of means, focusing on the processes and practices to be employed. And though economic diplomacy may be largely concerned with actions taken by the state, it also considers the dynamic environment in which the state operates (Okano-Heijmans, 2011: 15–17). This finds support in Bayne's (2008: 1) definition for economic diplomacy as the 'method by which states conduct their external economic relations. It embraces how they make decisions domestically, how they negotiate internationally, and how the two processes interact'. Moreover, in a subsequent study (Bayne & Woolcock, 2011), the definition evolves into three levels of tension that need to be reconciled by governments for their policies to become mutually reinforcing, rather than conflicting with each other, that is, the tension between international economics and international politics, the tension between international and domestic pressures, and the tension between governments and other forces. As such, Economic diplomacy explores the dynamic processes integrating all actions across the economic-political spectrum. These actions include informal negotiation and voluntary cooperation through soft types of regulation (such as codes of conduct), creation and enforcement of binding rules, economic security, commercial diplomacy, and economic statecraft. These are considered as methods of economic diplomacy in action within the dynamic environment in which the state operates, both domestically and externally (Okano-Heijmans, 2011).

The fall of the Berlin Wall resulted in, among other outcomes, a situation where economic diplomacy was no longer prioritized only by official governmental representatives of a limited number of states. As a matter of fact, with the former communist states becoming more market-oriented and participatory, to a larger extent, in the world's single economic system, the phenomenon of globalization was accelerated (Held et al., 1999; Reich, 2010; Saner & Yiu, 2003; van Bergeijk & Oldersma, 1990). These newly emerging markets tend to focus on the specific role of commercial policy in their development process, making economic diplomacy a priority in foreign policy (Bayne & Woolcock, 2011; Lee & Hudson, 2004). Moreover, economic diplomacy increasingly also started to operate more within the domestic sphere, and influence local politics (Held et al., 1999; Reich, 2010; Saner & Yiu, 2003).

Considering the role of non-state actors, specifically the Multinational Enterprises (MNEs), consumer groups, and Non-Governmental Organizations (NGOs), together with the dominance of states, van Bergeijk (2009: 14) offers three distinctive elements of economic diplomacy:

- Commercial Policy—Bilateral economic diplomacy using political influence and relationships to promote or influence bilateral international trade and investment, improve on functioning of markets and/or address market failures and reduce costs and risks of cross-border transactions;
- Economic Security—The use of economic assets and relationships to increase the cost of conflict and to strengthen the mutual benefits of cooperation and politically stable relationships; and
- Trade Diplomacy—the domain of the supranational organizations and institutions covering multilateral negotiations, considering ways to consolidate the correct political climate and international political-economic environment to facilitate and institute these objectives.

Indeed, it is economics that is the core ability of nations to project power according to economic diplomacy. The integration of economics into the international system resulted in a clear linkage between economics and national security. The integration of new markets into the system together with the unprecedented levels of products and production, global warming, the occurrence of new forms of conflict, such as transnational terrorism, and the emergence of new security concerns following September 11, are all issues of interrelation between economic diplomacy and economic security that have risen to the top of the international policy agenda (van Bergeijk, 2009: 2–7, 17–18).

2.3.1 *Economics as Power*

> If any Member of the League breaks or ignores these promises with regard to arbitration and discussions, what happens, War? No, not War but something more tremendous than war. Apply this economic, peaceful, silent, deadly remedy and there will be no need for force. The boycott is what is substituted for war. A nation that is boycotted is a nation that is in sight of surrender. (US President Woodrow Wilson, 1919 in: Schrijver, 1993)

Economic strategies are prominent foreign policy instruments. Following the end of the Cold War, the economic sanctions regime proliferated, mainly through United Nations resolutions (Reisman, 2009). There are various types of economic sanctions, such as trade sanctions, that is, restrictions on imports from or exports to the target country; investment sanctions, which include restrictions on capital flows to the target or, in some cases, mandatory disinvestment; and more narrowly targeted, so-called smart sanctions, such as freezing the offshore assets of individual members of the target nation's ruling elite, or travel bans on government officials and party cadres. The sanctions are not necessarily imposed to inflict maximum economic damage to the target but are also used for expressive or demonstrative purposes. In all cases, the economic sanctions are expected to impose some level of pain on the target country, and particularly on its ruling regime. This may compel the regime to alter its policies in order to comply with the sender's demands and thereby avoid further damage (Halcoussis et al., 2021; Kaempfer & Lowenberg, 2007).

Throughout history, states have often resorted to economic sanctions to achieve political ends, whether as peacetime instruments belonging to *jus pacis*, or during armed conflict (Schrijver, 1993). Trade essentially provides states with a tool they would not otherwise have when disputes arise, with economic sanctions imposed to achieve all sorts of political means, as well as the prospects of these potential sanctions affecting state decisions. As such, it is the coercive potential of trade that can be argued as the reasoning for reducing conflicts (Stein, 2003).

'Demonstration of resolve' has often been the driving force behind the imposition of sanctions. The behaviour of the US post-World War II offers numerous examples of deploying sanctions to assert its leadership in world affairs (Hufbauer et al., 2009: 5–6). While military measures may indeed be too excessive to use by dominant states, as also claimed by Keohane and Nye (1973), and diplomatic protests are too meagre, economic sanctions provide a popular middle path for powerful actors to impose new norms in international diplomacy. Sanctions are often conceived by world leaders as satisfying theatrical display and yet ones that avoid the high costs of war. Sanctions have at least one of the five aims of compliance, subversion, deterrence, international symbolism, and domestic symbolism, and often succeed both as international and domestic symbols (Hufbauer et al., 2009: 30–34).

Since the early 1960s, sanctions have been deployed in support of numerous other foreign goals than the pursuit of war, peace, or political destabilization. Sanctions have also been used to protect human rights, to halt nuclear proliferation, to settle expropriation claims, and to combat international terrorism, as well as in negotiation efforts for overcompensation of expropriated property (Hufbauer et al., 2009: 5–6). Further, since the end of the Cold War, sanctions have been serving a wide range of purposes, such as being the centrepiece of efforts to repel aggression, restore democracy, condemn human rights abuse, and punish regimes harbouring terrorist and international war criminals (Lopez & Cortright, 2018). The schemes of collective security, measures for the prevention or containment of armed conflicts, and the enforcement of international law in the world regime brought to the front the concept of collective sanctions. Collective sanctions are defined as collective measures imposed by organs representing the international community, involving far-reaching reactions in response to perceived unlawful or unacceptable conduct by one of its members and meant to uphold standards of behaviour required by international law (Schrijver, 1993).

In a rising interdependence of global society, the pursuit of any positive or negative interest cannot be done without taking other's interests into account (Ananyev, 2019). The level of global economic interdependence already increased following WWII. It was the 1973 oil crisis that brought the economic conflict to the centre stage, demonstrating that conflicts in an interdependent world involve both 'guns and butter' (Nye, 1999: 186–195). Indeed, deterrence and coercion can take the form of actual or threatened economic sanctions and can be either in a positive or a negative form. While positive sanctions are treats in return for the target sanction country either adopting or neglecting to make specific policy changes, negative sanctions are measures that either impose costs or withhold benefits from the target sanctions country for pursuing or failing to pursue certain policies. Both negative and positive economic sanctions are needed for an optimal economic sanctions policy (Alexander, 2009). Sanctions can be perceived as a general measure for strengthening friendships and weakening enemies. However, for future demands to be conditioned by sanctions, van Bergeijk (2009: 162) argues for positive sanctions on cases of intangible exchange, such as the sharing of specific technologies and infrastructures. Also, the positive sanctions entail an international transfer of purchasing power.

In an interdependent world of guns and butter, the importance of economics as both a punitive and incentive tool is more central than ever, particularly since international conflicts are now on the rise and becoming more protracted, violent, intractable, fragmented, and asymmetric in nature. Economic diplomacy acknowledges the balance of power as being greater than the sum of its parts, however economic incentives, such as more positive sanctions, should be given special attention at the international level, specifically in situations of inherent asymmetricity as these are in many ways the representations of the global 'butter'.

2.4 A Conflict and Its Resolution

Modern conflicts are asymmetric by nature. While most of these conflicts take the shape of civil wars or intrastate conflicts, other forms are guerilla warfare, extreme violence, or counterinsurgency (Arreguín-Toft, 2012; Murshed, 2010: 3). In these types of conflicts, the stronger parties usually enjoy state authority, legitimacy, sovereignty, and institutionalized alliances, and hold economic, political, and military power. Consequently, to a large extent, the stronger side may determine the rules of the game. On the other hand, the weaker party most often lacks these large-scale resources, while power mobilization is based on mutual grounds and commitments to goals as resistance of domination, exclusion, persecution, dispossession of land, and loss of resources, among others (Habeeb, 1988: 8; Zartman, 1995: 7–8).

The origin of asymmetric warfare can be attributed to the evolution of modern states throughout history. The creation of nationalism was led by principles of sovereignty and national self-determination, and conceived in ethnic, religious, or national terms. The end of World War II marked a key turning point in the formation of modern asymmetric conflicts. During the 1950s and 1960s, wars of national liberation, mainly ideological in character and associated with decolonization, took place around the world. During the 1970s and 1980s, internal wars emerging in the successor states gradually shifted to post-colonial civil wars. These wars took place in the context of the bipolar warfare between the United States and the *Union of Soviet Socialist Republics—the Soviet Union (USSR)*, with the superpowers' intervention being part of a continuing geopolitical struggle for power and influence. In the 1990s, the further evolution in prevailing patterns of conflicts would be viewed through these lenses as the third phase of national wars. These post-Cold War wars are known as peoples' wars, revolutionary wars, or wars of the third kind, and share a pattern resembling medieval wars characterized by their lack of differentiation between state and society, soldier and civilian, war and organized crime (Ramsbotham et al., 2011). As these conflicts are highly antagonistic, and prone to anarchy, they evoke extreme notions of security and identity (Barak, 2005). Whether defined as uprising, insurgency, guerrilla warfare, ethnic cleansing or genocide, the primary goal of the belligerents is political independence, making territory inevitably central. Furthermore, all of these conflicts have shared consequences, driving up the number of refugees and internally displaced persons, increase in civilian deaths in comparison with military deaths, and are associated with regional instability, political fragmentation, and fragile state structure (Fixdal, 2012; Ramsbotham et al., 2011).

The prohibition of using force at the international level painstakingly evolved from the beginning of the twentieth century. The United Nations Charter of 1945, for the very first time, prohibited threat or use of force outright (Schrijver, 2005: 32–33). Furthermore, with the end of World War II new structural and procedural arrangements, such as the Marshall Plan and the European Economic Community (EEC) were established, giving rise to a new form of community, one wider than national belonging (Ackermann, 2003). These communities emerged as a stable form of interstate politics among democracies in the Global North, grounded in a reliable expectation of peaceful change, domestic rule of law, stable international institutions, and intensive societal interactions (Moravcsik, 1997), termed by Deutsch et al. (1957) as *pluralistic security community, complex interdependence* by Keohane & Nye (1973), or *liberal security community* (Moravcsik, 1997).

The end of the Cold War brought a shift in the fundamental patterns of power division between the East and West. Boundaries of nascent security communities, whether already existing or newly emerging, started to blur and extend more than even before. A stable and more peaceful international order was promoted through shared understandings and transnational values in building new communities (Russett, 2011: 129–130). With the deepening of those shared values and transnational linkages, security became both a condition and a quality for these communities. Power, accordingly, adapted to include the ability of a community to defend its values against external threats. Whereas security once meant a military threat, in the post-Cold War world states have been identifying a variety of security issues, ones that revolve around economic, environmental, and social welfare concerns (Adler & Barnett, 1998: 4). Indeed, the nation state has become the focal point of globalized and localized pressure, leading to the imagining of new forms of communities. The security and well-being of growing numbers of people is being imagined based on shared values, norms, and common understanding of proper behaviour in both international and domestic arenas. These communities are bound by the sense of community, mutual sympathy, and common interest, as was claimed for any 'Imagined Community' originally portrayed by Anderson (1983), and bordered where shared understanding and common identity ends (Adler, 1997: 250–251). As such, neither states nor social networks carry changes of social structures across functional and geographical boundaries, but communities of practice, defined as likeminded groups of practitioners who are informally as well as contextually bound by a shared interest in learning and applying a common practice. Security communities are a type of communities of practice that allow not merely a change, but one that is as peaceful as desired (Adler, 2008).

Already prior to the end of the Cold War early in 1990, policy measures of economic reforms based on the recommendation of the World Bank (WB) and International Monetary Fund (IMF) were requested by the Soviet government. Thus, following the end of the Cold War, while collective security was brought centre stage, similarly significant was the fact that the Western international financial institutions also became at least as important as the nation states. This process of globalization of the world economy strengthened the interconnectedness between political, military, and economic conditions resulting in economic security becoming inseparable from the collective one (Kaufmann et al., 1991: 138).

2.4.1 *Trade as Development*

The 1944 Bretton Woods conference, followed by its agreements' ratification, established the post war international economic and financial system through which the financial economic order was developed (Held & McGrew, 2000: 163–167). In the post-World War II era, successive rounds of trade negotiations were carried out under the auspices of the GATT leading to trade liberalization and expansion, and to the increasing linkages of the global economy (Gilpin & Gilpin, 2001: 96–98). The process by which economies become highly integrated leads to the formation of a global economy and is known as globalization (Bordo et al., 2007; Todaro & Smith, 2009: 589–592).

In this global economic system, interventionism and protectionism are abandoned in favour of laissez-faire policies and international openness in free trade, out of the belief that this will enable the aspired level of development. In this context, globalization, trade, development, and international political economy have become mutually embedded.

Since the 1990s, the move towards greater openness and reductions in trade barriers has been taking place not only among the industrialized countries, but also the developing ones. The end of the Cold War leading to the opening of Eastern European economies with the introduction of the New World Order (NWO),[5] and the successful conclusion of the multilateral trade negotiations under the GATT (the Uruguay Round in 1993), which led to the creation of the World Trade Organization (WTO), contributed to further extension of trade liberalization, and worldwide trade relations, with many more countries becoming a part of it (van Bergeijk, 1994: 4–6; Held & McGrew, 2000; Milner, 1999).

The integration of rapidly growing emerging market economies into the international trading system led to the tripling of global output of trade in 2010 as compared to early 1950s (IMF, 2011). The tremendous

[5] The New World Order (NWO) that had replaced the bipolar politics of the Cold War era was introduced by former US president George Bush during the 1990–1991 Persian Gulf crisis.

growth in international trade has shaped contemporary economies, with few, if any, economies able to become self-sufficient (Ma & Lu, 2011). The massive increase in the scope of trade also encouraged many transformations in trade regulations around the world, involving the tearing down of trade barriers erected by governments to promote national economic development. This was believed to be the way to enable the course for mutual benefits and enhancement of development across all borders (Fligstein, 2005; Swedberg, 2005).

Still, for achieving accelerated growth and sustainable development, that is, 'sustained growth', minimal civic and economic/social human rights are a precondition. Thus, the general economic policies, and specifically the promotion of free trade, were associated with environmental and political policies from the end of the Cold War onwards (Kaufmann et al., 1991: 138). Additionally, the increase in global conflicts during the 1990s, marked by heightened violence and widespread wars, along with the influence of Western liberal values strengthened by the international supremacy of the US, led to a shift in development policy. As a result, from a 'narrow' economic policy perspective, development assistance became the instrument to pursue the promotion of social progress, peace, and reconciliation to achieve human development in countries emerging from violent conflict. Since prevention of violence and conflict eruption are post-conflict policies that also foster peace promotion, development should be understood not only as a post-conflict tool, but also a preventive conflict instrument to achieve inclusive human security (Uvin, 2002).

The 1992 Agenda for Peace of the United Nations Secretary-General (UNSG) Boutros Boutros Ghali 47/277, underpins the relations between economic development and peace to address causes of violent conflict through economic and social development in order to achieve peace (United Nations General Assembly (UNGA), 1992).[6] Complex emergencies and reflexive modernization have led to development being reinvented, acquiring a new strategic role. As such, for example, according to the European Commission (EC) (1996) development is seen as having a capacity for conflict resolution. The Development Assistance Committee (DAC) of the Organization for Economic Cooperation and Development

[6] UNGA (1992) Report 47/277, UNSC Report 24111, *An Agenda for Peace: Preventive diplomacy, Peacemaking and peace-keeping: Report of the Secretary-General pursuant to the statement adopted by the Summit Meeting of the Security Council on 31 January 1992*, A/47/277; S/24111 (31 January 1992).

(OECD) guidelines on evaluating conflict prevention and peacebuilding activities primarily focuses on addressing the roots of violent conflicts through long-term structural preventive measures, which are formed into the developmental assistance programmes (OECD, 2002). And, according to the UNGA Resolution 70/1 (2015), the 2030 Agenda for Sustainable Development Goals defines development as being:

> a plan of action for people, planet and prosperity (…) seeks to strengthen universal peace in larger freedom. (…) a world free of poverty, hunger, disease and want, where all life can thrive (…) equitable and universal access to quality education at all levels, to health care and social protection, where physical mental and social well-being are assured (…). A world where human habitants are safe, resilient and sustainable (…) a world of universal respect for human rights and human dignity, the rule of law, justice, equality and non-discrimination (…) a world in which every country enjoys sustained, inclusive and sustainable economic growth and decent work for all (…). One in which democracy, good governance and the rule of law, as well as an enabling environment at the national and international levels, are essential for sustainable development, including sustained and inclusive economic growth, social development, environmental protection and the eradication of poverty and hunger.[7]

The concept of development has come a long way from the original definition of being purely economic in essence. Yet, in the evolution of development policy as the way for peace, the economic component has remained essential in all the different forms and variations over the years. Indeed, growth and poverty alleviation are necessary and even crucial, but without economic development, efforts to sustain peace will not suffice (World Bank Group and United Nations, 2018). As for trade, the outcomes of the global trend towards trade liberalization have shown, at least to some extent, evidence supporting the implementation of this policy. In their analysis, Wacziarg and Welch (2008) illustrated empirical evidence of higher average annual growth rates due to trade liberalization, while Bekaert et al. (2005) demonstrated that equity market liberalizations, on average, lead to a 1 per cent increase in annual real economic growth. Moreover, not only does enough economic evidence exist to support this

[7] UNGA (2015) Resolution 70/1, *Transforming our world: The 2030 agenda for sustainable development*, A/RES/70/1 (21 October 2015).

policy, studies showed that conducting free trade policies is indeed helpful in promoting other fields.[8]

Free trade is being contested for shifting from 'comparative' to 'competitive' advantages, with the development and implications of trade strategies undermining support of trade liberalization (Gilpin & Gilpin, 2001: 196–198). Nonetheless, policies in promotion of free trade cannot be overlooked as free trade agreements (FTAs) are covering every sphere of our lives from agriculture and rules of origin, to services and intellectual property rights. These are being negotiated in larger and more exclusionary scales than ever before. Some examples from recent years are: Transatlantic Trade and Investment Partnership (TTIP), Trans-Pacific Partnership (TPP), EU-Canada comprehensive trade agreement (CETA), EU-Africa multiple Free Trade Agreements and Economic Partnership Agreements (EPAs)[9], and EU-China Comprehensive Agreement on Investment (CAI), among others. At the same time, the notion that free trade is the best of all possible policies is part of the neoclassical case for laissez-faire in a market economy, and rests on the proposition that markets are efficient. However, models emphasizing increasing returns and imperfect competition have been supplementing the constant returns and perfect competition that characterize international trade theory, including the comparative advantage theory. These models are a result of new approaches that provide a more enriched understanding of the causes and consequences of trade, as the geography and trade approach, or the industrial-organization one (Krugman, 1987).

[8] An example of this can be observed when examining how the implementation of free trade policies impact environmental preservation. A meta-analysis of 149 studies published before May 2018, investigating economic variables and their effects on environmental emissions, finds a negative effect between the control of trade openness (Demena & Afesorgbor, 2020).

[9] Five Economic Partnership Agreements between the EU and 14 Sub-Saharan African countries:

EU-Southern African Development Community (SADC) EPA, EU-Eastern and Southern Africa EPA: Madagascar, Mauritius, Seychelles, Zimbabwe and Comoros—the so-called ESA 5, EU-Cote d'Ivoire EPA, EU-Ghana EPA, EU-Cameroon EPA, EU-Cariforum EPA, and EU-Pacific EPA; and four FTAs as part of the Association Agreements with North African countries as part of our common Union for the Mediterranean space (European Commission (EC), 2023).

2.4.2 *Distance Does Matter*

Technological changes have been argued to revolutionize the world economy by reducing, if not eliminating, the impact of spatial separation (Disdier & Head, 2008). Indeed, the technological improvement in mobility has affected the convergence in wages. However, mobility is not movement, and as such, the geography of commerce has not changed (Leamer, 2007).

A meta-analysis of the gravity model of 1467 estimates from 103 papers for the years 1880–2000 found an elasticity of 0.9 for trade. This indicates that on average bilateral trade is nearly inversely proportional to distance. While a slight decrease has been seen between 1870 and 1950, it was followed by a rise from there onwards. Moreover, the analysis shows that distance effects on trade have been found in a wide range of samples and methodologies and are not declining even in studies employing more recent data (Disdier & Head, 2008). Another key factor affecting the costs of distant trade is the accessibility of information. Yet, despite the reduction in transport costs, and a significant improvement in communication technologies, results of disaggregated bilateral trade data regressions for 776 industries in 100 countries from 1985 onwards, confirm that the importance of distance in regard to trade is very significant, and the distance-related costs effect on trade has remained roughly unchanged for most industries (Berthelon & Freund, 2008).

Understanding cultural etiquette and building trust is essential for establishing trade agreements (Leamer, 2007). Common cultural and/or religious background reduces transaction costs between trading partners (Đào & van Bergeijk, 2022). Language, as claimed by Lameli et al. (2015), is the most identifiable factor for the promotion of international trade relations as evident in their standard gravity analysis of trade relations between East and West Germany. In addition to common language, colonial ties may be perceived as those being 'at best [an] imperfect representation of cultural similarity'. These factors are all representatives of cultural attributes, and at the state level, translate into social and institutional dis/similarity, and/or information asymmetries represented by the trust level (Tadesse & White, 2010: 238). Given that the quality of the institutions encourages the norms of behaviour, greater institutional similarity among trading partners leads to higher levels of trust (De Groot et al., 2004).

The negative effects of distance on bilateral trade are not contested. It is the transformation processes in the world and the spread of globalization that have been argued to reduce the distance effect on trade (Borchert & Yotov, 2017). As globalization alters the world from being round to flat, the world is merely a 'global village' with costs and barriers of geographic distance becoming negligible (Friedman, 2006). Nevertheless, as Leamer (2007) argued, a flat world represents the open market for goods and services of globalization. Globalization, however, is the pace at which ideas are spread as ideas determine the rate of progress. These ideas are defined by van Bergeijk (2015) as 'unseen walls' or 'invisible walls', that create a very strong impact on the real economy. Thus, in a world in which cultural differences are increasingly becoming cultural poles between the East and West, and pluralism and totalitarianism, not only does that distancing effect remain on bilateral trade, but in some respects has increased it tremendously. Indeed, and in contrast to popular beliefs, estimations of the distance effect on trade repeatedly show beyond the polarization of the West and East, that the distance-related variables have become more important instead of less (van Bergeijk & Brakman, 2010: 2).

With globalization referring to developments of integration between the spheres of economics, social, and political structures through the international system, a new world order has emerged. This new world order has not only brought international entities and alternative society formations such as the security community to the centre stage, it has also made conflicts more protracted, violent, intractable, fragmented, and asymmetric in nature. At the same time, the new world order has also ushered in new ways of conflict resolution, other than traditional military ones.

Bibliography

Ackermann, A. (2003). The idea and practice of conflict prevention. *Journal of Peace Research, 40*(3), 339–347.

Adler, E. (1997). Seizing the middle ground: Constructivism in world politics. *European Journal of International Relations, 3*(3), 319–363.

Adler, E. (2008). The spread of security communities: Communities of practice, self-restraint, and NATO's post—Cold War transformation. *European Journal of International Relations, 14*(2), 195–230.

Adler, E., & Barnett, M. (Eds.). (1998). *Security communities*. Cambridge University Press.

Alexander, K. (2009). *Economic sanctions law and public policy*. Palgrave Macmillan.

Ananyev, B. (2019). Sanctions in IR: Understanding, defining, studying. *International Organisations Research Journal, 14*(3), 136–150.
Arel, D., & Driscoll, J. (2023). *Ukraine's unnamed war: Before the Russian invasion of 2022.* Cambridge University Press.
Arreguín-Toft, I. (2012). Contemporary asymmetric conflict theory in historical perspective. *Terrorism and Political Violence, 24*(4), 635–657.
Bandeira, L. A. M. (2019). *The world disorder: US hegemony, proxy wars, terrorism and humanitarian catastrophes.* Springer.
Barak, O. (2005). The failure of the Israeli–Palestinian peace process, 1993–2000. *Journal of Peace Research, 42*(6), 719–736.
Barbieri, K. (2002). *The liberal illusion: Does trade promote peace?* University of Michigan Press.
Barbieri, K., & Schneider, G. (1999). Globalization and peace: Assessing new directions in the study of trade and conflict. *Journal of Peace Research, 36*(4), 387–404.
Bayne, N. (2008). Financial diplomacy and the credit crunch: The rise of central banks. *Journal of International Affairs, 62*, 1–16.
Bayne, N., & Woolcock, S. (2011). *The new economic diplomacy: Decision-making and negotiation in international economic relations.* Ashgate Publishing, Ltd.
Bekaert, G., Harvey, C. R., & Lundblad, C. (2005). Does financial liberalization spur growth? *Journal of Financial Economics, 77*(1), 3–55.
Benoit, K. (1996). Democracies really are more Pacific (in general) reexamining regime type and war involvement. *Journal of Conflict Resolution, 40*(4), 636–657.
Berthelon, M., & Freund, C. (2008). On the conservation of distance in international trade. *Journal of International Economics, 75*(2), 310–320.
Borchert, I., & Yotov, Y. V. (2017). Distance, globalization, and international trade. *Economics Letters, 153*, 32–38.
Bordo, M. D., Taylor, A. M., & Williamson, J. G. (2007). *Globalization in historical perspective.* University of Chicago Press.
Boutros-Ghali, B. (1995). *An agenda for development 1995: With related UN documents,* [ST/]DPI/1622/DEV, United Nations: New York.
Boutros-Ghali, B. (1996, December 20). United Nations General Assembly (UNGA) Report 51/761 *An agenda for democratization,* New York: UN Department of Public Information [ST/]DPI/1867, A/51/761. Retrieved December 20, 2020, from https://documents-dds-ny.un.org/doc/UNDOC/GEN/N96/371/60/PDF/N9637160.pdf?OpenElement.
Bremer, S. A. (1992). Dangerous dyads: Conditions affecting the likelihood of interstate war, 1816–1965. *Journal of Conflict Resolution, 36*(2), 309–341.
Chan, S. (1997). In search of democratic peace: Problems and promise. *Mershon International Studies Review, 41*(1), 59–91.

Covell, C. (1998). The definitive articles of perpetual peace. In *Kant and the law of peace: A study in the philosophy of international law and international relations.* Palgrave Macmillan.

D'Anieri, P. (2022). Conflict studies and the war in Ukraine, 2014–2022. *Journal of Soviet and Post-Soviet Politics and Society, 8*(2), 117–152.

Đào, K. T., & van Bergeijk, P. A. G. (2022). Winds from the East: Ancient Asian views on international trade. ISS working papers. General series, no. 705, International Institute of Social Studies (ISS), Den Haag.

De Groot, H. L., Linders, G. J., Rietveld, P., & Subramanian, U. (2004). The institutional determinants of bilateral trade patterns. *Kyklos, 57*(1), 103–123.

De Mesquita, B. B., Morrow, J. D., Siverson, R. M., & Smith, A. (1999). An institutional explanation of the democratic peace. *American Political Science Review, 93*(4), 791–807.

Demena, B. A., & Afesorgbor, S. K. (2020). The effect of FDI on environmental emissions: Evidence from a meta-analysis. *Energy Policy, 138*, 111192.

Deutsch, K. W., Burrell, S. A., Kann, R. A., Lee, M., Lichterman, M., Lindgren, R. E., Loewenheim, F. L., & van Wagenen, R. W. (1957). *Political community and the North Atlantic Area: International organization in the light of historical experience.* Princeton University Press.

Disdier, A. C., & Head, K. (2008). The puzzling persistence of the distance effect on bilateral trade. *The Review of Economics and Statistics, 90*(1), 37–48.

Doyle, M. W. (1986). Liberalism and world politics. *American Political Science Review, 80*(4), 1151–1169.

Doyle, M. W. (1997). Ways of war and peace: Realism. *Liberalism, and Socialism, 219*, 24–25.

Doyle, M. W. (2005). Three pillars of the liberal peace. *American Political Science Review, 99*(3), 463–466.

Duncombe, C., & Dunne, T. (2018). After liberal world order. *International Affairs, 94*(1), 25–42.

European Commission (EC). (1996). *Communication of April 30 from the commission to the council and the European Parliament on Linking, Relief, Rehabilitation and Development (LRRD).* Commission of the European Communities.

European Commission (EC). (2023). *Economic partnerships.* Retrieved August 19, 2023, from https://policy.trade.ec.europa.eu/development-and-sustainability/economic-partnerships_en.

Fixdal, M. (2012). Introduction: Peacemaking in asymmetrical conflicts. In M. Fixdal (Ed.), *Ways out of war: Peacemakers in the Middle East and Balkans* (pp. 1–30). Palgrave Macmillan US.

Fligstein, N. (2005). The political and economic sociology of international economic arrangements. In *Handbook of economic sociology* (pp. 183–204). Princeton University Press.

Friedman, T. L. (2006). *The world is flat [updated and expanded]: A brief history of the twenty-first century*. Macmillan.

Fukuyama, F. (2022, March 4). Putin's war on the liberal order. *Financial Times*.

Gartzke, E. (1998). Kant we all just get along? Opportunity, willingness, and the origins of the democratic peace. *American Journal of Political Science, 42*(1), 1–27.

Gartzke, E. (2007). The capitalist peace. *American Journal of Political Science, 51*(1), 166–191.

Gartzke, E., & Hewitt, J. J. (2010). International crises and the capitalist peace. *International Interactions, 36*, 115–145.

Gilpin, R., & Gilpin, J. M. (2001). *Global political economy: Understanding the international economic order*. Princeton University Press.

Gleditsch, N. P. (2008). The liberal moment fifteen years on. *International Studies Quarterly, 52*(4), 691–712.

Habeeb, W. M. (1988). *Power and tactics in international negotiation: How weak nations bargain with strong nations*. Johns Hopkins University Press.

Halcoussis, D., Kaempfer, W. H., & Lowenberg, A. D. (2021). The public choice approach to international sanctions: Retrospect and prospect. In P. A. G. van Bergeijk (Ed.), *Research handbook on economic sanctions* (pp. 152–166). US Edward Elgar Publishing Limited; Edward Elgar Publishing, Inc.

Hayes, J. (2012). The democratic peace and the new evolution of an old idea. *European Journal of International Relations, 18*(4), 767–791.

Hegre, H. (2000). Development and the liberal peace: What does it take to be a trading state? *Journal of Peace Research, 37*(1), 5–30.

Held, D., Goldblatt, D., McGrew, A., Perraton, J., & Hampson, F. O. (1999). Global transformations: Politics, economics and culture. In C. Pierson & S. Tormey (Eds.), *Politics at the edge: The PSA yearbook 1999* (pp. 14–28). Palgrave Macmillan UK.

Held, D., & McGrew, A. (2000). *The global transformations reader*. Polity Press.

Helleiner, E. (2014). *Forgotten foundations of Bretton Woods: International development and the making of the postwar order*. Cornell University Press.

Holsti, K. J. (1991). *Peace and war: Armed conflicts and international order, 1648–1989*. Cambridge University Press.

Hufbauer, G. C., Schott, J. J., Elliott, K. A., & Oegg, B. (2009). *Economic sanctions reconsidered* (3rd ed.). Peterson Institute for International Economics.

Hughes, G. (2014). Ukraine: Europe's new proxy war. *Fletcher Security Review, 1*(II), 105–118.

Ikenberry, G. J. (2011). *Liberal leviathan: The origins, crisis, and transformation of the American world order*. Princeton University Press.

Ikenberry, G. J. (2014). The illusion of geopolitics: The enduring power of the liberal order. *Foreign Affairs, 93*, 80–92.

International Monetary Fund (IMF). (2011, June). *Changing Patterns of Global Trade.*
Kaempfer, W. H., & Lowenberg, A. D. (2007). The political economy of economic sanctions. In T. Sandler & K. Hartley (Eds.), *Handbook of defense economics Volume 2 Defence in a globalized world* (pp. 867–911). North-Holland.
Kaufmann, J., Leurdijk, D. A., & Schrijver, N. (1991). *The world in turmoil: Testing the UN's capacity*. Academic Council on the United Nations System.
Keohane, & Nye, (1973). *Power and interdependence.* Pearson.
Krugman, P. R. (1987). Is free trade passé? *The Journal of Economic Perspectives, 1*(2), 131–144.
Lameli, A., Südekum, J., Nitsch, V., & Wolf, N. (2015). Same same but different: Dialects and trade. *German Economic Review, 16*(3), 290–306.
Leamer, E. E. (2007). A flat world, a level playing field, a small world after all, or none of the above? A review of Thomas L Friedman's the world is flat. *Journal of Economic Literature, 45*(1), 83–126.
Lee, D., & Hudson, D. (2004). The old and new significance of political economy in diplomacy. *Review of International Studies, 30*(3), 343–360.
Lombardo, C. E. (2001). The making of an agenda for democratization: A Speechwriter's view. *Chicago Journal of International Law, 2*(1), 253–266.
Lopez, G. A., & Cortright, D. (2018). Economic sanctions in contemporary global relations. In D. Cortright (Ed.), *Economic sanctions panacea or peacebuilding in a post-cold war world?* (pp. 3–16). Routledge.
Ma, J., & Lu, Y. (2011). Free trade or protection: A literature review on trade barriers. *Research in World Economy, 2*(1), 69–76.
Maoz, Z., & Russett, B. (1993). Normative and structural causes of democratic peace, 1946–1986. *American Political Science Review, 87*(3), 624–638.
McDonald, P. J. (2007). The purse strings of peace. *American Journal of Political Science, 51*(3), 569–582.
McDonald, P. J. (2009). *The invisible hand of peace: Capitalism, the war machine, and international relations theory.* Cambridge University Press.
McDonald, P. J. (2010). Capitalism, commitment, and peace. *International Interactions, 36*(2), 146–168.
Mearsheimer, J. J. (2014). Why the Ukraine crisis is the West's fault: The liberal delusions that provoked Putin. *Foreign Affairs, 93*, 77–89.
Milner, H. V. (1999). The political economy of international trade. *Annual Review of Political Science, 2*(1), 91–114.
Moravcsik, A. (1997). Taking preferences seriously: A liberal theory of international politics. *International Organization, 51*(4), 513–553.
Moravcsik, A. (2010). *Liberal theories of international relations: A primer.* Princeton University.
Mousseau, M. (2013). The democratic peace unraveled: It's the economy. *International Studies Quarterly, 57*(1), 186–197.

Mousseau, M., Hegre, H., & O'neal, J. R. (2003). How the wealth of nations conditions the liberal peace. *European Journal of International Relations, 9*(2), 277–314.

Mousseau, M., & Mousseau, D. Y. (2008). The contracting roots of human rights. *Journal of Peace Research, 45*(3), 327–344.

Müller, H., & Wolff, J. (2004). Dyadic democratic peace strikes back, 5th Pan-European International Relations Conference, The Hague.

Murshed, S. M. (2002). Conflict, civil war and underdevelopment: An introduction. *Journal of Peace Research, 39*(4), 387–393.

Murshed, S. M. (2010). *Explaining civil war: A rational choice approach.* Edward Elgar Publishing.

Murshed, S. M. (2011). Economic dimensions of the liberal peace and its implications for conflict in developing countries. In S. Tadjbakhsh (Ed.), *Rethinking the liberal peace: External models and local alternatives* (pp. 164–179). Taylor & Francis.

Naz, A. (2023). Continued hostilities between Russia and Ukraine (2015–2022). *Pakistan Review of Social Sciences (PRSS), 4*(1), 70–84.

Nye, J. S. (1999). *Understanding international conflicts: An introduction to theory and history.* Longman.

OECD. (2002). Development co-operation Report 2001: *Efforts and Policies of the Members of the Development Assistance Committee*, OECD Publishing, Paris.

Okano-Heijmans, M. (2011). Conceptualizing economic diplomacy: The crossroads of international relations, economics, IPE and diplomatic studies. *The Hague Journal of Diplomacy, 6*(1–2), 7–36.

Oneal, J. R., & Russet, B. M. (1997). The classical liberals were right: Democracy, interdependence, and conflict, 1950–1985. *International Studies Quarterly, 41*(2), 267–293.

Owen, J. M. (1994). How liberalism produces democratic peace. *International Security, 19*(2), 87–125.

Paris, R. (2002). International peacebuilding and the 'mission civilisatrice'. *Review of International Studies, 28*(4), 637–656.

Peterson, J. W., & Kuck, S. (2014). Civil War in Ukraine: Ethnic conflict, authoritarian leadership, and outside involvement. *Contemporary European Studies, 1*, 23–44.

Polachek, S. W. (1980). Conflict and trade. *Journal of Conflict Resolution, 24*(1), 55–78.

Polacheck & McDonald (1992). Strategic trade and the incentive for cooperation. In *Disarmament, economic conversion, and management of peace*, 273–284.

Polachek, S. W., & Seiglie, C. (2007). Trade, peace and democracy: An analysis of dyadic dispute. In T. Sandler & K. Hartley (Eds.), *Handbook of defense economics Volume 2 Defence in a globalized world* (pp. 1017–1073). North-Holland.

Ramsbotham, O., Miall, H., & Woodhouse, T. (2011). *Contemporary conflict resolution*. Polity.
Reich, R. B. (2010). *The work of nations: Preparing ourselves for 21st century capitalism*. Vintage.
Reisman, W. M. (2009). Sanctions and international law. *Intercultural Human Rights Law Review, 4*, 9–20.
Richmond, O. P. (2006). The problem of peace: Understanding the 'liberal peace'. *Conflict, Security and Development, 6*(3), 291–314.
Richmond, O. P. (2009). A post-liberal peace: Eirenism and the everyday. *Review of International Studies, 35*(3), 557–580.
Risse-Kappen, T. (1995). Democratic peace—warlike democracies? A social constructivist interpretation of the liberal argument. *European Journal of International Relations, 1*(4), 491–517.
Rosato, S. (2003). The flawed logic of democratic peace theory. *American Political Science Review, 97*(4), 585–602.
Rosecrance, R. N. (1986). *The rise of the trading state: Commerce and conquest in the modern world*. Basic Books.
Rousseau, D. L., Gelpi, C., Reiter, D., & Huth, P. K. (1996). Assessing the dyadic nature of the democratic peace, 1918–88. *American Political Science Review, 90*(3), 512–533.
Russett, B. (1994). *Grasping the democratic peace: Principles for a post-Cold War world*. Princeton University Press.
Russett, B. (2011). *Hegemony and democracy*. Taylor & Francis.
Saner, R., & Yiu, L. (2003). International economic diplomacy: Mutations in post-modern times. Discussion Paper in Diplomacy No. 84, SSN 1569-2981, Netherlands Institute of International Relations "Clingendael".
Schneider, G., & Gleditsch, N. P. (2010). The capitalist peace: The origins and prospects of a liberal idea. *International Interactions, 36*(2), 107–114.
Schrijver, N. (1993). *The use of economic sanctions by the UN Security Council: An international law perspective*. Centre for Development Studies.
Schrijver, N. (2005). Challenges to the prohibition to use force: Does the straitjacket of Article 2 (4) UN charter begin to gall too much? In N. M. Blokker & N. Schrijver (Eds.), *The security council and the use of force* (pp. 31–45). Brill Nijhoff.
Schrijver, N. (2006). The future of the charter of the United Nations. In A. V. Bogdandy & R. Wolfrum (Eds.), *Max Planck yearbook of United Nations Law Online* (Vol. 10, pp. 1–34). Brill.
Stein, A. A. (2003). Trade and conflict: Uncertainty, strategic signaling, and interstate disputes. In E. D. Mansfield & B. Pollins (Eds.), *Economic interdependence and international conflict: New perspectives on an enduring debate* (pp. 111–126). University of Michigan Press.

Swedberg, R. (2005). Markets in society. In N. J. Smelser & R. Swedberg (Eds.), *The handbook of economic sociology*. Princeton University Press.
Tadesse, B., & White, R. (2010). Does cultural distance hinder trade in goods? A comparative study of nine OECD member nations. *Open Economies Review, 21*, 237–261.
Todaro, M. P., & Smith, S. C. (2009). *Economic development*. Pearson Education.
Turan, İ. (2023). The Ukraine-Russia crises of 2014 and 2022 on the axis of the perception of the "other". In A. Kara & R. Bazancir (Eds.), *Pioneer and contemporary studies in social, human and administrative sciences* (pp. 207–220). Duvar Publishing.
United Nations (UN). (1945, October 24). Charter of the United Nations and Statute of the International Court of Justice. Retrieved March 17, 2023, from https://www.un.org/en/about-us/un-charter.
United Nations General Assembly (UNGA). (1992, January 31). *Report 47/277*. United Nations Security Council (UNSC) *Report 24111. An agenda for peace: Preventive diplomacy, peacemaking and peace-keeping, Report of the Secretary-General pursuant to the statement adopted by the Summit Meeting of the Security Council on 31 January 1992*, A/47/277-S/24111. Retrieved December 20, 2020, from https://documents-ddsny.un.org/doc/UNDOC/GEN/N92/259/61/PDF/N9225961.pdf?OpenElement.
United Nations General Assembly (UNGA). (2015, October 21). *Resolution 70/1. Transforming our world: The 2030 agenda for sustainable development*, A/RES/70/1. Retrieved January 11, 2023, from https://documents-dds-ny.un.org/doc/UNDOC/GEN/N15/291/89/PDF/N1529189.pdf?OpenElement.
Uvin, P. (2002). The development/peacebuilding nexus: A typology and history of changing paradigms. *Journal of Peacebuilding & Development, 1*(1), 5–24.
van Bergeijk, P. A. G. (1994). *Economic diplomacy, trade and commercial policy: Positive and negative sanctions in a new world order*. Edward Elgar Publishing.
van Bergeijk, P. A. G. (2009). *Economic diplomacy and the geography of international trade*. Edward Elgar Publishing.
van Bergeijk, P. A. G. (2015). Visible and invisible walls: World trade patterns and the end of the Cold War. *Acta Oeconomica, 65*(2), 231–247.
van Bergeijk, P. A. G. (2019). *Deglobalization 2.0: Trade and openness during the great depression and the great recession*. Edward Elgar Publishing.
van Bergeijk, P. A. G., & Brakman, S. (2010). Introduction: The comeback of the gravity model. In P. A. G. van Bergeijk & S. Brakman (Eds.), *The gravity model in international trade: Advances and applications* (pp. 1–26). Cambridge University Press.
van Bergeijk, P. A. G., & Oldersma, H. (1990). Détente, market-oriented reform and German Unification: Potential consequences for the World Trade System. *Kyklos, 43*(4), 599–609.

Wacziarg, R., & Welch, K. H. (2008). Trade liberalization and growth: New evidence. *The World Bank Economic Review, 22*(2), 187–231.
Weede, E. (2005). *Balance of power, globalization and the capitalist peace.* Liberal-Verlag Berlin.
Weede, E. (2011). 14 The capitalist peace. In C. J. Coyne & R. L. Matehrs (Eds.), *The handbook on the political economy of war* (pp. 269–274). Edward Elgar Publishing Limited.
Williams, M. C. (2001). The discipline of the democratic peace: Kant, liberalism and the social construction of security communities. *European Journal of International Relations, 7*(4), 525–553.
World Bank Group and United Nations. (2018). *Pathways for peace inclusive approaches to preventing violent conflict.* International Bank for Reconstruction and Development.
Zartman, I. W. (1995). *Elusive peace: Negotiating an end to civil wars.* Brookings Institution Press.

CHAPTER 3

Framing the Israeli-Palestinian Conflict through Economic Relations

The Israeli-Palestinian conflict has long been discussed throughout the literature. This may be even more applicable to the Oslo peace process as a historical breakthrough in decades, if not centuries, of deep-rooted rivalry, with a focus on the historical, cultural, and political aspects. Nonetheless, though this chapter presents the course of events leading to the Oslo breakthrough, the focus offered here is through the lens of economic diplomacy while presenting the political-economy history of Israel-Palestine relations, from the time of occupation until the signing of the peace accord, 1967–1993.

3.1 Background

The Israeli-Palestinian conflict is one between two national claims, that of the Jewish people to self-determination in its ancestral land, and the right of the native Arab majority in Palestine to political independence (Arieli, 2009). The origin of conflict traces back to the start of the 1900s, with the British Empire taking over the ruling of Palestine under the mandate from the League of Nations and committing to prepare the country for both a future Arab self-rule and a Jewish national state (Wanis-St, 2011: 1). Since the early 1920s, eruptions of violence in various forms and varying degrees of intensity have been taking place between the conflicting sides (Kelman, 1997). Both societies have contested each other over goals and interests, such as

L. Lahar, *The Economic Diplomacy of Peace in the Middle East*, https://doi.org/10.1007/978-3-031-93991-4_3

social identity, territory, natural resources, and values. This gave birth to psychological repertoire and the perception of the sheer identity, where the mere existence of the other side represented a threat to one's own identity and existence. All of these factors have shaped the dynamics and relationship between the two sides, leading to the perception of the conflict as a zero-sum, and, as such, intractable (Kelman, 2007; Oren & Bar-Tal, 2007).

In 1947, the United Nations General Assembly adopted Resolution 181(II), with the partition plan,[1] creating both a Jewish and an Arab state (Fig. 3.1). The state of Israel was established on 14 May 1948. However, the Arab countries rejected the resolution, claiming it as unjust and inequitable (Watson, 2000: 21–22). According to the Plan of Partition, both territories of the West Bank and Gaza Strip were planned to become a part of the (to be established) Arab state. The rejection of the plan by the Arab leaders and Governments resulted in the territories of the West Bank and Gaza Strip being incorporated, respectively, into the new State of Jordan, and Egypt (Fig. 3.2) (Al-Botmeh & Kanafani, 2006). While the West Bank became an integral part of Jordan, both politically and economically, the Gaza Strip was only administrated by Egypt. At the time, Eastern Europe[2] was the main trading partner of Egypt, and Gaza had enjoyed economic links both with Egypt and Eastern Europe. The economic ties between the West Bank and Gaza Strip themselves were non-existent. Not only this, the two territories were being attributed to different official authorities, but they were also geographically separated by a territory belonging to the State of Israel. There were no economic contacts taking place between either of those territories and Israel. This state of affairs lasted until 1967 (Arnon & Weinblatt, 2001; Kanafani, 2001).

Indeed, between 1949 and 1967 the Palestinian cause was mostly in the hands of the Arab states, with the Palestinian issue being constructed as one facet of the comprehensive Arab-Israeli conflict (Barak, 2005). Thus, the Israeli understanding of the conflict at the time was that of a territorial dispute, not of the rights of the Palestinian people for an independent state (Arieli, 2009). The 1967 Arab Israeli War, the Six-Day War, radically changed the 1949 map and, along with it, the political atmosphere in the

[1] UNGA (1947) Resolution 181 (II), *Future Government of Palestine-Plan of Partition with Economic Union,* GA RES/181 (II) (29 November 1947).

[2] The Council for Mutual Economic Assistance (Comecon)—an economic organization from 1949 to 1991 under the leadership of the Soviet Union that comprised the countries of the Eastern Bloc along with a number of socialist states elsewhere around the world (Schiavone, 1981).

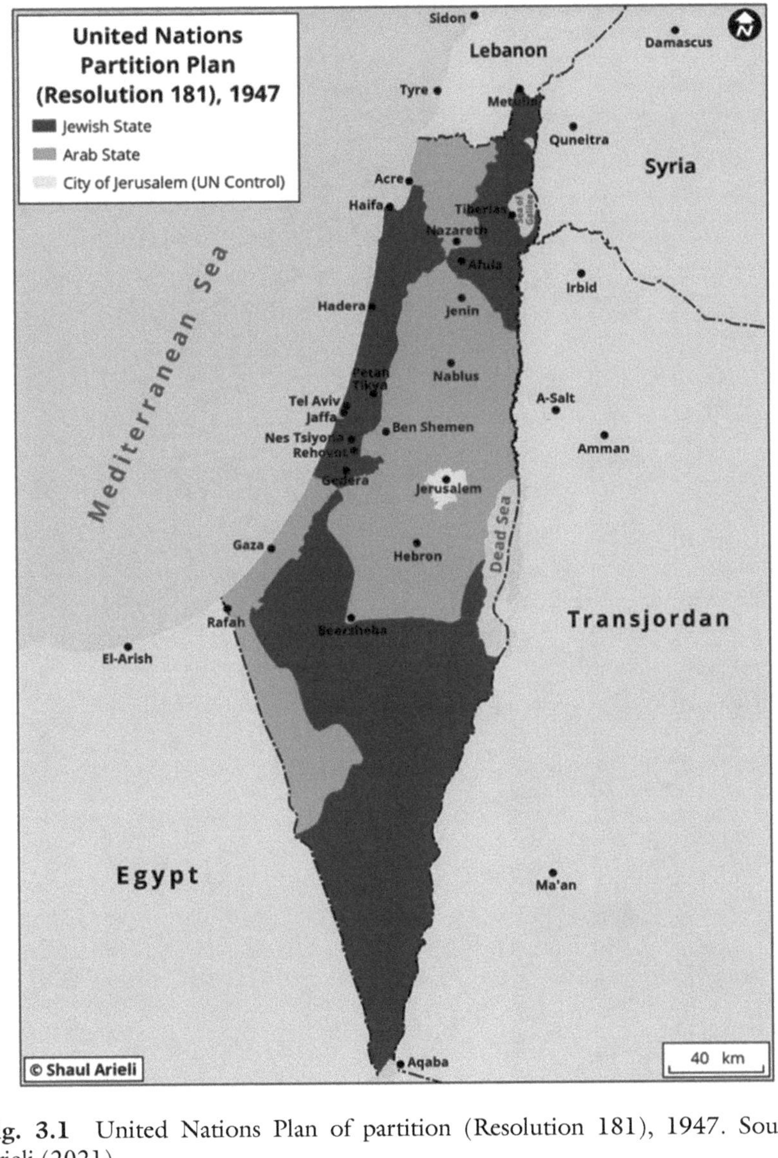

Fig. 3.1 United Nations Plan of partition (Resolution 181), 1947. Source: Arieli (2021)

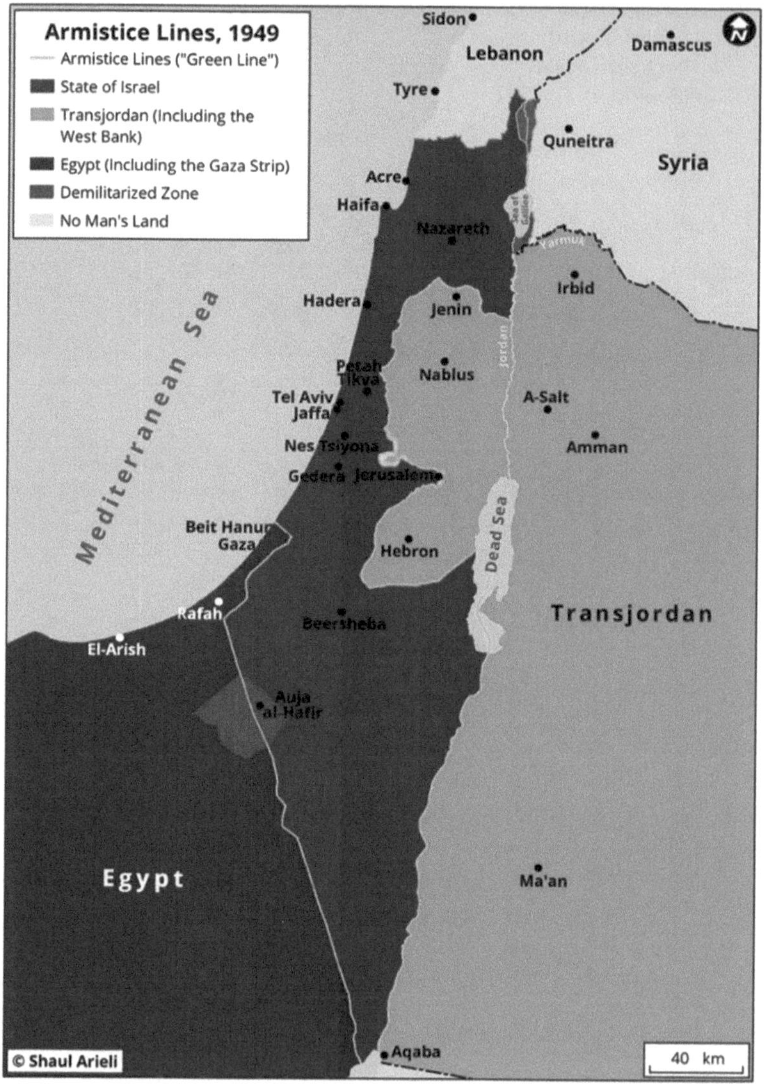

Fig. 3.2 Armistice lines, 1949. Source: Arieli (2021)

Middle East. At the end of the Six-Day War, Israel occupied the formerly part of Jordan, namely the West Bank, Gaza Strip and the Sinai Peninsula, which were previously administrated by Egypt, and the Golan Heights, Syria's former territory (Fig. 3.3). This new geopolitical and strategic situation led to the *Palestinization* of the Arab-Israeli conflict, bringing it back to its origin as a conflict between two peoples 'over and increasingly within the land they both claimed' (Kelman, 2007: 289). I think it might be better to have this paragraph before all three maps then it also solves the in text reference not appear before the figure itself issue.

In the aftermath of the 1967 War, the occupied West Bank and Gaza Strip Territory had to face a new economic reality. While Israel did not allow a flow of goods from Jordan to the Occupied Palestinian Territory, the rules of the Arab boycott for Israel limited on their side the flow of goods from the territories to Jordan. For the rest of the Arab world, both territories of the West Bank and Gaza Strip together became extensively linked to Israel. At the same time, while the territories became isolated from each other, their respective economic ties with Jordan and Egypt also diminished (Arnon & Weinblatt, 2001; Elmusa & El-Jaafari, 1995). In 1967, the GDP in the West Bank, which had a population of 600,000 inhabitants, was 2.5 per cent of Israel's GDP. Similarly, the GDP in Gaza, with a population of 380,000 inhabitants, was only 1 per cent of Israel's GDP; and the living standards in the Palestinian economy were much lower than those of Israel (Arnon, 2007). The closure of the occupied territories from their previous markets without offering alternatives would have caused a rapid deterioration of economic life and a sharp drop in the standards of living in WBGS, leading to unrest. The government and military of Israel strived to maintain the status quo and opened the trade relations between the occupied territories and Israel (Aix Group, 2004; Arnon, 1997; Arnon, 2007). Thus, shortly after the 1967 war, most of the barriers to the movement of people and goods between the Palestinian territories and Israel were removed leading to a forced economic integration between Israel and the occupied territories (Kleiman, 1999).

The repercussions of the two wars in 1967 and 1973 led the Arab states to gradually withdraw from the military struggle against Israel, essentially leaving it to the Palestinians themselves. The Palestinians, on their part, already prior to the 1967 War, had started to take repossession of their own struggle, assuming responsibility for liberating their homeland with the rise to prominence of Palestinian resistance groups. This forced the Arab leadership to take the Palestinian demands into account, with the Arab League establishing in 1964 the Palestine Liberation Organization

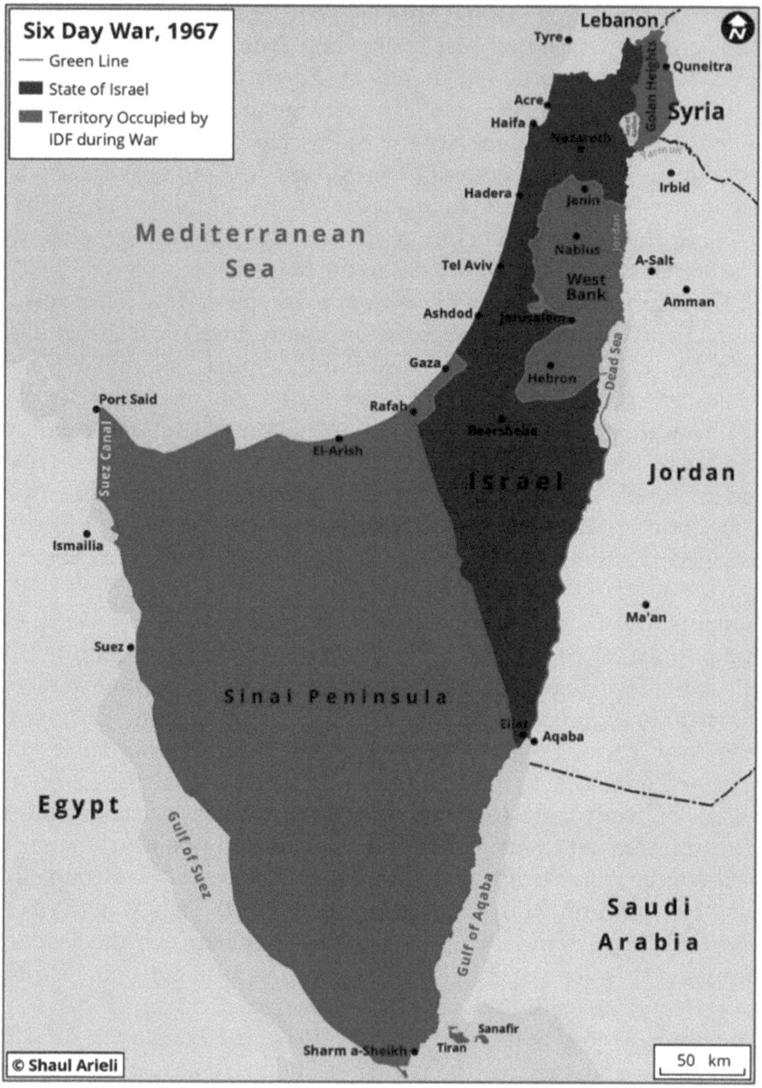

Fig. 3.3 Six-Day war, 1967. Source: Arieli (2021)

(PLO)—a multiparty confederation of Palestinian political parties (Gelvin, 2005: 346; Kelman, 2007). For the Arab countries, originally, the creation of the PLO was intended to co-opt and restrain the Palestinian resistance movement, rather than give expression to the Palestinian desire for self-determination (Abusada, 2017). For the Palestinians, however, from the start, the PLO was intended to lead the fight to recapture the Palestinian homeland. Fatah group, the Palestinian National Liberation Movement, led by Yasser Arafat emerged predominantly among the factions within the PLO (Ghanem, 2017), with Arafat becoming the leader of the PLO as of 1969 (Gelvin, 2005: 346; Kelman, 2007).

From the early 1970s onwards, after the PLO's acceptance of the Palestinian state comprising the West Bank and Gaza territories,[3] the organization also gained Arab and international recognition. In February 1974, the PLO received full membership at the Organization of Islamic Cooperation (OIC) (Abusada, 2017). On 28 October 1974, during the Arab League summit in Rabat, Morocco, the PLO was recognized by the Arab states as the 'sole legitimate representative of the Palestinian people'. This move signalled that the Arab states viewed the PLO as an independent actor and that the future peace of the region would depend on the emergence of an independent Palestine not controlled by any of the other Arab countries (Wanis-St, 2011: 23–24). As for the international approach, 1974 marked the beginning of a new phase in the Palestinian problem. Until that year, the Palestinian issue was that of refugees, as adopted by the UNGA Resolution 194(III) (1948).[4] In November 1974, Arafat was invited to address the United Nations General Assembly (Parsons, 2005: 33), followed by the adoption of the UNGA Resolution 3236 (XXIX) (1974) on the inalienable rights of the Palestinian people, including the right to self-determination without external interference and the right to national independence and sovereignty.[5] This resolution has been reaffirmed in various ways ever since (UN CEIRPP, 2014). The Assembly also adopted Resolution 3237(XXIX) (1974)[6] granting observer status to

[3] The prerequisite to a two-state solution was the 1988 official Declaration of Independence. However, unofficially the change already occurred from early-mid 1970s with the pro-PLO elite in the WBGS advocating for the PLO to accept the two-state solution (Massad, 1999).

[4] UNGA (1948) 194(III), *Palestine—Progress Report of the United Nations Mediator*, GA RES/194(III) (27 November 1948).

[5] UNGA (1974a) *Resolution 3236(XXIX). The Question of Palestine*, GA RES/3236(XXIX) (22 November 1974).

[6] UNGA (1974b) *Resolution 3237(XXIX). Observer Status for the Palestine Liberation Organization*, A/RES/3237(XXIX) (22 November 1974).

the Palestine Liberation Organization and invited the PLO, as the representative of the Palestinian people, to participate in all of the sessions, conferences, and work of the Assembly in all organs of the UN. The UNGA Resolution 3376 (XXX) in 1975[7] followed with the establishment of the Committee on the Exercise of the Inalienable Rights of the Palestinian People (CEIRPP), requesting the Committee to recommend 'a programme of implementation to enable the Palestinian people to exercise their inalienable rights to self-determination without external interference, national independence and sovereignty; and to return to their home and property from which they had been displaced'. A special unit on Palestinian Rights in the United Nations Secretariat is to assist the Committee in its work in accordance with Resolutions 32/40 B (1977), and 33/28(A-C) (1978) of the GA.[8,9]

Israel, the Arab world, and the international arena had a change of perception regarding the conflict. This new approach merely emphasized what have always been the core issues of the conflict. Though centralized around the fate of a disputed territory, from its emergence, the conflict revolved around deep-rooted identity issues linked to the security and economy of both sides. The 1948 War defined the three main issues at the heart of this conflict: border, Jerusalem, and refugees. A solution to these issues would necessarily dictate the solution of the fundamental issues: recognition of the right of each side for an independent state of its own, which exists in secure and recognized borders, and in which each side can maintain its national identity, character, and regime (Arieli, 2009).

3.2 Establishing the Relationship Between Israel and the PLO

Following the 1967 Israeli occupation of the West Bank and Gaza Strip, the PLO leadership had to move its headquarters from the Occupied Territory into Jordan. In 1970, the PLO was then forced out of Jordan to

[7] UNGA (1975) *Resolution 3376(XXX). Question of Palestine*, GA RES/3376 (XXX) (10 November 1975).

[8] UNGA (1977) *Resolution 32/40(B). Assist in the Establishment of the Special Unit on Palestinian Rights*, A/RES/32/40(B) (2 December 1977).

[9] UNGA (1978) *Resolution 33/28(A-C). Palestine question/ Committee on the Exercise of the Inalienable Rights of the Palestinian People (CEIRPP)/ Special Unit on Palestinian Rights (SUPR)*, A/RES/33/28(A-C) (7 December 1978).

Lebanon,[10] and in 1982 had to find a new safe haven, in Tunis. In the early 1980s, Peres' associate, Yossi Beilin, and his close colleague, Yair Hirschfeld, a senior lecturer on Middle East affairs at Haifa University, established contacts with West Bank residents. Their primary interest was economic, as they were interested in studying the potential for economic self-sufficiency of the Occupied Territory. This interest had quickly become political. Their main contacts were Faisal Husseini, a Jerusalem native and one of the original founders of the PLO, and academic Hanan Ashrawi, two of the dominant local leaders of the Palestinians in the territories. In 1986, however, the PLO was outlawed in Israel, with the 'Law of Association'[11] banning any communication between Israel and members of the PLO passed in the Israeli parliament, the Knesset. Moreover, PLO supporters in the Territory were arrested and Israel's official stand was a refusal to negotiate with any other Palestinians than those living in the West Bank or Gaza Strip. This together with Beilin's securing official position as deputy minister of finance in the Israeli government came to stand in the way of these contacts (Beilin, 1997: 25–31; Lundberg, 1999).

The year 1987 marked the start of the Intifada, a revolt of angry young Palestinians against the Israeli occupiers. On 8 December 1987, spontaneous demonstrations against Israeli occupation in the Gaza Strip became widespread. These spread to the West Bank, turning into an organized and coordinated resistance in the following weeks and months (Abusada, 2017). The national self-determination-driven uprising was accompanied by calls for economic independence, manifested through various Palestinian self-reliance initiatives. Some of these initiatives included voluntary protests, encouraging Palestinian workers to abstain from their jobs in Israel and the settlements, calls for boycotting Israeli-imported agriculture and manufactured goods, promotion of 'national' substitutes consumption, and advocacy for a resurgence in the agriculture sector with a return to farming, and a tax strike (Taghdisi-Rad, 2014).

For the Palestinians, the Intifada gave rise to a radical new Palestinian organization called Hamas—Islamic Resistance Movement—founded in February 1988, which rejected the PLO as ineffectual and outdated

[10] In 1970 King Hussein of Jordan, worried by the threat of domestic instability forced the PLO representatives out of Jordan to Lebanon, in what is known by Palestinians as 'Black September'.

[11] Amendment No. 2 (1986) to the Prevention of Terrorism Ordinance No. 33 (23 September 1948).

(Abusada, 2017). Following this, from 1991 onwards the Intifada increasingly became radicalized (Weinberger, 2006: 18). Moreover, the Intifada demonstrated the capability of the local Palestinians to fight Israeli occupation themselves, while marginalizing the role of exiled PLO leaders in Tunis. At the same time, the Intifada spurred a growing interest among both Israelis and Palestinians in bringing the occupation to an end by reaching a political understanding along the guidelines laid out in the Camp David Accords.[12] All these events drove the PLO to opt for a diplomatic route (Behrendt, 2007; Israeli, 2017: 13; Kaye, 1998; Waage, 2012).

In November 1988, the Palestinian National Council (PNC), the ruling body of the PLO, met in Algiers, the capital of Algeria. At the meeting, the PNC finally agreed to the original 1947 UN partition plan for Palestine and endorsed UN Security Council Resolution 242 (1967)[13] and 338 (1973).[14] The endorsement had profound significance: it meant that the PLO accepted Israel's right to exist. The PLO also called for an international peace conference. The PLO had freed its own officials to pursue contact with Israelis. With this, the PLO had made itself an acceptable partner within the global community of nations. The United States had been consistently refusing to hold discussions with the PLO until it would meet three conditions:

- accept UN Security Council Resolutions 242 and 338;
- recognize Israel's right to exist in peace and security; and
- renounce terrorism.

[12] Camp David Accords—the Egypt-Israel peace treaty signed on March 26, 1979. During negotiations regarding the Palestinian issue, Israel argued for a five-year interim period of Palestinian autonomy in some of the occupied territories, followed by the possibility of sovereignty. Though never coming to fruition, this proposal served as the benchmark for future patterns of Arab-Israeli diplomacy on the Palestinian issue.

[13] UNSC (1967) *Resolution 242. Situation in the Middle East*, S/RES/242 (22 November 1967). The Resolution calls for the withdrawal of Israeli troops from the occupied territories, acknowledges the claim of sovereignty, territorial integrity and political independence of every state in the region and calls on the UNSG to appoint an Envoy to facilitate an acceptable solution to the conflict.

[14] UNSC (1973) *Resolution 338. Ceasefire in the Middle East*, S/RES/338 (22 October 1973). The Resolution calls for all parties to cease all firing and terminate all military activities immediately. The parties should implement Security Council Resolution 242 (1967) in all of its parts and immediately and concurrently with the ceasefire, start negotiations with an aim to establish a just and durable peace in the Middle East.

After Arafat confirmed publicly that the PNC had resolved to do all three, the US opened a formal channel to the PLO, and in 1989 proposed a plan for Israeli-Palestinian negotiations. But the then Prime Minister of Israel Shamir, rejected the US plan, as he had the Peres-Hussein proposal of 1987.[15] Then, in March 1990, the US again suspended relations with the PLO following a terrorist attack on Israel (Aggestam, 2012; Lundberg, 1999; Watson, 2000: 38).

The PLO's acceptance of Israel's right to exist motivated Beilin to engage again with peace-minded Palestinian leaders. Following a successful meeting in 1989, with leading Palestinians from the West Bank headed by Faisal Husseini, Beilin then decided to pursue a new opportunity of contact, this time directly with the PLO. The Dutch government had offered to host secret 'proximity talks' between the PLO and Israel, in which the two sides would never actually meet face to face, and Beilin took advantage of an official trip to The Hague to accept the offer, with Hirschfeld accompanying him. Former Dutch Foreign Minister Max van der Stoel shuttled messages between the hotel rooms of the Israeli and PLO participants. On the Israeli side were Beilin and Hirschfeld, while the PLO representatives were Hassan Asfour, a PLO political advisor, Abdullah Hourani, a member of the PLO executive committee, and Afif Safieh, the PLO representative in the Netherlands also addressed as Holland. The participants agreed on a document establishing principles for opening negotiations between the two sides. The document foundered on PLO reservations, but this exercise helped Beilin come to the decision that it is counterproductive to pretend that the centre of Palestinian power lies anywhere but with the PLO (Beilin, 1997: 37–39; Hirschfeld, 2000: 63–64; Lundberg, 1999).

As for Israel's society, the Israeli military reactions during the Palestinian uprising led to negative diplomatic repercussions in the form of international condemnation, but moreover vehement reaction within Israeli society, and raised questions regarding the costs of retaining total control over the territories. With the election in mid-1992, the Labour Party-led government ruled for the first time in 15 years, Prime Minister Yitzhak Rabin

[15]The London Agreement between King Hussein of Jordan and Israeli Foreign Affairs Minister Shimon Peres outlined the framework for an international peace conference hosted by the United Nations with the purpose of finding a peaceful solution for the Arab-Israeli conflict based on resolutions 242 and 338, and a peaceful solution to the Palestinian problem. The agreement was signed during a secret meeting held in London on 11 April 1987 (Peres, 1995: 423).

pledged to reach a settlement with the Palestinians within nine months. Thus, the Palestinians' Intifada uprising had given the Palestinian cause new international prominence (Lundberg, 1999).

3.2.1 *The Road to Peace*

The year 1991 marked the culmination of several historical processes. All of these together played a role in leading the road to the Israeli-Palestinian peace process, known as the 'Oslo Accords'. The first one was the breakdown of the USSR, effectively leaving the PLO without a superpower sponsor (Parsons, 2005: 13). Since the establishment of the state of Israel in 1948, the region had been engulfed in the global conflict between the Soviet Union and the United States, with no room for collaboration. The end of the Cold War left Russia severely weakened without the capacity to continue the game of rivalry in the Middle East, which enabled the search for cooperation between the two superpowers and established new opportunities for Arab-Israeli peacemaking.

The end of the Persian Gulf War in February 1991, with the defeat of Saddam Hussein and the restoration of Kuwait as an independent state, was the second historical event. With the elimination of the threat of an Iraqi attack against Saudi Arabia, as well as re-establishing the security of other Arab Gulf states as a result of the war, the regional political landscape of the Middle East was now profoundly altered, and new regional alignments were to be born (Behrendt, 2007; Kaye, 1998: 60–62; Waage, 2012). The US-led coalition in the war against Iraq included the majority of the Arab states, Russia, and Israel, among other states. The PLO under Chairman Arafat's leadership, however, sided with Iraq. The Iraqi defeat cost the PLO both the loss of support of many Arab states, as well as loss of funding. Subsidies from wealthy Arab states tumbled from $350 million a year in 1988 to $40 million by 1993. In 1993 the PLO was on the verge of bankruptcy, and the exiled PLO leadership in Tunis also became marginalized in the regional scene (Abusada, 2017; Lundberg, 1999). These, together with the Intifada uprising and growing support for extremist groups, including Hamas and Islamic Jihad in the occupied territories, threatened to compromise the position of Arafat and the PLO, both politically and strategically (Waage, 2012; Watkins & Lundberg, 1998).

The results of the Gulf War strengthened the United States' influence on many regional players in the Middle East, be it the Arab countries that chose to join the Gulf coalition or those that supported Saddam Hussein.

Syria

Syria, under the leadership of Hafez el-Assad, joined the Gulf coalition against Saddam Hussein, thereby opening up to American diplomacy. Though President Hafez el-Assad had ambitions regarding negotiations with Israel over the Golan Heights, the General Secretary of the Communist Party of the Soviet Union Mikhail Gorbachev, refused to back him up on this issue. The importance of this to Assad can be seen in the meeting held between the Syrian leadership and the Americans before the war came to a halt, in which Assad stressed the US duty to address the Arab-Israeli peace after reversing Iraqi aggression. Moreover, according to D. Ross (2005: 141), this view was commonly heard in the form of argument that if the United States forged a coalition for war, it should also forge a coalition for peace after the war, which indeed became a part of US mantra in justifying the coalition against Saddam, during the George Bush 41st presidency.

Jordan

Jordan, which had supported Saddam Hussein, emerged from the war not only politically isolated but also economically devastated. This prompted King Hussein bin Talal to take steps to overcome the strained US-Jordanian relations, which would involve an effort to assist Washington in pursuing a peace policy in the region.

PLO

While inside the Palestinian Liberation Organization chairman Arafat sided with Saddam Hussein against the US-led coalition, others among the PLO leadership seated in the West Bank headed by Faisal Husseini and Hanan Ashrawi wanted to get negotiations with Israel underway, and used the new conditions to gain maneuvering space and undermine the power of Arafat. This led Arafat to the realization that in order to re-establish his own legitimacy inside the organization he had to allow the Palestinian inside leadership to move forward with the negotiations.

Israel

As for Israel, Prime Minister Shamir understood that the interests of Israel would be best served when going along with the American diplomatic initiative. Likewise, Shamir understood that Israel could obtain an important upgrade in the US-Israeli security relationship and was determined to convince Washington to rebuild a strong alliance relationship with Amman (Hirschfeld, 2014: 95).

The US advocating for the liberation of Kuwait in support of the right of people to live free from occupation provided a compelling reason to seek a settlement for the Palestinian question (Cleveland & Bunton, 2016: 500). Furthermore, the new perception of the Americans as the guarantor of the regional stability, together with its unprecedented show of force, provided the United States leverage to push forward new initiatives (Kelman, 1997; Ross, 2005: 53; Kaye, 1998: 47). Thus, following the end of the Gulf War by late 1990 vigorous calls were made by American leaders about the need to tackle the Arab-Israeli conflict (Kaufmann et al., 1991: 63–64). Undoubtedly, the result of the Gulf War brought with it a 'window of opportunity' which was ripe for diplomatic peace initiatives in the Middle East. Whether the international community alone perceived this 'window of opportunity' ripe for diplomatic initiatives, as Aggestam (2012) argued, or whether the disputants themselves saw this as the culmination of a psychological transformation leading to the recognition that the conflict had reached a hurting stalemate (Watkins & Lundberg, 1998), did not affect the subsequent events. The United States was again motivated to pursue a lasting solution to the Middle East conflict. This came to fruition in the form of a co-sponsored conference by the United States and Russia held in Madrid, in October 1991, known as the Madrid Peace Conference.

3.2.2 *The Madrid Peace Conference*

The Madrid conference was the first step in the framework set by the United States to put in motion peace negotiations between Israel and the Palestinians, and Israel and its Arab neighbours—Syria, Lebanon, and Jordan. The gathering witnessed the coming together of Israelis with representatives from numerous Arab states. This included both her immediate neighbours and the larger Arab world as observers, delegations from the Gulf states and North Africa, sanctioned by the presence of the European Community,[16] and observers from the United Nations.[17] The meeting sent a clear message by itself. But even more than the symbolic act of bringing all sides to the table, the Madrid conference established a negotiation framework and launched the Madrid peace process that would lay the groundwork for all future peace process advances (Freedman, 1993: 69–70; Hirschfeld, 2014: 97; Kaye, 1998: 47–48; Waage, 2007).

The establishment of the talks reflected the emerging concept of cooperative security in the post-Cold War era, with a greater emphasis on tackling the root causes of conflict and promoting confidence, rather than relying primarily on deterrence or containment. Cooperation, it was hoped, would foster a fundamental change in attitudes and result in the convergence of expectations and the institutionalization of norms of behaviour (Peters, 1999). In American eyes, this process was a quest for a comprehensive regional peace.

> Our objectives must be clear (…) it is not simply to end the state of war in the Middle East and replace it with a state of non-belligerency. This is not enough; this would not last. Rather, we seek peace, real peace. And by real peace I mean treaties. Security. Diplomatic relations. Economic relations. Trade. Investment. Cultural exchange. Even Tourism.

These are the words of former US President George Bush, as stated on 30 October 1991, at his Opening Addresses in Madrid.[18] The conference was an unprecedented example of conference diplomacy, aimed to establish two tracks in parallel—a bilateral track and a multilateral one (Kaufmann, 1996: 168). The bilateral track aimed to promote negotiations on the Israeli-Arab conflicts to solve them bilaterally through formal and direct diplomatic links between Israel and its Arab neighbours: between Israel

[16] The European Economic Community (EEC) took part in the Madrid conference as a full participant, sitting at the conference table, and taking the floor through the statement addressed by the Netherlands Foregoing Minister van den Broek, representing the EC presidency (the role of the EC was constrained as it did not have at the time a foreign policy (Kaufmann, 1996: 170).

[17] At the Madrid conference the UN attended only as a silent observer. From 1992 onwards, the UN Secretariat was represented in all the multilateral meetings, and other international organizations as the World Bank and United Nations Development Programme (UNDP) joined the appropriate multilateral groups (Kaufmann, 1996: 171).

[18] Remarks by Mr. George Bush—President of the United States, 30 October 1991 (Bush, 1991).

and a Jordanian-Palestinian delegation, between Israel and a Syrian delegation, and between Israel and a Lebanese delegation. These bilateral tracks were to be continued with American mediation later in Washington. However, while several rounds of talks were convened in Washington between the various parties, all were inconclusive.

As for the multilateral track, the Madrid conference also invited regional parties, including Arab states which do not share borders with Israel, to join a multilateral peacemaking track that would focus on region-wide issues, such as combating proliferation and regional security, water, environment, economic development, and other mutual interest issues while looking into the future of the region (Freedman, 1993; Hirschfeld, 2014: 9; Waage, 2007). This track was formally launched in a conference sponsored by the United States and Russia to be held in Moscow in January 1992. At least 36 parties attended the conference, including 11 Arab states comprising Egypt, Jordan and the Palestinians, Arab states from the Gulf and North Africa, as well as Israel (Fig. 3.4).

The Moscow meeting initiated five working groups focused on regional problems, each chaired by an extra-regional party:

- Arms Control and Regional Security (ACRS), chaired by the United States and Russia;
- Regional Economic Development (REDWG), chaired by the European Union (EU);
- the Environment (EWG), chaired by Japan;
- Water Resources (WWG), chaired by the United States; and
- Refugees (RWG), chaired by Canada.

A steering group co-chaired by the United States and Russia was also established to oversee the operations of the overall process and its respective working groups. After Moscow, starting in the spring of 1992, the multilateral working groups began to meet separately and developed distinct agendas and goals, with varying degrees of success. Israel and its Arab partners, with the encouragement and funding of their extra-regional sponsors, developed regional projects, and new regional institutions. The working process of all working groups began with occasional plenary sessions where the entire range of issues within a particular group might be discussed at a general level. Over time, each working group increased their interaction by meeting in smaller, more focused intersessions between the larger plenaries, sometimes on a monthly basis. While these sessions were

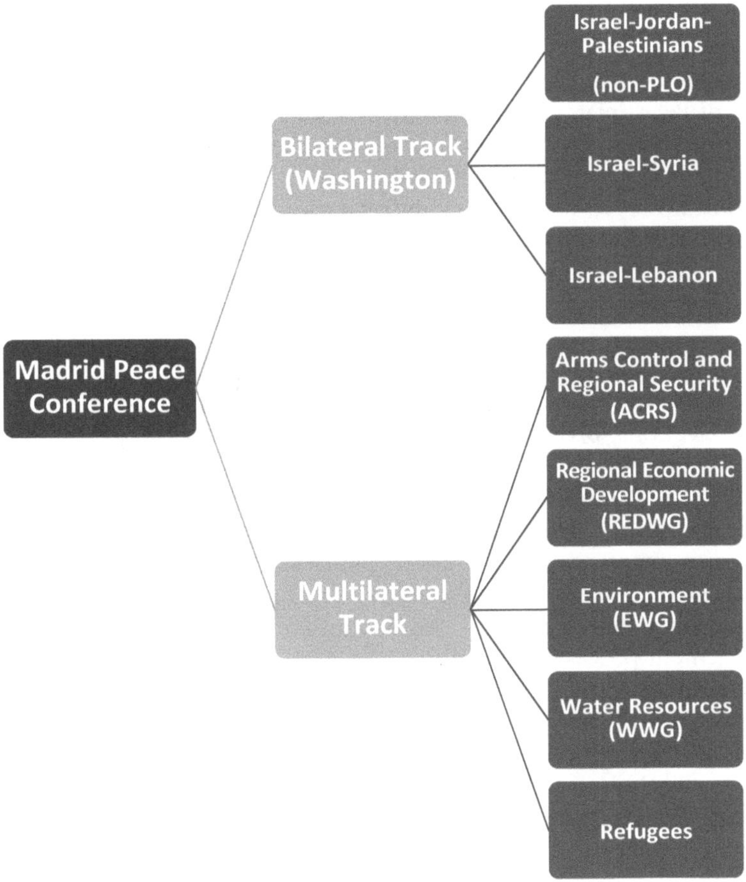

Fig. 3.4 The Madrid peace process—structure

being held under the multilateral track, many concepts discussed in them found their way into Israel's bilateral peace agreements with Jordan and the Palestinian Authority (Kaye, 1998; The Madrid Peace Conference, 1992).

As for PLO's participation, it was not obvious that the Palestinians would participate in the Madrid Conference. Due to the diplomatic efforts of former US Secretary of State James Baker, the Israelis did agree to a Palestinian presence, but the Likud-led government set stringent conditions of no PLO representative joining the delegation, and that the Palestinians would only be half of a joint Jordanian-Palestinian delegation to be established (Lundberg, 1999; Massad, 1999). The talks with the Palestinians foresaw two stages of talks, modelled on the arrangements first spelled out in the Camp David agreement aimed at establishing some form of Palestinian autonomy. The first stage of negotiation would establish a five-year interim self-government, while the second stage would deal with the permanent statute of a Palestinian entity. The US-led peace negotiations, however, were plagued by obstacles from the very beginning, and within a few months, the talks with the Palestinians were bogged down at both the bilateral and multilateral level (Lundberg, 1999; Waage, 2012).

3.2.3 *The New Middle East*

Shimon Peres, appointed as the Foreign Minister of Israel following the 1992 elections, brought with him to the table the concept of '*The New Middle East*'. Peres envisioned the future of the world as one to be reorganized via economic clusters. The trend of economic communities that started with the European Community after the end of World War II had gained momentum with the fall of the Iron Curtain, and the collapse of the USSR. The process of economic communities grew wider while embracing different parts of the world. This, for instance, included the enlargement process within the European Community of former Eastern European countries, the Free Trade Area between the United States, Canada, and Mexico-NAFTA, the Organization of the American States—OAS, and signs of regional economic arrangement in Asia.

The political-economic sphere of the individual states in the Middle East enables limited opportunities. Indeed, to achieve the aspirational rise in living standards, there is a need for regional economic cooperation. It is through this mechanism that the region would be able to address the challenges it faces, for example, starvation, overexploitation of limited natural resources, and desertification. This could be the tool to counter the rise of political extremism and fundamentalism in the region. Thus, there are four pillars upon which the regional framework should be established—stabilization, economics, national security, and democratization, with two parallel operational branches of security and economics.

The regional economic system would be established through a gradual process creating a community of states on the lines of the Western Europe Community. As Germany and France joined forces against a common enemy, the USSR, Peres saw poverty as the common political enemy of the Middle East. He argued that poverty is the root cause of fundamentalism and radicalism phenomena that poses a threat to any plausible progress, development, liberty, and welfare that the future could bring. The final goal is the creation of a regional community of states, sharing a common market and selective central institutions like those of the European Community. But the history of the Middle East dictates that progress in this direction should be made one step at a time, with interstate projects between at least two countries per project, addressing issues that affect the quality of life in the region. These collaborations should be established through a gradual cooperation, with the first level being the formation of joint institutions to deal with the desolateness of the region's landscape and build desalination facilities. The second level would be to involve multinational companies to lead initiatives and projects that require large-scale investments, such as the Mediterranean-Dead Sea Canal project. In this project, a canal will connect the Mediterranean Sea and the Dead Sea while establishing a free trade zone and tourist attractions. Not only this, Israel, Jordan, and Saudi Arabia will be using a port to utilize the energy from the water streaming down the canal for electricity and desalination purposes, further enhancing the development of the Dead Sea factories. This, like other future projects, would create a vast interest in keeping the peace among countries in the region. The third stage would deal with stabilization of the community through institutionalism.

Indeed, the choice is either between leading the region towards the path Western Europe has taken, or towards a Balkanization of the region to perpetuate hatred. Allocation of thoughts, beliefs, and resources from a strategy of military superiority towards a strategy of economic cooperation can lead to the right path. As for doubts regarding the feasibility of a free trade zone in the region, Peres offers four economic-political topic clusters—water, biotechnology, and fighting desolateness; development of the tourism industry; regional transportation and communication infrastructures; and slowing down the arms race in the Middle East (Peres & Naor, 1993: 61–63, 67–72, 89–93).

As for the Palestinians, and specifically the peace process, Peres believed that it is in Israel's interest to assist in relations to economic development as a neighbour in a good, stable condition ensures the same for his neighbours. In his view, a political success that is not accompanied by economic promotion is in danger of collapsing. Political success can be declared loud and clear but would not provide food for hungry children (Peres & Naor, 1993: 34). The world is shifting away from the classic security notion leaning on arms and weapons, to a new perception of security that must lean on political agreements as well as include a component of international security and economics (Peres & Naor, 1993: 37).

With the ongoing Madrid Peace Process, the question of how to build the New Middle East was already in focus. The unexpected breakthrough in the process by means of the secret Oslo track, foregrounded the vision of the new Middle East, making it seem viable more than ever. A couple of weeks following the signing of the Oslo I Accord in September 1993, this was then presented in Peres' address to the 48th General Assembly of the United Nations:[19]

> The Middle East which has been an important agenda of the United Nations history, must become prosperous, not only peaceful. To construct a modern Middle East, we need wisdom not less than financial support.
>
> We have to rid ourselves of the costly follies of the past and adopt the principles of modern economy…We can and should turn to the promises of scientific development, of market economy, of comprehensive education. We must base our industry, our agriculture, our services on the height of the current technologies (…)
>
> If we want to represent their (young generation) hopes, we have to combine wise policies and regional security with market economies (…)

3.2.4 *The Road to Oslo*

In 1992, during a side meeting convened simultaneously to the Madrid process multilateral talks, a European representative approached Dr. Yair Hirschfeld while presenting him a paper on economic cooperation in the region written by Abu Ala, a high-ranking economic expert official in the Palestinian exiled government in Tunis. The paper, much to Hirschfeld's surprise, talked about several future economic cooperation projects suggested for implementation in the region, which were all taken from a paper published earlier by Tel Aviv University, one that Hirschfeld himself took part in writing.[20]

On 19 April 1992, Beilin and Terje Rød-Larsen had lunch together in Tel Aviv. Larsen was a Norwegian social scientist, with close ties to the Norwegian government, and the founder and director of a Norwegian

[19] Address by Foreign Minister Peres to the United Nations General Assembly, 28 September 1993 (Peres, 1993).

[20] Hirschfeld, Interview, 2 January 2017.

research institute, known as Fafo,[21] who grew interested in the conflict. Larsen had heard of Beilin and his efforts to promote dialogue with the Palestinians and wanted to meet him in person. During their meeting, Larsen told Beilin he was in a position to offer Norwegian assistance in setting up an unofficial channel of communication between Israelis and Palestinians. He explained that his wife, Mona Juul, was a diplomat in the Foreign Ministry and a personal assistant to Deputy Foreign Minister Jan Egeland. Following this, they discussed the idea of a Beilin-Husseini meeting. To encourage Larsen, Beilin proposed that he would contact Beilin's long-time associate Yair Hirschfeld to develop the idea. Larsen and Hirschfeld met and in what is recalled by Larsen as a slip of the tongue, Hirschfeld also told Larsen that if he were ever to meet a PLO member, he would like him to be Abu Ala, the unofficial finance minister for the Palestinians. This was two months after Larsen had the chance to meet Abu Ala during his visit to Oslo. Nonetheless, the official focus still was on West Bank Palestinians. Shortly after, Larsen arranged a gathering for himself, Beilin, Hirschfeld, and Husseini, in which they discussed the option of Norway hosting secret Israeli-Palestinian negotiations. All agreed it would be useful to meet in Norway. But before any further moves towards peace could be contemplated, the Israelis had to elect a new government (Beilin, 1997: 64–66; Lundberg, 1999).

In June 1992, the Labour Party came to power in Israel. Upon assuming office, the then-new Prime Minister, Yitzhak Rabin, explicitly expressed his aim to engage in a political process that would bring the Intifada to an end in peaceful ways within nine months from the time elected. Shimon Peres was appointed as the Foreign Minister, and Beilin as the Deputy Foreign Minister. Mahmoud Abbas, known as Abu Mazen, a founder of Fatah, and the Director of the PLO Department for National and International Relations, and a trusted lieutenant of Yasser Arafat, saw an opportunity with this new government and worked through the Egyptians to establish contacts with both Rabin and Peres (Aggestam, 2012; Watkins & Lundberg, 1998).

[21] Fafo Research Foundation (Forskningsstiftelsen *Fafo*)—the Norwegian Institute for Applied International Studies is an independent social science research foundation that develops knowledge on the conditions for participation in working life, organizational life, society and politics, the relationship between politics and living conditions, as well as on democracy, development, and value creation. It was co-founded by Larsen, who also served as its director until 1994 (see also: Fafo, n.d.).

Jan Egeland, the Deputy Foreign Minister of Norway, had an official trip to Israel planned for September and was intending to use this opportunity and pursue Larsen's offer—the possibility that Norway might provide a back-channel for Israeli-Palestinian negotiations. On 12 September 1992, Egeland conducted a secret meeting following an official dinner in Tel Aviv. The few guests included Fafo director Terje Larsen, Egeland's assistant Mona Juul, Yossi Beilin, his assistant Shlomo Gur, and Yair Hirschfeld. At this meeting, Egeland renewed Larsen's offer that Norway would act as sponsor of back-channel talks between Israel and the Palestinians. He confirmed that Norwegian Foreign Minister Thorvald Stoltenberg knew of, and officially endorsed the offer. The understanding was that Beilin and Husseini would be the chief participants. According to Beilin, they agreed to establish a parallel track to the ongoing Washington talks 'in the form of a series of conversations between myself and Faisal Husseini, with the intention of dismantling the obstacles currently blocking progress in the Washington talks' (Beilin, 1997: 91). Under this plan, the track would remain secret, and problems solved within the framework would be offered to the official delegations in Washington to present as their own breakthrough.

On 14 September, two days after the meeting with Egeland took place, Beilin prepared to tell Peres about the Norwegian offer to host confidential talks with Husseini in Oslo. However, before he could broach the subject, Peres informed him that Rabin, much to Peres' dismay, had forbidden Peres to meet Husseini to discuss the stalemate in Washington. Beilin was dumbfounded. If Peres was banned from meeting with the West Bank leader, surely Beilin himself could not ask for permission to do so. Despite this, a few weeks later Beilin told his long-time colleague Prof. Hirschfeld that he should consider going to Oslo in Beilin's place. Beilin left it up to Hirschfeld whether he would go, and with whom he might meet in Oslo, Husseini or someone else. At the same time, Beilin and Hirschfeld remembered Husseini's own urging, dating back many months, that Israel contact the PLO directly (Lundberg, 1999).

Meanwhile, frustration among the Palestinian team in Washington was growing. Hanan Ashrawi, who served at the time as the spokesperson for the Palestinian delegation to the Washington talks, approached Hirschfeld and suggested he would go to London on 3–4 December 1992, and meet with the PLO representative, Abu Ala. These dates in London clashed with the meeting of the steering committee responsible for the multilateral talks on economics, associated with the Madrid process. Abu Ala was expected there in order to guide the Palestinian delegation. Yossi Beilin as the Israeli Deputy Foreign Minister also planned to attend the meeting. Larsen was to be in London on the same dates as well to attend a trade union conference, regardless of the multilateral peace process (Waage, 2002).

According to Pundak, who was an academic working with Hirschfeld in the Economic Cooperation Foundation (ECF)[22] at the time, and engaged in the meetings with the Palestinian local leadership, Ashrawi and Faisal, always delivered the message of:

> "Go to the PLO. (The Washington delegation) can't deliver (a peace agreement)". She (Ashrawi) knew exactly what we were doing, and she saw a very interesting possibility: that if we are dealing with economic issues, if we are close to Yossi (Beilin) who is dealing with multilateral issues officially, maybe a meeting can bring something in order to get the PLO engaged. It was illegal, but we were academics and we thought maybe we could get away with it. (Pundak interview with Prof. Michael Watkins, Tel Aviv, June 25, 1995, in: Lundberg, 1999: 25)

Thus, as Pundak retrospectively indicated:

> A very important point both for when examining the sequence of events and how this (Oslo) had started is the meeting on November 30, 1992, at Ashrawi's, which for us (Pundak and Hirschfeld) was a critical junction, as then the meeting with Abu Ala was set. During the meeting, Ashrawi pointed out two points: first that we should meet Abu Ala, who was not involved in the bilateral negotiation track at the time, and the second point was that the only way for achieving progress is through an American-Israeli-Palestinian back-channel in Washington, while the Palestinian representatives will include PLO representatives. (Pundak, *Getting to the table—Oslo part B* 1998: -11:49:10)

[22]The Economic Cooperation Foundation (ECF) was founded by Dr. Hirschfeld, and the then-former Minister of Justice Dr. Beilin, at the end of 1991, in order to promote the NWO in the ME region. Van der Stoel, and other high-ranking officials in the EEC supported and advised in the establishment of the organization (Beilin, 1997: 53). The ECF was founded as a non-profit, non-governmental track II think tank, whose objectives are to build, maintain and support Israeli-Palestinian and Israeli-Arab cooperation in the political, economic, and civil society spheres in support of creating a sustainable Permanent Status based on a two-state solution (see also: ECF, 2015).

But Rabin's September injunction against any Peres-Husseini meeting had put an end to that process. Hirschfeld had not forgotten, however, the Norwegian offer to host confidential meetings. Knowing that Abu Ala would be at the multilateral meeting in London Hirschfeld, who was scheduled to attend a seminar in Switzerland later that week, decided to stop in the British Capital en route and meet the Palestinians. He and Pundak informed Ashrawi, who called Abu Ala personally and asked him to meet Hirschfeld. Hirschfeld did not, however, inform Beilin about the decision. Says Pundak 'We didn't want to tell Yossi [Beilin] that we were going to meet Abu Ala. The reason was we wanted neither to receive a yes nor a no. A yes could make problems for him; a no could make problems for us. So, this was probably the first and last time we did something related to the process without telling him' (Pundak, interview with Prof. Watkins, Tel Aviv, 25 June 1995 in: Lundberg, 1999: 50).

Hirschfeld, arriving in London on 3 December, scheduled a meeting with Abu Ala the next day, as well as meeting Larsen ahead for an early breakfast. Taking what he acknowledged was a risk, Hirschfeld decided to tell Larsen during their meeting of the impending meeting planned with Abu Ala. Hirschfeld: 'I said "I'm about to meet Abu Ala. If this works well, I will want to meet him again. Can you help me?" his answer was "I'll get you any help you want from the Norwegian government. We will do everything you need." He couldn't have been clearer.' Abu Ala, for his part, had been highly reluctant to meet Hirschfeld. A subsequent call to Ashrawi from Faisal Husseini plus one from an old friend, Akram Haniye, persuaded him otherwise. Abu Ala, who brought with him Safieh, who by then was appointed as the PLO London representative, and Hirschfeld talked from 10 a.m. to 1 p.m. Hirschfeld says he learned later that after the meeting, Safieh dismissed it as nothing new, similar to hundreds of other meetings. But Abu Ala felt encouraged. That evening Hirschfeld went to tell Beilin about the meeting. Recalls Hirschfeld: 'Yossi was in a double funny position.' Minutes before, Beilin had suggested to two American State Department officials that they should start back-channel talks with the PLO. They turned the suggestion back to him, saying they could not, but that someone should. Continues Hirschfeld: 'Then I come five minutes afterwards and say, "you know, I've established a back-channel."' Beilin encouraged him to pursue it. (Besides the US, Beilin had approached Britain about sponsoring a back-channel. Britain was encouraging but responded so officially that Beilin feared it would be difficult to keep a negotiations channel secret.) At the end of the second meeting with Abu

Ala, this time in the Hilton coffee shop, Hirschfeld suggested the men meet yet again in Oslo, and by the time the two men parted, they had agreed in principle to make arrangements as soon as possible. On 7 December, Abu Mazen instructed Abu Ala to pursue his secret contacts. At the same time, Larsen flew to Tunis with his government's approval and officially invited Abu Ala to Oslo (Hirschfeld, interview with Lundberg, Ramat Ishai, 31 March 1998 in: Lundberg, 1999: 27).

In Larsen's meeting with Chairman Arafat, in reply to Larsen's questions about assistance, Arafat said: 'You know, Mr Larsen, that the American-Palestinian dialogue started in Sweden, which is a Scandinavian country next door to you. Accordingly, you can play a role as well with all the bona fides you have. You can contribute something similar. We are in need of all you can offer' (Qurei, 2006: 51).

For his part, Beilin remembers approving Norway as a rendezvous location for two reasons: first, because the government could finance the meetings, and second, it set no preconditions. Other governments he had approached had wanted, for their own political protection, assurances that Rabin and Peres were behind the secret initiative. This Beilin could not provide. Serving in an official position, Beilin could not become directly involved with the PLO. Hirschfeld and Pundak, on the other hand, were private people, not carrying official office. Thus, in the event of an information leak or breakdown in negotiations, it would be possible to deny the whole mission. If the two teams in Oslo would manage to resolve outstanding differences, the plan was to inform the State Department, which could introduce the compromise into the Washington talks as a US-sponsored measure. Then, the two sides were to give their formal approval.

It was an intersection of a sequence of coincidences combined at the right time, at the right place, and with the right people that led to the Oslo track, according to Beilin (1997: 153). This track, as history has it, would soon transform from back-channel negotiations in support of the Washington talks, to the main track leading to the peace accords.

On 19 January 1993, the Knesset finally repealed the 'Law of Association' banning contact with the PLO. Hirschfeld and Pundak left the following morning. They would not have to break the law to attend the Norwegian seminar. Abu Ala brought with him Hassan Asfour, who had also taken part in the 1989 'proximity talks' with Hirschfeld and Beilin in The Hague, The Netherlands. Asfour was a former communist whom the Syrians had jailed. Later, he joined the radical Popular Front for the Liberation of Palestine, before Abu Mazen chose him as a political advisor. Asfour also served as secretary to the negotiations committee in Washington. The third member of the PLO team was Abu Ala's economic advisor, Maher Elkurd, who spoke fluent English (Lundberg, 1999; Waage, 2002).

The first meeting of what would become the Oslo Peace Process took place on 21–22 January 1993, Sarpsborg, Norway.

3.3 Economic Component of the Oslo Accord

> During the negotiations the guideline that we laid down was that of the New Middle East. We, more accurately, Yair put on the table the vision of the Middle East as according to Beilin and Peres (…) thus, it is not the exact wording and paragraphs of the agreement that are of most importance, only the key structure that set its tone. The text [the first paper to be drafted during the Oslo back-channel negotiations] could have been comprised out of security issues and only two lines on the declaration of principles, that clearly representing one side's interests; or one with a significant economic focus and an extended declaration of principles, which clearly indicate engaging more with the future than the past (…) (Pundak, *Getting to the table—Oslo part B* 1998: -11:48:47)

Hirschfeld (2000: 117) states that the Israeli-Oslo perception was based on the belief that there is a need to promote economic development in the West Bank and Gaza Strip, and that economic cooperation between the Palestinians and Israeli should and would be promoted. This line of thinking together with the perception regarding the future of the region in the spirit of the Madrid process, as well as Hirschfeld's exposure to Abu Ala's paper prior to initiating the Oslo track, laid the ground for promoting economic cooperation in Oslo's talks.

During the first meeting in Norway on 21–22 January 1993, Abu Ala, head of the Palestinian delegation, in his opening remarks asked the Israelis to take an approach of moving on as soon as possible from a theoretical approach to more tangible and practical matters. As such, he asked if Israel would consider carrying out some practical confidence-building measures in the economic sphere. He suggested examples, including giving consent to the establishment of a Palestinian development bank, or enabling economic infrastructure ventures in the Palestinian Territory, such as a cement factory, a commercial seaport in Gaza, or undertaking housing projects (Qurei, 2006: 62, 65). Moreover, according to Abbas, Abu Ala also suggested a free trade area, a maritime canal, a gas pipeline, and advocated for a mini 'Marshall Plan' of global economic assistance for the Palestinians (Abbas, 1995: 121). As Hirschfeld recalls, during this session Abu Ala offered what Israel demanded earlier in previous occasions—a Gaza-first agreement based on three understandings:

1. Israel would agree to withdraw from Gaza 'in two to three years';
2. An economic development 'Marshall Plan' would be immediately introduced for the Gaza Strip; and
3. A structure for Israeli-Palestinian economic cooperation would be immediately created.

For implementing these understandings, the Palestinian team presented several ideas for economic cooperation, which would build on existing resources, and help to develop new ones. These include the construction of an Israeli-Palestinian-Egyptian water desalination plant and a power station on the Gaza-Sinai border; a free trade zone between Ashdod and Gaza to connect the two harbours; cooperation to develop the Dead Sea's natural resources, the creation of a joint Israeli-Palestinian automobile factory to make cars for the Arab world; and the construction of gas and oil pipelines and refineries, incorporating the existing Tap Line. The Palestinians assumed (correctly) if not knew, these would suit Israeli Foreign Minister Peres (Hirschfeld, 2014: 108–109). In using such language, asserted Uri Savir, Abu Ala was 'speaking Peres' language. Abu Ala had read Peres' book. The whole thing with a Marshall Plan etc., these were buzz words' (Savir, interview with Lundberg, Tel Aviv, 30 March 1998, in Lundberg, 1999: 32).

Following the first meeting and upon return to Israel, Hirschfeld and Pundak submitted their report on the meeting to Beilin, who asked them in return to draft a paper for use in the next meeting to explore common positions and gaps between the teams. In February 1993, Hirschfeld prepared a document titled 'The Principles of an Israeli-Palestinian Negotiating Plan', which included three draft components:

1. A Declaration of Principles;
2. An Israeli-Palestinian Cooperation and working program; and
3. 'Preparing a Marshall Plan for the West Bank, Gaza Strip, and the Region'

['The principles of an Israeli-Palestinian Negotiating Plan', paper submitted in Sarpsborg, February 1993] (Hirschfeld, 2014: 110).

Presenting this paper during the second meeting in Oslo in February 1993, the Palestinians felt that the Israelis tried to 'bypass the Gaza withdrawal issue by putting forward a broad and vague set of proposals', in Abu Ala's words, to improve economic and social conditions in both the West Bank and Gaza, without referring directly to suggestions made by them in the previous meeting. However, Hirschfeld's presentation of a draft Declaration of Principles was based upon the ten points the Palestinian presented at the previous session, while this was accompanied with a further proposal for economic measures, including a 'Marshall Plan' for the Gaza Strip (Qurei, 2006: 85). Responding to this, Pundak stated that Israel intends to revitalize the economy of the territories. Steps taken in this direction would include a tax holiday for new industrial projects, the encouragement of investment by Palestinians from abroad, who would be granted entry permits, and the encouragement of exports by cutting duties. Then Pundak put forth plans to establish eight industrial zones, five in Gaza and three in the West Bank, as well as permits in both territories for new building projects, preliminary studies for the construction of the proposed cement factory and for construction of a flour mill (Qurei, 2006: 87).

Based on the proposal of the Israeli team in Norway in February 1993, 'Principle of an Israeli-Palestinian Negotiating Plan', a joint paper was composed. It read:

> it is suggested that the US Secretary of State will go to Jerusalem and will submit to the Government of Israel on the one hand, and to the Palestinian leadership (Faisal Hesseini and Hanan Ashrawi) on the other hand, an American draft for a DOP (Declaration of Principles); an outline of a proposed Israeli-Palestinian CWP (Cooperation and Working Plan); and an outline of a proposed 'Marshall Plan' for the West Bank, the Gaza Strip and the Region. (Hirschfeld, 2014: 110)

During these first few meetings, the Israeli and Palestinian delegations were simultaneously examining each other's teams. 'Yair put on the table the philosophic perception of how the Middle East should be formed according to Beiliin's and Peres' doctrine.' Indeed, this was the right timing as in January, on the Palestinian side Abu Ala raised during the negotiations the economic cooperation projects. These were presented as the foundation for the economic cooperation and the Marshall plan between Israel and Palestine (Pundak, *Getting to the table—Oslo part B* 1998: -16:23:10). The unofficial talks that initially dealt with economic cooperation, quickly broadened into a dialogue about a joint Declaration of Principles (Shlaim, 1994).

The DOP, the outcome of Oslo negotiations to be signed in September 1993, contains several articles and annexes relating to economic cooperation (Declaration of Principles on Interim Self-Government Arrangements ISR-PA, 1993).[23] The economic provision of the DOP, even more than other parts of the agreement, is to reflect the hope that trade and wider economic cooperation would strengthen the Palestinian economy, and lead to cooperation in other fields (Watson, 2000: 157). Appendixes III and IV to the DOP address the different forms of the Israeli-Palestinian cooperation (Hirschfeld, 2000: 117). This includes a joint economic committee (JEC) to promote cooperation on trade, industry, finance, labour relations, social welfare, transport and communications, energy, and electricity amongst other fields, as well as a regional development plan involving the G-7, and other interested states and international organizations (Watson, 2000: 157). Hirschfeld attests to writing the final text of these annexes based on the ideas expressed in the Israeli-Palestinian Cooperation and Working Program, and the Draft for Preparing a Marshall Plan for the West Bank, respectively. The aim was to use economic development and cooperation to rebuild grassroots support and legitimacy for the peace-making and Palestinian state-building effort, and to overcome the hate and resentment that had erupted as a reaction to the 1987–93 Intifada (Hirschfeld, 2014: 137).

Abu Ala, even before the negotiations, had expressed a perception that is not far from the one Peres held, that Israeli-Palestinian cooperation opens the region to both parties of the conflict. Indeed, that is why Abu Ala was one of the biggest supporters of the regional development plans, especially the Casablanca Summit,[24] the regional bank, and the cooperation with Jordan. Moreover, Savir adds:

> The issues discussed were not of importance because they did not address security, nor settlements, nor Jerusalem. However, the fundamental approach that led Oslo onwards (and still leads until this day), is that of the

[23] See Appendix A: Article XI Israeli-Palestinian Cooperation in Economic Fields; Article XVI Israeli-Palestinian Cooperation Concerning regional Programs; Annex III Protocol on Israeli-Palestinian Cooperation in Economic and Development Programs; Annex IV Protocol on Israeli-Palestinian Cooperation Concerning Regional Development Programs in: Declaration of Principles on Interim Self-Government Arrangements ISR-PA (13 September 1993), United Nations General Assembly (UNGA), United Nations Security Council (UNSC), A/48/486, S/26560 (11 October 1993).

[24] Casablanca Summit—First Middle East North Africa (MENA) Economic Summit, 1994, part of a series of summits held subsequent to signing of Declaration of Principles and Israel-Jordan peace agreement; see also Chap. 7, Sect. 7.1.1 Promoting peace through economic incentives.

> Israeli-Palestinian cooperation that to open the region in the best way possible for achieving growth. The choice for this approach as that leading the process came in fact from the Palestinians, and that is why it was so powerful (…) (Savir, *Getting to the table—Oslo part B* 1998: -11:49:15)

3.4 A Shift of Gears

With the Oslo negotiations getting more attention at the then Israeli Prime Minister's desk and becoming a real option to the stagnated Washington talks, Israel stepped up the level of negotiators with first Uri Savir, and shortly after Yoel Singer, joining the team (Rød-Larsen et al., 2014; Shlaim, 1994, 2005).

Beilin was familiar with Yoel Singer, a former IDF colonel in charge of the defense ministry's legal team who had moved to Washington about a year before the Oslo process began. Singer had worked on the Taba Arbitration talks in the 1980s and was trusted by Rabin (Mitchell, 2014: 35–36). Beilin reached out to Singer at a point where he thought the document conceived by Hirschfeld and Pundak was almost complete, asking Singer to review it. This was the draft Declaration of Principles. After Singer reviewed the document, a meeting between Singer, Beilin, Hirschfeld, and Pundak took place, in which they provided him with the background regarding the secret talks. Only then did Savir join the meeting as well. Except for Beilin, it was the first time Singer met all the others (Cohen-Almagor, 2018). Singer's reaction to the proposed declaration of principles was that 'It's not the draft of an agreement! It's a blob of raw mush!' as quoted by Savir (1998: 27). This, however, did not compromise the contribution of both Hirschfeld and Pundak to the success of Oslo, which was indisputable. Indeed, in Savir's view, Hirschfeld and Pundak's detachment from the customary manner in which international diplomacy is conducted is, in fact, what led to the success of the negotiation process (Shlaim, 1994). At the same time, it is these characteristics that were posing challenges to the nature of the draft document.

From Singer's viewpoint, the draft agreement he received was vague and unclear. Furthermore, there were many discrepancies between his perception of the agreement and what Hirschfeld and Pundak attempted to explain during the meeting. From a legal perspective, important things were missing according to Singer. He attests to having had a vague impression of being slightly unsure of what was going on at the time. Primarily because the terminology used in the document, and the manner in which things were presented to him, all were very different from his previous experience in international negotiations related to the West Bank and Gaza Strip. For Singer, the conversation revolved around economic cooperation and projects. And as Hirschfeld, Pundak, and Beilin kept talking, he was thinking:

> We're talking about the PLO. When you negotiate an agreement with an enemy, there are so many other things to deal with. Economic cooperation, projects and fishponds and agriculture, yes that's important, but where is everything else that is much more important? (Singer, interview with Cohen-Almagor, Washington DC, 29 August 2014, in: Cohen-Almagor, 2018: 738)

Between May and early June 1993, after Singer met Rabin and expressed his professional view on the document and the process, the shift of gears from what had started as academic non-governmental discussions, to an official back-channel track led by government representatives, was complete (Cohen-Almagor, 2018).

The pre-negotiation phase of Oslo ended on 20 May 1993, with Savir joining the talks and elevating them to official status (Savir, 1998: 22). However, it was only after Singer had joined the team that the change of focus took place (Cohen-Almagor, 2018). For everyone involved, it was clear that the future trajectory of the process depended, for better or worse, on Singer's recommendations, and it was the meeting of Singer with Rabin that would tilt the scales one way or the other (Hirschfeld, 2000: 125). Despite the document's vagueness and ambiguity, Singer realized that a historical breakthrough was within reach. As such, he decided to endorse the document, leading to receiving the official blessing from Rabin (letter from Singer to Peres, handed on 5 June 1993, Hirschfeld personal archive in: Hirschfeld, 2000: 126). As the negotiations became official, the focus shifted from political-economic issues to political-security aspects, as all official negotiations were focused on security issues (Pundak, *Getting to the table—Oslo part B* 1998: -11:49:20).

Thus, the economic cooperation and mutual benefits served as catalysts fostering a shared vision. Arguably, these economic incentives brought the Israelis and Palestinians to the Oslo negotiation table. However, though these incentives served as catalysts of the shared vision, once established politics took over the process, including in relation to the design of the economic agreement, the Paris Protocol.

References

Abbas, M. (1995). *Through secret channels: The road to Oslo; Senior PLO Leader Abu Mazen's revealing story of the negotiations with Israel.* Garnet.

Abusada, M. (2017). Palestinian diplomacy: 'Past and present'. In G. Gürbey, S. Hofmann, & F. I. Seyder (Eds.), *Between state and non-state: Politics and society in Kurdistan-Iraq and Palestine* (pp. 197–212). Palgrave Macmillan.

Aggestam, K. (2012). The psychology of peacemaking: Terje Rød-Larsen. In M. Fixdal (Ed.), *Ways out of war: Peacemakers in the Middle East and Balkans* (pp. 71–90). Palgrave Macmillan US.

Aix Group. (2004). *Economic road map: An Israeli-Palestinian perspective on permanent status.* Aix-en-Provence, Jerusalem.

Al-Botmeh, S., & Kanafani, N. (2006). The Paris economic protocol and beyond–in search of an optimal trade arrangement. *The Palestine Yearbook of International Law Online, 14,* 75–97.

Arieli, S. (2009). *Israel and Palestine, a brief history of the negotiations. Babylon Nordisk tidsskrift for Midtøstenstudier.*

Arieli, S.. (2021). *Shaul Arieli the Israeli-Palestinian conflict maps.* Retrieved August 3, 2023, from https://www.shaularieli.com/en/maps/political-arrangements.

Arnon, A. (1997). *The Palestinian economy: Between imposed integration and voluntary separation.* Brill.

Arnon, A. (2007). Israeli policy towards the occupied Palestinian territories: The economic dimension, 1967–2007. *The Middle East Journal, 61*(4), 573–595.

Arnon, A., & Weinblatt, J. (2001). Sovereignty and economic development: The case of Israel and Palestine. *The Economic Journal, 111*(472), 291–308.

Barak, O. (2005). The failure of the Israeli–Palestinian peace process, 1993–2000. *Journal of Peace Research, 42*(6), 719–736.

Behrendt, S. (2007). *The secret Israeli-Palestinian negotiations in Oslo: Their success and why the process ultimately failed.* Routledge.

Beilin, Y. (1997). *Touching peace: From the Oslo Accord to a final agreement.* Miskal-Yedioth Ahronoth Books and Chemed Books.

Bush, G. H. W. (1991, October 30). Remarks by Mr. George Bush—President of the United States, The Madrid Conference opening speeches October 30–31, 1991. Retrieved April 20, 2020, from https://www.gov.il/en/Departments/General/remarks-by-mr-george-bush-president-of-the-united-states-30-october-91.

Cleveland, W. L., & Bunton, M. (2016). *A history of the modern Middle East.* Hachette UK.

Cohen-Almagor, R. (2018). The Oslo peace process: Interview with Joel Singer. *Israel Affairs, 24*(5), 733–766.

Declaration of Principles on Interim Self-Government Arrangements ISR-PA. (1993, September 13). United Nations General Assembly (UNGA), United Nations Security Council (UNSC), A/48/486, S/26560 (11 October

1993). Retrieved May 14, 2020, from https://www.un.org/unispal/document/auto-insert-180015/.
ECF. (2015). *Overview*. Retrieved July 7, 2020, from https://ecf.org.il.
Elmusa, S. S., & El-Jaafari, M. (1995). Power and trade: The Israeli-Palestinian economic protocol. *Journal of Palestine Studies, 24*, 14–32.
Fafo. (n.d.). *Fafo and our history*. Retrieved July 7, 2020, from https://www.fafo.no/en/about-fafo/fafo.
Freedman, R. O. (1993). *The Middle East after Iraq's invasion of Kuwait*. University Press of Florida.
Gelvin, J. L. (2005). *The modern Middle East: A history*. Oxford University Press.
Ghanem, A. A. (2017). Historical Background of the State-Building Process in Palestine. In G. Gürbey, S. Hofmann & F. I. Seyder (Eds.), *Between State and Non-State: Politics and Society in Kurdistan-Iraq and Palestine* (pp. 43–58). Springer.
Hirschfeld, Y. (2000). *Oslo: A formula for peace*. Am-Oved.
Hirschfeld, Y. (2014). *Track-two diplomacy toward an Israeli-Palestinian solution, 1978–2014*. Woodrow Wilson Center Press.
Israeli, R. (2017). *The Oslo idea: The euphoria of failure*. Routledge.
Kanafani, N. M. (2001). Trade—A catalyst for peace? *Economic Journal, 111*(472), 276–290.
Kaufmann, J. (1996). *Conference diplomacy: An introductory analysis*. Springer.
Kaufmann, J., Leurdijk, D. A., & Schrijver, N. (1991). *The world in turmoil: Testing the UN's capacity*. Academic Council on the United Nations System.
Kaye, D. D. (1998). *Beyond the handshake: Multilateral cooperation in the Arab-Israeli peace process, 1991–1996*. Columbia University Press.
Kelman, H. C. (1997). Group processes in the resolution of international conflicts: Experiences from the Israeli–Palestinian case. *American Psychologist, 52*(3), 212–2020.
Kelman, H. C. (2007). The Israeli-Palestinian peace process and its vicissitudes: Insights from attitude theory. *American Psychologist, 62*(4), 287–303.
Kleiman, E. (1999). Fiscal separation with economic integration: Israel and the Palestinian authority. In A. Razin & E. Sadka (Eds.), *The economics of globalization policy perspective from public economics*. Cambridge University Press.
Lundberg, K. (1999). *The Oslo channel: Getting to the negotiating table* (p. 1333). John F. Kennedy School of Government Case.
Massad, J. (1999). Return or permanent exile? Palestinian refugees and the ends of Oslo. *Critique: Journal for Critical Studies of the Middle East, 8*(4), 5–23.
Mitchell, T. G. (2014). *When peace fails: Lessons from Belfast for the Middle East*. McFarland.
Oren, N., & Bar-Tal, D. (2007). The detrimental dynamics of delegitimization in intractable conflicts: The Israeli–Palestinian case. *International Journal of Intercultural Relations, 31*(1), 111–126.

Parsons, N. (2005). *The politics of the Palestinian Authority: From Oslo to Al-Aqsa*. Routledge.
Peres, S. (1993, September 28). Address by Foreign Minister Peres to the United Nations General Assembly. Retrieved August 4, 2020, from https://embassies.gov.il/MFA/InternatlOrgs/Speeches/Pages/Address%20by%20FM%20Peres%20to%20the%20UN%20General%20Assembly-%2028.aspx.
Peres, S. (1995). *Battling for peace: A memoir*. Random House.
Peres, S., & Naor, A. (1993). *The new Middle East*. Harper Element.
Peters, J. (1999). Can the multilateral Middle East talks be revived? *Middle East Review of International Affairs (MERIA), 3*(4), 90–99.
Qurei, A. (2006). *From Oslo to Jerusalem: The Palestinian story of the secret negotiations*. IB Tauris.
Rød-Larsen, T., Laiq, N., & Aidan, F. (Eds.). (2014). *The search for peace in the Arab-Israeli conflict: A compendium of documents and analysis*. Oxford University Press, USA.
Ross, D. (2005). *The missing peace: The inside story of the fight for Middle East peace*. Farrar, Straus and Giroux.
Savir, U. (1998). *The process: 1,100 days that changed the Middle East*. Vintage.
Schiavone, G. (1981). *The institutions of Comecon*. Springer.
Shlaim, A. (1994). The Oslo Accord. *Journal of Palestine Studies, 23*(3), 24–40.
Shlaim, A. (2005). The rise and fall of the Oslo Peace process. *International Relations of the Middle East, 285*, 241–261.
Taghdisi-Rad, S. (2014). The economic strategies of occupation: Confining development and buying-off peace. In M. Turner & O. Shweiki (Eds.), *Decolonizing Palestinian political economy* (pp. 13–31). Springer, Palgrave Macmillan.
The Madrid Peace Conference. (1992). *Journal of Palestine Studies, 21*(2), 117–149.
United Nations Committee on the Exercise of the Inalienable Rights of the Palestinian People (UN CEIRPP). (2014). *The origin and evolution of the Palestinian problem Part V (1989–2000)*. New York: United Nations, 2014.
United Nations General Assembly (UNGA). (1947, November 29). Resolution *181 (II). Future government of Palestine-Plan of partition with Economic Union*, GA RES/181(II). Retrieved April 5, 2020, from https://documents-ddsny.un.org/doc/RESOLUTION/GEN/NR0/038/88/PDF/NR003888.pdf?OpenElement; https://www.un.org/unispal/document/auto-insert-185393/.
United Nations General Assembly (UNGA). (1948, November 27). Resolution *194 (III). Palestine—Progress Report of the Unite Nations Mediator*, GA RES 194 (III). Retrieved April 17, 2020, from https://documents-dds-ny.un.org/doc/RESOLUTION/GEN/NR0/043/65/PDF/NR004365.pdf?OpenElement.
United Nations General Assembly (UNGA). (1974a, November 22). *Resolution 3236(XXIX). Question of Palestine*, GA RES/ 3236(XXIX). Retrieved August 19, 2023, from https://documents-ddsny.un.org/doc/RESOLUTION/GEN/NR0/738/38/PDF/NR073838.pdf?OpenElement.

United Nations General Assembly (UNGA). (1974b, November 22). *Resolution 3237(XXIX). Observer status for the Palestine Liberation Organization*, GA RES/3237(XXIX). Retrieved August 19, 2023, from https://documents-dds-ny.un.org/doc/RESOLUTION/GEN/NR0/738/38/PDF/NR073838.p df?OpenElement.

United Nations General Assembly (UNGA). (1975, November 10). *Resolution 3376(XXX). Question of Palestine* (1975), GA RES/3376 (XXX). Retrieved August 19, 2023, from https://documents-dds-ny.un.org/doc/RESOLUTION/GEN/NR0/ 000/89/PDF/NR000089.pdf?OpenElement (Accessed 19 August 2023).

United Nations General Assembly (UNGA). (1977, December 2). *Resolution 32/40(B). Assist in the Establishment of the Special Unit on Palestinian Rights*, A/RES/32/40(B). Retrieved December 3, 2022, from https://www.un.org/documents/ga/res/32/ares32r40.pdf.

United Nations General Assembly (UNGA). (1978, December 7). *Resolution 33/28(A-C). Palestine question/Committee on the Exercise of the Inalienable Rights of the Palestinian People (CEIRPP)/ Special Unit on Palestinian Rights (SUPR)*, A/RES/33/28(A-C). Retrieved August 19, 2023, from https://www.un.org/unispal/document/auto-insert-189135/.

United Nations Security Council (UNSC). (1967, November 22). *Resolution 242. Situation in the Middle East*, S/RES/242. Retrieved May 7, 2020, from https://documents-ddsny.un.org/doc/RESOLUTION/GEN/NR0/240/94 /PDF/NR024094.pdf?OpenElement.

United Nations Security Council (UNSC). (1973, October 22). *Resolution 338. Ceasefire in the Middle East*, S/RES/338. Retrieved May 7, 2020, from https://documents-dds-ny.un.org/doc/RESOLUTION/GEN/NR0/288/65 /PDF/NR028865.pdf?OpenElement.

Waage, H. H. (2002). Explaining the Oslo backchannel: Norway's political past in the Middle East. *The Middle East Journal, 56*(4), 597–615.

Waage, H. H. (2007). The 'Minnow' and the 'Whale': Norway and the United States in the peace process in the Middle East. *British Journal of Middle Eastern Studies, 34*(2), 157–176.

Waage, H. H. (2012). Proactive peace diplomacy: Jan Egeland. In M. Fixdal (Ed.), *Ways out of war* (pp. 91–116). Palgrave Macmillan US.

Wanis-St, J. A. (2011). *Back channel negotiation: Secrecy in the Middle East peace process*. Syracuse University Press.

Watkins, M., & Lundberg, K. (1998). Getting to the table in Oslo: Driving forces and channel factors. *Negotiation Journal, 14*, 115–135.

Watson, G. R. (2000). *The Oslo Accords: International law and the Israeli-Palestinian peace agreements*. Oxford University Press.

Weinberger, P. E. (2006). *Co-opting the PLO: A critical reconstruction of the Oslo Accords, 1993–1995*. Lexington Books.

CHAPTER 4

Oslo through an Economic Lens—The Paris Protocol

The Protocol on Economic Relations between Israel and Palestine has been analysed and discussed in the academic and professional literature numerous times, as being the legal framework defining the relations from 1994 onwards, until today. In this sense, this chapter is no different and presents the main issues of the agreement, that is, trade, labour, taxation, and monetary and fiscal issues. However, taking into account the asymmetricity of the balance of power, the focus of the analysis here is on the scale of trade-offs between economic and political spheres the Paris Protocol has set at the time the Oslo I Accord was signed.

4.1 Setting and Framing

At the beginning of 1993, the Minister of Finance in Israel, Avraham 'Baiga' Shochat, nominated Haim Ben Shahar[1] to establish an Economic Consulting Team. This team was asked to prepare a report that would provide recommendations and help form the government's policy

[1] An Israeli economist who served in prominent positions in the private and public sector in Israel, amongst others: Chair of the 1975 Committee for Tax Reform Government of Israel; Chair of the Steering Committee of the University Armand Hammer Fund for Economic Cooperation in the Middle East; Chairman of the Committee on Economic Relations between Israel and the proposed Palestinian Authority and more. References to the 'Ben Shahar' report in this work will be to the report of the 'Committee on Economic Relations between Israel and the proposed Palestinian Authority'.

L. Lahar, *The Economic Diplomacy of Peace in the Middle East*,
https://doi.org/10.1007/978-3-031-93991-4_4

regarding the economic negotiations with the Palestinians, if and when this would come to term. Ben Shahar served as head of the Committee, and the work of the committee was in full coordination with governmental offices, the Bank of Israel (BOI), and Civil Administration,[2] basing its work on professional considerations. Recommendations were submitted to the government in July 1993, a few weeks before the signature on the Oslo Accord took place in Washington. The main guidelines for the committee's work were defined as follows:

1. Israel has an interest in economic welfare in the territories.
2. During the interim period of self-governance, no physical borders are to be established between the territories and Israel, with exception for security needs, in accordance with the circumstances and situation on the ground.
3. The purpose is to guarantee the free movement of goods, labour, and capital between the territories and Israel. Alternatives covering specific issues deviating from this guideline would be examined.
4. The financial aspects that are currently under the responsibility of the Civil Administration are to become the responsibility of the financial authorities of the Autonomy, subjected to the agreements to be achieved.
5. The committee will not address issues related to land and water, and act according to the assumption that the migration rate to the territories will remain the same as the current rate.
6. A linkage between the interim economic agreement with the Autonomy, and the future agreement with Jordan is desirable.
7. The current agreement should not limit Israel's freedom of decision regarding the permanent agreement, to be negotiated at the end of the interim period.
8. The preferable agreements would be those requiring the minimum direct involvement of the State of Israel. Unless it is required for either political or security reasons (Ben Shahar, 1995; Report of the Economic Advisory Team July, 1993: 4–5).

[2] Civil Administration—an Israeli military organ entrusted with the role of looking after the needs of the civil population in the Palestinian territories occupied by Israel as a result of the 1967 war and having a completely independent budget. The Civil Administration is subordinate to a larger entity known as Coordinator of Government Activities in the Territories (COGAT), which is a unit in the Defense Ministry of Israel.

The committee based its recommendations on the presupposition that a border, including an economic border, would not exist during the interim stage, with this political framing heavily affecting the alternatives available (Arnon, 2002). At the same time, the work of the committee was based on the realization that though trade relations between Israel and the Occupied Territory would have very little impact on the Israeli economy, it will largely affect the economy of the territories. Hence the desirable trade regime should be examined according to standards allowing the achievement of economic welfare in the territories, including taking into consideration the number of habitants to be employed in Israel, while minimizing the potential of negative effects on the Israeli economy and its international obligations (Box 4.1). These led to recommendations on keeping no economic borders between the two sides for reaching the maximum economic welfare conditions in the OPT (Report of the Economic Advisory Team July, 1993: 7–8). The guidelines leading the work of the committee were approved by the head of the Israeli delegation to the negotiations on the interim agreement (Ben Shahar, 1995).

Following the signature of the Declaration of Principles, the Israeli team for the economic negotiations was formed. The Minister of Finance, Shochat, headed the economic negotiation team. Some members of the Ben Shahar consulting team became members of the Israeli negotiations team to the economic agreement, including David Brodet, Budget Director in the Ministry of Finance (1991–1994) who served as Chief Israeli Negotiator for the Paris economic agreement between Israel and the PLO; as well as appearing before the Ministry of Finance team to further advise on issues covered in the report;[3] and the Ben Shahar recommendations becoming simply 'the Blueprint' in Kleiman's words[4] for the economic agreement between Israel and the Palestinians, known as the Paris Protocol.

Though the Ben-Shahar committee was the first official preparatory body for future economic negotiations, research regarding future economic relations had already been taking place in Israel since the late 1980s. Avi Ben Basat, who served as the head of the research unit at the BOI, led a research team focused on issues of Palestinian foreign trade and monetary topics.[5] Kleiman on his part refers to other preparations he was a part

[3] Oz, Interview, 4 August 2021; Shochat, Interview, 8 August 2021.

[4] Kleiman, Interview, 4 October 2018.

[5] Arnon, Interview, 27 July 2021; Ben Basat, Interview, 2 January 2017.

Box 4.1 Economic Relations Between Israel and OPT 1967–1993
The 1967 occupation shaped the economic relations between Israel and the Palestinian Occupied Territory. Trade and labour were the main economic links (Kleiman, 1999). The period between 1967–1993 was one of economic integration in which the Palestinian trade policy had to be fully aligned with the Israeli trade policy. Thus, all the tariffs, levies, and standard requirements that Israel adopted on imports from third parties were automatically, in effect, imposed on the West Bank and Gaza Strip (Astrup & Dessus, 2001). The external borders were controlled by Israel and a 'de-facto, one-sided customs union' (Al-Botmeh & Kanafani, 2006), or a quasi-customs union, was imposed as Israel created one sided barriers to trade between her and OPT with Israeli products having free access to the Occupied Territory's markets while free movement of goods and capital of Palestinian products were subjected to Israeli constraints; and a revenue sharing mechanism which is usually part and parcel of every customs union did not exist (Aix Group, 2005; Arnon, 1997: 2; Arnon, 2002). Agricultural exports from the WBGS to Israel were practically prohibited, except as a buffer to meet any shortages in supply from Israeli sources (Aminoff, 1991; Rivlin, 1992). Manufactured exports were subject to multiple administrative controls and non-tariff barriers (Al-Botmeh & Kanafani, 2006). And Palestinian farmers and manufactures were effectively excluded from the various forms of public subsidies extended to their Israeli counterparts. Administrative means were implemented by Israel in order to hamper the establishment of industrial plants that could compete with Israeli firms (Kleiman, 1999).

of during the early years of the 1990s which due to political sensitivity amongst other things, fell through.[6] All the preparatory work came to a culmination and was discussed during the formation of the Ben Shahar committee with both Ben Basat and Kleiman, among others, being a part of the professional committee teams.

[6] Kleiman, Interview, 4 October 2018.

During the official preparations on the framework of the committee, scenarios were conducted by the Israeli specialist, based on two assumptions: one is that both sides to the negotiations are rational actors and want to reach an agreement; the second is that as both sides are professionals, they will acknowledge the limitations of the other, as well as those derived from the DOP to which the agreement is subject. The simulations allowed the Israelis to estimate the spectrum of debate with which they would come to the negotiation table. While some conditions were defined for the Israeli team as being non-negotiable, other conditions enabled a certain degree of flexibility, which they examined during preparation.[7] Indeed the spirit of the preparatory discussions was led by principles of free movement of goods and labour, a viable and independent economic system in the OPT, including collecting and receiving funds that will support the future Palestinian Authority establishments.[8]

> The Israeli team prepared for the negotiations on the understanding and assumption that if Autonomy were to be established it would need to be economically successful, and though during the preparations there were some debates regarding the economic regime, it became clear early on that the Oslo agreement left only one viable option on the table in the form of a customs union.[9]

The Israeli team arrived at the negotiation table with firm stands, and even more, a clear distinction of what was indeed feasible in the framework of the agreement.[10] The Israeli delegation comprised representatives of all the financial institutions in Israel. Among others were representatives of the Ministry of Finance, BOI, and Ministry of Economy and Industry. Also, the head of the Coordinator of the Government Activities in the Territories (COGAT), Major General Rothschild, the person in charge of the OPT economy served as Baiga's right hand, in order to ensure that any economic decision being discussed was indeed feasible.[11] As the negotiation progressed, and with the focus turning to specific issues, more experts joined specific rounds of negotiations. For the Palestinians, the situation was completely different as they lacked the toolbox required for

[7] Gabai, Interview, 2 January 2017.
[8] Shochat, Interview, 8 August 2021.
[9] Brodet, Interview, 3 January 2017.
[10] Ben Basat, Interview, 2 January 2017.
[11] Shochat, Interview, 8 August 2021; Rothschild, Interview, 18 August 2021.

running either a state or an autonomous authority, or anything else for that matter. Nonetheless, though their number of experts was lesser, they were very talented economists and professionals,[12] also according to Brodet 'though they had the professional background, they were short on professional qualifications'.[13]

Abu Ala, serving as head of the economic department of Fatah, was appointed to head the Palestinian economic negotiation team. He assembled the Palestinian economic negotiation delegation with the notion that its members should be from the territories themselves, as these were the ones who knew the situation on the ground when it came to economic development.[14] Indeed, to Abu Ala it was clear that the Palestinians on the negotiation team should also be professionals with an economic background, like him. These two criteria, especially considering that Abu Ala himself was not in the Occupied Territory,[15] meant that it took time to identify the members of the negotiations' delegation. Thus, the negotiations started a month later than planned (following the signing of the DOP the two other scheduled parallel tracks, the general and civilian negotiations, started a month before the economic negotiations).[16]

Prof. Yusif A. Sayigh, who was a famous Palestinian economist, prepared the PLO's Palestinian development plan published in 1993. This guiding document contradicted the Ben Shahar recommendations, and endeavoured to set economic borders around the green line,[17] meaning that all exchange of goods and services between Israel and the OPT would be subjected to some form of inspection at the borders, which 'of course was rejected by the Israeli delegation'.[18] Sayigh, as Elkurd, was part of the PLO leadership in Tunis, and though he headed the multilateral economic track and was one of the best professors and economists of the Arab world, the proposed plan was not in line with the economic reality on the ground,

[12] Shochat, Interview, 8 August 2021.

[13] Brodet, Interview, 3 January 2017.

[14] Hulileh, Interview, 13 December 2018; Brodet, Interview, 3 January 2017.

[15] Abu Ala was part of the exile PLO leadership in Tunis (see Chap. 3, Sect. 3.2 Establishing the relationship between Israel and the PLO).

[16] Brodet, Interview, 3 January 2017.

[17] Green Line—the 1949 Armistice Agreement's demarcation line between Israel and Egypt, Jordan, Lebanon and Syria, set out as the de facto Israeli borders between 1949–1967, also referred to as the '1967 borders'. The line received its name because of the green marker with which it was drawn.

[18] Elkurd, Interview, 27 August 2018.

due to the physical separation between the PLO exiled leadership from the territory. Samir Hulileh was the only member out of the Palestinian multilateral economic track to also become a member of the negotiation team to the Protocol. And as a part of the internal Palestinian leadership in the West Bank, in Hulilehs' view, Abu Ala's approach demonstrated a deep understanding of the complexity of the situation, and the need to deal with key issues relating to the situation on the ground, in the West Bank and Gaza Strip, and not the issues addressed in 'generic papers' at the macro level discussing issues related to the 'hypothetical state of Palestine'.[19] Support for Abu Ala's approach to the negotiations can be found in Arafat's lack of limitations given to the economic team for the negotiations, 'as they were the professionals in the field, with the authority on all economic decisions delegated to Abu Ala'.[20]

4.2 The Protocol on Economic Relations

The Protocol on Economic Relations between Israel and the Palestinian Liberation Organization, also known as the Paris Protocol, sought to regulate the interim economic arrangement between Israel and the Palestinians while covering the West Bank and the Gaza Strip, pending the formation of a permanent agreement between the two sides. The Protocol was signed by the Israeli Finance Minister, Avraham Shochat, and the Palestinian Chief Negotiator, Ahmed Qurei, in Paris, on 29 April 1994. This Protocol was incorporated into the Gaza-Jericho Agreement, known as the Cairo Agreement, signed on 4 May 1994, and with minor amendments later on into the Interim Agreement, Oslo II, signed on 28 September 1995.

The Protocol set a concrete framework concerning the integration of the Israeli and Palestinian economies on issues related to import tax policies, monetary and financial issues, direct and indirect taxation, labour relations, agriculture, industry, tourism, and insurance, as well as a Joint Economic Committee as the mechanism in charge of the implementation of the Protocol.

[19] Hulileh, Interview, 13 December 2018.
[20] Abu Kosh, Interview, 15 September 2018.

> The two parties view the economic domain as one of the cornerstone in their mutual relations with a view to enhance their interest in the achievement of a just, lasting and comprehensive peace. Both parties shall cooperate in this field in order to establish a sound economic base for these relations, which will be governed in various economic spheres by the principles of mutual respect of each other's economic interests, reciprocity, equity and fairness.
>
> This protocol lays the groundwork for strengthening the economic base of the Palestinian side and for exercising its right of economic decision-making in accordance with its own development plan and priorities. The two parties recognise each other's economic ties with other markets and the need to create a better economic environment for their peoples and individuals.
>
> Source: Preamble, Protocol on Economic Relations between the Government of the State of Israel and the P.L.O., representing the Palestinian people (Paris Protocol), Paris, April 29, (1994)

The Protocol, like the DOP and the agreements to follow, states clearly that the aim is to establish a sound economic base and new economic relations between the two parties accompanied by the anticipation that the Palestinian economy would thrive (Arnon & Weinblatt, 2001; World Bank and The United Nations, 1999). The Protocol provided scope for the Palestinians to adapt prices of products, to engage freely in commerce with both external markets and Israel, which together with the relatively high levels of Palestinian education, human capital endowment and the close realities with Israel's development economy would enable the Palestinians to build their own viable economy (World Bank and The United Nations, 1999). Furthermore, promotion of economic development through the Protocol and the newly created prosperity it would bring with it, were expected to support the peace process in its later stages (Aix Group, 2005).

4.2.1 *Trade Relations*[21]

The key to the whole agreement is the freedom of movement of agriculture and industrial goods, with certain exceptions, and the common customs and import regime formed 'the operational nexus' of both the economic negotiations and the agreement itself (Kleiman, 1994: 359). The Protocol establishes a single customs envelope[22] covering both Israel and the areas under the control of the Palestinian National Authority (PNA, commonly known as PA) (Al-Botmeh & Kanafani, 2006; Kleiman, 1999). The key economic principles defining the economic relations between the two sides are the free access for the WBGS agriculture and industrial products to the Israeli market (Box 4.2). The exceptions to this are five agriculture commodities of poultry, eggs, potatoes, cucumbers, and tomatoes, on which increasing quotas were imposed up to 1997;[23] and to melons imported into the territories from Israel. Also, dairy products could be limited 'in principle', which Kleiman (1994: 356) refers to as a 'hint at restricting competition'; and the movement of agricultural products would also be subjected to veterinary and phytosanitary requirements. The right of the West Bank and Gaza Strip to undertake independent and direct trade relations with the outside world, either via its own special crossing points (to Jordan and Egypt) or via the Israeli international port where the Palestinian goods 'will be given equal trade and economic treatment', and the external trade of the territories would be subjected to Israeli trade policy and regulations. The customs tariffs and import regulations applying both in Israel and the Palestinian Territory have to be the same in order not to provide a means of circumventing Israeli import policy, and for enabling the free unrestricted movement of goods between the two. This refers to the rates of customs tariffs and all other imposed levies on imports, and to the international procedures adopted by Israel for the classification and valuation of goods for customs purposes, as well as to standard requirements and import licensing

[21] See Appendix B: Article III, Import Tax and Import Policy clause 10; Article VIII, Agriculture clause 1; Article IX, Industry clause 1 in: The Protocol on Economic Relations between the Government of the States of Israel and the P.L.O., representing the Palestinian people (29 April 1994), UNGA, UNSC, A/49/180, S/1994/727 (4 May 1994).

[22] The term customs envelope was suggested by Zeif, Director of Customs Directorate of Israel at the time. This structure is one of a kind based on an internal free trade area and the common external tariff key principles of a customs union, yet with exceptions.

[23] These products constituted approximately 60 per cent of the agricultural production of Gaza Strip, and were the most competitive with Israel's agricultural products (Roy, 1998: 10).

Box 4.2 Israel's Economic Policy in the OPT 1967–1993
The forced union with Israel, from the stranpoint of the Occupied Territory, opened a huge market on their doorstep, which had the potential to more than compensate for the loss from traditional trade partners in the Arab world. Nonetheless, the highly protective farm policy preventing the main export potential of agricultural produce; prevention of industrial plants that would present competition to the Israeli ones; and the unofficial policy to protect the shares of Israeli firms in the OPT's market itself, took their course regarding the level of economic development reached in Palestine (Abed, 1990; Kleiman, 1994). Further, the large number of obstacles related to customs, transportation, and infrastructure prevented the 'open bridges' Israeli policy following the 1967 occupation from working. The 'open bridges' enabled the Palestinian exports to Arab and regional countries through the Jordan River bridges, stimulating Palestinian trade relations with non-Israeli partners (Taghdisi-Rad, 2014).

policies. To these there are two exceptions. First, Palestine has the right to its own import policy (customs and other import charges as well as standard specifications) on quantities designed to meet the WBGS's own market needs of specified goods. Second, Palestine has the right to impose its own import charges (but not standards specifications) on imports from another list of goods (Kanafani, 2001; Kleiman, 1994).

Arnon and Spivak (1995a) defined the level of cooperation as a hybrid form of cooperation that lies between the EU on the one hand, and the NAFTA, on the other. On the one hand, the EU agreement includes the free movement of raw materials, labour, and capital, but at the time of the Protocol entering into force, the EU did not yet have a common currency. NAFTA countries, on the other hand, implemented the free movement of goods and capital but limited the movement of labour. Also, the country members of NAFTA do not share a common currency. Prior to the signing of the Protocol, Israel and the Occupied Territories implemented almost full free movement of goods, large volume of movement of labour, and limited movement of capital. As for the currency, the Israeli Shekel is one of two currencies to be used, with the other being the US dollar.[24]

The customs envelope structure includes three lists (addressed below). The terms for the lists were restricted to ensuring that these imports would not filter into the Israeli market. These lists were the exception to a customs union, and resembled an FTA between Israel and Palestine enabling each partner to import under its own rules and restricting the free trade between them to locally produced goods or to those that complied with the ultimate importer's tariff. In the event of imports finding their way to the Israeli market, the arrangement will be equivalent to some preferential trade agreement between Israel and the countries in which they originate, Jordan and Egypt in particular (Kleiman, 1994). Yet, it is a shared framework of monetary, fiscal and trade regulations that both economies share, with this framework reflecting the broader economy and trade preferences of Israel. Thus, the customs envelope has a structural bias towards the more advanced Israeli economy and the interests of its producers, and as such it is in fact more of an economic union (Samour, 2016). Indeed, one of the key goals of the Palestinian delegation was for the interim agreement to define that the (final) economic agreement between the two sides is in the form of an FTA. Since this entailed the establishment of economic borders, which clearly did not take place, there is no doubt that the agreement could not be addressed in the same way as other preferential trade agreements.[25]

The Palestinians aspired to formulate a new Palestinian trade policy according to their own priorities during the negotiations. The Israelis tried to convince the Palestinians that a more protectionist policy would reduce the Palestinians' chances of building a prosperous economy. This correlated with, yet not necessarily required, the creation of trade borders between the two economies (Box 4.3) (Arnon & Weinblatt, 2001). Nevertheless, the question of whether it should be a customs union-based system or an FTA was not really on the negotiation table, since Israel was opposed to any defined border (Arnon, 2007). Rabin, the Prime Minister of Israel at the time, gave strict instructions on this issue with no room for manoeuvre—a physical border is not acceptable under any circumstances. And this automatically means a customs envelope.[26] The Palestinians tried

[24] Jordanian dinar is also being used.
[25] Elkurd, Interview, 27 August 2018.
[26] Kleiman, Interview, 4 October 2018.

to fend off Israel's argument about the need for a defined border by suggesting other alternatives that amounted to some type of national border arrangement. Their perspective was that an economic border can be argued as national if taxes are associated with passing from one fiscal jurisdiction to another. The distinction between the jurisdictions then depends on some evidence other than that of crossing a given physical line. Yet, for such an arrangement to be at all considered, there has to be considerable trust between the fiscal authorities of the relevant jurisdictions. Given that the absence of borders was a strict demand, and the continuation of access to the Israeli market was desired by both sides, there was no other alternative than an arrangement in the form of a 'customs union' (Kleiman, 1994). 'It goes without saying' said Ben Basat referring to the arrangement in the form of a 'customs union' as being the only possible alternative. With the lack of established borders, the taxation cannot be differential. From an economic perspective, this left the Israeli team no other choice for consideration. Furthermore, even if a decision about the borders would have been taken, establishing the borders would have taken years. Thus, it became clear to the Palestinians, as it was already evident to the Israelis prior to the start of the negotiation, that a form of a 'customs union' indeed is the only option.[27] The decision about the economic border is argued by Arnon and Weinblatt (2001) as the upshot of wider political decisions in Israel to put off, or even consciously avoid the need to agree on the demarcation of borders.

Despite the political restrictions and a 'no border' policy, the disparity in the sizes of the respective economies of Israel and Palestine implied that a customs union would be able to benefit the Palestinian economy (Kleiman, 1994). The Palestinians, like many of the Israelis, held the perception that a 'union' between large and small economies necessarily meant the exploitation of the small economy by the large one. Indeed, a large powerful economy is prone to use its power and, in many ways, exploit the small economy, extorting concessions. However, a 'customs union' agreement is the exception.[28] At the same time, Israel wanted to protect itself against the possible adverse consequences of open borders, such as the OPT becoming a channel for circumventing its import regime or providing tax shelters for Israelis; and to reserve the right to regulate the number of Palestinians employed in Israel for internal economic and

[27] Ben Basat, Interview, 3 January 2017.
[28] Kleiman, Interview, 4 October 2018.

social reasons (Kleiman, 1994). The negotiators were told they would be personally held responsible for the protection of Israel's economy, and every non-paper is to be signed directly by them. Gabai attested to taking a hawkish stance in his recommendations during the negotiations, purely out of professional considerations for the benefit of the Israeli tax system. In an internal discussion, for example, regarding the possibility of having a customs crossing point fully controlled by the Palestinians, Prime Minister Rabin asked Gabai if from his professional point of view, solely as a taxation specialist without any political consideration to be taken into account, he would authorize this. Gabai on his part recalls not being able to support this as if and where there is a tax loophole from his professional point of view, it will be taken advantage of by the business sector, no matter if it is the Israeli or Palestinian one. Rabin's conclusion from this discussion was not to approve the full control of customs checkpoints by the Palestinian Authority. 'We were told that no borders are to be established at the time of the negotiations thus, the axiom is that customs borders have to be unified for both sides.'[29]

From the Israeli point of view it was clear that the unified import and export policies would be according to Israel's requirements, from the first month of the negotiations.[30] Yet the trade regime was the main issue of contest throughout all of the negotiation process with the majority of discussions revolving around the specifications and adaptations to the customs union-like arrangement, which was the only possible arrangement, given the no-borders framework.[31] Without a border the Palestinians were compelled to transport imports and exports through Israeli ports, and not Jordanian as they demanded. Also, they refused to accept the Israeli VAT rate, and moreover, demanded that the excise tax should be used as their state's revenues and not transferred to the Israeli government. As these were irreconcilable points of discussion, Rothschild suggested the lists. Indeed, as head of COGAT he acknowledged the importance of preserving the secured OPT budget, and this received Baiga's support.[32] The lists, the agricultural exceptions, trade relations with third countries, the tax collection mechanism, division of taxations, all the practical issues derived out of the customs envelope. These and all other issues to be discussed

[29] Gabai, Interview, 2 January 2017.
[30] Elkurd, Interview, 27 August 2018.
[31] Brodet, Interview, 3 January 2017.
[32] Rothschild, Interview, 18 August 2021; Shochat, Interview, 8 August 2021.

were to be implemented for the five-year period, and with the final arrangement, the economic agreement would be revised and renegotiated according to developments and results on the ground.[33] It was clear to the Palestinians as it was to the Israelis that 'this is an interim arrangement, not a permanent one'.[34]

Box 4.3 Israel-Palestine Trade Relations 1967–1993
The occupation of the territories led to the full control of Israel on the trade relations of WBGS, from restrictions imposed regarding trade partners to trade operations through Israeli entry points, and to Israeli export and import agents. At the same time, from the time of the occupation and for over two decades practically free movement of people and goods between the Palestinian territories and Israel took place. Despite an increase of nearly 80 per cent in the Palestinian population between 1968 and 1992, GNP per capita grew, on average, by 5.7 per cent annually in real terms over those 24 years. Though much of that growth represented income from work in Israel, the GDP figures, which do not include income from abroad, also registered a respectable 4.2 per cent annual growth during that period, about 50 per cent higher than that of Israel itself. Part of that growth was due to the expansion of exports to the newly accessible and relatively very large Israeli market. Israel came to absorb nearly three-quarters of all Palestinian merchandise exports (Kleiman, 1999). Since 1967 Israel has been the biggest channel for Palestinian imports and exports as well as the main trading partner of the Palestinian Authority. The value of Palestinian purchases from Israel accounts for about two-thirds of total Palestinian imports, while the value of Palestinian sales to Israel accounts for about 81 per cent of total Palestinian exports. In contrast, trade with the Palestinian Authority is only equivalent to a small percentage of the Israeli foreign trade (Kanafani & Taghdisi-Rad, 2012; Bank of Israel, 2014).

[33] Brodet, Interview, 3 January 2017.
[34] Ben Basat, Interview, 3 January 2017.

It was only after more than a month from the start of the negotiations that the 'real' talks started, once both sides were on the same page regarding the constraints and possibilities with no border to be established under the DOP. 'The negotiations were concessions of Israel regarding the customs envelope. The negotiation process from here onwards was debated over the range of these concessions. We did not think about the process in terms of peace, we looked at it from the professional prism. As such, for instance when the Palestinians demanded to import from countries such as Iraq, Iran, and Libya our response was that this was against the law as these countries are defined as enemy countries. Rabin asked me if from my professional point of view as a taxation specialist this would bother me and I said of course not, on the contrary, we wanted to enable cheap imports as much as possible for their benefit. They, however, hardly used it in the end. Indeed, this shows that it was purely motivated by professional economic considerations.'[35]

4.2.2 Lists A1, A2, B[36]

The Palestinians did not want to remain restricted to the Israeli import regime. They wanted to have the freedom to import from cheaper sources, and from Arab and Muslim countries, the majority of which maintained no trading relations with Israel. Also, Palestinians did not want to be subjected to the Israeli safety and quality specification requirements. Moreover, they wanted to be able to encourage their infant industries which according to them had been exposed in the past to unfair competition from Israel by means of protective tariffs, especially against imports from the latter (Kleiman, 1994). The main exceptions of the customs envelope were in the form of three lists comprised of goods giving the Palestinian Authority flexibility to some degree to apply independent import regulations in trade with third countries, specifically the integration of Palestine's economy into the region, with Jordan and Egypt as key trading partners (Samour, 2016).

All exceptions to the Israeli import regime, including rates of customs tariffs and all other imposts levied on imports, also to the international procedures adopted by Israel for classification and valuation of goods for

[35] Gabai, Interview, 2 January 2017.

[36] See Appendix B: Article III, Import Tax and Import Policy, clauses 2.1, Protocol on Economic Relations 1994.

customs purposes, as well as standard requirements and import licensing policies are divided into four categories:

1. Limited quantities of goods of certain origin with respect to which the Palestinian Authority is to exercise complete discretion over both tariffs and levies, but not value added tax (VAT), imposed on them and all other conditions of importation (except those pertaining to the classification and evaluation for customs purposes);
2. certain goods with respect to which the PA is to have discretion only with regard to the rate of import taxes, but not to the evaluation procedures etc., or to other aspects of the import regime, such as standards requirements or licensing;
3. motor vehicles, where the PA is authorized not only to determine the level of the import taxes, but also to allow imports of used passenger cars (no more than four years old), currently not allowed to be imported into Israel;
4. fuels, which the agreement allows the Palestinians to import from Jordan, a country with which, at the time of signature, Israel had no trade relations (Kleiman, 1994).

Products under category (a) are products on list A1 and A2, mainly consumer goods, for which the Palestinian Authority has full discretion over tariff setting, but the total amount of import from third parties is limited by quotas. Category (b) relates to products on list B to the agreement, mainly equipment goods, and consists mostly of machinery, equipment and tools, with some semi-processed pharmaceuticals and raw materials for the wood industry for which the Palestinian Authority can set any tariff rate, but the products must meet Israeli standards requirements, and there are no quotas for the goods on this list (Astrup & Dessus, 2001; Kleiman, 1994). Under these exceptions to the lists, the Palestine government could enter into trade agreements with countries with which Israel has no relations according to the Protocol, though these agreements in practice should not create a challenge to the operation of the Protocol (Samour, 2016).

Forming of the lists A1, A2, and B, might have been the most original contribution, but even more, the most important one to the negotiations.[37] Many discussions revolved around the lists and quantities

[37] Kleiman, Interview, 4 October 2018.

since it had a symbolic role but the sheer fact that these lists even exist undermines the concept of a customs union on its own.[38] The Israeli criteria for the products and quantities to be included was that these would not harm the Israeli market; for the Palestinians, the criteria were 'sovereignty plus cheaper prices to some extent'. These lists are in essence de facto sovereignty that Israel could support, in the following forms: a variety of products for which import tax was already in a certain low range, and also with no purchasing tax. Products addressing these two requirements are those that Israel could easily adapt taxes for in accordance with the Palestinians. Products with high import taxes or protective tariffs were not to be included in these lists (A1); electricity products to be imported from Jordan or Egypt with a limitation of quotas per year (A2); and a list of imported goods from enemy countries with limited quotas defined (B). In the end, the only list actually implemented was the one regarding imports from Jordan and Egypt. Also, a range of prices to be used for VAT and petrol was decided on, for which the Palestinians could adapt the taxes, but this was never used as well.[39]

Goods to be excluded from the customs envelope include those deemed not to affect the local market of each jurisdiction, despite different taxations, or those for which smuggling prevention was considered possible even in the absence of economic borders. These included motor vehicles, for which registration provides a national border, allowing customs to be collected when ownership, rather than the good itself, passes across jurisdictions. The other exemptions were for limited quantities of certain imports from Arab countries that the Palestinian Authority wished to make available at low cost to its public, and which it expected to be willing and able to prevent from finding their way onto the Israeli market. In one case, that of gasoline, the exemption was conditional on the price to consumers in the Palestinian territories not being lower than that in Israel by more than a certain stipulated margin (15 per cent). For the rest, the tariffs applied in the areas under the PA's tax jurisdiction were to be the same as those in Israel. Because effective tariffs and thus the protections provided for industries are functions not only of the formal tariff rates but also of the commodity-classification system and the valuation methods used for customs purposes, those as well had to be the same (Kleiman, 1999).

[38] Brodet, Interview, 3 January 2017.
[39] Gabai, Interview, 2 January 2017.

Regardless of the importance of the lists and what they stood for, the structure of a customs union with the exception of the three lists—the customs envelope—was in fact a compromise. For Israel, an arrangement in the shape of a 'customs union' was the only viable option. Thus, it was a political precondition for the negotiators. For the Palestinians, a free trade agreement was opted for. Yet even with the acceptance of this 'hybrid' form of trade regime for the interim period, for the Palestinians three issues remained a key problem. First, only at the end of the interim agreement, with the permanent one signed, would Palestine establish its own customs tariff. Second, the quotas of products the three lists addressed required statistical findings that were not in the possession of the Palestinian side. This led to a three-week delay in the quotas' negotiation in which the Palestinian team looked for relevant data in order to form their proposal. Third, though the charges relating to list B items were subject to Palestine's decision, these items were required to meet the Israeli standards. This became clear to the Palestinians while negotiating fuel import. Fuel stated Hulileh, was the most important item on the lists for their part. At the same time this was bound also to be the most problematic item to be negotiated. The Palestinians insisted on the fuel issue. The Israeli team accepted it, with the exception of differentiating the fuel by colouring. Thus, for fuel to be imported from Egypt and Jordan, it required green colouring, while Israel's is blue. However, Egypt's and Jordan's fuel has a high lead component which is not in accordance with the Israeli standard, thus as well limiting this list's import options.[40]

4.2.3 *Labour*[41]

Since 1967, movement of labour from WBGS has been more important than the export of goods, with the ratio of net factor incomes from employment abroad to GDP being almost equal, yet higher than the GDP from exports of goods (Astrup & Dessus, 2005; Kleiman, 1999). Until the beginning of the 1990s over a third of the Palestinian work force was

[40] Hulileh, Interview, 13 December 2018.

[41] See Appendix B: Article VII, Labor, clause 1, Protocol on Economic Relations 1994.

employed in Israel and unemployment rates were less than 5 per cent both in the West Bank and Gaza Strip (Aix Group, 2005). At the beginning of the 1990s, as a result of the outbreak of the first Intifada, the free labour movement of Palestinian workers had been subjected to the imposed restrictions of Israel on the Palestinian labour flow by means of a permit system, required for entry to Israel (Taghdisi-Rad, 2014).

The report of the economic advisory team (1993) cites a figure of 60,000 Palestinians working in Israel annually, with an estimated number of Palestinians expected to continue employment in Israel in the long run of 100,000–120,000 annually. As such the intention of 'normality of movement' on the Israeli side was of 70–100 thousand Palestinians working in Israel (Arnon & Weinblatt, 2001). At the time of Oslo around 130,000 Palestinian workers were employed in Israel and though closures were already implemented at that time, there were very few disruptions of the workers' flow. The disruptions that did take place during the first Intifada in the number of workers entering Israel were mostly because of strikes and demonstrations on the Palestinian side, not because of Israeli restrictive measures (Box 4.4).[42]

During the negotiations, the Palestinians wanted to retain, if not broaden the access they had to the Israeli market. They were 'acutely aware' of their inability to create a sufficient number of jobs in the OPT in the short run to provide an alternative to employment in Israel. Thus, despite their desire to ultimately reduce their dependency on the Israeli labour market their immediate objectives were to have the latest restriction on the number of workers admitted to Israel lifted, or at least greatly relaxed (Kleiman, 1994). Though the agreement clearly foresees the continuation of Palestinian employment in Israel, unlike in the case of goods, it does not provide for them doing so in defined or unlimited numbers. The ambivalence of the phrasing of the agreement stating, 'attempt to maintain the normality of movement of labor between them, subject to each side's right to determine from time to time the extent and conditions of the labor movement into this area' (Article VII, Paris Protocol 1994)

[42] Brodet, Interview, 3 January 2017.

became a bone of contention, especially in light of the relatively new permit system issued by the Israeli authorities (Cobham, 2001; Kanafani, 2001; Kleiman, 1994; Levine, 1996).

Box 4.4 Palestinian Workers in Israel Following the 1967 Occupation
Shortly after the occupation took place, Palestinian workers were allowed to enter the Israeli labour market. Within five years of Palestinians starting to work in Israel, a 'steady-state equilibrium' was reached with about a third of Palestinian employment being in Israel since then (Aix Group, 2005; Dessus & Bulmer, 2004; Kleiman, 1994). From 1972 to 1990 there was a 64 per cent increase in the Palestinian labour force in Israel, while only a 28 per cent increase in the domestic Palestinian labour (Roy, 1998). This high employment rate of Palestinians in Israel, with remittances constituting approximately 30 per cent of GDP in WB and more in GS, has contributed to high growth rate in WBGS during the 1970s and 1980s, and at the same time provides a partial explanation to the slow and weak performance of the Palestinian economy, as well as to the trade deficit partially financed by wages earned in Israel, hindering competitiveness (Aix Group, 2005; Dessus & Bulmer, 2004; Kleiman, 1994). In 1968 the ratio between the wages of Palestinian workers in Israel's labour market and in Palestine was approximately 2:1; by 1972 the ratio had decreased to 1.2:1 and remained at this level until the outbreak of the First Intifada in 1987 (Arnon & Weinblatt, 2001).

'Clearly, the phrasing of this article was intentionally vague' states Kleiman. A free labour movement is not expected to be allowed by any country. However, it also cannot be ignored that the text article of the agreement states that both sides will be able to keep the mobility of the labour market. What this implied was clear to all; thus, it could not have simply been disregarded.[43] As there were already precedents for closures imposed by Israel, it was made clear to the Palestinians that the free movement of labour is subjected first to the security needs, as the past has already shown, and second to the economic condition as the negotiation

[43] Kleiman, Interview, 4 October 2018.

team wanted to keep the possibility of determining the number of foreign workers in case of high unemployment rates. The 'Normal movement' as defined in the agreement was explained and cleared as subjected to these two conditions.[44] The Palestinians opted for guarantees from the Israeli team that the quotas of working permits would grow. The Israelis on their part, indeed said that they would be able to expand the quotas from an economic perspective, keeping in mind that this all is subject to the security situation, and that Israel is the sole decider in this regard.[45] From the Israeli professional team perspective the freer the movement of labourers, the better it is for the market. The labour movement quotas were more of a political consideration, hence the limitations on movement.[46] The closures, adds Brodet, did not result in fewer foreign workers in Israel, they only resulted in the change of origin of these employees. Indeed, the current number of foreign workers in Israel is more or less the same as it was at the beginning of the 1990s.[47]

As the trading framework was defined by a customs envelope, from the Palestinians' perspective this meant free movement and free access. 'They have an obligation to allow our workers into Israel… so they decided it is a customs union from their side, but not where security reasons are concerned.' From February onwards, according to Hulileh, the consistency in the Israeli stand started to shift from the Palestinian perspective. Concerning the labour issue, while until February it was clear to the Palestinian negotiators that the movement of labourers to and from Israel was fully guaranteed, free, open, and not conditioned by any means, from February onwards, it became linked to the security situation, thus enabling Israel to limit the number of workers as it deemed fit.[48]

Arnon and Weinblatt (2001) stated (with reservation, as no official record had been published in this regard) that during the final stage of negotiations, an FTA was proposed by the Israeli team, which was a complete reversal from the customs envelope discussed earlier. This offer, which was more in line with the Palestinian proposal was made as a bargaining chip, because it included the stipulation that under an FTA the flow of labour would not be as free as under the customs envelope. It

[44] Brodet, Interview, 3 January 2017.
[45] Ben Basat, Interview, 3 January 2017.
[46] Gabai, Interview, 2 January 2017.
[47] Brodet, Interview, 3 January 2017.
[48] Hulileh, Interview, 13 December 2018.

brought to the forefront the possible contradiction between political sovereignty and economic prosperity. The Palestinians opted for the customs envelope package. Arnon (2007) argued that 'the temptation that was offered to the Palestinians for their acceptance of the customs envelope was the continuity of the work of Palestinians in Israel'.

Besides the first paragraph of Article VII, all other paragraphs of the article solely focus on the transfer of payments to the Palestinian Authority to be made by legal Palestinian workers to the Israeli National Insurance (social security), and medical insurance systems. The levying of the equivalents of Israel's national insurance premia and other welfare imposed on the wages of legally employed Palestinians in Israel had been a bone of contention. The intention was to equalize the costs of Israeli and Palestinian labour to the employer, in order to reduce incentives for employers to prefer the latter. However, only Israeli nationals were eligible for national insurance benefits, and only a very small fraction of the payments conferred upon the Palestinians the rights to any social benefits. The rest of the money went towards the expenditure of the Israeli Civil Administration in the OPT. The agreement provides for the continuation of this arrangement with future funds to be transferred from then on to the Palestinian Authority, setting a formula for reimbursing the PA for part of the direct taxes the Palestinian workers in Israel pay. These funds according to the agreement are to be used for social benefits and health services for the employees and their families (Al-Botmeh & Kanafani, 2006; Kleiman, 1994).

Labour movement was a much higher priority for the Palestinians than the issues of the trade regime. Yet in the final agreement on labour issues, two issues are unfairly addressed from the Palestinian perspective claims Hulileh. One is the conditioning of movement to security; the other is the conditioning of transfers due to the workers to a parallel social security institute when this is established. The Israeli team insisted on the establishment of a proper institute dealing with social benefits in Palestine. It took more than 20 years following the adoption of the agreement for this to be established in Palestine according to Hulileh. Further, many other disagreements regarding these payments including among others the amount and interest rate took place between the teams resulting in this section being deemed 'improper'.[49]

[49] Hulileh, Interview, 13 December 2018.

4.2.4 *Taxation*[50]

The tax provisions were intended to provide a relationship between an established political and administrative entity and an entity that had not yet come into existence. Insofar as fiscal arrangements were concerned, the Protocol gave the PA a completely free hand in determining those parts of its tax regime that could be expected to have little or no direct diversionary effect on the Israeli economy. But it did spell out very close coordination, requiring that the two systems would be almost identical in some areas (Kleiman, 1999). According to the agreement up to a two-percentage points difference in VAT between Israel and Palestine was acceptable, as long as the cost of any of the material does not exceed a total of 30 per cent difference. This divergence in the tax burden and VAT was according to Israel, because of its market's exposure to smuggling.[51] Moreover, stated Gabi, the difference of up to two percentage points in VAT did not make a difference for the Israeli team, as it was unclear whether the Palestinians would even collect the local VAT.[52]

If until Oslo, the OPT were part of Israel when it came to taxation, it was clear that once the Palestinian Authority was established it would oversee its own administration. Israel would keep control of security aspects. Thus, following the signing of the agreements all the customs checkpoints within the OPT, held until then under Israeli control, were transferred to Palestine administration. The tax revenue mechanism established in the agreement[53] would then enable the viability of Palestine from then onwards for the interim period.[54]

From 1967 until 1994 all revenues from import taxes were transferred for the most part to the Israeli treasury without any arrangement for the division of revenues. Considering the annual import surplus with Israel in the ten years prior to the agreement fell in the range of $600–900 million US, then at a tax rate of 17 per cent, the VAT revenues alone would amount to $100–150 million each year. The annual budget of the Civil Administration for comparison was just over $300 million (Box 4.5). This

[50] See Appendix B: Article V, Direct Taxation, clauses 1–5; Article VI, Indirect Taxes on Local Production, clauses 1,2, in: Protocol on Economic Relations 1994.

[51] Hulileh, Interview, 13 December 2018.

[52] Gabai, Interview, 2 January 2017.

[53] See Appendix B: Article III, Import taxes and Import policy, clause 15 in: Protocol on Economic Relations 1994.

[54] Zaif, Interview, 2 January 2017.

was a very large sum, and the lack of which greatly restricted its operations (Kleiman, 1999). The agreement defined the arrangement for revenue sharing, which was acceptable to all (Aix Group, 2004). All revenues from taxes and fees levied on imports were cleared on a monthly basis and the accurate amount of import taxes would subsequently be transferred to the Palestinian Authority through the revenue clearance mechanism. These revenues would be calculated on the basis of destination and not on point of entry as was done in the past, in which all revenues on imports from third parties were accrued to the Israeli Treasury. As the majority of customs declaration of goods destined for the WBGS take place at Israeli points of entry and is carried out by Israeli customs officials, the definition of the place of destination as the defining measure of imports revenues implied that funds would be transferred to the Palestinian public treasury from now on. Also, VAT on all Israeli-Palestinian transactions is cleared through the mechanism, as are direct taxes on for example, Palestinian workers employed in Israel. Israel would have a 3 per cent administrative fee on all revenues to be transferred through the clearance system (Astrup & Dessus, 2001; Samour, 2016).

The clearance revenue mechanism is the main change the Paris Protocol founded. With the establishment of this mechanism from 1994 onwards the Palestinians would be able to reclaim value-added taxes and customs duties through it, in order to finance Palestine during the interim period and enable building their own independent state. 'It is this mechanism of revenue clearing that constitutes 90 per cent of the objectives of the Protocol and is the core essence of it' adds Elkurd, and it is according to this that the agreement should be judged.[55]

For Hulileh on the other hand, unlike the labour agreement, in relation to the finance, an agreement between the two sides on most of the components was in place; yet, the revenue mechanism is perceived as the most problematic part of this section. The Palestinian team wanted to have a border bonded with houses in the West Bank where all the quantities will be collected. Thus, the Palestinians would be controlling it at the border itself. It was clear to the Palestinian team that establishing this would require time and would not be able to be implemented immediately, yet they wanted this to be already included in the agreement. The Israelis did

[55] Elkurd, Interview, 27 August 2018.

Box 4.5 Israel Taxation Policy in Palestine 1967–1993
Following the 1967 occupation almost all direct and indirect taxes imposed on the inhabitants of the WBGS were transferred to the Israeli Treasury. Direct and indirect taxes were collected on the basis of 'origin' or place of payment, rather than on the basis of 'destination' and residency. Import taxes and excises paid on goods consumed by the Palestinians in the WBGS, but imported via Israeli ports, were also kept by Israel. The procedure was the same for purchase taxes and other charges imposed on Israeli-manufactured products sold in the WBGS. These led to the WBGS being in a position of excessive resource deficit and more dependent on labour exports, mainly to Israel, and on unrequited transfers from abroad. The WBGS ended up with the economic structure of an extremely poor productive base, weaker than in typical 'low-income countries' but with a per capita GNP at the top of the range for 'lower middle-income countries'. The Occupied Palestinian Territory became the second most important single market for Israeli exports, after the US (Al-Botmeh & Kanafani, 2006; Kanafani, 2001).

accept this according to Hulileh in principle, yet, it was not officially added to the written agreement.[56]

4.2.5 *Monetary and Financial Issues*[57]

The Protocol enabled the establishment of financial institutions in the WBGS, agreement on legal currencies, and the creation of the Palestine Monetary Authority (PMA) to supervise financial institutions and act as the sole financial agent of the PA (Al-Botmeh & Kanafani, 2006). The two sides agreed to create a PMA to solve the problems of financial intermediation. The PMA was granted all the powers typically vested in a central bank vis-à-vis the banking system, but not the authority to issue an independent Palestinian currency. Being a symbol of a declaration of independence, the currency was postponed for the permanent stage of the negotiations. There were now two legal tenders in the Palestinian

[56] Hulileh, Interview, 13 December 2018.

[57] See Appendix B: Article IV, Monetary and Financial Issues, clauses 1,6, in: Protocol on Economic Relations 1994.

economy: the Jordanian Dinar, and the Israeli Shekel (Arnon & Spivak, 1995b; Arnon & Weinblatt, 2001).

For the negotiations over the banking system, Hulileh served as the Palestinian chief negotiator. For preparations he was advised to turn to the Basel Accords[58] as terms of reference. Following this he worked closely with Ben Basat, his Israeli counterpart to formalize the agreement. In Hulileh's view, this topic out of the whole agreement was one of the issues to be handled most properly. For his part, he thoroughly familiarized himself with the first and second Basel Accords, and then engaged with Ben Basat in a three-month negotiation process over the banking system that was concluded almost without any controversies. The agreement led to the dismantling of the Israeli banking sector in the West Bank which up to 1994, had around 12 Israeli banks operating in each city in Palestine.[59] Ben Basat reinforced the successful negotiations around the banking system. Israel agreed to pass all authorities to the Palestinians. Moreover, it was in the Israeli interest to make sure that a viable and properly operating system was established.[60]

As for the currency, this was the second central issue of high importance to the Palestinians, in addition to the FTA. The Palestinian team opted for the establishment of a Palestinian national currency, offering the dinar, or a currency in the form of the pre-1948 Palestinian dinar, but this as others was rejected.[61] Bordet recalls the currency as the second out of the two central issues defining the negotiations. 'This was all a political discussion. I as the chief negotiator of the Israeli team had been directly ordered by Rabin (the Prime Minister) not to give the currency; I was going back and forth to report to him from every round of negotiations and he was explicit about this. He said that currency is a symbol of sovereignty, and this would be given at the end, with the permanent agreement. They received other symbols of sovereignty—a flag, passport, and stamp. The Palestinians for their part throughout the entire process wanted to

[58] Basel Accords are three series of banking regulations set by the Basel Committee on Bank Supervision (BCBS). The committee provides recommendations on banking regulations, specifically, concerning capital risk, market risk, and operational risk. The accords ensure that financial institutions have enough capital on account to absorb unexpected losses.

[59] Hulileh, Interview, 13 December 2018.

[60] Ben Basat, Interview, 3 January 2017.

[61] Elkurd, Interview, 27 August 2018.

achieve independence at all costs. Thus, an independent currency, with value determined according to the Israeli Shekel, and many other proposals, were all derived, and rightly so, out of the perception that this is a central economic (and political) symbol. Nonetheless, Rabin insisted, as the agreement established autonomy and not a state.'[62]

Ben Basat recalls as well having a relatively large amount of freedom during the negotiations in regard to a variety of issues, besides this. The currency issue was one to be decided directly by the Prime Minister while the Israeli negotiation team was not to allow under any terms an independent currency. Nonetheless, he recalls that his impression was that though the Palestinian team put a lot of pressure on the matter, it was not very strong. It was at a certain point an issue of at least one of the two for them—either currency or a stamp, and Rabin approved the team to agree on a Palestinian national stamp. A Palestinian stamp is symbolically important, yet a currency is beyond a symbol, de facto this can be perceived as the Israeli acknowledgement of Palestine's independence. Thus, even though from a professional side the Israeli team had no concrete reservations in relation to a Palestinian currency, it was beyond their authority.[63] The one to object from an economic perspective, adds Gabai, was King Hussein of Jordan, even though Jordan was not a party to the negotiations.[64] Indeed, with the rejection of a Palestinian currency, the Palestinian team opted for the Jordanian dinar to be the official currency in the OPT. Rothschild presented the issue to the Minister of Finance of Jordan on behalf of the Israeli government. However, this was not open for discussion on Jordan's part.[65]

Once the issue was settled, with a currency postponed to the permanent status agreement, following the approval of the political level, the Israeli team told the Palestinians that they could raise the issue of currency again in a year or two. If they would want to discuss the currency then, and the political level would allow it, the Israeli team would work with them to find a suitable arrangement on currency to be acceptable to all.[66]

[62] Brodet, Interview, 3 January 2017.
[63] Ben Basat, Interview, 3 January 2017.
[64] Gabai, Interview, 2 January 2017.
[65] Rothschild, Interview, 18 August 2021.
[66] Brodet, Interview, 3 January 2017.

4.3 Economics as Sovereignty

The protocol in many ways may seem as regulating the economic regime implemented in the territories unilaterally by Israel since 1967 (Arnon, 2002; Astrup & Dessus, 2001). The agreement defined the de jure regime for an interim period of five years, setting the economic arrangements in accordance with the Israeli demand that no border would be defined during the interim stage of negotiations (Arnon & Weinblatt, 2001). The de facto integration regime created after 1967 imposed a uniform external trade envelope, no internal trade borders and a restricted and ambiguous labour arrangement. This trade regime correlated with the conceptual framework of a customs union but was one-sidedly implemented upon Israel's decision (Aix Group, 2004). This was legitimized with the agreement of both sides and with the finalization of the Protocol in Paris, 1994, has been the official economic regime to which both sides were obliged ever since (Aix Group, 2005).

The Preamble of the Protocol clearly states that the economic framework set in the Protocol embodies the vision of a partnership between equals (Kanafani, 2001). But more than that, the Protocol resulted in giving the Palestinians some control over their future for the first time; the Protocol acknowledged that there were two parties living side-by-side, with possible divergence in their interests and priorities, and moreover, it made a clear distinction between the decision-making bodies representing each side (Aix Group, 2005). The title of the agreement itself can be seen as evidence of the efforts made to present it as an agreement being drawn up between two equal partners, in spite of the fact that one party was a state and the other an organization (Arnon & Weinblatt, 2001: 295); and the agreement clearly states that the authority to unilaterally determine the economic policy in the Territories was expropriated out of the hands of the Government of Israel (GOI) (Aix Group, 2004), a change that could not simply be dismissed in regard to the unilateral arrangements that were in place up to this point (Astrup & Dessus, 2001). The Protocol also provided an opportunity not only to reduce the economic dependency of the WBGS on the Israeli market but moreover, to revive the trade relations with neighbouring markets and reduce the trade diversion, which has been taking place since the occupation of the Territories. While the old trade structure had been created by imposed constraints, a proper working customs envelope should enable the WBGS to restructure its trade and revive old regional relations, with the absence of borders benefitting the WBGS exports in the long run (Kanafani, 1996).

Before the economic agreement, Palestine's economy was completely in the hands of Israel. It is through the Israeli Civil Administration that all the decision-making affecting the Palestinian economy took place with regard to both the West Bank and Gaza Strip. Following the agreement, though far from being at full capacity, the Palestinian economy came under the responsibility of the Palestinians themselves. Trade relations with Arab countries that were not a possibility up until 1994, such as the imports of goods from Jordan, petrol from Saudi Arabia and/or other Gulf states, became a viable option.[67] Indeed, the currency and economic borders were rejected. This became clear during the first few weeks of the negotiations. However, the temperament was clear, these two issues were to be postponed to the permanent status agreement. Thus, for the Palestinian team as the general lines and direction were agreed between the two teams, postponing the currency and borders until the time of the permanent agreement was an obstacle that could be passed for the time being.[68] As stated by Abu Ala, head of the Palestinian negotiation team, in relation to the concessions and compromises '…the spirit of the agreement was of an interim five-year agreement. Therefore, whatever we are unable to take now, we will take in five years with the finalization of the permanent agreement.'[69]

Yet, the protocol was subordinate to the DOP which stopped short of holding out a promise of a sovereign state (Falk, 2016), leading the Palestinians to be eager 'for even the slightest tokens of sovereignty, and for any expression of the separateness of their new entity from Israel' (Kleiman, 1994: 351). While the Palestinians sought to acquire as many attributes of sovereignty as possible, the Israeli leadership wanted to defer as many decisions as possible to the final status negotiations. The different positionings of both delegations were derived from both economic and political reasoning from the start (Arnon & Weinblatt, 2001). Indeed, it is these gaps between political and economic, and between the interests of Israel and Palestine in regard to each of these spheres, that shaped the framework of the negotiations, agreement, and implementation in many ways.

[67] Abu Ala, Interview, 27 August 2018.
[68] Elkurd, Interview, 27 August 2018.
[69] Abu Ala, Interview, 27 August 2018.

The negotiations in Paris were held over approximately four months and from start to end were political alongside professional in nature according to Bordet. However, while the Israeli team was prepared for professional negotiations out of the realization that if and when autonomy were to be established it should be economically successful, the Palestinians, though supporting this purpose, were focused on symbolic political achievements, endorsing the feeling of achieving the closest result possible to autonomy. As such, most of the negotiation rounds and content discussed per issue were revolving around the aspirations of Palestinians to define autonomy more as a state,[70] though the Oslo agreement specifically determined the establishment of Autonomy for the interim period. This gap in the political will versus political reality led to the main discussion in the economic negotiations: while the Israeli team was obliged to work towards a customs union, the Palestinians were aiming for the definition of economic independence as much as possible.[71] Indeed, there was a thin line between the issues for which the Palestinians could determine their own economic policy and those which would result in compromising Israel's economic interests.[72] The lists and revenue clearance mechanism, the one-of-a-kind mechanisms leading to a customs envelope, were the result of this tension between sovereignty and economics. These were the only solutions possible for agreement to be reached under the political constraints. Rothschild, as the person heading the OPT budget suggested it, and though Zaif firmly objected, Baiga took the decision to pursue this, out of a genuine belief that this would best serve the Palestinian state-to-be during the interim period.[73]

As such the Palestinian team also wished to minimize the amount of times Israel is mentioned as the standard of reference in the Protocol for arrangements to be adopted by Palestine (Kleiman, 1994). This, stresses Abu Kosh, was because the Palestinian negotiation team wanted to reframe the perception of the Palestinian developing economy being a satellite of the Israeli developed economy. It was not with the purpose to dislodge the economic relations of Palestine with Israel, only to start a new phase of

[70] Hirschfeld reports on a conversation he had with Abu Ala in December 1994 during a lunch the day after the Nobel prize ceremony in which Abu Ala shared that the focus of the Palestinians demand was on national symbols including Palestinian passports, currency, and an international telephone zip code (Hirschfeld, 2000: 154).

[71] Brodet, Interview, 3 January 2017.

[72] Sharvit Baruch, Interview, 26 July 2021.

[73] Rothschild, Interview, 18 August 2021; Shochat, Interview, 8 August 2021.

cooperation between the two economies on an equal level. 'The Palestinian economy would not be merely a subsidiary to the Israeli economy, or just a market to be exploited... there would be two equal economic partners, like the mutual recognition'.[74,75]

Constructive ambiguity is a tactic purposely implemented in texts of international agreements. It is used to save a deal from falling apart and is the result of the negotiating parties being unable to resolve a few remaining issues that stand in the way of reaching an agreement. Under the circumstance in which the ambiguity is deliberately introduced, it is considered constructive (Singer, 2020). Its origins in relation to the Middle East conflict is with the contradictory pledges Great Britain made to both Jewish and Arab national movements, following World War I (Weinberger, 2006: 32). In Middle East peace negotiations, the negotiation's progress almost always includes three stages:

1. Resolving all issues for which the text language used by both sides is different but essentially identical;
2. Resolving issues on which the parties hold different positions on substantive matters, but are able to compromise and reach a text with an agreement on its meaning and;
3. Agreeing on the adoption of ambiguous text for the remaining issues that cannot be resolved (Singer, 2020).

The purposed ambiguity of the DOP, that is the frame of reference for the economic protocol, helped bring out the differences between the negotiating parties. This ambiguity of the Oslo I Accord was aimed to serve Israel from balking at any formulation which might prejudice future negotiations for a permanent settlement by suggesting territorial borders.[76] However, it is the same ambiguity that was used in the terminology of the Protocol to relax and make flexibilities by the negotiations' teams regarding others. *Autonomy* (as in the context of Palestinian Autonomy) thus, does not appear in the Protocol. It is '*areas under Palestinian*

[74] Abu Kosh, Interview, 15 September 2018.

[75] The mutual recognition letters were a series of official letters of recognition exchanged between the GOI and its Prime Minister Yitzhak Rabin and the Palestine Liberation Organization's Chairman Yasser Arafat as part of the Oslo process dated 9 September 1993.

[76] Israeli (2017: 2–3) claimed that the DOP's ambiguity was much more than ambiguity, leading to the document only offering principles for negotiations and not concrete substance of agreements.

Jurisdiction' that the agreement addresses which either related to personal jurisdiction, or to territorial jurisdiction, depending on the specific context (Kleiman, 1994).

In many ways, the constructive ambiguity used in the Protocol led to the appearance of an agreement between equals. For the Palestinians, the wish for the agreement to appear as one between equals led to the insistence on phrases emphasizing symmetry or reciprocity, even if they were completely empty of meaning. As such, the article addressing labour speaks of movement in both directions, though all the articles that follow, dealing with workers, insurance etc., refer exclusively to Palestinian employment in Israel. With respect to the gradual relaxation of restrictions on the sale of agricultural produce on both sides, no mention is made of these applying, only to imports into Israel; and, for the sake of symmetry, an item freely traded in the opposite direction has been added to the list of restrictions which are to be phased out within a span of four years. The Israeli side on the other hand eschewed words or phrases that could even suggest political independence in regard to terms such as imports and exports when describing the trade between the Autonomy and Israel (Kleiman, 1994).

Despite the tokens and appearances of equivalence, the Palestinian delegation had no illusions about the existing balance of power. It is stated in the Protocol that there is a free movement of goods, labour, and services between the two sides, yet one customs and one importation policy for both sides, argues Abu Kosh. The agreement reflected the implementation of the Israeli policy on both sides, not a new customs book, nor a policy jointly shaped, with the exceptions to the customs union simply being 'a way of indulging the Palestinians'.[77] While Brodet defined the Protocol in essence as 'a compromise between the political will and the political reality' of the Palestinians for sovereignty, and that of the gradual process defined in Oslo for the interim period respectively.[78] For the Palestinian team, more than perhaps emphasizing the gaps between the two sides, it was the way for achieving as many tokens as possible of their political aspiration for sovereignty yet to come. This indeed is best represented through the discussion revolved around the reasoning for the use of the term 'customs envelope'. The Israeli-Palestinian customs envelope, also known as a

[77] Abu Kosh, Interview, 15 September 2018.

[78] Brodet, Interview, 3 January 2017.

modified customs union, or alternatively, a quasi-customs union is a one-of-a-kind trade regime with a hybrid form combining both a customs union and free trade. Though the name of the customs envelope represents some of its economic features, it also bears political significance.

The term *customs union* does not appear in the agreement. It is a *customs envelope* not because of the exception to a customs union through the three lists, but mostly if not merely, because of political reasoning, argues Kleiman. The Palestinians did not have to ask or say something specific about that, it was obvious that 'union' could not appear in the agreement according to Kleiman. Customs envelope on the other hand is a more neutral term less subjected to political interpretations.[79] Hulileh, however, emphasizes that though the Israelis did call it a customs union, the Palestinians never accepted that. A customs union has no exceptions. They had the exceptions embodied in the three lists, and the Palestinians aspired to enlarge them. Furthermore, this was a clear demonstration that it is indeed two separated economies, two markets. True, the separation was not yet 'crystal clear'. However, if Palestine can import products based on its own standards, import policy, and customs from other third countries, then you cannot refer to the Israeli and Palestinian economies as one.[80]

> We tried to take everything that related to an independent entity, we tried but it was not possible because both sides accepted an interim period not exceeding five years.[81]

References

Abed, G. T. (1990). The economic viability of a Palestinian state. *Journal of Palestine Studies, 19*, 3–28.

Aix Group. (2004). *Economic road map: An Israeli-Palestinian perspective on permanent status*. Aix-en-Provence, Jerusalem.

Aix Group. (2005). *Israel and Palestine: Between disengagement and the economic road map*. Centre d'Economie Régionale, de l'Emploi et des Firmes Internationales (CEREFI), Faculté d'Economie Appliquée, Université de Droit, d'Economie et des Sciences d'Aix-Marseille III, France.

[79] Kleiman, Interview, 22 October 2018; Kleiman, Interview, 4 October 2018.

[80] Hulileh, Interview, 13 December 2018.

[81] Abu Ala, Interview, 27 August 2018.

Al-Botmeh, S., & Kanafani, N. (2006). The Paris economic protocol and beyond–in search of an optimal trade arrangement. *The Palestine Yearbook of International Law Online, 14*, 75–97.

Aminoff, N. A. (1991). The United States–Israel free trade area agreement of 1985: In theory and practice. *Journal of World Trade, 25*, 5–42.

Arnon, A. (1997). *The Palestinian economy: Between imposed integration and voluntary separation.* Brill.

Arnon, A. (2002). The implications of economic borders between Israel and Palestine. *Palestine-Israel Journal of Politics, Economics, and Culture, 9*(3), 32.

Arnon, A. (2007). Israeli policy towards the occupied Palestinian territories: The economic dimension, 1967–2007. *The Middle East Journal, 61*(4), 573–595.

Arnon, A., & Spivak, A. (1995a). Notes on the protocol on economic relations between Israel and the PLO—The Monetary aspect. *The Economic Quarterly, 42*(1), 155–159.

Arnon, A., & Spivak, A. (1995b). A seigniorage perspective on the introduction of a Palestinian currency. *The Economic Quarterly, 42*(1), 180–197.

Arnon, A., & Weinblatt, J. (2001). Sovereignty and economic development: The case of Israel and Palestine. *The Economic Journal, 111*(472), 291–308.

Astrup, C., & Dessus, S. (2001). Trade options for the Palestinian economy: Some orders of magnitude. World Bank Mid-East and North. Africa Working Paper.

Astrup, C., & Dessus, S. (2005). Exporting goods or exporting labor?: Long-term implications for the Palestinian economy. *Review of Middle East Economics and Finance, 3*(1), 39–61.

Bank of Israel Research Department. (2014). *Recent economic developments 137 October 2013–March 2014.* Ayalon Press, Israel: Bank of Israel.

Ben Shahar, H. (1995). The economic consulting team to the political negotiations—1993. *Quarterly for Economics*, 135–154.

Cobham, D. (2001). Economic aspects of the Israeli-Palestinian conflict: Introduction. *The Economic Journal, 111*(472), 249–253.

Dessus, S., & Bulmer, E. R. (2004). 'The choice of trade regime depends on multiple other factors. In D. Cobham & N. M. Kanafani (Eds.), *The economics of Palestine: Economic policy and institutional reform for a viable Palestine state.* Routledge.

Falk, R. (2016). After Oslo: A legal historical perspective. In P. Bauck & M. Omer (Eds.), *The Oslo Accords a critical assessment* (pp. 67–79). The American University Cairo Press.

Hirschfeld, Y. (2000). *Oslo: A formula for peace.* Am-Oved.

Israeli, R. (2017). *The Oslo idea: The euphoria of failure.* Routledge.

Kanafani, N. M. (1996). Trade relations between Palestine and Israel: Free trade area or customs union. *Jerusalem and Ramallah: MAS.*

Kanafani, N. M. (2001). Trade—A catalyst for peace? *Economic Journal, 111*(472), 276–290.

Kanafani, N. M., & Taghdisi-Rad, S. (2012). *The Palestinian economy: Macroeconomic and trade policymaking under occupation*. United Nations Conference on Trade and Development.

Kleiman, E. (1994). The economic provisions of the agreement between Israel and the PLO. *Israel Law Review, 28*(2–3), 347–373.

Kleiman, E. (1999). Fiscal separation with economic integration: Israel and the Palestinian authority. In A. Razin & E. Sadka (Eds.), *The economics of globalization policy perspective from public economics*. Cambridge University Press.

Levine, M. (1996). Palestinian economic progress under the Oslo agreements. *Fordham International Law Journal Fordham, 19*, 1393–1418.

Report of the Economic Advisory Team for the Political Negotiations submitted to the Government of Israel. (1993, July).

Rivlin, P. (1992). *The Israeli economy*. Westview Press.

Roy, S. (1998). *The Palestinian economy and the Oslo process: Decline and fragmentation*. Emirates Center for Strategic Studies and Research.

Samour, S. (2016). *Review and assessment of Palestinian trade policy options*. Palestine Economic Policy Research Institute (MAS).

Singer, J. (2020). The case of constructive ambiguity in Israel-Arab peace negotiations. In Y. Dinstein (Ed.), *Israel yearbook on human rights, volume 50* (pp. 305–347). Brill Nijhoff.

Taghdisi-Rad, S. (2014). The economic strategies of occupation: Confining development and buying-off peace. In M. Turner & O. Shweiki (Eds.), *Decolonizing Palestinian political economy* (pp. 13–31). Springer, Palgrave Macmillan.

The Protocol on Economic Relations between the Government of the State of Israel and the P.L.O., Representing the Palestinian People. (1994, April 29). United Nations General Assembly (UNGA), United Nations Security Council (UNSC), A/49/180, S/1994/727 (4 May 1994). Retrieved May 14, 2020, from https://www.un.org/unispal/document/auto-insert-185298/.

The World Bank and the United Nations Office of the Special Coordinator in the Occupied Territories (UNSCO). (1999). *The promise, the challenges, and the achievements donor investment in Palestinian development 1994–1998*. The World Bank West Bank and Gaza Resident Mission Jerusalem; United Nations Office of the Special Coordinator in the Occupied Territories, Government House, Jerusalem.

Weinberger, P. E. (2006). *Co-opting the PLO: A critical reconstruction of the Oslo Accords, 1993–1995*. Lexington Books.

CHAPTER 5

The Oslo Spirit

A negotiation process as part of a peace process, in itself, is a stand-alone process that plays a crucial role, even more in regard to asymmetric conflicts. The Oslo I Accord was criticized throughout the years, by both sides, as an agreement that only contributed to the further deterioration of the situation between Palestine and Israel. Unlike traditional analysis of the accord and its results, this chapter analyses the dynamics and components that defined the negotiation, that is, gradualism, win-win, secrecy, and trust building, to explore whether and how they have contributed to the balance of power asymmetry. Acknowledging that a negotiation process can be used to empower the weaker side and reduce asymmetricity, or have the opposite outcome; and that these dynamics have the potential to affect the level of asymmetricity in later stages, the dynamics of the Oslo negotiations process, as the legal framework of the Protocol, and those of the Protocol, are viewed through the prism of the balance of power.

5.1 Barriers to Peace in the Middle East

From the emergence of the Israeli-Palestinian conflict during the years of the British Mandate in Palestine, the search for peace has been a part of the Israeli-Palestinian trajectory. Major diplomatic efforts undertaken by the United States, the United Nations, and others, followed each of the 1948, 1956, 1967, 1973, and 1982 Arab-Israeli wars. Following the 1967

L. Lahar, *The Economic Diplomacy of Peace in the Middle East*,
https://doi.org/10.1007/978-3-031-93991-4_5

turning point in the conflict, intervening events in the region, including among others the Egyptian-Israeli peace treaty; the Intifada of the late 1980s, and the first Gulf War further contributed to its intractability (Kelman, 2007; Wanis-St, 2011: 23). Though in the 1978 Camp David Peace Accord between Egypt and Israel, the Palestinian right to autonomy, based on an interim period of self-rule to be followed by a permanent status agreement, was agreed for the first time (Lundberg, 1999). Fifteen years later, with the Oslo Accords, a fundamental breakthrough was reached through the achievement of mutual recognition of nationhood between Israel and Palestine, with the commitment of both sides to the peace process (Kelman, 1997). The DOP signed on 13 September 1993 resulted on the Palestinian side in the establishment of a Palestinian Authority in the West Bank and Gaza and the return of the exiled leadership from Tunis (Hirschfeld, 2014: 134). For Israel's part, the Oslo process brought about a historical change in the Arab-Israeli conflict: the peace agreement with Jordan; a process of recognizing Israel's legitimacy by the Arab world; and security and trade relations for those Arab states that preferred to maintain an informal relationship with Israel. More than that, the peace process paved the way for much more intense US-Israeli security cooperation and an upgrade of Israeli technological capacities. Also, it had a large contribution to opening Israel to worldwide markets, enabling a sustainable increase in the Israeli gross national product per capita within only a few years (Hirschfeld, 2014: 135; Pundak, 2001). Indeed, reaching a formal agreement, with the signing of the Oslo I Accord, was an unprecedented breakthrough.

1992–1993 marked a hurting stalemate for the PLO, and especially Arafat. The exiled PLO leadership status was challenged by new Palestinian movements gaining focus during the Intifada, while also dealing with financial strains and the loss of funding sources following the 1991 Gulf War. To regain control and preserve their status the PLO needed to return to the territories (Mitchell, 2014: 11–12). Further, the warming relations between Israel and Jordan, and the possibility of a peace agreement to be signed between them would only isolate the Palestinian cause, and especially Arafat himself. Arafat had no expectations that King Hussein[1] would coordinate any of his peace moves with the PLO (Cohen-Almagor, 2018).

[1] Hussein bin Talal- King of Jordan 1952–1999, see also Chap. 3, Sect. 3.2.1 The road to peace.

From the commencement of the secret talks, the desire of the PLO for a peace agreement was intertwined with the strengthening of its position as the exclusive leadership of the Palestinian people. The Madrid peace process, likewise, with the following talks in Washington, raised the profile of Palestinian leaders other than Arafat with Palestine being represented by delegators from the occupied territories. While they remained loyal to the leadership in Tunis and headed its instructions, this was conceived by Arafat as a potential threat to his monopoly. Oslo was the sole track where PLO official representatives were sitting at the negotiation table and as such Arafat delivered the message to the Israeli envoys involved that in this track he would be prepared to compromise (Pearlman, 2009; Savir, 1998: 18). Indeed, the success of Oslo according to Abu Ala was due to it being 'the free choice of the two partners themselves, in contrast to the negotiations in Madrid and Washington' (Qurei, 2006: 290).

Furthermore, a determining factor of the Oslo success was not only engaging in a negotiation process directly with PLO representatives and not their agents, but also Peres' willingness to allow the return of Arafat with the PLO leadership in exile to the Gaza Strip, acknowledging the PLO under Arafat leadership as a legitimate ruling future governance representing the Palestinian people, and even more regaining control over its land (Israeli, 2017: 4).[2]

> It was agreed in Paris that there is mutual recognition of the PLO and Israel. But just before the signing ceremony we discovered that the papers which were supposed to be signed in the White House did not specifically name the PLO, only the Palestinian side, causing a lot of trouble and jeopardizing the whole arrangement, with Arafat refusing to go ahead with the signing ceremony if this would not to be amended.[3]

Even though the PLO representatives were part of the negotiations, disagreements about the official definition and recognition in the Palestinian leadership continued to be a stumbling block during the signing ceremony taking place in Washington DC in September 1993. With Israel striving to maintain the upper hand and control of the situation, and the Palestinians striving for independence and self-determination as the motivational forces, perhaps there could have been no other alternative

[2] Hirschfeld, Interview, 2 January 2017.
[3] Abu Kosh, Interview, 15 September 2018.

besides that of the interim agreement as achieved. Nevertheless, would a negotiation process culminating in the preservation of the power relations between state and non-state be considered as successful? Would the relations established in the accords indeed enable a future change in the power relations towards those to be more balanced? And, would the negotiation process itself be a tool for narrowing the asymmetry in the balance of power, even when the accords themselves are not those to be signed between equals? The answer to all would be yes according to participants in the negotiations due to several characteristics the process adopted. These special ingredients are known as the '*Oslo spirit*'.

5.2 The Oslo Way

All those involved in the initial discussions in Norway held the understanding that there was a need to lead a change in the relational barriers between the two sides. Considering the many years the relations were locked in a zero-sum pattern, a conventional negotiation approach would pose an almost insurmountable obstacle. Thus, values of fairness, equity, and common objectives were those to set the tone of all dialogues, as much as possible; and these were all reflected both in the character of the negotiations, the basis for all personal relationships between negotiators, and in the preferred solutions and implementations (Pundak, 2001).

> A few ground rules were established; though they were not officially defined as such, these became the guidelines to all discussions taking place around the table… it was clear that we all want to hold brainstorming sessions and discussions about future relations, and not dwell on past events. We did not intend to 'fix' the past or convince the other side that our narrative perception is righter, only to try and create a new start and provide tools for a better future, one that would end a tragic bloody history prevailing between two nations. (Pundak, 2013: 97)

In addition to seeing eye to eye on the importance of the economic aspect and that an agreement should also include economic cooperation, for the implementation of the vision described by Pundak, in the first couple of meetings four guiding and overarching principles evolved between the two teams:

- first, the process followed a step-by-step approach termed 'gradualism', which started with an interim agreement;
- second, the negotiations prioritized substance over procedure, focusing on mutual benefits to avoid a zero-sum mindset;
- third, the intention was not to replace the Washington negotiations. The establishment of the back-channel negotiations was aimed at supporting the official negotiation track. By assimilating the results of the back-channel into the Washington track, the role of the PLO, which was a crucial element for successful outcomes, could be kept secret;
- And fourth, for these all to become feasible, trust had to be built out of the realization that for both sides an expressed understanding of the other side's needs had to take place (Aggestam, 2012).

Gradualism as defined by Hirschfeld, clearly has always been the Israeli strategy taken towards the Palestinian issue, from the time of the Camp David Accords (1978) onwards. Thus, there is no question regarding the strategic perception that should be adopted by an Israeli negotiation team, as gradualism allows Israel to maintain the upper-hand position throughout the process in parallel with the achievement of progress, one step at a time, towards understanding and ultimately a final agreement. This strategy not only led to the Camp David achievement being the first peace accord ever signed with an Arab neighbouring country but also to one that reached an understanding regarding the Palestinian issue.[4] Despite being heavily criticized throughout the years following Oslo, Gradualism, according to Savir was the main strength of the Oslo process (1998: 348). From day one of the negotiations the talks were pervaded by a sense of realism conveyed by the gradualism principle. This has been the most important factor enabling the success of Oslo (Shlaim, 1994). Gradualism intentionally did not provide for the conclusion of a comprehensive Interim Agreement on Palestine's self-government. Thus, it enabled the maintenance of all necessary conflict mechanisms for Israel and made clear provisions for Palestinian empowerment which made the mutual recognition and Declaration of Principles feasible. The signing of all six follow-up agreements that have been concluded within the framework of the Oslo process is proof of the success of gradualism (Hirschfeld, 2014: 112, 134–135):

[4] Hirschfeld, Interview, 2 January 2017.

- The Paris Agreement (April 1994), which would regulate the economic relationship between the emerging Palestinian Authority and Israel;
- The Cairo Agreement, or the Gaza-Jericho Agreement (May 1994), which provided for the detailed implementation of the DOP and the return of Yasser Arafat to Gaza;
- The Oslo II Agreement (September 1995), which established the Palestinian Authority;
- The Hebron Protocol (January 1997), which provided for Israel's withdrawal from parts of Hebron and defined further steps in the negotiating process;
- The Wye River Agreement (October 1998), which provided for an agreed-on Israeli redeployment of forces and for an agreed-on prisoner release; and
- The Sharm el-Sheikh Protocol (September 1999), which summed up the achievements and agreements made until then and defined the agreed-on next steps.

As part of the DOP, it was declared that within two months of the signing ceremony a withdrawal of the Israeli military from Gaza and Jericho should be reached and within four months it should be completed. This would establish a Palestinian Authority for self-rule that would first gain control over Gaza and Jericho and then gradually expand into the West Bank (Rød-Larsen et al., 2014). Israel would retain overall responsibility for external security and foreign affairs while internal security in Gaza and Jericho would be under the responsibility of a Palestinian police force. In parallel Israel would transfer power to authorized Palestinians in the fields of education, health, social welfare, direct taxation, and tourism. Elections for the Palestinian Council to take office should be held within nine months and the Council would assume responsibility for most government functions except in the areas of defence and foreign affairs. Within two years, Israel and the Palestinians agreed to commence negotiations on the final status of the territories, and at the end of five years, the permanent settlement was to come into force. However, the DOP did not specify the permanent settlement and only set it in motion, with the agreement of both sides to a five-year transition period without a clear commitment from Israel as to the nature of the permanent settlement (Shlaim, 2005; Watson, 2000: 41–43). Eisenberg and Caplan (2010: 255) claimed that the ambiguity concerning the final parameters of the settlement was deliberated by the negotiation teams and continued following the signing of the DOP as Rabin and Arafat proceeded to regale their followers with conflicting assertions as to the inviolability of unified Jerusalem as Israel's capital versus the destiny of East Jerusalem as the capital of the Palestinian state. Barak (2005) identified the major structural limitation to the end-point of the negotiation as the lack of an explicit commitment to a two-state solution. Though the two-state solution was implicit throughout the negotiations, the final decision was meant to be taken only at the end of the interim period. For Beilin, Hirschfeld, and Pundak, the 'Oslo Architects', however, the result of the process taking its firsts steps was never questionable. Indeed, despite the gradualism strategy, the finish line being that of two states was the underlying assumption of all Oslo I negotiations. ,

> They referred to five years of an interim period, but it was clear to all that it could also be seven years or eight years. These are processes and processes take time, but it all came down to the fact that at the end there will be two states.[5]

5.2.1 *Win-Win?*

'Oslo, by contrast [to the ongoing zero-sum relations pattern], was guided from the start by efforts to create as many win-win situations as possible, notwithstanding a balance of power that was tipped heavily in Israel's favour' (Pundak, 2001: 33). Claims of both sides during past negotiation attempts were based on the different narrative held by each of the sides to the conflict, providing them the moral justification. Oslo was the exception with the two sides agreeing to put aside the past differences for the sake of achieving a forward-looking framework agreement (Savir, 1998: 347–348). The new political thinking leading to the signing of Oslo, according to Kelman (2007), is not to be perceived as attitude change but rather as attitude formation. The new attitudes developed; yet the relationship in which they were embedded did not entirely replace the old attitudes, characterized by fear and distrust of the other and negation of the other's identity. Rather they developed alongside the existing attitudes, with only limited confrontation between the new and old attitudes and reorganization of the attitude framework. As such, the second

[5] Hacker, Interview, 21 August 2019.

principle of the negotiation process was reaching as many mutual benefits as possible. For this, a conscious decision taken during the Oslo negotiations was to leave the most sensitive issues to the permanent status negotiations. These outstanding issues included Jerusalem, refugees, settlements, security arrangements, borders, relations and cooperation with neighbours, and other generic issues such as water and economics. With Oslo being the starting point of a process ending with a permanent agreement, the decision to postpone the core issues of disagreement for further negotiation stages, was in Pundak's view what made the Oslo achievements possible (Pundak, 2001).

For Ashrawi representing the Palestinian local leadership, the postponement of all core issues was perceived as nothing else than the continuation of occupation, as she expressed to Abu Mazen during their meeting held in August 1993 in which the final draft of the agreement was shared with her and Faisal Husseini

> You postpone the settlement issue and Jerusalem without even getting guarantees that Israel would not continue to create facts on the ground that would preempt and prejudge the final outcome. And what about human rights? There's a constituency at home, a people in captivity, whose rights must be protected and whose suffering must be alleviated. What about all our red lines? (Ashrawi, 1996: 260)

Indeed, agreements are only achieved if they reflect the actual power relations. Thus, a wide balance of power between the two sides requires scrutinizing the outcome over time. Relatively to the power balance, and time passing the results of the agreement should be re-evaluated as just and/or desirable for both sides (Albin & Jarblad, 2012). Leaving the most difficult issues of the conflict: Jerusalem, the Palestinian refugees, the Jewish settlements in the Territories, and the Palestinian state and its borders, out of the negotiation table for the 'final negotiation' phase, has been heavily criticized. By doing so Israel could have regarded the negotiations as negotiations between equal powers as if two states were sitting around the negotiation table and not as an asymmetric process: Jerusalem could have implied that the conflict was an identity-based conflict, in addition to it being a territorial dispute; Refugees were liable to evoke the conflicting narratives of the 1948 War and the needs of the Palestinians in the diaspora; the issue of settlements and a Palestinian state could have revealed the magnitude of the former and how it effectively obstructed the latter, that is, the 'facts on the ground' created by Israel in the Territories have caused both groups to become intertwined (Barak, 2005).

Nonetheless, according to Pundak, the Oslo way was that all issues, especially the most sensitive and problematic ones, had to be placed on the negotiation table. 'Postponement of any of them was possible but had to be agreed by both sides', meaning Oslo defined these issues as part of the permanent status while adopting the gradualism tactic to reach willingness and trust that will allow reaching it, with the 'end state' of a permanent status agreement not being put under scrutiny (Pundak, 2001: 39). The US special negotiator during the Camp David negotiation of 1978, Sol Linowitz, asserted that considerable progress was made on his negotiations with the Israelis over the power to be assumed by the eventual Palestinian National Authority. Yet, also under this negotiation capacity the issues of territorial sovereignty, water rights, internal/external security responsibilities, or the fate of East Jerusalem, all critical to the viability of a peace process, could not be managed to be resolved (Wanis-St, 2011: 25–26).

There is no question that if it were a permanent agreement that was to be negotiated then it would have to result in an independent Palestinian state and an independent Palestinian economy. However, within the designated framework of an interim agreement, the results more than served the Palestinian purposes during the preparatory period of state building.[6] The interim period was for both sides to adjust and prepare, each according to its needs for the negotiations on the permanent agreement, whether referring to building institutions or reorganizing those in place for future changes. Examination of all cooperation to be established, decisions to be taken, and the understandings reached should be with this in mind and serving as the main objective.[7]

The gradualism principle, the Israeli strategy that would enable the breakthrough of stagnation is by definition one that would inherently preserve the inequality of the balance of power between the two sides until progress on the ground would enable movement towards a permanent agreement in the form of the establishment of a Palestinian state. The road to equality could only be paved by a strategy that preserves the balance of power until it would be demonstrated otherwise. Together with gradualism though, the second principle of 'win-win' being endorsed may seem

[6] Abu Ala, Interview, 27 August 2018.
[7] Elkurd, Interview, 27 August 2018.

at first glance as contradictory in relations to the balance of power. As argued by L. Ross (2014), it is an inherent belief on the Israeli side that maintaining the asymmetricity with Palestine is the way to secure a 'bearable' future for Israel. While one principle maintains the power relations, the other strives to reach mutual benefits to reinforce the Palestinian side. However, gradualism as a strategy is not what is being questioned. It is whether within the gradualism framework, considering its set of boundaries on the balance of power, the balance of power could have been narrowed. Indeed, gradualism implies constraints on the level of (a)symmetry, yet it does not necessarily prevent having more symmetric relations than the pre-agreement ones. The 'win-win', the aspired mutual benefits, were not those necessarily narrowing the power gap, only benefits in absolute terms. While for an interim limited period this might have been sufficient, for a permanent condition it is not nearly enough.

5.2.2 *Oslo vs Washington*

The Oslo back-channel negotiations were held in parallel to the official Washington bilateral track. Originally, from the Israeli perspective the Oslo channel was intended to serve as a secret track in support of the Washington official negotiations (Beilin, 1997: 71–72; Bentsur, 1997: 167; Pundak, *Getting to the table—Oslo part A*, 1998: -10:39:15 min). Despite being a non-official support channel, once started the negotiations in Oslo soon began to demonstrate real progress, thus were quickly upgraded, resulting in the Oslo channel being a mixture of official and unofficial negotiators (Kelman, 1995; Waage, 2012).

For the success of the first stage of the back-channel negotiation track, with unofficial negotiations taking place, Hirschfeld identifies five essential components:

> maintaining complete deniability, demonstrating our relevance to the official decision making process, refraining from exploiting the other side's internal political rivalries, creating a great degree of reliability, and being aware of what can and cannot be done in these types of negotiations. (Hirschfeld, 2014: 124)

For a successful back-channel negotiation track, both understanding what can be done, and the scope of the negotiation issues are important. For that, four parallel tasks should be pursued simultaneously, as implemented during the Oslo negotiations (Hirschfeld, 2014: 131–132):

1. Develop an agreed-on framework for a proposed agreement, as the framework proposed in the first paper the Israeli team submitted to Abu Ala in Norway.
2. Identify the deal-making concession that the other side is keen to obtain, as in the offer for Arafat to come to Gaza and the proposed empowerment of the Palestinians.
3. Define the red lines that will need to be respected later on when the negotiations move to the official track-one setup. The source of authority was evident to stay with Israel in the Oslo case, which meant maintaining Israeli control with regard to security, settlement, and Jerusalem.
4. Leave sufficient space to allow for additional demands or even a change of concept later on. This phase occurred in the Oslo negotiations when Singer joined the negotiating effort.

From Hirschfeld's analysis, it is evident that the success of the unofficial back-channel relied on the personal relationships and trust-building measures taken by the negotiators. These apply both towards their counterpart negotiating team, as well as in relation to the official policy decision-makers they reported to. Achievement of a successful back-channel process through the four elements identified above by Hirschfeld, furthermore, requires complete and explicit clarity in place from the start.

The back-channel negotiators of Oslo were close to their respective decision-makers, enjoying a higher level of autonomy than front-channel negotiators in the Washington official track (Wanis-St, 2006). During the first phase of the negotiations the Israeli team, Hirschfeld and Pundak, updated Beilin on every step of the negotiations, and meetings with him and Peres were in place; for the second phase with Singer and Savir joining the negotiation team, Singer, in addition, had personally updated Rabin on the progress. Rabin then was compelled to embrace the Oslo track because of his high opinion and respect for Singer's professional view, based on their prior working relations.[8]

As for the Palestinians, the Washington negotiators were the Palestinian leaders who lived in the West Bank or Gaza Strip in accordance with Israel's demand, and lacked a true mandate to negotiate as consent was required from the PLO leadership in Tunis (Aggestam, 2012; Waage, 2012).

> In Washington the non-PLO Palestinian delegation was controlled by the PLO. The PLO was sitting in the next room and giving them instructions, so the non-PLO delegation was like a puppet that you put on your hand and the puppet 'talks', but the PLO's hand is playing the puppet. So, the PLO was the puppeteer, and the non-PLO Palestinian delegation was the puppet. And in any event, there are no negotiations. (Singer, interview with Cohen-Almagor, Washington DC, 29 August 2014 in: Cohen-Almagor, 2018: 742)

From Arafat's point of view, as long as the PLO was excluded from the process, he would not allow the Palestinian delegation to make any progress (Bentsur, 1997: 166–167; Lundberg, 1999; Waage, 2012). In Oslo however, the Palestinians personally reported on every step to Abu Mazen and held briefing updates upon their return from each round with him and Arafat.[9] Moreover, unlike the Washington delegation which was struggling to reach consensus within the Jordanian-Palestinian delegation, the Palestinian delegation to Oslo spoke with one voice, that of Arafat's exiled leadership (Israeli, 2017: 11).

The primary objective of the Oslo back-channel was to foster confidence building and establish ownership between the parties through facilitation and communication. The purpose of this goal was to help the parties see the possibility of finding a negotiated compromise. For that, Larsen maintained that throughout the whole process, the teams should consist of a few permanent negotiators, focusing his facilitative role mainly on psychology, communication, and personality (Aggestam, 2012). 'What

[8] Singer and Rabin had worked together before for many years in the army. Singer, an international law expert, as someone who was raised and educated in the military, the 'defence establishment' as he refers to it, shared the same line of thinking as Rabin. Further, as Singer was not one of the 'Blazers' (the nickname that Peres' protégés were known by, with both Beilin and Savir among these), from the time he joined the team the regular update meetings came to be between him, Rabin, and Peres; with Beilin only joining some (Cohen-Almagor, 2018).

[9] Abu Kosh, Interview, 15 September 2018; Elkurd, Interview, 27 August 2018; Hirschfeld, Interview, 2 January 2017.

I wanted was a pre-negotiating phase, because I thought there had to be confidence established on an emotional basis… I thought if they were to get to know each other, they had to be in a remote place and they should be with one another around the clock' (Terje Roed-Larsen, interview with Prof. Michael Watkins, Gaza, 24 June, 1995 in: Lundberg, 1999: 30). The official-level Israelis, and supposedly 'non-PLO' Palestinians' (led by Hanan Ashrawi and Faisal Husseini), meeting in Washington versus the Israeli and PLO delegates meeting in Norway—reveals that both the Israeli and PLO teams in Norway proved more flexible in their positions and more willing to compromise than their counterparts in Washington. The D.C. negotiators were labouring under old priorities, the Madrid constraints, and the media's constant glare.

The secrecy itself as well had a significant part with the Oslo secret talks proving to be more crisis-resistant than the public ones in Washington (Stedman, 1997; Eisenberg & Caplan, 2010: 173). Being subjected to intense media scrutiny, and the recurrent leaks compromised progress in the Washington talks. Thus, by the beginning of 1993, it seemed that the Madrid process had reach a point of total stagnation (Bentsur, 1997: 166–167; Lundberg, 1999; Waage, 2012). During the Oslo talks, despite substantial progress, the Israeli-level upgrade, and Foreign Minister Holst's firm guidance of the Norwegian mediation, secrecy prevailed (Waage, 2012). This 'top secrecy' being respected by both sides of the negotiation table as well as the Norwegians' commitment to it, held the full weight of the success of the process.[10] As such, even the Israeli delegation to the bilateral track in Washington was caught completely by surprise when the Oslo track became public.[11] Egeland highlighted two key aspects of the Oslo mediation process. First, the Oslo peace negotiations involved two coherent teams, each under firm control: Yasser Arafat's full authority over his handpicked men, and equally the overall power of Israel's Prime Minister Yitzhak Rabin and Foreign Minister Shimon Peres over their delegation. Second, the whole process was conducted under a deep veil of secrecy, with no one from the outside aware of these proceedings. Thus, the Oslo process held a unique combination of classical facilitator-based diplomacy, with utmost secrecy and selective central participation (Waage, 2012).

[10] Abu Kosh, Interview, 15 September 2018.

[11] Sharvit Baruch, Interview, 26 July 2021.

The Oslo process secrecy, however, may be argued not only as that to enable the agreement, but also at the same time to be the core of its failure (Daigle & Wittes, 2012). Indeed, the Oslo I Accord came as a surprise for the domestic political scene both in Palestine and Israel, as well as to many regional and international actors. Yet, both the decisions regarding the gradualism strategy with an interim adjustment period, as well as that of leaving all the core issues to the final stages of negotiations to be conducted in a front-channel negotiation with full transparency and visibility on the permanent status agreement, may be perceived as countering the negative effects of spoilers.

5.3 Norway's Role

Trust building was a key principle leading the Oslo negotiation path. Although this needed to be established between the Palestinians and Israelis, it could not have taken place, especially in the way that it did without Norway's assistance. Both the Norwegian actors and the state of Norway had a significant influence on the way trust was established in the Oslo track.

The idea of Norway as a 'peace nation' has deep historical roots. The building of both the Norwegian state and nation revolved around international status-seeking, and peace activism, combined. The link between Norway and peace is tautological—Norway works to promote peace because it is a peaceful nation, and Norway is a peaceful nation because it works to promote peace (Johnsen, 2015).

The Norwegian policy of involvement, Norway's engagement with international peace negotiation, peacekeeping, and humanitarian aid, derives from three elements:

1. The long-standing self-understanding and self-perception of Norway as a peaceful nation;
2. The emergence of awareness regarding the possibilities this stance offers;
3. The associated instrumental gains and benefits that this involvement policy holds.

This foreign policy, more than providing a good conscience, was meant to serve Norway's aspirations in the international arena. During the Cold War, the mutual border Norway shared with the Soviet Union was a central consideration in the development of Norwegian foreign policy, resulting in various forced restrictions. With the end of the Cold War, Norway was no longer confined regarding its foreign policy, and revitalization of the involvement policy took place. This policy was aimed to give Norway a better reputation internationally, and the acknowledgement of peer and great powers. Thus, the policy of involvement became central in Norway's foreign policy from the early 1990s onwards (de Carvalho & Lie, 2015).

Norway had close relations with Israel since 1948, and a one-sided pro-Israel policy in regard to the Middle East Peace Process throughout the 1950s and 1960s. Formation of strong ties between the two states took place and a positive attitude towards the new Jewish state had a grasp across the entire Norwegian political spectrum, especially as Norway was a state with a deep-seated religious foundation (Waage, 2000, 2002, 2012). Following the 1967 War between Israel and its Arab neighbours, Norway continued to support Israel in the international arena. Being in the minority when voting on issues relating to the Middle East in international forums such as the United Nations, while in parallel being considered as holding one of the most restrictive policies towards the PLO in the whole world, Norway found itself isolated both in Europe and within the international community during the 1970s (Waage, 2002, 2012, 2016). This isolation together with criticism being domestically raised on Norway being too pro-Israel following the outcomes of the 1967 War, resulted in a change of policy towards a more balanced one in regard to the Middle East throughout the 1970s. Improvement took place in the shape of Norway's contacts with the PLO, support of in his efforts to address the United Nations, and allowing the PLO to open an office in Oslo. These relations were further developed during the 1980s and 1990s and had been accompanied by a higher level of confidence and trust for Norway among the Palestinians (Lundberg, 1999; Waage, 2002, 2012).

The idea of Norway as a mediator was raised for the first time in 1979 by Arafat in relation to the Camp David agreement. Arafat was in need of a country that maintained friendly relations as well as was trusted by Israel, on the one hand, and had strong ties with the Americans, on the other hand. The United States would have a crucial role in any form and shape of a peace settlement that would become viable in the Middle East. Hence, the mediator would not only need to have the trust of the strongest party in the conflict, but also the trust and confidence of the superpower behind the regional strongest party. Norway qualified on both terms. Furthermore,

Arafat grasped Norway as a country that would not primarily promote its own national interests. Thus, though at the time this has not come to term, Arafat requested to keep the door open for approaching Norway in the future if needed for a secret back-channel to the Israelis. Knut Frydelnund, the Norwegian Foreign Minister was positive and willing to serve as a potential back-channel option, and during the 1980s this idea was addressed on several occasions without being put into action. In 1989 Arafat specifically asked the Norwegian foreign minister to convey a message to Israel's foreign minister, suggesting Norway as a venue for direct talks. Though Norway passed this proposal on to Israel, Israel on her side gave it little consideration (Waage, 2002, 2005, 2012, 2016).

In 1991, despite the previous reluctance of Israel, Arafat sent Norway's officials several emissaries on the PLO's interest in direct negotiations with Israel (Egeland, 1994). The requests were the result of Sweden's attempts to encourage the PLO to continue strengthening its contacts with Norway. In the late 1980s the Swedish government, and Sten Andersson in particular, as the foreign minister, had been assisting in facilitating direct contacts between the PLO and American Jewish Peace organizations in order to help establish the groundwork for the acceptance of a two-state solution by Israel, and Israel's recognition by the PLO. In 1991 the Swedish Social Democratic Party lost the election and with it, Andersson had to step down. Having to leave the Foreign Affairs office Andersson advised the PLO to seek assistance from Norway and Stoltenberg (Abbas, 1995: 23, 113; Aggestam, 2012).

The foreign policy of Norway, led by Foreign Minister Thorvald Stoltenberg, was focused on peacemaking efforts as a foreign policy instrument, with Norway's role as a bridge-builder. In 1990 Jan Egeland was appointed the State Secretary. Egeland was under the belief that being a small, wealthy, well-respected, friendly and non-threatening country, Norway was much more suitable to advocate for human rights and mediate peace agreements around the world (Waage, 2002, 2005, 2012). This was presented in the *Potent Small States, Impotent Superpowers* PhD thesis Egeland wrote in 1985 (de Carvalho & Lie, 2015). These all supported on its part to Norway's will to contribute to getting the Middle East peace process back on track (Waage, 2002, 2005, 2012).

The positive image and reputation in the international arena; not being a former colonial power; holding close relations with the United States; being a loyal member of NATO; not being a member state in the European Community; and being one of the most generous countries in the world when it comes to granting economic assistance to developing countries, all were in Norway's favour. These, together with the close friendship Norway held with Israel's Labour Party, and Stoltenberg's efforts to nurture personal relations with Arafat, on the other hand, all supported Norway as becoming a feasible third-party option for the conflicting sides to turn to (Waage, 2007, 2016).

For the adversaries, it was Norway's will above all that played the determinative factor. Other countries had better advantages to use as the venue for a secret negotiation process according to both the Israeli and Palestinian perspectives. On this matter, Shaath recalls addressing Hans van den Broek, the Foreign Minister of Holland. While starting to show increasing interest in the Middle East peace process, Van den Broek felt that it was too much for Holland ('Interview I: Nabil Shaath' December, 2013). Beilin reached out to two other governments before the Norwegian option came to life, trying to convince them to take the lead on a secret negotiation channel, which they refused because of fear of failing (Beilin, 1997: 38). When the Norwegian option came to the table, he could not simply let it slip away:

> I was haunted by the many opportunities for peace that had been missed in the past. I had learned about them, taught about them, written about them, and sworn to myself that I would never let such an opportunity slip through my hands, should I ever be in a position of influence. (Beilin, 1997: 83)

As for Norway, the motivation to foster peace between Israel and Palestine was as compelling as the desire to carve out a new international role for itself. Thus, the Norwegians invested great efforts in achieving their goal. The Oslo channel was perceived to be a significant achievement for Norway, especially for the 'new involvement' Norwegian foreign policy, promoting the Stoltenberg-Egeland activist foreign policy approach (Waage, 2002). The success of this involvement policy in the form of Oslo promoted the perception of Norway as a good power, one that can be trusted, and that has a staying power enhanced its international visibility while giving it access to new clubs (de Carvalho & Lie, 2015).

5.3.1 *From Facilitator to Mediator*

'It was clear. Oslo meant money.'[12]

At first, the Norwegians took the role of facilitators, providing funds and a supportive informal environment. They facilitated bringing the parties together, arranging the flights, accommodations, transportation, and covering all other associated travel costs, from meals to local transportation, as well as assist with organizing the meetings, ensuring the negotiations continuation, and perhaps most importantly, maintaining the secrecy by holding the meetings in isolated locations, compelling the negotiators to spend the majority of their time during the session together, and using Norway's research foundation—Fafo mechanism as a cover (Aggestam, 2012; Waage, 2012, 2016). Having the direct support of the Norwegian Foreign Ministry in the process according to Pundak was 'a crucial factor in determining the course of history' as he and Hirschfeld had no source of funding to enable them to hold the meetings as private persons, and they could not turn and ask for Beilin's support nor approach any other official source with a request for money (Pundak, *Getting to the table—Oslo*, 1998, part B, -11:49:32). As Larsen pointed out before leaving the room at the first session on 21 January 1993, that if the two sides want to live together, they have to solve their own problems. The Norwegians will give any assistance they may need, from practicalities to communications, and nothing more (Qurei, 2006: 58).

The Norwegians used their good offices to promote trust between the two sides by creating an informal and cosy atmosphere that would foster the development of friendships, helping to overcome existential obstacles, resolving misunderstandings, and bridging communication gaps (Waage, 2005). All of them from the very beginning operated as the middleman between the Israelis and Palestinians, whenever difficulties during negotiation sessions arose, and especially during the time gaps between negotiation rounds taking place in Norway, making sure of the continuation of the process.[13]

Larsen was the communicator and messenger both during the meetings and the break between one negotiation session to another. In his point of view, the principal key to success was with both sides directly involved in

[12] Beilin, *Getting to the table—Oslo* part B 1998: -11:49:34.
[13] Abu Kosh, Interview, 15 September 2018.

solving their problems. This would be the only way to build trust. Larsen constantly reassured both sides that they were negotiating in good faith, often by rephrasing contentious issues with more nuanced rhetoric and installing optimism among the negotiators. His efforts were put into supportive, impartial, and non-judgmental talks after the negotiation session: being a shoulder to cry on, a shock absorber, and a punching bag while managing the fraught expression of emotions the negotiation process brought with it, as described by Singer (Aggestam, 2002).

Even more than the facilitation of trust building, balancing the power relations and symmetrizing were needed. While the process of symmetry, on the one hand, enabled the Palestinian delegates to feel empowered, and thus equal to their Israeli counterparts, it was equally important for the Israeli delegates who held no official status. The Norwegians did everything possible in their power as facilitators to ensure a symmetrical process, by providing the Israelis and the Palestinians the same of everything (Waage, 2005, 2007).

> I also decided to treat the Israelis and the Palestinians exactly the same way: they should have the same cars, the same hotel rooms, the same food; they should use exactly the same amount of time. If I was rude with one of them in the presence of the other, I had to be just as rude to the other. (Terje Roed-Larsen, interview with Prof. Michael Watkins, Gaza, 24 June 1995 in: Lundberg, 1999: 30)

The clear division of responsibilities between the Norwegian team members during the negotiations also affected the feeling of symmetry between the Israelis and Palestinians. Terje Rød-Larsen played a central role, being present at every meeting; Mona Juul was designated the official Foreign Ministry liaison to the talks. The Foreign Ministers (Thorvald Stoltenberg followed by Johan Jørgen Holst) alongside State Secretary Jan Egeland, exemplified Norway's government's high-level endorsement and backing. As the process got underway, though Juul was the official liaison officer Egeland also attended in several negotiating rounds. His participation could be attributed both to hope arising to reach an agreement, as well as Norway actively aspiring to legitimize the talks, especially in light of the level gap between the teams. Egeland's presence appeared to lend authority to the proceedings, with him joining the group already in the first day of meeting for lunch (Lundberg, 1999; Watkins & Lundberg, 1998; Waage, 2012). This, recalls Pundak, sent a critical signal.

'It put the whole session at the ministerial level. It told the Palestinians that the Norwegians are taking the Israelis very seriously. After all, the PLO was ministerial level. We were no level. They were officials, we were non-officials' (Ron Pundak interview with Prof. Watkins, Tel Aviv, 25 June 1995 in: Watkins & Lundberg, 1998: 130).

With the appointment of Johan Jørgen Holst as the new foreign minister of Norway in April 1993, Norway's role as facilitator, ranging from providing good offices to advancing communications, gradually started to change into that of a mediator, thereby influencing the terms of engagement (Beilin, 1997: 130). Holst immediately made clear his intentions to play an active role with a hands-on personal involvement in the process. As such, not only did he attend the fifth round of talks on 8–9 May, but even more, he directly participated in the negotiation talks taking place from then onwards. In the realm of peacemaking Norway felt it benefitted from a neutral public image that could serve her as a mediator as Egeland puts it: 'We either have no image, because nobody knows we exist or we have a good image' (Jan Egeland interview with Prof. Watkins and Lundberg, Cambridge, MA, 23 March 1995 in: Lundberg, 1999: 18). When Holst stepped into the process his main concern was focused on protecting Norway's role and the Norwegian peace project at stake. Not long after Holst was appointed, Israel upgraded the negotiations. This, together with the Norwegian channel no longer being a secret, with the United States involved, and the signing ceremony already scheduled, meant that both Holst's personal prestige and Norway's place as an international peacemaker was now even more on the line (Waage, 2005, 2016).

In mid-June Holst travelled to Israel to explore the extent of Israel's commitment to the process; in July he used an official visit to Tunisia as a cover to meet with Arafat, following the crisis that erupted with Abu Ala during the back-channel talks. In the meeting, at the PLO Headquarters on 13 July, in which Egeland and Juul were also present, Holst negotiated with Arafat the demands raised by the Palestinian team during the last meeting while offering solutions for the conflicted point. Afterwards, Holst reported to the Israelis trying to actively push the two sides back to the negotiation table. This was followed by intense Norwegian activity and intervention with both sides keeping the channel open and closing the gap in order to reach an agreement (Peres, 1995). At this point it seemed that Holst was prepared 'to do anything in his power to prevent the talks from collapsing' (Beilin, 1997: 126). The efforts of the Norwegians were highly appreciated by the Israelis, in particular those of Holst. In mid-August, Peres made use of an official visit to Stockholm and asked the Norwegians to meet him there in order to help expedite matters. They telephoned Tunis, where Abu Ala stood next to Arafat while on the line and held a seven-hour telephone conversation throughout the night finalizing all the issues still pending. By the end of that night, an agreement was achieved. This was very much due to Holst throwing the 'full weight of his energy and expertise into the issue of mutual recognition, and the phone lines to Tunis and Jerusalem were hot' (Beilin, 1997: 134–135); Holst was not merely the messenger, he was the formulator. In terms of the Norwegian participation, the negotiations over the mutual recognition text, reaching their peak in Stockholm were entirely Holst's show. According to Waage (2005), following his appointment Norway left behind its role as a facilitator, fully embracing the role of active mediation during the overnight negotiation session. Peres describes his relations with Holst as very close. He saw him as a positive figure who did not try to control things and had a very constructive approach to the matter. From his point of view, Holst getting involved in the negotiations, and putting a lot of weight on it, was the turning point in the process (Peres, *Getting to the table—Oslo part A* 1998: -14:35:10).

Thus, Holst stepping into the negotiation process brought not only a change from facilitation to mediation but also a change of approach from one based on teamwork to one dominated by Holst. By the end of July 1993, the role of Deputy Foreign Minister Egeland had almost vanished, as well as that of Larsen and Juul. Though they continued to be important for practical matters, they were no longer the centre of what was happening. This change of approach came at a time of high-stakes politics as the peace process reached its climax, with the three top leaders in Jerusalem, Tunis, and Oslo increasingly taking over (Waage, 2005).

5.3.2 *Resolutions of Asymmetry?*

Norway, unlike the United States, had few, if any, strategic interests in the Middle East. It was flexible in quickly and discretely funding pre-negotiation discussions and was able to provide a secure environment for secret talks to take place. Yet, all the qualities that gave Norway the upper hand as a facilitator in the early stages of the negotiations, were those limiting her power as a mediator in later stages. Norway had very little if any leverage with both of the conflicting sides, especially not in relation to Israel, unlike a powerful mediator would have had (Watkins & Lundberg,

1998; Waage, 2002, 2012). This lack of leverage as a mediator could be claimed to take its toll on the asymmetry in relations Norway had implemented as a mediator, in contrast to the perfect symmetry it reinforced as a facilitator (Waage, 2007). Whereas relatively in regard to Israel, Norway had neither sticks nor carrots, in regard to the Palestinians it had both: the stick being the argument that if the Palestinians failed to strike a deal, they would ruin their chances for peace; the carrot being getting a foothold in Palestine or winning Israeli recognition. Furthermore, Norway made clear that if the Palestinians were to accept the proposal put forward by Israel, it could also offer economic assistance from Norway as well as raise support from others in the international community (Waage, 2005, 2012).

Norway had become an active mediator. However, its mediation role did not involve being on equal terms with each of the involved parties. During this official phase of the negotiations in the summer of 1993, the Norwegians took a clear stand on questions related to the DOP and on the negotiations over mutual recognition: Norway agreed with Israel that it was Arafat and the PLO that were slowing down the negotiations and jeopardizing the whole enterprise. The Palestinians were not sufficiently eager to achieve a peaceful solution. Israel's demands were 'red lines' and they had to be understood and accepted. If not, there would be no deal. No evidence has been found showing or even suggesting that the Norwegians argued in the same way towards the Israelis as they did towards the Palestinians (Beilin, 1997: 123–126; Waage, 2007).

Due to the inherent imbalance of strength and power between the parties involved in the conflict, the outcome was bound to be peace based on terms of the stronger side. While the terms of an agreement being dictated by the stronger side is not unique to asymmetric conflicts, peace taking place after a war is usually within the framework of established statehood safeguarding the basic rights of the weaker side. However, in asymmetric conflicts, the weaker party's position is much more vulnerable. Thus, in order to avoid cementing the weaker side's disadvantaged position, external mediators need to take this structural imbalance into account. Mediators in these situations are faced with the dilemma of having to consider solutions that may promote peace at the expense of justice. The decision rests partly on prioritizing either the cessation of conflict or its continuation in anticipation of a more just peace in the future. Furthermore, it hinges on the probability of future negotiations yielding a better agreement, and whether an alternate mediator would be willing and capable of securing concessions from the strong side (Fixdal, 2012: 9–10). Realizing that a deal had to be accepted, first and foremost, by the stronger party, both for the sake of the process as well as to protect its own role, Norway acted invariably on Israel's premises (Waage, 2005, 2016).

Moreover, though as a facilitator Norway's role was to assist the parties to reach an understanding using an incremental approach, the result in the form of the DOP which might be claimed to be more of an agenda for future negotiations rather than a comprehensive agreement, emphasized ever more the asymmetry while mediating (Waage, 2007, 2016; Weinberger, 2006: 38–39). Nonetheless, given the gradualism precondition principle framing the terms of negotiations Norway could be perceived as breaking the historical pattern by which a powerful third party perpetuated the conflict by permitting one or both sides to maintain unrealistic hopes of having its preferred solution imposed on the other by an outside arbitrator (Eisenberg & Caplan, 2010). Rejection of the gradualism principle entailing the realistic perspective on what is indeed feasible to be negotiated would have prevented, as in many other attempts before, the understandings achieved, and the culmination of the peace accords.

'An imperfect peace was better than a perfect war' according to Egeland (Waage, 2005: 17). In his personal view, as well as Norway's top priority was to keep the negotiation process going. Instead of focusing on post-negotiation issues, the emphasis was given to keeping the parties engaged in the process, finding original ways forward, and employing diplomatic pressure when needed (Waage, 2012). Out of the belief that trust could be built between the conflicting sides with positive developments leading towards a lasting peace in the Middle East, the Norwegians perceived an irreversible negotiation dynamic as the catalyst for advancing the peace process (Waage, 2002).

Following the success of Oslo, Norway successfully repositioned itself on the global stage. Norway's reputation became that of being able to act in order to solve difficult conflicts, and of a state with consistent involvement in international peacekeeping operations. Norway was asked to contribute to mediating conflicts all over the world and played a role in peace processes in Guatemala, Sudan, Sri Lanka, Cyprus, Colombia, and the former Yugoslavia, amongst others. And Oslo gained recognition as the 'Capital of Peace' (de Carvalho & Lie, 2015; Waage, 2005, 2012). Indeed, for Norway, the Oslo process was a success.

5.3.3 *Strawberries and Whipped Cream*

An important part of the 'Oslo Spirit' should be attributed to the unique personal chemistry between all of the Oslo participants which 'descended' upon Israelis, Palestinians and Norwegians, alike (Aronoff & Aronoff, 1998; Waage, 2002). With the Norwegians not merely providing secrecy but also creating a sense of intimacy, putting an emphasis on breaking down stereotypes, and on the solidarity of purpose, an atmosphere of friendship and humour was fostered among the teams (Hirschfeld, 2014: 133–134; Waage, 2007, 2012). Larsen held the conviction that personal relations lead to trust building. He dedicated his work to cultivating strong interpersonal relationships, encouraging the negotiators to engage in informal conversations outside the formal negotiation talks, take walks together in the forest, and share about their personal lives and families (Aggestam, 2012).

The centrality of this unique atmosphere perhaps is best demonstrated by the reaction of those already involved in the negotiation process to Uri Savir, Director General of the Israel Ministry of Foreign Affairs joining the Israeli team, thus making the negotiations official. Pundak and Hirschfeld had no previous acquaintance with Savir before he joined the negotiations:

> We [referring to him and Hirschfeld] feared that he would be a bull in a china shop and crush the whole thing into pieces being a technocrat. It was clear to us that if this is to happen, the content and issues he would strive to address would not make any difference and this whole process would collapse…the ability to immediately grasp the atmosphere and what we are all trying to achieve was the greatness of Savir being the one to join the process. (Pundak, *Getting to the table—Oslo part B* 1998: -13:14:10)

Larsen, acutely aware of the impact Savir would have on the negotiators, and determined to retain the continued success of the Oslo channels, indoctrinated Savir into the spirit of the talks:

> (…) He explained that humor was an important element in the talks, and that the interchange should be informal, as it had been so far with the two professors. For Terje, the essence of the Oslo channel was to come up with creative solutions by a process of free thinking, not traditional hard-nosed bargaining. (Savir, 1998: 25–26)

At Larsen's suggestion, the two chief negotiators, Abu Ala and Savir went for a walk in the woods during their first encounter, which gave them the first opportunity to engage in informal talks. This first encounter resulted in an extraordinary personal chemistry which was consolidated with a great sense of humour between the two for many years to come (Aggestam, 2012). Savir used to share stories of the long nights he and Abu Ala had in Oslo—laughing, and talking about their families while enjoying strawberries and whipped cream until almost dawn. This friendship later extended to visiting each other in Tel Aviv and Gaza with their families, for many years to come.[14]

5.4 The Oslo Spirit in Paris

The negotiations on the economic agreement taking place in Paris were held in accordance with the premise of a five-year interim agreement period, with no official borders being established throughout this interim period, setting the tone of the agreement framework. Though these negotiations were on professional grounds, the power relations between the negotiating teams were no less evident than in the political process, and it was the personal relations, trust, and mutual respect that played a significant role in reaching understandings, much like during the Oslo negotiations.

Baiga as head of the Israeli delegation, asked Rothschild, head of COGAT to join him from the start. As Rothschild was the head of the Authority governing the OPT, including in charge of its budget, Baiga needed him to approve the feasibility of economic decisions on the ground. Unlike Baiga, Rothschild was well acquainted with Abu Ala from before the Madrid process, back in 1991.[15] As well as having Rothschild as a familiar and friendly face on his side, during the first night after arriving in Paris, Baiga and Abu Ala held a three-hour-long tete-a-tete that covered professional as well as personal matters.[16] As for the Israeli negotiators, Baiga's instructions were very specific; as those holding the upper hand, the Israeli delegates were instructed to be extra careful and not to take advantage of the situation in any way. The Palestinian negotiators held professional theoretical backgrounds as economists but had limited knowledge of the economics of the State of Israel, no experience of practically running a state's budget and finance, and lacked access to rules, data and

[14] Stories Savir and his wife shared on different occasions throughout my time at the Peres Center working with both. (Also, other descriptions attesting to the personal close relations between Abu Ala and Savir can be found in Savir, 1998.)

[15] Rothschild, Interview, 18 August 2021.

[16] Shochat, Interview, 8 August 2021.

regulations, which put them in a weaker position leading to misunderstandings and the need to clarify many differences and nuances.[17]

Being a bit 'in the dark' and not having access to any Palestinian records of prior economic data of the Palestinian territories led Abu Ala, head of the Palestinian delegation, to urge the delegation members to probe throughout the whole negotiations, on a variety of matters to be discussed, both during the official rounds as well as during the breaks and social engagement between the two teams. In his view, the negotiations were an opportunity to learn from the Israelis, and as such asked the negotiators neither to judge nor take specific stands during the first stage of the negotiations. Moreover, the purpose was for the Palestinian delegation to gain as much knowledge and information for a comprehensive understanding that would allow them to better prepare for the decision-making phase later on.[18]

'This was agonizing for them, but for us, it was a prerequisite, it was a must.'[19]

The probing, perhaps more accurately in this case—the 'learning' stage, consumed the majority of time in the first few months of the negotiations. For the Israelis, it was time spent on bringing the Palestinian team to the same level as the Israeli professionals. Indeed, though the Palestinians were economists, they were not necessarily experts or specialists in the different fields addressed and lacked specific knowledge.[20] The Palestinians delayed the presentation of their position on all issues during the first four months of the negotiations, from November to February, while only reacting to position papers presented by the Israelis.

The Israelis were very helpful, and very informative, demonstrating a lot of patience towards the Palestinian team implementing this probing tactic. However, after approximately three months the Israelis started to lose their temper and their tolerance as there was no progress in negotiations. Nonetheless, probing while not committing or posing a clear stand on any of the issues, was a result of the imbalance of power, with the Palestinians being aware from day one that not only were they coming shorthanded to the negotiations, but moreover, they should not rely on

[17] Brodet, Interview, 3 January 2017; Kleiman, Interview, 4 October 2018.
[18] Hulileh, Interview, 13 December 2018.
[19] Hulileh, Interview, 13 December 2018.
[20] Ben-Bassat, Interview, 3 January 2017; Brodet, Interview, 3 January 2017.

any external third party for advice, including Arab neighbouring countries. This together with having almost no official international protocols as references due to the exceptional economic arrangement being formed, left the Palestinian delegation with the Israeli team as their main source of information, both as those sharing the same goal, as well as because of a lack of other better alternatives.[21]

It was clear that a few factors played a role in choosing this negotiation tactic including cultural etiquettes, and differences in mentality;[22] yet with continuously reopening and renegotiating issues that had already been discussed and agreed upon, and this practice becoming the standard negotiation tactic for the Palestinians, there was growing frustration among the Israeli team. Furthermore, the Palestinians rarely initiated proposals and merely reacted to those already being put on the table by the Israelis, making reservations without offering alternatives.[23]

Also, throughout the process many crises emerged, all in light of demands and political pressure Arafat tried to impose directly connected to the parallel ongoing security negotiation track taking place at the time in Cairo.[24] When such crises occurred either the entire Palestinian delegation would come down with a 'diplomatic illness' causing them to abstain from participating in sessions for an entire day, or they would delay the sessions scheduled for the next few hours, thus dragging negotiation rounds late into the night and exhausting their counterparts.[25] As for tactics used during the discussions and bargaining stage these could easily be perceived not as tactics per se but merely as cultural etiquettes used by both sides. The only difference was that the Israeli side was more tenacious thus managing the negotiation game better.[26]

Nonetheless, though the process seemed as if for each step forward, there were more steps backwards, the atmosphere remained very friendly and positive throughout the whole process. Accepting the Palestinian tactic and considering the complexity and sensitivity of the situation, the Israelis continuously demonstrated patience, repeatedly renegotiating and explaining what was indeed feasible within the limitations given. While well aware of their limitations and the boundaries established ahead of the

[21] Hulileh, Interview, 13 December 2018.
[22] Gabai, Interview, 1 January 2017; Hacker, Interview, 21 August 2019.
[23] Hacker, Interview, 21 August 2019; Kleiman, Interview, 4 October 2018.
[24] Gabai, Interview, 1 January 2017; Rothschild, Interview, 18 August 2021.
[25] Kleiman, Interview, 4 October 2018.
[26] Gabai, Interview, 1 January 2017.

negotiations, the Israelis did make a continuous effort to make as many adjustments as possible within the boundaries given, in accordance with the importance stressed by the Palestinian team.[27] [28] Indeed, perhaps the most prominent one was Baiga's decision, against the strong objection of the Israel Tax Authority Director, Zaif, who argued that with the lists the agreement has 'more holes than a Swiss cheese'.[29] The Palestinians on their side showed respect for the Israelis, most being much older as well as more experienced than the Palestinians involved in the process, for taking the time and putting in the effort to explain and teach the Palestinians as much as possible. Moreover, though the Israelis had a clear stand on where the negotiations were heading from day one, the approach taken by the Palestinians was not to resist what was presented for the sake of resistance per se. With the Palestinians needing and wanting to learn as much as the Israelis were willing to teach, both parties felt they were working towards a shared cause.[30]

Out of the negotiators participating in the Oslo back-channel track, only Abu Ala and Abu Kosh were to be involved in the negotiations on the economic agreement. Indeed, the majority of the negotiators had no prior contact with their counterparts. In this regard, Kleiman was the exception, knowing many of both the Israeli and Palestinian negotiators, resulting from his capacity as a professor and economic advisor.[31] As such, in the first few days Kleiman attests that he served as the 'social secretary' working hard to introduce everyone to one another on the two negotiating teams and helping to break the ice. After a couple of weeks, this was not needed anymore. The atmosphere quickly turned to informal relations during official sessions, taking the 'Middle Eastern' way with shouting turning quickly to laughter, and personal relations and friendships being deepened during free time. This informality, accompanied by affection, respect, and appreciation for one another, was the most significant contribution to the negotiation process: helping to ease tensions and disagreements around professional matters, encouraging both sides to stretch even

[27] For example, Brodet himself approached Rabin personally on the issue of currency as this had the utmost importance to the Palestinian delegation as discussed in Chap. 4, Sect. 4.2.5 Monetary and financial issues.

[28] Hacker, Interview, 21 August 2019.

[29] Rothschild, Interview, 18 August 2021; Shochat, Interview, 8 August 2021.

[30] Ben-Bassat, Interview, 3 January 2017; Hulileh, Interview, 13 December 2018.

[31] Gabai, Interview, 1 January 2017; Hulileh, Interview, 13 December 2018; Kleiman, Interview, 4 October 2018.

Fig. 5.1 Paris protocol negotiations session. First from the left: Samir Hulileh; Second from the left: Abu Ala (Ahmad Qurei); first from the right Tamar Hacker; Second: Ephraim Kleiman; third from the right: Avraham, 'Baiga', Shochat; Fourth: David Brodet; Centre of the table from the right: Yoram Gabai; Center of the table to the left: Arie Zeif (Sources: Kleiman, Interview, 4 October 2018; Hacker, Interview, 21 August 2019)

further and put in the effort in order to come up with outside the box solutions and alternatives, and perhaps most of all overcome the gap in the balance of power, with the Palestinians putting their trust in the Israelis despite everything. Furthermore, these feelings were what enabled them to come through difficult times resulting from events taking place on the ground. Added to that, the personalities of Abu Ala and Baiga as those heading the teams, with their unpresumptuous attitude and great sense of humour perhaps were the biggest asset of all (Fig. 5.1).[32]

Indeed, throughout the negotiation process, Kleiman held a unique position as he was told by some of the Palestinians that they could confide

[32] Hacker, Interview, 21 August 2019; Hulileh, Interview, 13 December 2018; Kleiman, Interview, 4 October 2018; Sharvit Baruch, Interview, 26 July 2021.

in him and trust his opinion. An example of that can be seen following the Ibrahimi Mosque/Cave of the Patriarchs massacre on 25 February 1994.[33] News about the massacre started to arrive that Friday after the round of negotiations was concluded for that week and discussions were to be resumed only the following Monday after the weekend. Meetings, as to be expected, did not take place on Monday, Tuesday or Wednesday and then Kleiman was asked to call his friend and make initial contact to check about the possibility of resuming the talks. He reached out to one of the Palestinian team members who was a 'protégé' of his and they had a long talk, which was the first contact between the delegations after this horrifying act of violence.[34]

5.5 Where There's a Will There's a Way

Oslo, like many other prominent events defining the course of history, was the culmination of multiple tracks happening alongside each other, without necessarily having any overlaps or coordination between them. In Gil's view it was the merging of four parallel tracks: the geopolitical situation in the sub-region (the result of the 1991 Gulf War); the ideological position, eventually coming to fruition in the ideas the accords were based upon (the New Middle East Vision of Peres shared by Abu Ala); the various efforts for the establishment of a direct channel with the PLO (unofficially as a private initiative of Beilin, with Hirschfeld and Pundak as proxies); and the political receptiveness with the consent and legitimacy of Premier Rabin (Gil, *Getting to the table—Oslo part B* 1998:-10:08:32). With this last one, Rabin's clinch towards an agreement with the PLO alone resulted from four other specific evolutions coincidently taking place between the end of May and July 1993: the advice of the head of the Israeli delegation to the bilateral talks with Syria, that the only way to attain a settlement with Syria is at the cost of a full Israeli withdrawal from the Golan Heights; reports about the lack of influence of the local Palestinian leadership; the assessment of the Chief of military intelligence of the Israeli defence forces that the dire situations and possibly imminent collapse of control made Arafat the most convenient interlocutor for Israel

[33] On 25 February 1994, right-wing settler Baruch Goldstein killed 29 Palestinians praying in the Ibrahimi Mosque (Cave of the Patriarchs) in Hebron. A few others later died of their wounds (Schenker, 2018).

[34] Kleiman, Interview, 4 October 2018.

at that particular juncture; and the reports about the progress made in the Oslo channel (Shlaim, 1994).

> The whole time we gambled on a borderline case… This whole business [the Oslo back-channel negotiation track] really was not conducted in an organised fashion where there is a captain who sets the tone and has the authority, working together with his team, then together they can administer the deal, and there are technocrats who conduct the negotiations in their name. It was just an upside-down story. (Beilin, *Getting to the table—Oslo part A* 1998: -15:12:02)

From the macro to the micro, the global and regional events, to the way Oslo negotiations themselves were conducted, there was nothing inevitable in the way the Oslo process unfolded. Furthermore, other paths if taken further might have been in the end those leading to the signing of the accords between the contending parties. All of these, however, are not to say that the Oslo peace process was neither random nor particular (Watkins & Lundberg, 1998). Indeed, the success of Oslo I can be attributed to various circumstances. Yet, these did not necessarily result in a tangible shift in the balance of power between the two sides; it was the intangible change of perception from asymmetricity to symmetricity around the negotiations table.

'One could never tell' what led to the success of Oslo, Hirschfeld was quoted as saying in 1994. Yet, he added, beyond the contribution of the preservation of absolute secrecy, the excellent working conditions provided by the Norwegian hosts, and the personal chemistry between the individuals involved, there was also a sense of realism that pervaded the talks. During the first phase of the negotiations, rather than seeking solutions with the Palestinians, Hirschfeld and Pundak put their efforts and focus on explaining their point of view to the Palestinian team. Above all the purpose of this was to convey to the Palestinians a sense of the limits of what indeed is possible, and not let them develop false hopes or illusions. The principle of gradualism framing the discussion and decisions to come was clear from the start (Shlaim, 1994).

In a negotiation process *holding the other side's object of value hostage* occurs when one side knows what is most important to the other side and exploits it to extract concessions. In past negotiations between Israel and Palestine, both sides had items of value that they exploited yet failed to make a trade-off on. However, in the Oslo negotiations though neither of the sides was in a position to grant what the other side needed—security for the Israelis and the end of occupation for the Palestinians, the Israelis and Palestinians succeeded (Mitchell, 2014: 13–14).

Trust is an essential ingredient in all types of relationships, let alone between sides in an exchange relationship, such as negotiations. In these relationships, mutual trust serves as a fundamental condition for the advancement of the parties' interests. Moreover, the development of mutual trust is equally essential in conflict resolution efforts, and transforming the relationship between enemies into a relationship characterized by sustainable peace and cooperation. In a deep-rooted protracted conflict between identity groups, such as the Israeli-Palestinian conflict, when trust is being built between parties caught in an existential conflict, the kind of trust to be built should not be expected to be the same as that developed from personal relationships. It is a working trust—a trust in the other side's seriousness and sincerity, for a genuine commitment to finding a mutually acceptable accommodation. This trust is increasing to the extent each side is convinced that the other is moving in a conciliatory direction out of its own interests (Kelman, 2005). Furthermore, genuinely eroding suspicions of the opposite requires that no suggestions of triumphalism or condescension will take place (Darby & Ginty, 2000). And if a third party is to be involved in these negotiation processes, it is its fundamental role to serve as a repository of the trust (Kelman, 2005).

The Israeli-Palestinian conflict is replete with political symbolism not least because of the very deep emotional attachments displayed by both sides to the notions of land, statehood, security, and survival. These symbolic and historical elements are zero-sum, rather than the practical features of conflict resolution. As each side focuses on its own exclusive interpretation of the conflict, the elements are those that usually determine the trajectory and decision regarding the peace process at the political and grassroots levels, for both societies (Hermann & Newman, 2000). Yet, Oslo despite the untraditional process, multiple events aligning coincidently, and moreover being the 'underdog' channel to the official channel taking place in Washington, not only managed to achieve progress between the two sides, but also managed to build the kind of trust that enabled the pursuit and maintenance of the process by those involved in the Protocol's negotiations, even more despite the latter's faults.

Above and beyond the exceptional personal chemistry that the Oslo negotiators developed, it was the feeling of equality between all those sitting around the negations table that prevailed throughout both the Oslo and the Protocol's negotiations.[35] This feeling of equals, of a shared cause and vision of the two peoples' future despite the evident power relations, trickled down to the executive level in the years to follow while those who were a part of the negotiation were in charge. Maher Elkurd and David Brodet never met during the negotiations as while Brodet was the acting head of delegation in Paris, Maher was the liaison person of the Palestinian delegation to Arafat back in Tunis. The close cooperation both of them had and the professional trust and respect for each other at later stages of the agreement's implementation as Director General of the Ministry of Finance (Brodet) and Deputy Minister of Economy (Elkurd), led to the development of personal relations and growing affection throughout time.[36] Furthermore, as Baiga attests, even when the security situation on the ground deteriorated, and for many more years to come after his term as Minister of Finance ended, and Abu Ala retired from political life after his term as Prime Minister of Palestine,[37] they kept exchanging warm greetings during the high holidays of each side and also met in person when the opportunity occurred.[38]

Indeed, as long as the ongoing communication channels between the operational teams were open, and the Joint sub-committees' part of the JEC established in the Paris Protocol, as well as other Joint Committees focusing on other issues met and worked together, the cooperation advanced. The members of these committees, being 15–20 professionals from a variety of governmental offices from each side of the agreement, meeting on a weekly or biweekly basis, either in Jerusalem or Ramallah, with exchanges of dozens of emails and phone calls in between meetings, solved multiple problems and situations that arose on the ground on a daily basis.[39,40]

Ultimately, 'what killed the Oslo peace process was that we were caught out by history and by counter forces. We ended up, not with a peace

[35] Abu Ala, Interview, 27 August 2018.

[36] Brodet, Interview, 3 January 2017; Elkurd, Interview, 27 August 2018.

[37] Between October 2003 and January 2006 Abu Ala served as the second Prime Minister of the PNA.

[38] Shochat, Interview, 8 August 2021.

[39] Elkurd, Interview, 27 August 2018.

[40] This finds additional support in Jayousi (2010: 48) analysis of the temporary Joint Water Committee (JWC) established according to Article 40 in Oslo II Accord relating to 'good will and genuine spirit of equality' prevailing during implementation as crucial.

agreement, but with a five-year roadmap, and in the five-year period the whole thing was torn apart by history and terror, and counter forces', suggests Egeland (Waage, 2012).[41] However, the change of the political ruling party in Israel shortly after Oslo was signed, in 1996, did not result in immediate withdrawal from the agreements. Only with the breakout of the second Intifada in 2000 was it evident that the process had reached a deadlock.[42]

The Oslo process and the path it paved for a permanent status agreement may have been faulty by design. Rather, the Oslo approach and objectives that were never truly implemented, led to the collapse of the peace process in Pundak's view. Though the 'Oslo Spirit' had influenced the highest levels of both Israeli and Palestinian leaderships, it had permeated neither to the level of the Israelis who formulated the complicated system of the implementation agreements (the 'Gaza and Jericho agreement' and the Interim Agreement of September 1995), nor to the Israeli officials who were in charge of negotiating with the Palestinians in translating the agreements into concrete actions (Pundak, 2001). The imbalance of power, which was not addressed in the DOP, being only the first step in the way for a permanent agreement, was 'preserved and reproduced at the expense of the Palestinians' (Weinberger, 2006: 39).

'Sometimes it was forced on them or came from another level, and we understood that' states Hulileh, with regard to the subjectivity of the Protocol to both the political and the security level. The problem for the Paris Protocol and its implementation in the years to follow should not be addressed as a result of a lack of respect or friendship, or to the Israeli counterparts not offering the right options or proper policies; it was with the Israeli team themselves being exploited and misused by the system. Even though pursuing the right policies they were often misinterpreted.[43] Yet, as long as there was a feeling of a shared purpose and progress, even if only to some extent, in goodwill the Palestinians were willing to trust the process, even though the status quo of the balance of power remained without much change, if any at all.

[41] On 4 November 1995, Israel's Prime Minister Rabin was murdered by a right-wing Israeli-Jew extremist opposed to the Oslo Accords. In the 1996 elections following the assassination, the opposition leader from Likud, Benjamin Netanyahu became the Prime Minister (see further discussion in Chap. 6, Sect. 6.3.2 Spoilers of peace in the Middle East).

[42] Abu Ala, Interview, 27 August 2018; Ben-Bassat, Interview, 3 January 2017; Brodet, Interview, 3 January 2017.

[43] Hulileh, Interview, 13 December 2018.

> The Oslo Spirit was aimed to change the nature of relations between the two sides for years to come. This however was not achieved. Agreements were signed, spheres of authority and various responsibilities were passed on to the Palestinians in the following years, but it was the patronizing Israeli attitude towards the Palestinians—one of occupier to occupied that continued unabated. (Pundak, 2001)

Not because of faulty gradualism, leaving the core issues unresolved, or the balance of power not being narrowed, nor political paralysis, it is more the loss of trust in sharing a joint purpose leading to a viable Palestinian state that ultimately put the final nail in the peace process coffin, a decade after Oslo was signed. With a partner that would have gained the Palestinians' trust and confidence as a supporter of the end of occupation everything was, and still is possible, even during challenging times of political hardships for the Palestinian people, as attested by the former Premier of Palestine not long before he received his nomination.[44]

References

Abbas, M. (1995). *Through secret channels: The road to Oslo; Senior PLO Leader Abu Mazen's revealing story of the negotiations with Israel.* Garnet.

Aggestam, K. (2002). Quasi-informal mediation in the Oslo Channel: Larsen and Holst as individual mediators. In *Studies in international mediation: Essays in honor of Jeffrey Z. Rubin*. Palgrave Macmillan.

Aggestam, K. (2012). The psychology of peacemaking: Terje Rød-Larsen. In M. Fixdal (Ed.), *Ways out of war: Peacemakers in the Middle East and Balkans* (pp. 71–90). Palgrave Macmillan US.

Albin, C., & Jarblad, A. (2012). The sustained dialogue approach: Harold H. Saunders. In M. Fixdal (Ed.), *Ways out of war: Peacemakers in the Middle East and Balkans* (pp. 53–70). Palgrave Macmillan US.

Aronoff, M. J., & Aronoff, Y. S. (1998). Domestic determinants of Israeli foreign policy. In O. R. Freedman (Ed.), *The Middle East and the peace process: The impact of the Oslo Accords*. University Press of Florida.

Ashrawi, H. (1996). *This side of peace: A personal account.* Simon & Schuster.

Barak, O. (2005). The failure of the Israeli–Palestinian peace process, 1993–2000. *Journal of Peace Research, 42*(6), 719–736.

Beilin, Y. (1997). *Touching peace: From the Oslo Accord to a final agreement.* Miskal-Yedioth Ahronoth Books and Chemed Books.

Bentsur, E. (1997). *The road to peace goes through Madrid.* Yediot Books.

[44] Shtayyeh, Interview, 2 October 2018.

Cohen-Almagor, R. (2018). The Oslo peace process: Interview with Joel Singer. *Israel Affairs, 24*(5), 733–766.

Daigle, C., & Wittes, T. (2012). Peacemaking as interstate diplomacy: Samuel Lewis. In M. Fixdal (Ed.), *Ways out of war: Peacemakers in the Middle East and Balkans*. Palgrave Macmillan US.

Darby, J., & Ginty, R. M. (2000). Introduction: Comparing peace processes. In J. Darby & R. M. Ginty (Eds.), *The management of peace processes*. Palgrave Macmillan UK, United States of America: St. Martin's Press LLC..

de Carvalho, B., & Lie, J. H. S. (2015). A great power performance: Norway, status and the policy of involvement. In B. de Carvalho & I. B. Neumann (Eds.), *Small state status seeking Norway's quest for international standing* (pp. 56–72). Routledge.

Egeland, J. (1994). Norway's Middle East peace channel: An insider's view. *Security Dialogue, 25*(3), 349–351.

Eisenberg, L. Z., & Caplan, N. (2010). *Negotiating Arab-Israeli peace: Patterns, problems, possibilities*. Indiana University Press.

Fixdal, M. (2012). Introduction: Peacemaking in asymmetrical conflicts. In M. Fixdal (Ed.), *Ways out of war: Peacemakers in the Middle East and Balkans* (pp. 1–30). Palgrave Macmillan US.

Hermann, T., & Newman, D. (2000). A path strewn with thorns: Along the difficult road of Israeli-Palestinian peacemaking. In J. Darby & R. M. Ginty (Eds.), *The management of peace processes* (pp. 107–153). Palgrave Macmillan UK, United States of America: St. Martin's Press LLC Springer.

Hirschfeld, Y. (2014). *Track-two diplomacy toward an Israeli-Palestinian solution, 1978–2014*. Woodrow Wilson Center Press.

'Interview I: Nabil Shaath' (2013, December). In B. Scheller, R. Wildangel, & J. Paul (Eds.), *20 years since Oslo: Palestinian perspectives. Perspectives political analyses and commentary from the Middle East & North Africa*, Issue 5, 23–29.

Israeli, R. (2017). *The Oslo idea: The euphoria of failure*. Routledge.

Jayousi, A. (2010). The Oslo II accords in retrospect: Implementation of the water provisions of the Israeli and Palestinian Interim peace agreements. In A. Tal & A. Abed-Rabbo (Eds.), *Water wisdom preparing the ground for cooperative and sustainable water management in the Middle East* (pp. 43–49). Rutgers, The State University.

Johnsen, I. (2015). Gifts favour the giver: Norway, status and the Nobel Peace Prize. In B. de Carvalho & I. B. Neumann (Eds.), *Small state status seeking Norway's Quest for international standing* (pp. 108–126). Routledge.

Kelman, H. C. (1995). Contributions of an unofficial conflict resolution effort to the Israeli-Palestinian breakthrough. *Negotiation Journal, 11*, 19–27.

Kelman, H. C. (1997). Group processes in the resolution of international conflicts: Experiences from the Israeli–Palestinian case. *American Psychologist, 52*(3), 212–2020.

Kelman, H. C. (2005). Building trust among enemies: The central challenge for international conflict resolution. *International Journal of Intercultural Relations, 29*(6), 639–650.
Kelman, H. C. (2007). The Israeli-Palestinian peace process and its vicissitudes: Insights from attitude theory. *American Psychologist, 62*(4), 287–303.
Lundberg, K. (1999). *The Oslo channel: Getting to the negotiating table* (p. 1333). John F. Kennedy School of Government Case.
Mitchell, T. G. (2014). *When peace fails: Lessons from Belfast for the Middle East.* McFarland.
Pearlman, W. (2009). Spoiling inside and out: Internal political contestation and the Middle East peace process. *International Security, 33*(3), 79–109.
Peres, S. (1995). *Battling for peace: A memoir.* Random House.
Pundak, R. (2001). From Oslo to Taba: What went wrong? *Survival, 43*(3), 31–45.
Pundak, R. (2013). *A ruts Hasha'i: Oslo, ha-Sipur ha-Male' [Secret Channel: Oslo, The Full Story*]. Yediot Books.
Qurei, A. (2006). *From Oslo to Jerusalem: The Palestinian story of the secret negotiations.* IB Tauris.
Rød-Larsen, T., Laiq, N., & Aidan, F. (Eds.). (2014). *The search for peace in the Arab-Israeli conflict: A compendium of documents and analysis.* Oxford University Press, USA.
Ross, L. (2014). Barriers to agreement in the asymmetric Israeli–Palestinian conflict. *Dynamics of Asymmetric Conflict, 7*(2–3), 120–136.
Savir, U. (1998). *The process: 1,100 days that changed the Middle East.* Vintage.
Schenker, H. (2018). Oslo then and now-what's next? *Palestine-Israel Journal of Politics, Economics, and Culture, 23*(2/3), 5–7.
Shlaim, A. (1994). The Oslo Accord. *Journal of Palestine Studies, 23*(3), 24–40.
Shlaim, A. (2005). The rise and fall of the Oslo Peace process. *International Relations of the Middle East, 285*, 241–261.
Stedman, S. J. (1997). Spoiler problems in peace processes. *International Security, 22*(2), 5–53.
Waage, H. H. (2000). Norwegians? Who needs Norwegians?: Explaining the Oslo back channel: Norway's political past in the Middle East. *Royal Norwegian Ministry of Foreign Affairs, 9.*
Waage, H. H. (2002). Explaining the Oslo backchannel: Norway's political past in the Middle East. *The Middle East Journal, 56*(4), 597–615.
Waage, H. H. (2005). Norway's role in the Middle East peace talks: Between a strong state and a weak belligerent. *Journal of Palestine Studies, 34*(4), 6–24.
Waage, H. H. (2007). The 'Minnow' and the 'Whale': Norway and the United States in the peace process in the Middle East. *British Journal of Middle Eastern Studies, 34*(2), 157–176.
Waage, H. H. (2012). Proactive peace diplomacy: Jan Egeland. In M. Fixdal (Ed.), *Ways out of war* (pp. 91–116). Palgrave Macmillan US.

Waage, H. H. (2016). Champions of peace? Tools in whose hands? Norwegians and peace brokering in the Middle East. In P. Bauck & M. Omer (Eds.), *The Oslo Accords 1993–2013: A critical assessment* (pp. 13–29). The American University in Cairo Press.

Wanis-St, J. A. (2006). Back-channel negotiation: International bargaining in the shadows. *Negotiation Journal, 22*(2), 119–144.

Wanis-St, J. A. (2011). *Back channel negotiation: Secrecy in the Middle East peace process.* Syracuse University Press.

Watkins, M., & Lundberg, K. (1998). Getting to the table in Oslo: Driving forces and channel factors. *Negotiation Journal, 14*, 115–135.

Watson, G. R. (2000). *The Oslo Accords: International law and the Israeli-Palestinian peace agreements.* Oxford University Press.

Weinberger, P. E. (2006). *Co-opting the PLO: A critical reconstruction of the Oslo Accords, 1993–1995.* Lexington Books.

CHAPTER 6

Framing the Paris Protocol through Political-Economic Relations

While preferential trade agreements are usually assessed by their effects on bilateral trade relations, and as pointed out by Kanafani (2001), in regard to the Israeli-Palestine economic relations this should not be considered the sole appropriate criterion. Indeed, it is through the lens of political economy that economic change, and furthermore economic policy, should be assessed. Notwithstanding the gradualism and the inherent limitations on Palestine's access to resources of power, the aalysis offered in this chapter aims to explore whether, within this framework, the Paris Protocol could have been instrumental in encouraging the Palestinian statehood capacity potential, as declared in its preamble. In order to accommodate that, this chapter offers a political-economy analysis exploring the role of the Protocol within the peace process institution.

6.1 Barriers to Trade in Paris Protocol

Throughout the history of the region, the establishment of two national states, the Palestinian and Jewish, has been considered by various international bodies. The plans and proposals were all accompanied by recommendations of similar economic arrangements to a customs union. The 'common tariff over the widest possible range of imported articles' of the 1937 British Royal Commission on Palestine and the customs union with a joint currency system of the partition plan adopted by the United

L. Lahar, *The Economic Diplomacy of Peace in the Middle East*,
https://doi.org/10.1007/978-3-031-93991-4_6

Nations in 1947 are prominent examples (Kleiman, 1999). The customs envelope established in the Protocol was based on the free movement of goods and labour as the catalysator for Palestine's economic development. Free trade with Israel was expected to enhance growth, while the continuation of free labour movement to Israel, to generate high employment (Arnon, 2002).

Whether in practice the Custom Unions and/or the FTAs lead to trade creation and an increase or reduction in welfare is debatable with different approaches (Panagariya, 2000). In many ways, the strong economy may be inclined to exploit the weaker economy and extort concessions. Nevertheless, when a customs union is formed between a strong and weak economy, this should not be the case. On the contrary, a customs union mechanism for these cases finds support in both theoretical and practical perspectives. Thus, according to Kleiman though with no physical border, it was the only trade agreement possible, the poor economic performance of the Palestinian economy should not be seen as resulting from it.[1]

In order to examine if a customs union is economically the preferable arrangement there is a need to look beyond the adapted policies. To address this, the focus should be given to the actual form this arrangement has taken. The limited political autonomy established through the Oslo Accords could only find expression in a narrow margin of an independent import policy in the form of the lists (El-Jafari, 1997). At the same time, these exceptions of sovereignty could be argued to contribute to the overall poor economic results. The Protocol established a hybrid, one-of-a-kind form of customs union, also more appropriately named 'customs envelope', leading to the Protocol being comprised of ambiguities through and through.

Despite addressing the economic relations as the cornerstone of the Israeli-Palestinian relations, and strengthening the Palestinian economy, the Protocol's preamble 'stops short of declaring any free-trade areas or common market' (Watson, 2000: 158). Also, while establishing a JEC[2] to pursue economic cooperation, it falls short of establishing other institutions that would have been expected of a common market. These include mechanisms that formulate a common agriculture policy, a common industrial policy, deal with anti-competitive practices, and harmonize

[1] Kleiman, Interview, 4 October 2018.

[2] See Appendix B: Article II, The Joint Economic Committee, Protocol on Economic Relations 1994

commercial law or contract law, none of which are addressed in the Protocol. While in many ways the Protocol is pursuing a customs union, it is less than complete. Moreover, in regard to certain issues as the revenue-sharing mechanism, it clearly points towards a free trade arrangement (Watson, 2000: 158–161).[3]

Though this was the result of good intentions, out of consideration for the Palestinian sovereignty aspiration within the political limitations, and an attempt to show good faith and goodwill from the Israeli team, it led according to Hulileh to 'an impossible economic structure'.[4] The absence of defined borders in the Oslo I Accord and as such in the Protocol is what 'lies in the core of the problems facing the Palestinian economy' from day one, as claimed by Roy (1998: 12). Already during the negotiation problems related to this mechanism were starting to surface. The issue of lack of border was 'overwhelming' in relation to each and every issue to be discussed. More than that, as this situation of a gradual process without agreeing on the final borders was without precedence, there was no international reference or standard addressing these issues. As in traditional economics when a trade policy is formed between two separate economies, the lack of a border crosscuts all aspects of international trade and economic relations, from the rules of origin defined by the World Customs Organization (WCO) to the banking regulations set in the Basel Accords. This resulted in both teams struggling to find solutions, being creative in finding ways to mitigate this, while rounding the corners on each and every issue. As stressed by Hulileh, this leads to '*always not having the right solution*'. The lack of international references as yet this is a one-of-a-kind structure, made the agreement not able to support a standard environment that will help promote the relationship from day one. Indeed, in Hulileh's view, this can be grasped as bearing the full responsibility for the economic process.[5]

Despite the complications posed by the lists, they were not to prevent the trade preference in favour of the Israeli products created by the Protocol. These products, unlike products from other countries, are exempted from duty, creating significant protection for local goods while undermining trade with third countries (Arnon & Spivak, 1995). Thus, following the institutionalization of the customs envelope an increase in

[3] The road accident law is harmonized in the Protocol (Paris Protocol, Art. XI).

[4] Hulileh, Interview, 13 December 2018.

[5] Hulileh, Interview, 13 December 2018.

the bilateral trade of Palestine with Israel has been taking place (Cobham & Kanafani, 2004: 2; Samour, 2016).

Indeed, from a Palestinian perspective, the success of the Paris Protocol should be measured by its ability to restructure Palestine's trade relations, with the diversification of trading partners and entering new economic markets. This would have facilitated higher levels of autonomy for the economy. A customs envelope arguably from this perspective might have been counterintuitive as it reinforces the integration with Israel and not with other partners (Samour, 2016).

> Everything goes through Israel. This is increasing the control on the Palestinian economy, and in addition, does not give you the best comparative advantage (…)[6]

Whichever economic policy is to be held accountable for the Palestinian economic trajectory, whether it be the customs union, or the one-of-a-kind 'customs envelope', a consensus is in place on the role politics holds, in the form of access to power, for either success or failure.

6.1.1 Tariff Barriers

During the 1990s Israel was going through a steady process of trade liberalization, with import taxes gradually being reduced to a rate of 0–12 per cent, and all import quotas (except for food products) being cancelled.[7] The trade liberalization was appropriate for the Israeli matured economy. For the Palestinian economy, however, these modifications were not in its best interest (Bamya, 2013; Misyef, 2017). The Palestinian economy was struggling to mobilize its own resources and assets and pursue the development of domestic productive capacity and autonomous trade relations with the world (Misyef, 2017).

Article III (6)[8] of the Protocol addresses Israel's obligation to notify the Palestinian government ahead of any changes made to the tariff policy. This is one of the two policy restrictions the agreement entails on Israel (Arnon & Weinblatt, 2001). Despite the specific reference in the

[6] Shaath, Interview, 13 September 2018.

[7] Gabai, Interview, 2 January 2017.

[8] See Appendix B: Article III Import Taxes and Import Policy, clause 6, Protocol on Economic Relations 1994.

agreement to mutual consultations regarding the changes, Israel constantly made changes to the trade regime, for example, reduction of taxes on imports, a purchase tax, and customs tariffs over time, without coordinating with the Palestinian government (Bamya, 2013). On its part, the Palestinian government in response to each of the tariffs' reduction in return, simply updated the tariff book in accordance with the Israeli modifications (Misyef, 2017).

The Palestinians also ended up making very little use if any of their autonomy to set their own tariffs. One of the few times this was indeed implemented is with the adoption of decision no. (13/46/14) by the Cabinet of the Palestinian Authority on 12 March 2013, to customize the tariffs applied to 212 imported commodities, that is, apparel and garments, shoes, furniture, and aluminium production sectors, that established a rise in tariffs. An analysis of the effect of the changes in local production in these sectors between the years 2013–2015 conducted by Misyef (2017) shows an increase in the value of output, and the number of establishments, thus, also in the workers in part of these branches. The change in Palestinian tariff was the only industrial tool aimed at supporting the concerned branches to be deployed since 2013. Yet, for a development-led approach to trade, industrial policy should be one of the main strategies to be employed. As such, according to the report, the differences in the performance between the branches addressed in the decision demonstrate that a raise in tariff alone is not sufficient, only that this policy should also be accompanied by effective customs control mechanisms.

Whether the change in tariff rate alone damages the Palestinian economy, and if so, to what extent is not the core issue according to Bamya (2013: 64). The unilateralism in Israel's decision-making in itself 'intended to rob the Palestinian Authority of the capacity to formulate trade policy'. Thus, not only is this a complete violation of the agreement of the Paris Protocol, it also violates the spirit of the agreement.

With a clear balance of power heavily tilted towards Israel, these acts of consultations, even if they were only for the sake of appearance, were not only an abuse of power but also had a symbolic meaning serving as proof of the Oslo intentions being broken.

6.1.2 *Non-Tariff Barriers and Trade Impediments*

Article III (10)[9] presents the second trade policy restriction imposed on Israel, with a one-sided amendment to the trade policy imposed by Israel being conditioned as those not constituting a non-tariff barrier (NTB). In the past, Israel used NTBs to protect local production, which may be considered the reason for this reservation (Arnon & Weinblatt, 2001).

While preparing for, and during the Protocol negotiations themselves, the Palestinians did not have official data and statistics regarding the economic and trade parameters in the West Bank and Gaza Strip. The only available data regarding the Territories was that of the Israeli Bureau of Statistics,[10] and this was described according to Hulileh as 'generic and general'. Thus, the decisions regarding quantities and quotas taken during the negotiations were agreed to be revised between six months and a year after the signing of the agreement. As the revision meetings did not take place, the Palestinians perceived this as Israel taking advantage of the circumstances not to adapt the agreement in accordance with the Palestinian needs.[11] Between the signing of the Protocol and 2013, the original lists were only expanded twice (Bamya, 2013).

Besides the lists established in the agreement, Israel has imposed import quotas on agricultural and non-agricultural products including meat products, live animals, dairy products, cement, and carpets. Palestine receives a portion of these quotas depending on the product, for example, 20 per cent of the milk products quota, and 25 per cent of the live animal one. Also, there is an export quota in Israel for its international trade agreements. As Palestinian products are identified as domestic according to the Rules of Origin, they do not benefit from the international agreements Israel is part of. Thus, no amount of this quota is being allocated to Palestine (Khalidi & Taghdisi-Rad, 2009; Misyef, 2017).

Clearance of goods imported by Palestinians, along with the utilization of Israeli ports and airports being on equal footing with Israeli importers

[9] See Appendix B: Article III Import Taxes and Import Policy, clause 10, Protocol on Economic Relations 1994.

[10] From 1967 to 1994–5 Palestine's economic data was part of Israel's economic data, solely collected by the Israeli Bureau of Statistics. The Palestinian Central Bureau of Statistics (PCBS) was established in 1993, following the Oslo Accord. The World Bank and other international mechanisms relied until 1994–5 on the Israeli Bureau of Statistics as the data source.

[11] Hulileh, Interview, 13 December 2018.

and exporters was also a key construct of the Paris Protocol and the Oslo Agreement. Palestinian products, however, were discriminated against at the ports and airport, including when it came to issues such as security procedures, the prevention of Palestinian cargo from being shipped on commercial passenger planes and the application of extraordinarily cumbersome technical standards and testing procedures, all resulting in delays and an increase in costs for Palestinian trade (Bamya, 2013). Indeed, the dependency of the trade relations of Palestine on the necessity to obtain Israel's approval leads to Palestine's economic loss every time an extensive closure is imposed on OPT, as all the permits needed for trade are cancelled by Israel. This was often the case between 1994–1997, and 2000–2008 (Khalil, 2009; Weinberger, 2006: 220).

To this array of impediments, the Israeli side put in place the process of moving goods from Palestinian to Israeli trucks at security checkpoints which later developed into actual border crossings, that surely violate the Paris Protocol and the Oslo Accord. This unloading and reloading process known as back-to-back, adds to the cost of transportation and increases the potential for delays in the movement of goods. Israel also created a list of 'dual-use goods' that cannot be imported into Palestine since an alternative use could pose a security threat. This list includes a large number of items, which are basic inputs to the productive process of industry, including items such as hydrogen peroxide, which is used by the food industry as well as in leather tanning and textile production. The fact that the producers need to find replacement materials amasses higher costs for the production process, thereby increasing production costs and affecting competitive capacity (Bamya, 2013).

The tight envelope of customs procedures for trade with third countries under the veil of the Protocol is merely a political instrument. Thus, when Shaath was appointed as the Minister of Planning and International Cooperation it was his priority to create a more export revenue-oriented economy, which would create lesser dependency on Israel.[12]

Article III (10) relates to the existing international obligations Israel held at the time of concluding the agreement as a party to GATT and having free trade agreements in force with the European Community, and the US. If the Palestinian Authority is to become an independent political entity, a situation might arise where, with the Palestinians taking advantage of their right to impose VAT at a lower rate, Israel could be accused

[12] Shaath, Interview, 13 September 2018.

of discriminating in indirect taxation against imports. On the other hand, in case Palestine is not acknowledged as a separate political entity, its accession to the European and or North American markets requires extending them the preferential status Israel holds (Kleiman, 1994). Thus, according to the Protocol, Palestine is allowed to sign trade agreements with other trade partners, as long as there is no divergence from the principles of the customs envelope on which the Protocol was based, and it complies with Israel's agreements (Bamya, 2013; Misyef, 2017). The Palestinian trade with other countries, however, is to continue to be handled through Israeli sea and airports, or through the border crossings between Palestine, Jordan and Egypt, which are controlled by Israel (Khalil, 2009).

The Palestinian Authority's explicit policy objective being pursued when entering into trade agreements is to reduce the high dependency on the Israeli market and diversify the trading partners. The existing trade preferences granted to Palestine can be classified into three categories:

1. Those that are dependent on the Paris Protocol and an extension of the bilateral trade agreement with Israel, for example, the US Presidential Proclamation of 1996 and the Joint Canadian Palestinian Framework for Economic Cooperation and Trade of 1999.
2. Those that are interlocked in the context of the European regional strategy and Euro-Mediterranean Partnership of 1996,[13] for example, the Palestinian trade agreements with the EU, the European Free Trade Area (EFTA) with Turkey and the Agadir Agreement,[14] are embedded with this wider initiative, and
3. Those that are stand-alone agreements, for example, the Greater Arab Free Trade Area (GAFTA) of 1997 (Misyef, 2017).

Yet while Israel engages with global trade and is now a member of the WTO, this status does not benefit Palestinian trade. Indeed, Israel does not recognize the free trade agreements that Palestine enters into with other countries. The numerous trade agreements Palestine has entered,

[13] Euro-Mediterranean Partnership is the implementation of the multilateral aspects of the 1995 Barcelona Declaration, which serves as the framework for political, economic, cultural and social ties between the European Union and 12 Mediterranean countries: Algeria, Cyprus, Egypt, Israel, Jordan, Lebanon, Malta, Morocco, Palestinian Authority, Syria, Tunisia, and Turkey.

[14] The Agadir Agreement is a free trade agreement between Egypt, Jordan, Morocco, and Tunisia, singed in February 2004 and came into force in March 2007 (Bilaterals, 2017).

their total impact on exports, inter-sectorial, and intra-sectorial allocation of resources, have had limited impact on upgrading the Palestinian economy. And these contributions to reducing the Palestinian trade dependency on Israel are negligible (Misyef, 2017).

Once these agreements were signed, the political decision to thwart this agreement resulted in the Israeli customs authorities not clearing the imports under these agreements. This led to additional costs and delays, as well as a competitive disadvantage to the Palestinian businessman (Bamya, 2013). Thus, not only has Palestine's dependency on the Israeli market not decreased from 1993 onwards, but the high transaction costs led to the price increase of this dependency (Roy, 1998: 21). Also, the bilateral FTAs Palestine has formed with other countries are not recognized by Israel because of the customs union. Thus, Israel collects the customs duties from Palestinian imports, which are then refunded by the PA (Misyef, 2017). As Israel's considerations for not recognizing Palestine's FTA agreements with third parties are politically motivated, the international community and Palestine both, try to use these as a means for pressuring Israel to align with a higher level of autonomy for Palestine.

The trade agreement with the EU is a clear example of that, as this was politically motivated par excellence. The Association Agreement with Palestine was negotiated and concluded in three months and two days. Egypt's agreement on the other hand took 13 years to be achieved.[15]

6.2 Barriers to Power

Following the outbreak of the first Intifada in 1987, towns, villages, and camps in the Occupied Territories sprang up to fill the widening gap in the officially supplied services. 'Popular committees' were then added to serve as quasi-governmental departments. This created a situation of a wide spectrum of services, for example, health, education, social welfare, manpower training, and medium-term agricultural and industrial development credit, being locally run mainly through a grassroot system. By 1990 the social aspects of living in the Territories were increasingly coming under the control of the Palestinian communities themselves. Over 400 local councils, charitable societies, professional associations, voluntary committees, and production cooperatives operating at the social level, despite obstructions from the Israeli authorities and the occupation (Abed, 1990).

[15] Shaath, Interview, 13 September 2018.

Despite the picture of a State in the making having already semi-established institutions at the time of the Oslo I Accord, there was a vast gap between stable established financial and legal institutions as would be expected in statehood conditions, and the reality on the ground in the Occupied Palestinian Territories. For the Palestinian delegation team, this was clearly reflected, if not during the negotiations themselves, then only shortly after. Yet, for the Israelis, it is only in retrospect that this gap seemed to be fully comprehensible.

During the economic negotiations the Palestinian negotiators felt that with time, they were indeed improving in the negotiation process. Through hard work, probing, learning, and posing questions time after time 'to check, to look, to compare'. Getting better, however, was still very far from being able to (easily) implement the agreement.[16]

> The lack of both experience and economic track records was overwhelming. You will build the customs authority, what does it mean? Or your ministry of trade and economy ...to do a trade policy, what is trade policy? who decides on the customs book? we do not know (...)[17]

The Israeli negotiation members on their part, at least partially, envisioned a situation similar to that existing for the Jewish people in Palestine, prior to the establishment of the state of Israel in 1948. The Jewish Agency for Palestine (following 1948—for Israel), the operational branch of the Zionist Organization in the land of Israel on its institutions, were the foundation for the Israeli state-to-be. This branch was a part of the World Zionist Organization founded in 1897, with the presidency, chairman, Jewish Colonial Trust, and Jewish National Fund among other institutions, all supporting the state-building institutionalization.[18] While the Jewish Agency was de facto running the state, with a functioning statehood in place for the Israeli state to be; the Palestinians had no prior experience in building state institutions, let alone knowledge regarding how to institutionalize the economy, or manage a state economy. This lack of full understanding of the gap between what was perceived to be the

[16] Hulileh, Interview, 13 December 2018; Abu Ala, Interview, 27 August 2018.

[17] Hulileh, Interview, 13 December 2018.

[18] For example, prior to the establishment of the State of Israel, enterprises such as the Palestine Electric Company, the Palestine Potash Company and the Anglo-Palestine Bank were established. These, following the declaration of Israel's independence, became the Israel Electric Company, the Dead Sea Works, and the Bank Leumi Le-Israel BM respectively.

situation on the ground, and the actual level of institutional development in the Territories, only in retrospect came to be acknowledged by the Israeli negotiators.[19] Perhaps, even because of the poor economic development level and the course of events following Oslo.

Another key obstacle was that the model formed in the Protocol did not include any provisions for a passage between the Gaza Strip and the West Bank, nor did it refer to special arrangements for moving products in or out of either location by way of Israel, which controlled the access to both, as was in the period from the time of occupation (Cobham, 2001; Kanafani, 2001; Levine, 1996).[20] This was in agreement with the Protocol being a part of Oslo I, *The Agreement on the Gaza Strip and the Jericho Area*. As intertwined in its name, it only addressed the DOP and the first step out of a future inclusive peace agreement between Israel and Palestine. The Protocol clearly states that what is to be concluded in its framework will be applied to all other interim agreements that will follow.

The West Bank and the relations between the two territories of Palestine were to be addressed in Oslo II, *The Interim Agreement on the West Bank and the Gaza Strip* (also known as the Taba Agreement), signed on 28 September 1995. Yet with Oslo II, the provisions of the agreement divided the West Bank into three areas of governance A, B, and C:

1. Area A, which included the cities and population centres inhabited by Palestinians, was placed in the Oslo Agreement under the security and administrative control of the Palestinian Authority.
2. Area B, on the other hand, which included villages and rural areas adjacent to Area A, were placed under the administrative control of the Palestinian Authority, while being at the same time under the security control of the Israeli side.
3. Area C, which comprises around 60 per cent of the total area of the West Bank, remained under the administrative and security control of the Israeli Occupation Forces (Bamya, 2013; Bauck, 2016).

This division entailed a tremendous impact on the development potential of Palestine's economy (Figure 6.1). The designation of Area C requires the approval of Israel for any work being done in it. This formed

[19] Oz, interview, 4 August 2021.

[20] The agreement did call the parties to negotiate the safe passage of people, for elaboration see Watson (2000: 144–148).

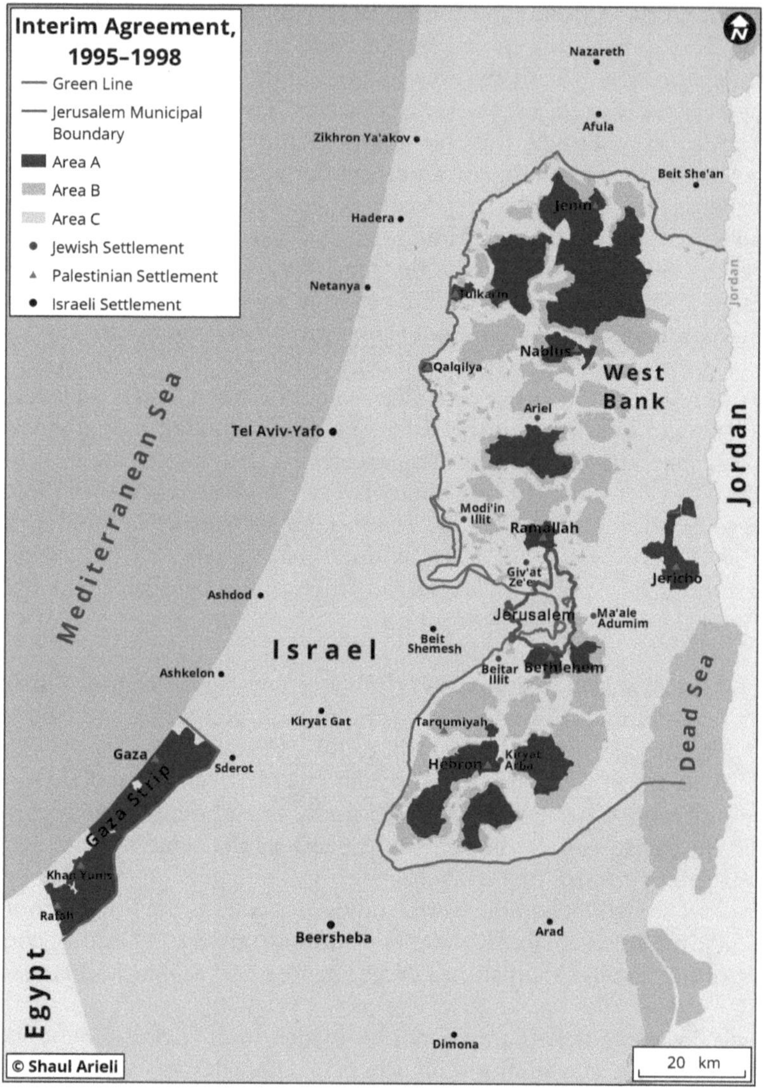

Fig. 6.1 Interim Agreement, 1995–1998. Source: Arieli (2021)

an impediment to basic infrastructure work such as telecommunications, electricity, water, and sewage lines, which could not be done without the constantly delayed or refused permits from the Israeli occupation army. Natural resources for example, water, stone, and marble quarries are also mostly located in Area C. Thus, an Israeli licence is required for accessing and establishing industrial or excavation operations (Bamya, 2013). Above all perhaps is that Area C represents 60 per cent of the Palestinian Territories and has the potential to increase Palestinian revenues, and thus reduce their dependency on external funding and donations.[21]

6.3 Politics of Economics

'All other non-economic issues arising from day one of the negotiations were those to determine the faith of the agreement; not this or that trade regime.'[22]

Following the signing of the DOP, decisions regarding the Oslo process negotiations framework needed to be taken. Deliberations about the structure and teams of the negotiations resulted in the formation of three thematic working groups:

- General negotiations[23] (including security arrangements), in Cairo, Egypt;
- Civil affairs, in el-Arish, Egypt;
- Economic arrangement, in Paris, France (Hirschfeld, 2000: 153).

For the negotiations on the economic arrangement, both the status of this working group and the location of meetings were issues for internal discussion. On both the Palestinian and Israeli sides, concerns were raised about the nature of hierarchical relations between the economic and the general negotiation teams. The importance of independence and the separation of the economic negotiations from the general ones, especially the security aspects, were points of extensive internal debate.

In Israel, Brodet who was asked by the Minister of Finance, Baiga, to lead the professional negotiations, and Oz as special advisor to the Minister

[21] Elkurd, Interview, 27 August 2018.
[22] Kleiman, Interview, 4 October 2018.
[23] Referred to by Abu Ala as 'the continuing negotiations' (Qurei, 2006: 288).

and coordinator of the delegation, strongly advised and lobbied for an independent framework. Both understood the centrality of economics and moreover the role of Palestinian economic development in determining the trajectory of the peace process. Thus, for the economic negotiations to be successful, and economic prosperity to be achieved for both, a full separation between the economic negotiation team and all other teams, was a must. For Brodet as the high-ranking economic expert leading the team, these were to be professional negotiations based on and requiring economic knowledge and expertise. As both qualities were not part of the competencies held by the security negotiation team, there was no justification thus, for the economic delegation to be subjected to the security one. As the Ministry of Finance was in charge of the state budget, Oz in his capacity as the advisor to the Minister anticipated that enormous pressure would be put on the delegation from different domestic stakeholders with a variety of economic interests. The economic negotiation team not being subordinated to other negotiation delegations would guarantee the 'right motivations' driving the decision taken by the Israeli negotiation team, that is, decisions that best serve the peace process itself and not those of interest groups. With Baiga's perception being aligned with these, he together with Brodet advocated the full independence of the economic delegation in consultations held about the structure of the delegation with Premier Rabin, and Minister of Foreign Affairs Peres.[24]

At the same time, similar discussions about the positioning of the economic delegation in the general process also took place in Palestine. Despite having no prior knowledge about each other's internal deliberations concerning the structure of the negotiations following the DOP, the need for independence of the economic delegation was a key issue on the Palestinian side. Abu Ala, appointed by Chairman Arafat to head the Palestinian economic delegation, demanded that the economic negotiation framework be an independent one, with reporting made directly to Chairman Arafat and not to the head of the 'main' delegation of the general negotiations, Shaath. Further to advocating for the separation of delegations and against a shared responsibility, Abu Ala also insisted on a physical separation between the security and economic delegations meeting points, requesting for the economic negations to take place in Paris, France.[25]

[24] Brodet, Interview, 3 January 2017; Oz, Interview, 4 August 2021.

[25] Brodet, Interview, 3 January 2017; Abu Ala, Interview, 27 August 2018.

Putting his full weight not only on a separation in delegations and authorities but also on a different geographical location may be perceived as an anecdote, though it entailed great significance in Brodet's view. Abu Ala not only served as the head of the Palestinian delegation to Oslo, but was also the only member of both teams who participated in the secret negotiations. The realization of the extent of Abu Ala's demands for full separation and complete independence of the Palestinian economic delegation, to the level of holding the negotiations outside the region, symbolized for the Israelis that both sides perceived the economic relations as central, and even crucial to the peace process as a whole.[26]

The shared point of view between the Israeli and Palestinian negotiation teams, however, did not correspond to the place these negotiations held within each of the domestic political scenes. On the Palestinian side, the expectations were for Abu Ala to be nominated as the head of the general negotiation delegation. His appointment as head of the economic delegation could directly indicate an internal political controversy between Abu Ala and Arafat, and indirectly also on the level of significance the economic negotiations held in Arafat's view on the peace process (Hirschfeld, 2000: 153–154; Savir, 1998: 116). During the negotiations this was evidently reflected, as following every obstacle, disagreement, hurdle, or conflict that was encountered during the security negotiations, the economic negotiations were put on hold by Arafat, yet not vice versa.[27]

Notwithstanding the political implications of Abu Ala's nomination, as the Palestinians' chief economist and as he attests on himself, this was to serve the economic negotiations (Qurei, 2006: 283). The other members of the Palestinian delegations to the economic negotiations—Amin Haddad, Attaf Alawi, Nasser Tahboub and Samir Hulileh, were selected by Abu Ala himself. The selection was based on their economic background; and more importantly on whether they had been living at the time in the OPT, and not in Tunis where the members of the PLO leadership in exile were situated. The motivation behind this decision was led by Abu Ala's desire to comprise a team from those who were familiar with the practicalities on the ground, and not with knowledge based on theory alone. Indeed, from an economic perspective, this thinking was for the greater good of the economic future of Palestine. Politically, however, it added additional layers of constraints. Abu al-Lutf who was 'the foreign

[26] Brodet, Interview, 3 January 2017.
[27] Gabai interview, 2 January 2017.

affairs minister of the PLO' in a sense, did not appreciate the exile representatives being compartmentalized, and asked Abu Kosh to join the delegation and report directly to him.[28] As a political nomination and lacking a professional economic background, Abu Kosh raised resentments and 'was never accepted neither by the Israelis nor by the Palestinian'.[29] While Abu Kosh perceived himself as leading the Palestinian team, in the eyes of both the Palestinians and the Israelis he was an outsider, neither fitting the social fabric nor the dynamics that were formed.[30] Yet, this was more than political rivalry between two high-ranking officials. This was a power struggle between the exile and local PLO leadership playing its role in the grand scheme of the Protocol.[31]

The struggle over power within the Palestinian leadership was also expressed in the reporting obligations the team was expected to fulfil. Besides the ongoing reporting routine following deliberations and each negotiation session, at the end of each negotiation round, over the weekends, the members of the Palestinian delegation had to travel to Tunis and report in person to the executive committee of the PLO. Only a few of the committee members were economists and/or experts in the relevant fields. They were 'all politicians trying to discuss the customs envelope of Israel-Palestine' advising the team on many of the topics discussed 'trying to scrutinize the delegation members' position at work'.[32] The power struggle continued until the very last minute. Following the conclusion of the Protocol's negotiations, final discussions were held in Taba in preparation for signing the Cairo agreement. During these, the Palestinian economists from the exiled Fatah leadership continued to strongly oppose the customs envelope while on the other hand, local Palestinian businessmen further pushed for continued access to the Israeli market (Lavie, 2013).

For the Israeli side, having the Ministry of Finance heading the negotiations was evidence of strength regarding the place economics held in the peace process. Other ministries had specific agendas and policy orientations. Overseeing the state budget, the Ministry of Finance had the leverage to see the full picture and held the power to pursue the state's

[28] Hulileh, Interview, 13 December 2018.

[29] Hulileh, Interview, 13 December 2018; Kleiman, Interview, 4 October 2018.

[30] Abu Kosh, Interview, 15 September 2018; Hulileh, Interview, 13 December 2018; Kleiman, Interview, 4 October 2018.

[31] Only on 1 July 1994 that Arafat and the PLO exiled leadership returned to Gaza.

[32] Hulileh, Interview, 13 December 2018.

interests in accordance.[33] Some sectors, particularly agriculture, that had been protected from competition from the territories in the past, would face considerable hardship if suddenly exposed. And some wanted to safeguard their existing positions in the markets of the territories themselves (Kleiman, 1994). Following the official decision for the Ministry of Finance to lead the negotiations, from day one of the preparatory stage to the signature, the majority of the economic and business sector expressed their objections, placing hurdles in any way possible, including personal threats aimed at the Minister and his team through letters, faxes, and calls.[34]

Beyond the direct implications on the Israeli and Palestinian markets, the agreement was bound to affect the trading relations in the region, especially with neighbouring countries, particularly Jordan. Oslo caught everyone off guard, leading to the feeling that they could not risk being kept in the dark from here onwards. The economic agreement had the potential to compromise the traditional trade relations between the West Bank and Jordan which was tilted more towards Israel, as well as to open the Palestinian economy to the world. Jordan wanted to keep its interests, and furthermore, benefit from the new trading relations and donations expected to the region. Throughout all of the negotiations' duration, Jordan put an immense amount of pressure through various means, publicly and behind the scenes, on the Palestinian delegation, demanding that the agreement include trade benefits between Palestine and Jordan. Hussein, King of Jordan was opposed to the agreement between Israel and Palestine,[35] more so the prospect of the Palestinians receiving their own currency as well as other economic instruments.[36]

Immediately after forming the economic delegation, 'brother' Arab countries Jordan and Egypt offered their advice to the Palestinians. Jordan sent two representatives from the Jordanian Central Bank to reside in Paris, whom the Palestinian delegation was expected to brief after each of the negotiation rounds. Prince Hassan[37] was very adamant about this. Egypt also sent two representatives from the customs authority who offered their help to the Palestinian delegation with the negotiations. The Egyptians were going back and forth to Paris, and seemed to be more

[33] Brodet, Interview, 3 January 2017; Oz, Interview, 4 August 2021.

[34] Oz, Interview, 4 August 2021.

[35] The economic agreement between Israel and Jordan was signed only in 1995.

[36] Brodet, Interview, 3 January 2017.

[37] Prince Hassan bin Talal is a member of the Jordanian royal family who was Crown Prince from 1965 to 1999.

genuine in their attempts to help, rather than only pursuing their own interests as were the Jordanians. Nonetheless, the Palestinians tried to maintain separation, as much as possible, between the representatives of the neighbouring Arab countries and the Palestinian delegation, including being adamant about all of them staying in different hotels from the Palestinians. The Governor of the Central Bank of Lebanon, and the regional director of the Arab bank in Paris on the other hand, were very instrumental in advising the Palestinians, and the Palestinian team felt that they could trust their opinions. [38]

Despite the enormous external pressure and attempts for interventions put on both Israel and Palestine, neither of them intended to let the economic negotiations become triangular instead of bilateral.[39] The Palestinian experience with the provision on Palestinian Autonomy in the Camp David framework with Egypt as the negotiator had already proved that no other third country, Arab states or other, could be counted on to represent and/or act for what was best for the Palestinian interests during negotiations with Israel (Wanis-St, 2011: 27). Thus, during the Protocol negotiations though aware of coming shorthanded to the negotiation table, they knew they could trust no one, let alone neighbouring Arab countries. As politics cannot be detached from economics, even though the neighbouring countries offered their experts and expertise, the Palestinians tried to avoid all external 'assistance'.[40] For their part, the Israelis were well aware of the complexities and implications this creates with the Arab world. Nonetheless, it seemed, at least in some ways that the Arab countries did not operate with the best intentions at heart towards the promotion of the Palestinian cause, as their interference in the negotiations was only out of their own economic interests. Paradoxically, Israel was the one they could trust and rely on most. As paraphrased by Gabai 'Better a close cousin than a bad brother'.[41]

> We thought ok the political side will continue (…) now that there is mutual recognition (…) but then with regard to the economic issue, we felt, and this is what we expressed, that it is the livelihood of the Palestinian side.[42]

[38] Hulileh, Interview, 13 December 2018.
[39] Brodet, Interview, 3 January 2017.
[40] Hulileh, Interview, 13 December 2018.
[41] Gabai, Interview, 2 January 2017.
[42] Abu Kosh, Interview, 15 September 2018.

The months before the signing of the Protocol were dominated by political tension and security instability in the region. Following the Ibrahimi Mosque massacre in February 1994, with the end of the mourning period, a few suicide bombing attacks were carried out in Israel. Hulileh refers to the first attack at the beginning of April as the turning point of the negotiations. Following the events, the Israeli delegation informed the Palestinians that the labour movement would be subjected to the security situation. This was the starting point of the economic factors, also those already under agreement, gradually becoming undermined by security events.[43] Indeed, the last point of contestation during the negotiations revolved around the free movement of Palestinian labourers. Abu Ala demanded that the agreement state unconditional free movement of the Palestinian labour force into Israel, while Baiga made it clear that from Israel's perspective, this is subjected to security needs. The discussions around the issue continued until 4 am on the night before signing, with no sight of agreements. In the end, this was resolved through the inclusion of a side letter to this clause, stating that the decision regarding the subjectivity of the Palestinian labour movement to Israeli security needs would be decided by Rabin and Arafat directly.[44]

At the beginning of April, a few weeks before the Protocol was signed in Paris, Abu Ala informed the Palestinian delegation that they needed to accelerate the negotiations as the negotiations on the general agreement were reaching their final stage.[45] The same was clear for the Israeli side while coordinating the last round of negotiations.[46] Nonetheless, many of the Israeli delegation members had no prior knowledge that the negotiation round at the end of April would be the last. Thus, they were caught by surprise when the signing of the Protocol happened at the end of the round, on 29 April 1994.

The rounds of negotiations were held on a regular basis between Monday and Thursday, allowing the Israeli team to catch the Thursday evening flight scheduled from Paris to Israel.[47] On Thursday the 28th discussions and negotiations continued into the night in order to reach a

[43] Hulileh, Interview, 13 December 2018.

[44] Shochat, Interview, 8 August 2021.

[45] Hulileh, Interview, 13 December 2018.

[46] Oz, Interview, 4 August 2021.

[47] Israeli governmental officials travelling on official business should not fly during Sabbath, hence the team had the Thursday evening flight booked for them regularly during the negotiations.

final agreement.[48] The signing of the protocol being held on a Friday delayed the Israeli delegation's flight and risked them not arriving to Israel before Sabbath's eve.[49] The French police closed the roads and cleared the way to the airport for the delegation members in order to make sure they would indeed catch the last available flight to bring them to Israel on time.[50] The change of flights, and the unusual setting accompanying it, left a mark on some of the Israeli delegation members, implying that there was a sense of urgency in the conclusion of the agreement, as well as an element of surprise, even if not for all.

With the conclusion of the negotiations over the implementation of the Declaration of Principles in the Gaza Strip and Jericho (Cairo agreement), the economic negotiations were to be concluded as well (Arnon & Weinblatt, 2001). While Premier Rabin informed the heads of the Israeli delegation that reaching an agreement at all costs was not in Israel's interest, Chairman Arafat ordered the Palestinian delegation to reach an agreement by the 28th as the general negotiations were coming to a conclusion.[51] For the Palestinians, and Arafat particularly, the stakes for not reaching an agreement were much higher. As such Arafat did not want to risk the general agreement not being reached, as his return and the return of the exiled Fatah Palestinian leadership in Tunis to the territories depended on it.[52]

From a positive start with the importance of economics being clear and agreed by all; despite the efforts to keep this track from being subjective to the general negotiations and especially the security aspect, the economic agreement had turned from an independent agreement to an annex of the general arrangement. The when, why, and how this shift took place (or if indeed it was an unplanned shift) is neither clear nor consensual. This is affected by personal perspectives and the memory being influenced

[48] Abu Kosh, Interview, 15 September 2018; Hacker, Interview, 21 August 2019; Oz, Interview, 4 August 2021; Shochat, Interview, 8 August 2021.

[49] The day according to Judaism begins and ends with sundown (for example, Sabbath begins with the sunset on Friday).

[50] Gabai, Interview, 2 January 2017; Hacker, Interview, 21 August 2019; Kleiman, Interview, 4 October 2018; Sharvit Baruch, Interview, 26 July 2021.

[51] Hacker, Interview, 21 August 2019.

[52] Abu Kosh, Interview, 15 September 2018.

by time. Furthermore, the rank of those involved in the peace process play a part as not all were exposed to the same level of information.[53]

A clear agreement is in place among the majority, if not all interviewees, regarding the economy being subjected to political constraints; and that being the case from the start. For those at the professional economic level, as well as all others comprising the negotiation team, the significance of the economic agreement, and establishing economic relations were more than clear. Nevertheless, the Protocol had taken a secondary place in the grand scheme of things. With the Protocol being an annex to the general agreement, the economic negotiations had to be finalized prior to the general negotiation arrangement. Yet as this was a deviation from what was originally understood and agreed by delegation members from both sides, it may be seen as the final stamp of the politization of economics.

The economic negotiations involved numerous experts from both sides, offering their expertise in specific fields to be discussed. From insurance to car plates, to eggs, to high resolution petrol. At the end of the day, though, the experts were not those calling the shots. It was politics that determined the decisions taken by both sides.[54] From the early days of the negotiation process, political opposition from within and from outside, expressed through personal to state-level interests, has been integrated into the Protocol.

6.3.1 Political (Ab)use of the Economic Agreement

> 'The economic field let's say is marginal at best. Though this is a very strong statement, it was the reality we experienced.' [55]

There was an overall understanding between the Israeli and the Palestinian negotiators, many of whom were soon to become those to implement the agreement in their official capacities, that in the forthcoming years until reaching the permanent agreement, the Palestinian economy would be supported by the Israeli economy. And the Israeli economy will benefit from this. The Israeli liberalization policy was promoted by those

[53]From the interviews it is clear (as well as to the interviewees themselves, for example, Sharvit Baruch, Interview, 26 July 2021) that not all were exposed to all matters regarding procedures and protocols, and it was in accordance with their respective position and role in the delegation.

[54]Abu Kosh, Interview, 15 September 2018.

[55]Gabai, Interview, 2 January 2017.

negotiating the Protocol. As this was the official policy of the Ministry of Finance, clearly the opening of the Israeli market to Palestinian goods would increase the competition and reduce prices. This served both Israel's and Palestine's interests during the interim period.[56]

In the years to follow the agreement, a construction materials industry developed in Gaza, with many small- and medium-sized businesses growing, creating competition for the Israeli producers. The construction materials industry had a high market share, with negligible transportation costs. In light of the increasing competition, the ceramic tile manufacturers in Israel filed a petition to the court of Israel claiming that the tiles produced in Gaza were not meeting the Israeli standards, which posed a danger to construction safety. The Supreme Court of Israel ruling sided with the need for measuring the standards to ensure they met the Israeli standards.[57] The Protocol clearly stated that the Israeli standards' measurements would not be enforced at the border.[58] Thus, despite the standardization differences, the Palestinian standardizations were agreed to be applicable in the Israeli market. Considering the lack of borders established in the Protocol this would not have made a difference and enable access of Palestinian goods to the Israeli market. Nonetheless the argument given by the Israeli Supreme Court was that as Israel is a state and Palestine is an Authority, it would be illegal for products not to comply with the Israeli regulations' standards.[59]

Another prominent example of the 'abuse' of mutual economic interests is with the agricultural sector. Not unlike other countries, this sector was protected and resisted opening the market to Palestinian products. Yet regardless of their livelihood, there was no question of misusing the agreement beyond that. The same as with the tiles, the Israeli farmers claimed that the phytosanitary conditions of the agricultural products originated in Gaza were very poor. At the start, the Israeli Ministry of Agriculture conducted inspections in the different crops to approve those that meet the phytosanitary conditions. However, a ruling of the Israeli court on this matter decided that in order to protect the health of the Israeli consumer, the inspection should be taken at the field level, and not per crop. In light of the poor phytosanitary agriculture conditions in Gaza, being subjected

[56] Gabai, Interview, 2 January 2017.
[57] Supreme Court of Israel 53/96, 16 March 1998.
[58] Kleiman, Interview, 22 October 2018.
[59] Gabai, Interview, 2 January 2017.

to inspection at the field level meant little to no chance of being able to keep importing agricultural products to Israel. Thus, even when import quotas of agricultural products were increased, the import to Israel was not to be made from Palestine. Referring to these rulings as undermining the agreement would be much more than an understatement.[60]

In 1998 the then-Israeli Minister of Industry and Trade pledged to ensure that Palestinian importers would only be able to sell the goods they were importing in the Palestinian market, while not applying this to Israeli importers in parallel (Bamya, 2013). This unilateral declaration reflects the political climate, enabling if not encouraging the continuation of segregation between the trading rights of both sides, regardless of what is good economics, or the bilateral obligations towards Palestine.

In addition to the abuse of the agreement from the Israeli side, in some fields, both sides had a mutual interest in keeping the pre-Protocol status quo. A key example of this is petroleum. Petrol was an exception in the agreement, with the Palestinians being able to import it from Jordan or Egypt. Yet following the signing of the Protocol Israeli representatives approached Arafat offering an exclusive contract with a special price for petrol to be imported to Palestine from Israel. The duration of the contract was approximately 20–25 years, which at that time in this crucial period for the Palestinian economy was equal to indefinite. Arafat thus, would benefit from the petrol taxes, and Israel would hold the Palestinian market captive.[61] This of course has wider consequences than just the Petroleum market, as maintaining the monopoly of Israel in one sector has far bigger implications on the Palestinian economy. With a single blow, all efforts to reduce the dependency of the Palestinian economy on Israel were dismissed, and the hard work of negotiating the economic terms went down the drain.[62]

Several other governmental monopolies in charge of importing goods were also established, including cement, which was another key commodity besides petrol, leading to losses in taxes and profits (Bauck, 2016; Khalidi & Taghdisi-Rad, 2009). During the negotiations, the Palestinians stated their intention to form a liberal open market. They told the Israelis they do not want to be like Israel in which big firms have control over

[60] Kleiman, Interview, 22 October 2018.

[61] The petroleum monopoly, as well as others, was managed by leading Fatah figures close to Arafat, who gained huge economic benefits from these monopolies (Bauck, 2016).

[62] Hulileh, Interview, 13 December 2018.

prices in some sectors. Yet it was the Palestinian Authority hand in hand with the Israeli companies that enabled the Palestinian import market to be controlled by Israeli traders. Neither the lists nor the range in VAT established in the Protocol were used by the Palestinian Authority. Driven by fiscal considerations and a desire to secure the revenues to be collected by Israel the Palestinian leadership supported Israeli monopolies taking over their economics.[63]

The economic sphere was central to the success of the exiled Palestinian leadership and its return to the Occupied Territories. The level of independence Palestine would hold was crucially dependent on Palestinian economic independence. Moreover, good economic policy and the ability to raise funds were key factors for Arafat's success in maintaining his rule and gaining the support of the population (Lavie, 2013). During the 1990s, the special relationship between certain Palestinian capitalists and ruling political circles within the PA led to the centralization of political and economic power in the hands of a few individuals, who rapidly managed to transform the national project into a game of interest politics. Monopolies protected by the PA cover over 25 key imported commodities, including flour, sugar, oil, frozen meats, cigarettes, live animals, cement, construction aggregate, steel, wood, tobacco, and petroleum (Bijaoui, 2014: 19–20).

Notwithstanding the various acts breaching the Protocol's purpose, thus, de facto operating against what would have been good economics on both sides; or perhaps because of these acts paving the way, it is unanimously agreed by all interviewees that the main violation of the agreement is that concerning the revenue sharing mechanism.[64] In the summer of 1997 the transfer of the clearance revenues was suspended during the closure of WBGS. The withheld revenues were transferred by Israel later that year (Watson, 2000: 162–163). In September 2000, in response to the outbreak of the second Intifada, Israel again suspended the transfer of clearance revenues, arguing that terrorist activities may have been supported out of the PA budget. The withheld funds were deposited in an account at the Bank of Israel and accumulated to about $500 million. Transfers were resumed in December 2002 after political pressure from the US and assurances from the PA to reform the internal auditing of expenditures. In March 2006, following Hamas winning the elections and

[63] Gabai, Interview, 2 January 2017.

[64] By both Israeli, and Palestinian interviewees.

forming the government, transfer was yet again suspended. Transfer of funds was resumed in July 2007 after the appointment of a new government led by Prime Minister Fayyad (Khalidi & Taghdisi-Rad, 2009; Kock & Qassis, 2011). In May 2011, in view of the signing of the reconciliation agreement between Fatah and Hamas, the Israeli government delayed the transfer of clearance revenues from April that year. The suspension was lifted after three weeks (Kock & Qassis, 2011). In October 2011, in response to the application of Palestine to the United Nations to be recognized as a state,[65] Israel withheld transferring the funds. In November 2012 as a result of Palestine's status being upgraded to a 'non-member state' by the UN, funds were yet again suspended (Bamya, 2013).

Throughout the years since signing the Paris Protocol, the clearance revenue mechanism monthly payments have been repeatedly interrupted or delayed owing to Israeli political considerations (Misyef, 2017). The numerous times funds were suspended in the years beyond the scope of this research resulted in turning this practice from ad hoc to being institutionalized. On 8 July 2018, the Israeli Knesset adopted the 'Freezing of Funds paid by the Palestinian Authority in Connection with Terrorism from Revenues Transferred by the Israeli Government' (FFPA) legislation (Law 5778-2018) (Law Library of Congress March, 2019).[66]

[65] UNGA (2012) *Resolution 67/19. Status of Palestine in the United Nations* (4 December 2012); see also Chap. 7, Sect. 7.4 The Liberal Way Forward- Summary and Conclusions.

[66] Law 5778-2018, FFPA Law, SH 5778 No. 2730 p. 732 (in Hebrew)—The FFPA Law requires that the Minister of Defense submit for the approval of the Ministerial Committee for Matters of National Security (Ministerial Committee) a report at the end of each year detailing the 'amount paid by the PA in connection with terrorism' in that year. In addition, the Minister must present the report to the Knesset Foreign Affairs and Defense Committee (3(a)).

The FFPA defines an 'amount paid by the PA in connection with terrorism' to include money or monetary value, paid by the PA directly or indirectly

1. [t]o a terrorist operative, during his imprisonment or detention or after his release, or to members of his family, for being a terrorist operative; [and]
2. [t]o a prisoner or a detainee who is not a terrorist operative during his imprisonment or detention or after his/her release, or to his/her family, due to the commission of or attempt to commit an offense that causes harm to state security or public security. (2)

For the purpose of implementing the FFPA, a 'terrorist operative' is generally defined as a person convicted or held in custody under charges of specified terrorism offences. (Id.)

The Clearance Revenue mechanism was the essence of the agreement not only as it was the main source of the Palestinian national budget, more so because for the first time since the 1967 occupation, these funds were to be managed by the Palestinians themselves.[67] Thus, the revenue mechanism was the embodiment of the first seeds of sovereignty in the form of an economic institution. Notwithstanding the economic ramifications the suspensions of funds have had on the Palestinian economy, it is the violation of the hidden promise of sovereignty. From a political 'kindergarten'[68] to an institutionalized rule, this as well, has become a pawn in the political game, though neither of the sides have a desire or interest in abolishing the revenue clearance mechanism. '(...) the economics, although it should be used as an instrument to support the peace process (...) became one of the results of the process, not a conducive part of it.' [69]

A complete political-economy assessment of the economic situations, however, requires that these acts of the Protocol's politicization through mechanisms and policies, be placed within both the regional political climate, as well as the domestic struggles over power.

6.3.2 *Spoilers of Peace in the Middle East*

Despite the historical achievement of the DOP signing, the gravity of the domestic opposition that the PLO and Israeli leaderships faced within their own communities was driven home already at the early stages of the process (Eisenberg & Caplan, 2010; Falk, 2016). Following the signing of Oslo, the Israeli and Palestinian leaders, like any other leaders pursuing peace, faced risks from adversaries that could exploit the settlement. These may evolve from stakeholders that perceive peace as contradicting their core values, or from excluded parties seeking to undermine or manipulate the process for their political gain (Waage, 2012).

The FFPA requires the freezing of an amount equal to one-twelfth of the total funds paid by the PA in relation to terrorism in the previous year from monthly revenues transferred by the GOI to the Palestinian Authority. Frozen funds may be transferred to the PA, in full or in part, in the event that the report indicates that the PA has not made payments in connection with terrorism in the year covered by the report. A decision by the Ministerial Committee to transfer frozen funds must be published (4(a–b).)

[67] Elkurd, Interview, 27 August 2018.

[68] Gabai, Interview, 2 January 2017.

[69] Hulileh, Interview, 13 December 2018.

In Israel, the extreme embodiment of the political controversy between political opponent sides was when Prime Minister Rabin was shot and killed by a young Jewish religious right-wing extremist, fanatically opposed to Israel relinquishing its biblical claim to the occupied territories in November 1995. The political leaders of the right-wing party, Likud, were blamed for contributing to the incendiary political climate that led to the murder, and even more of encouraging the incitements leading to it.[70] Rabin's assassination, the first ever of a prime minister in Israel's history, demonstrated the huge gap between the Rabin government's commitment to trading land for peace and the fervent rejection of that policy by those on the far right (Eisenberg & Caplan, 2010; Falk, 2016). In the elections held following the assassination,[71] in May 1996 Benjamin Netanyahu was elected Prime Minister of Israel. During the campaign, Netanyahu stressed his considerable dissatisfaction and scepticism about the Oslo process (Watson, 2000: 47).

In Palestine, opposition was from some of the parties within the PLO side, as well as by the political opposing parties (Savir, 1998: 108–109; Shlaim, 1994). Already during the Madrid bilateral negotiation track, the exiled PLO leadership headed by Arafat was challenged. With the internal Palestinian leadership representatives managing the official track, Arafat had no interest in the success of this track. Thus, from the start of this track, Arafat strove for its failure, in order to nullify any authority the internal PLO negotiators might otherwise gain (Massad, 1999). The PLO sought to forge direct contacts with Israel, with the Oslo secret negotiations unfolding according to their plans. Abu Mazen and Abu Ala both shared the ideology that salvation for the Palestinians 'would be realized through cooperation with Israel and not through cooperation with the Arabs (…)'.

[70] In the months prior to the assassination, Rabin had been branded as a traitor by political hard-liners, some calling for his death. Benjamin Netanyahu, then the opposition leader, Likud, has been accused of playing a role in the incitement of violence against Rabin, by personally participating in two of the most notorious incidents happing during the few weeks before the murder. The first was when Netanyahu participated in a demonstration where the protestors carried a coffin with the writing 'Rabin murders Zionism'; the second was when Netanyahu addressed a protest where demonstrators held posters depicting Rabin in an SS uniform.

[71] The elections were the first direct elections held in Israel for Prime Minister, in which Peres lost to Netanyahu.

They were looking for a suitable track to express it; and Oslo provided the way (Savir, *Getting to the table—Oslo part C* 1998: -10:28:42).[72]

Then, around the accord the PLO split between the Islamists and their supporters, with the radical nationalists from the Damascus-based Popular Front for the Liberation of Palestine (PFLP), and the Democratic Front for the Liberation of Palestine (DFLP) on one side, and Fatah and its affiliated organizations on the other (Falk, 2016; Shlaim, 1994; Mitchell, 2014: 13). Those resisting the agreement accused Arafat of abandoning the core principles of the movement to grab power. The agreement received the necessary majority for approval by the Executive Committee of the PLO, yet only after a bruising battle and the resignation of four of its members. The militant resistance movements Hamas and Islamic Jihad which regarded any compromise acknowledging the Jewish state's existence as anathema, were those in opposition from the outset (Shlaim, 1994).

From the early 1990s, the rapid hold Hamas gained in the WBGS, especially among the younger generation of Palestinians, posed a threat both to the PLO and to Israel. For the PLO which was until then the sole leader of the Palestinians, the new movement posed a challenge to their leadership for the first time, as well as a personal threat to Arafat as its leader (Abusada, 2017; Waage, 2012). As Arafat would not have dreamed of consulting or including his rivals, Hamas would never have dreamed of joining Arafat (Waage, 2012). Indeed, with the growing threat posed by Hamas, the PLO's motivation for pursuing an agreement with Israel was above all to discredit Hamas and maximize its own gains (Bauck, 2016; Lundberg, 1999; Pearlman, 2009; Waage, 2012).

Strengthening the PLO leadership at the expense of Hamas was also in the Israeli interest. Hamas constitutes a threat to Israel, carrying out military attacks against Israel, and encouraging people to fight until the liberation of all of Palestine (Abusada, 2017; Bauck, 2016). Reports of Hamas and the Islamic Jihad gaining more popularity in the Occupied Territories were presented to Premier Rabin, with both the army chiefs and the internal security chiefs repeatedly stressing to him the urgency of forging a political solution to the crisis in the relations between Israel and the

[72] While internal political power struggles in Israel also played a role in the pursuit of the Oslo track and direct negotiations with the PLO leadership, these are not addressed here as considerations affecting the final decision regarding reaching an agreement as Israel was an established democratic state. Ultimately, the final decision on whether and which track to pursue rested with Premier Rabin.

inhabitants of the occupied territories. These were all part of the decision to proceed with negotiations with the PLO, and Rabin's decision to embrace the Oslo track as official negotiations (Shlaim, 1994).

Initially, the balance of power favoured Fatah and the PLO. However, as building in settlements on the West Bank continued and the constant closures by Israel of the territories hurt the Palestinian economy, the balance began to shift (Mitchell, 2014: 13). During the peace process's early years, Hamas' attacks against Israel were in part a tactic for protecting its interests vis-à-vis its main political rivals: the PA, the PLO that gave rise to it, and the Fatah movement that dominated both. Just as the Palestinian leadership used support for the Oslo peace process to outmanoeuvre rivals and maintain dominance, it was predictable that those rivals would use their opposition to Oslo to outmanoeuvre the leadership and challenge that dominance. This struggle between the two political rivalries culminated in the split between the West Bank and Gaza Strip following the 2006 winning of the elections by Hamas.

The 2006 Palestinian parliamentary elections could have marked an unprecedented advance towards the establishment of a legitimate system of representation in the Palestinian territories. For the first time since 1996, an agreement between Hamas, Fatah, and other Palestinian groups was reached on the electoral system to be applied. However, Hamas' victory in the election led to strong opposition from both Fatah and international actors to a Hamas-led Palestinian government. The United States and the European Union announced that they would cut off aid until Hamas recognized Israel, denounced terrorism, and complied with all previous agreements. Israel refused to deal with the PA or transfer its customs revenues. Fatah rejected Hamas' invitation to join the government in what many viewed as an effort to ensure that Hamas failed on its own. Hamas refused to capitulate. Instead, it assumed power during a period of dire economic crisis, in which the payment of public employees' salaries was disabled, with more than a third of the Palestinian workforce dependent on it. At the same time, many Fatah members defied the Hamas government by disregarding its orders and creating havoc in the streets. The leadership struggle between Fatah and Hamas simmered for a year until the Saudi-brokered February 2007 Mecca agreement brought the factions together to form a unity government. Nevertheless, Israel and the United States again refused to recognize the government and the United States instead funded and armed Fatah to defeat the Islamists. The contestation over who had the right to represent the Palestinians continued until

June 2007. Following the capitulation of the pro-Fatah partisan sections of the Palestinian Security Force (PSF), Hamas forcibly seized complete control of the PA in the Gaza Strip. Palestinian President Abbas then declared a state of emergency, accusing Hamas of a violent coup leading to the collapse of the Hamas-Fatah unity government, and formed an emergency government in which Hamas had no representation. Salam Fayyad was appointed as the Prime Minister heading the new cabinet. Israel and the United States helped Fatah consolidate power in the West Bank, while Israel intensified its blockade of Gaza (Milton-Edwards, 2007; Pearlman, 2009). Hamas' violent takeover of the Gaza Strip in the summer of 2007 exposed the magnitude of that rift, pitting the West Bank (governed by the Palestinian Authority) against Gaza (ruled by Hamas) (Eisenberg & Caplan, 2010). These events, as stated by Milton-Edwards (2007: 301) 'were nothing short of civil war in Gaza between Fatah and Hamas'. Islamic groups viewed the Oslo Accords not only as an intolerable surrender of the Islamic land of Palestine but also as a threat to their existence. In carrying out violence against Israel, they sought, among other goals, to help secure a place in the new Palestinian political arena. This arena was characterized by a weakly institutionalized system of representation. In the absence of clear rules regarding how opposition groups could improve their bargaining position with Arafat, spoiler violence was as viable a means as any (Pearlman, 2009).

The Israeli and Palestinian societies were similarly torn between those who supported the peace process and those who wanted to destroy it (Eisenberg & Caplan, 2010). Both the split in the Palestinian society and the assassination of Rabin are the highest form of spoilers, though conversely it could also be argued that consulting with or including the Israeli or the Palestinian opposition would have irreversibly halted the Oslo Accords (Waage, 2012).

6.4 The Last One Standing

Tensions between the political and economic spheres have been a part of the Israeli-Palestinian peace process from its start. From the decision and division of authorities between the negotiation delegations on both sides, to decisions on meeting places, to delegates' appointees, all were a reflection of the political-economic balance of power.

The economic agreement, from negotiation to implementation, as an integral part of the peace process was not excluded from the political power struggles and considerations in regard to the domestic, bilateral, and regional layers within, and between both sides.

The Protocol, as entwined in its name, was designed as a framework establishing an interim period of economic relations of five years. In many ways, the agreement regulated the de facto economic regime already in place since the 1967 occupation into a de jure one, and though designed as an interim agreement in reality, it became the permanent framework shaping economic development until today. The circumstances, however, have changed, with borders of trade and labour existing both with Gaza and in different shapes with the West Bank, contradicting one of the primary assumptions in the Protocol. These borders resulting from restrictive security-related measures implemented by Israel as political means made the economy a pawn in the conflict. Thus, although the de jure regime is still the Paris Protocol, the de facto reality has deviated from the concepts upon which the Protocol was devised, calling for a rethink of the economic regime and the way to reach economic development separate from the political circumstances (Aix Group, 2005; Arnon, 2002).

Throughout the years, the Protocol has been subjected to multiple peace initiatives as sometimes considered as (almost) the 'last one standing' out of the Oslo Accords. It is the only agreement that has been fully implemented throughout the years since the time of signing and ratifying especially when taking into consideration the suspension of security coordination in recent times. At the same time, it is perceived as the bone of contention of the conflict, always being subjected to heavy criticism and controversy on several fronts, not solely because of the economic policies, but also due to the way implementation is subjected to politicians and political decisions. As such in 2012 the Protocol was among the main targets of the popular protests in Palestine with a mass march for 'Social Justice and the termination of the Paris Economic Protocol'.[73] Much like this case, the Protocol is often identified as a key instrument in the Israeli system of 'colonial control, occupation, and denial of sovereignty' (Husseini & Khalidi, 2013: 56). During the last few years the European Commission has been engaged in an independent revision of the Protocol; a newly emerging French initiative with the recent appointment of an envoy for the Middle East Peace Process in September 2020 focused on the Paris economic agreement; and a call to update the framework of the Protocol in light of COVID-19 effects on the Palestinian economy was

[73] '*Palestinians for Dignity*' pamphlet (Source: Kleiman, Interview, 4 October 2018).

made by the Special Coordinator for the Middle East Peace Process in June 2020 (World Bank Group June, 2020). These are only a few examples demonstrating the centrality of the Protocol in shaping the course of the conflict and that of Palestine's development, as considered both by the conflicting sides and the international community as one.

The Paris Protocol, nonetheless, and despite all, was the best result possible to be achieved at the time of its establishment. Considering the Oslo framework, political prohibitions, and above all that this was to be the agreement for the interim period, whether this be five years or a bit longer, it provided the Palestinians with the funds to build their political and economic institutions.[74] Indeed, the Protocol is the 'founding block' of the Oslo Accords that enabled the day-to-day management and governance of Palestine to be conducted by the Palestinians themselves in the wait for peace.[75]

While preferential trade agreements are usually assessed by their effects on bilateral trade relations, and as pointed out by Kanafani (2001), in regard to the Israeli-Palestine economic relations this should not be considered the sole appropriate criterion. Indeed, it is through the lens of political economy that economic change, and furthermore economic policy, should be assessed. Despite the numerous calls, proposals, and contests against the agreement, it can be argued it is the last one out of the Oslo agreements that has survived the test of time and political prohibitions. While the agreement has survived on paper, its spirit has been largely subverted in practice. More importantly, the political landscape in the region has undergone a profound transformation. The Protocol's viability, preserved by Israel and Palestine as well as the international community, and the economic situation in Palestine derived from the agreement's implementation, are both the result of a political-development nexus serving both of the conflicting sides and the international engagement in the political economy needs of MEPP.

[74] Abu Ala, Interview, 27 August 2018; Elkurd, Interview, 27 August 2018.
[75] Shochat, Interview, 8 August 2021.

Bibliography

Abed, G. T. (1990). The economic viability of a Palestinian state. *Journal of Palestine Studies, 19*, 3–28.

Abusada, M. (2017). Palestinian diplomacy: 'Past and present'. In G. Gürbey, S. Hofmann, & F. I. Seyder (Eds.), *Between state and non-state: Politics and society in Kurdistan-Iraq and Palestine* (pp. 197–212). Palgrave Macmillan.

Aix Group. (2005). *Israel and Palestine: Between disengagement and the economic road map.* Centre d'Economie Régionale, de l'Emploi et des Firmes Internationales (CEREFI), Faculté d'Economie Appliquée, Université de Droit, d'Economie et des Sciences d'Aix-Marseille III, France.

Arieli, S.. (2021). *Shaul Arieli the Israeli-Palestinian conflict maps.* Retrieved August 3, 2023, from https://www.shaularieli.com/en/maps/political-arrangements.

Arnon, A. (2002). The implications of economic borders between Israel and Palestine. *Palestine-Israel Journal of Politics, Economics, and Culture, 9*(3), 32.

Arnon, A., & Spivak, A. (1995). Notes on the protocol on economic relations between Israel and the PLO—The Monetary aspect. *The Economic Quarterly, 42*(1), 155–159.

Arnon, A., & Weinblatt, J. (2001). Sovereignty and economic development: The case of Israel and Palestine. *The Economic Journal, 111*(472), 291–308.

Bamya, S. (2013). The economics of the Oslo Accords. In B. Scheller, R. Wildangel, & J. Paul (Eds.), *20 Years Since Oslo: Palestinian perspectives. Perspectives Political Analyses and Commentary from the Middle East & North Africa*, Issue 5, 61–68.

Bauck, P. (2016). The Oslo Accords: A common savior for Israel and the PLO in exile? In P. Bauck & M. Omer (Eds.), *The Oslo Accords a critical assessment* (pp. 79–87). The American University Cairo Press.

Bijaoui, I. (2014). *The economic reconciliation process: Middle Eastern populations in conflict.* Springer.

Bilaterals. (2017). *Negotiations Agadir Agreement.* Retrieved August 12, 2023, from https://www.bilaterals.org/?-agadir-agreement-#:~:text=The%20Agadir%20Agreement%20is%20a,into%20force%20in%20March%202007.

Cobham, D. (2001). Economic aspects of the Israeli-Palestinian conflict: Introduction. *The Economic Journal, 111*(472), 249–253.

Cobham, D., & Kanafani, N. M. (2004). Introduction. In D. Cobham & N. M. Kanafani (Eds.), *The economics of Palestine: Economic policy and institutional reform for a viable Palestine state.* Routledge.

Eisenberg, L. Z., & Caplan, N. (2010). *Negotiating Arab-Israeli peace: Patterns, problems, possibilities.* Indiana University Press.

El-Jafari, M. (1997). Potential merchandise trade of the West Bank and Gaza Strip. *Journal of Economic Cooperation Among Islamic Countries, 18*(4), 23–55.

Falk, R. (2016). After Oslo: A legal historical perspective. In P. Bauck & M. Omer (Eds.), *The Oslo Accords a critical assessment* (pp. 67–79). The American University Cairo Press.

Hirschfeld, Y. (2000). *Oslo: A formula for peace.* Am-Oved.

Husseini, H. I., & Khalidi, R. (2013). Fixing the Paris protocol twenty years later: Some lessons for diehard reformers. In B. Scheller, R. Wildangel, & J. Paul (Eds.), *20 years since Oslo: Palestinian perspectives. Perspectives political analyses and commentary from the Middle East & North Africa*, Issue 5, 56–61.

Kanafani, N. M. (2001). Trade—A catalyst for peace? *Economic Journal, 111*(472), 276–290.

Khalidi, R. J., & Taghdisi-Rad, S. (2009). *The economic dimensions of prolonged occupation: Continuity and change in Israeli policy towards the Palestinian economy.* United Nations, UNCTAD.

Khalil, M. H. (2009). Guide to Palestine–Israel economic and trade relations, Czech Representative Office.

Kleiman, E. (1994). The economic provisions of the agreement between Israel and the PLO. *Israel Law Review, 28*(2–3), 347–373.

Kleiman, E. (1999). Fiscal separation with economic integration: Israel and the Palestinian authority. In A. Razin & E. Sadka (Eds.), *The economics of globalization policy perspective from public economics.* Cambridge University Press.

Kock, U., & Qassis, H. (2011). *West Bank and Gaza: Recent developments in clearance revenues.* International Monetary Fund.

Lavie, E. (2013). The Israeli-Palestinian economic agreement and current consequences. *Middle East Economy, 3*(1), 1–6.

Law Library of Congress. (2019, March). Israel: Law on freezing revenues designated for the Palestinian authority. (LL File No. 2019-017447), The Law Library of Congress, Global Legal Research Directorate.

Levine, M. (1996). Palestinian economic progress under the Oslo agreements. *Fordham International Law Journal Fordham, 19*, 1393–1418.

Lundberg, K. (1999). *The Oslo channel: Getting to the negotiating table* (p. 1333). John F. Kennedy School of Government Case.

Massad, J. (1999). Return or permanent exile? Palestinian refugees and the ends of Oslo. *Critique: Journal for Critical Studies of the Middle East, 8*(4), 5–23.

Milton-Edwards, B. (2007). The ascendance of political Islam: Hamas and consolidation in the Gaza Strip. *Third World Quarterly, 29*(8), 1585–1599.

Misyef, J. M. (2017). *National policy for Palestine—Analysis of tariff and industrial policy option.* Palestine Economic Policy Research Institute (MAS).

Mitchell, T. G. (2014). *When peace fails: Lessons from Belfast for the Middle East.* McFarland.

Panagariya, A. (2000) 'Preferential trade liberalization: the traditional theory and new developments', Journal of Economic literature, 38(2): 287–331.

Pearlman, W. (2009). Spoiling inside and out: Internal political contestation and the Middle East peace process. *International Security, 33*(3), 79–109.

Qurei, A. (2006). *From Oslo to Jerusalem: The Palestinian story of the secret negotiations.* IB Tauris.

Roy, S. (1998). *The Palestinian economy and the Oslo process: Decline and fragmentation.* Emirates Center for Strategic Studies and Research.

Samour, S. (2016). *Review and assessment of Palestinian trade policy options.* Palestine Economic Policy Research Institute (MAS).

Savir, U. (1998). *The process: 1,100 days that changed the Middle East.* Vintage.

Shlaim, A. (1994). The Oslo Accord. *Journal of Palestine Studies, 23*(3), 24–40.

United Nations General Assembly (UNGA). (2012, December 4). *Resolution 67/19. Status of Palestine in the United Nations.* Retrieved July 7, 2023, from https://documents-dds-ny.un.org/doc/UNDOC/GEN/N12/479/74/PDF /N1247974.pdf?OpenElement.

Waage, H. H. (2012). Proactive peace diplomacy: Jan Egeland. In M. Fixdal (Ed.), *Ways out of war* (pp. 91–116). Palgrave Macmillan US.

Wanis-St, J. A. (2011). *Back channel negotiation: Secrecy in the Middle East peace process.* Syracuse University Press.

Watson, G. R. (2000). *The Oslo Accords: International law and the Israeli-Palestinian peace agreements.* Oxford University Press.

Weinberger, P. E. (2006). *Co-opting the PLO: A critical reconstruction of the Oslo Accords, 1993–1995.* Lexington Books.

World Bank Group. (2020, June). *Economic monitoring report to the Ad Hoc Liaison Committee.*

CHAPTER 7

The Economic Diplomacy of Peace in The Middle East

In June 2019, during a US-led summit in Bahrain, the Economic Plan for the Middle East conflict was presented. This economic framework was part of US President Trump's peace initiative for the Middle East—'*Peace to Prosperity-a vision to improve the lives of the Palestinian and Israeli People*' (Trump White House, 2020). The plan, also known as the 'Deal of the Century', presented Trump's vision for achieving a comprehensive peace agreement between Israel and the Palestinians while structured from two separate frameworks—an economic, and political framework that was released later in January 2020. The Trump peace plan was not the first initiative to incorporate an economic roadmap alongside a political trajectory in regard to the Israeli-Palestinian conflict.

The *New Middle East Peace Process Initiative*, announced at the 1991 Madrid conference by US President Bush was comprised of a bilateral negotiation track, aimed at resolving the conflicts of the past; and multilateral negotiations that were meant to build the Middle East of the future comprising five working groups, including a working group on Economic Cooperation and Development.

The New Middle East vision of Peres, appointed in 1992 as Minister of Foreign Affairs of Israel, envisioned the region joining the reorganization of the global world in economic clusters through integrated economic projects crossing from Casablanca to Amman to Jenin (Peres & Naor, 1993).

L. Lahar, *The Economic Diplomacy of Peace in the Middle East*,
https://doi.org/10.1007/978-3-031-93991-4_7

The *Arab Peace Initiative*, also known as the *Saudi Initiative*, was proposed by Saudi Crown Prince Abdullah and endorsed for the first time at the Arab League Summit held in Beirut, Lebanon, in 2002,[1] as well as at the Arab League Summit held in Riyadh, Saudi Arabia, in 2007. The initiative calls for the normalization of relations between Israel and the Arab countries and security for Israel, in exchange for a full withdrawal of Israel from all occupied Arab territories—Golan Heights, West Bank including East Jerusalem, and Gaza Strip, as well as the return of the Palestinian refugees in accordance with UN General Assembly Resolution 194 (III) (1948).[2]

A Performance-based Road Map to a Permanent two-state solution to the Israel-Palestinian conflict, also known as the *Road Map for Peace* of the Middle East Quartet was adopted in 2003. Phase II out of III of the Road Map addressed the economic component calling on Arab states to restore pre-Intifada trade links to Israel, and a revival of multilateral engagement on issues of regional cooperation including economic development (UNSC, 2003a).[3]

> I call on the Arab countries to cooperate with the Palestinians and with us to advance economic peace. Economic peace is not a substitute for political peace, but an important element in achieving it. Together, we can undertake projects to overcome the scarcities of our region, like water desalination or to maximize its advantages, like developing solar energy, laying gas and petroleum lines, and transportation links between Asia, Africa and Europe (…)
>
> (…) if we join hands and work together for peace, there is no limit to the development and prosperity we can achieve for our two peoples — in the economy, agriculture, trade, tourism and education — most importantly, in providing our youth with a better world in which to live, a life full of tranquillity, creativity, opportunity and hope.[4]

[1] LAS Summit (2002), *Summit Resolution 14/221. Arab Peace Initiative* (28 March 2002).

[2] UNGA (1948) *Resolution 194 (III). Palestine—Progress Report of the United Nations Mediator,* GA RES 194 (III) (27 November 1948) in article 11 addresses the right of refugees wishing to return and live at peace with their neighbours should be permitted to so at the earliest practicable date.

[3] UNSC (2003a) *Resolution 2003/529. A Performance-based road map to a permanent two-State solution to the Israeli-Palestinian conflict,* S/2003/529 (7 May 2003). The Road Map was based on the 2002 'Vision for Peace' for a two-state solution to the Israeli-Palestinian conflict of President Bush (Bush, 2003).

[4] Address by PM Netanyahu at Bar-Ilan University, 14 June 2009 (Netanyahu, 2009).

This vision of economic peace was addressed by Netanyahu in 2009, shortly after being elected for the second time as Prime Minister (which would become the first time out of four terms in a row until June 2021, and six terms in total until 2024 as Prime Minister).[5]

The 2016 *French Peace Initiative* aimed at remobilizing the international community in support of peace between Israel and Palestine, promoted meaningful incentives that the international community could offer to the parties for the advancement of peace focusing on three fields: civil society; capacity building for the future Palestinian state; and economic incentives (Ministère de L'Europe et des Affaires Étrangères, 2017).

Indeed, in the many peace initiatives relating to the Israeli-Palestinian conflict incorporating economic roadmaps, focus was given to the economic development of Palestine. Yet, the Palestinians' economic development has been the focus of the international community since the end of the British mandate and the decolonization process following the end of World War II.

7.1 Promoting Development in Palestine—From UNRWA to AHLC

Assistance to the Palestinian people has been in place since the beginning of the 1950s. Following the 1948 war, on 8 December 1949 the UNGA adopted Resolution 302(IV) establishing the United Nations Relief and Works Agency for the Palestine Refugees in the Near East (UNRWA).[6] From its establishment to the early 1990s UNRWA remained the main source of aid to the Palestinian people (Hever, 2010: 21).

Following the 1967 War and the occupation of the West Bank and Gaza Strip a few Arab donor states started providing aid to the OPT. After the 1978 Camp David Accord between Israel and Egypt, donors such as the EC, the United States Agency for International Development (USAID), and the United Nations Development Programme (UNDP) started their support in the OPT (Turner, 2014).

[5] Benjamin 'Bibi' Netanyahu has been the longest-tenured Prime Minister in the history of Israel, with a total of six terms as follows: the first term took place between 1996–1999; the second to fifth term between 2009–2021; and currently in his sixth term as of 2022.

[6] UNGA (1949) *Resolution 320(IV). Assistance to Palestine refugees*, GA RES. 302(IV) (8 December 1949).

In 1979, the United Nations Conference on Trade and Development Resolution 109 (V) requested the Secretary-General of UNCTAD to initiate studies concerning the Palestinian people in collaboration with the Palestine Liberation Organization (PLO), representing the Palestinian people (UNCTAD, 1981).[7] This Resolution, *Assistance to National Liberation Movements recognized by regional intergovernmental organizations*, was an unprecedented resolution of the international community, for the first time focusing solely on economic development in the OPT. Following its adoption, the Assistance to the Palestinian People Unit (APPU) was established in 1985 by UNCTAD Resolution 146 (VI) to set up a special economic unit to monitor and investigate the social and economic impact of policies of the Israeli occupation authorities in the Palestinian Territories (UNCTAD, 1984).[8]

This mandate that extended to UNCTAD was expanded over the years by UNGA Resolutions 69/20 (2014),[9] 70/12 (2015),[10] 71/20 (2016),[11] 72/13 (2017),[12] and 73/18 (2018),[13] which requested UNCTAD to report to the General Assembly on the economic costs of the Israeli occupation for the Palestinian people.[14] The UNCTAD Programme of Assistance to the Palestinian People responds to paragraph 55 (dd) of *UNCTAD XIV* (Nairobi), which requests UNCTAD to 'continue to assess the economic development prospects of the Occupied Palestinian Territories and examine obstacles to trade and development (…) as part of the international community's commitment to building an independent Palestinian State' through: Trade and macroeconomic policies and

[7] UNCTAD (1981) *Resolution 109 (V)*. 'Assistance to the Palestinian People', TD/L.162 (7 May–3 June 1979), adopted on UNCTAD 5th session: 1979: Manila.

[8] UNCTAD (1984) *Resolution 146(VI)*. 'Assistance to the Palestinian people', TD/RES/146(VI) (2 July 1983)

[9] UNGA (2014) *Resolution 69/20. Committee on the Exercise of the Inalienable Rights of the Palestinian People*, A/RES/69/20 (25 November 2014).

[10] UNGA (2015) *Resolution 70/12. Committee on the Exercise of the Inalienable Rights of the Palestinian People*, A/RES/70/12 (24 November 2015).

[11] UNGA (2016) *Resolution 71/20. Committee on the Exercise of the Inalienable Rights of the Palestinian People*, A/RES/71/20 (30 November 2016).

[12] UNGA (2017) *Resolution 72/13. Committee on the Exercise of the Inalienable Rights of the Palestinian People*, A/RES/72/13 (30 November 2017).

[13] UNGA (2018) *Resolution 73/18. Committee on the Exercise of the Inalienable Rights of the Palestinian People*, A/RES/73/18 (30 November 2018).

[14] Mandate of UNCTAD's Assistance to the Palestinian People mandates (2000–2018) (UNCTAD, 2018).

development strategies; Trade facilitation and logistics; Finance and development; and Enterprise, investment and competition policy (UNCTAD, 2020).[15]

As of 1989, the General Assembly adopted annual resolutions entitled 'Assistance to the Palestinian people', from Resolution 44/235 (UNGA, 1989)[16] to Resolution 77/123 (UNGA, 2022).[17] In these resolutions, the Assembly affirmed the inability of the Palestinian people to develop their national economy as long as the Israeli occupation persisted. The Assembly also emphasized the importance of trade for the growth of the Palestinian economy through the above-mentioned resolutions and others. In these resolutions adopted between 1989 and 1993, the Assembly called for the granting of trade concessions and concrete preferential measures for Palestinian exports on the basis of Palestinian certificate of origin.

The Economic and Social Council (ECOSOC) had been expressing its concern about the development of the OPT and the assistance required towards this end. In its resolutions adopted from 1989 to 1994 (Resolutions 1989/96,[18] 1990/59,[19] 1991/69,[20] 1992/58,[21] 1993/78[22] and 1994/29[23]), the Council confirmed its rejection of Israeli restrictions on international assistance and 'called upon United Nations system agencies to mobilize resources to improve the social and economic conditions of the Palestinian people; it called upon neighbouring countries to facilitate the movement of Palestinian exports; and upon the international

[15] UNCTAD (2020) *Report on UNCTAD assistance to the Palestinian people: Development in the economy of the Occupied Palestinian Territory*, TD/B/67/5 (5 August 2020).

[16] UNGA (1989) *Resolution 44/235. Assistance to the Palestinian people*, A/RES/44/235 (22 December 1989).

[17] UNGA (2022) *Resolution 77/123. Assistance to Palestinian refugees*, A/RES/77/123 (12 December 2022).

[18] UN ECOSOC (1989) *Resolution 1989/56. Assistance to the Palestinian People*, E/RES/1989/96 (26 July 1989).

[19] UN ECOSOC (1990) *Resolution 1990/59. Assistance to the Palestinian People*, E/RES/1990/59 (26 July 1990).

[20] UN ECOSOC (1991) *Resolution 1991/69. Assistance to the Palestinian People*, E/RES/1991/69 (26 July 1991).

[21] UN ECOSOC (1992) *Resolution 1992/58. Assistance to the Palestinian People*, E/RES/1992/58 (31 July 1992).

[22] UN ECOSOC (1993) *Resolution 1993/78. Assistance to the Palestinian People*, E/RES/1993/78 (30 July 1993).

[23] UN ECOSOC (1994) *Resolution 1994/29. Assistance to the Palestinian People*, E/RES/1994/29 (27 July 1994).

community to make concessions for Palestinian merchandise' (UN CEIRPP, 2014: 73).

The culmination of the peace process with the signing of the Declaration of Principles in September 1993 provided both the prime rational and the political framework for international efforts to invest in foreign aid in the region, leading not only to a drastic increase in the level of assistance but also to a fundamental change in the approach towards assisting the Palestinians, aligning it with development of the OPT (Le More, 2005). With the aim of promoting an independent Palestinian economy between 1993 and 2000, development projects focused on economic development and job creation received five times more funding than humanitarian aid and crisis management (Hever, 2010: 22). And as such, multiple mechanisms and instruments were further established.

In November 1993, shortly after the signing of the Oslo I Accord, the first meeting of the Ad Hoc Liaison Committee (AHLC), a high-level group of key political donors, was convened. AHLC, also known as *Donor countries*, or *Donors*, is the principal policy-level framework setting the priorities of economic development, and the coordination of the development assistance in Palestine, between all the donor countries and aid institutions operating in the OPT (Le More, 2004). It comprises a 15-member committee, with Norway as the chair of the mechanism; the EU and US co-sponsors, and the UN, WB, and IMF participating alongside the donor countries (UNSCO, 2023a).

The December 1993 UNGA Resolution 48/213 adopted on March 1994 (UNGA, 1994) 'Assistants to the Palestinian people'[24]—to support the implementation of DOP including the economic development of the OPT:

> (...) Urges Member States, international financial institutions of the United Nations system, international intergovernmental and non-governmental organizations and regional and interregional organizations to extend, as rapidly and as generously as possible, economic and social assistance to the Palestinian people in order to assist in the development of the West Bank and Gaza, and to do so in close cooperation with the Palestine Liberation Organization and through official Palestinian institutions (...)

[24] UNGA (1994) *Resolution 48/213. Assistance to the Palestinian People*, A/RES/48/213 (15 March 1994).

This was followed by the adoption of a number of resolutions between 1994 and 2000 urging 'Member States to open their markets to exports from the West Bank and Gaza on the most favourable terms, consistent with appropriate trading rules' (UN CEIRPP, 2014).

From 1993 onwards, the Committee on the Exercise of the Inalienable Rights of the Palestinian People started to engage in activities that promoted assistance to the Palestinian people. In response to the General Assembly suggestion from 1993 onwards (that is, Resolutions 47/170,[25] 54/39[26] and 54/40[27]), and consistent with its mandate, the Committee started to convene annual seminars on assistance to the Palestinian people (UN CEIRPP, 2014).

In June 1994, the Secretary-General appointed Terje Rød Larsen from Norway, as Special Coordinator to OPT 'to serve as a focal point for all UN economic, social and other assistance to the Palestinians in the occupied territory', and with it, the United Nations Special Coordinator Office (UNSCO) for the Middle East Peace Process was established.[28] As part of its mandate, UNSCO has been producing annual reports on the economic and social conditions in the West Bank and Gaza Strip, analysing the challenges and opportunities of the business environment and the repercussions of adverse situations (UNSCO, 2023b).

From 1998 until 2003 the assistance of the United Nations to the Palestinian people was further extended towards the implementation of the Palestinian Development Plans of 1998–2000 (UNGA, 1998),[29] and 1999–2003 (UNGA, 2000c),[30] 'which included the following goals: infrastructure and natural resources management; institutional capacity-building; human resources and social development; and the development

[25] UNGA (1993) *Resolution 47/170. Assistance to the Palestinian People*, A/RES/47/170 (10 March 1993).

[26] UNGA (2000a) *Resolution 54/39. Committee on the Exercise of the Inalienable Rights of the Palestinian People* A/RES/54/39 (20 January 2000).

[27] UNGA (2000b) *Resolution 54/40. Division of the Palestinian Rights of the Secretariat* A/RES/54/40 (21 January 2000).

[28] UN Press Release (1994) 'Secretary-General appoints Terje Røed Larsen of Norway as Special Coordinator in the Occupied Territories' *Statement by Secretary-General Boutros Boutros-Ghali*, SG/A/585|SG/SM/5298 (1 June 1994).

[29] UNGA (1998) *Report 53/153.* UN ECOSOC (1998) *Report 1998/75. Assistance to the Palestinian people Report of the Secretary-General*, A/53/153, E/1998/75 (23 June 1998).

[30] UNGA (2000c) Report 55/137. UN ECOSOC (2000) *Report* 2000/95. *Assistance to the Palestinian people Report of the Secretary-General*, A/55/137, E/2000/95 para. 10 (24 July 2000).

of productive sectors'. The United Nations was involved in a wide range of activities aimed at assisting the Palestinian Authority in implementing the Palestinian Development Plans, while by the end of the decade, the UN was associated with projects in the Occupied Palestinian Territories valued at more than three-quarters of a billion dollars(United Nations CEIRPP, 2014: 74).

In 2002, the Quartet consisting of the United Nations, the United States, the European Union, and Russia was established. The Quartet's mandate is to help mediate Middle East peace negotiations and to support Palestinian economic development and institution building. In 2007 the office of the Quartet Representative with Tony Blair as the then representative was formed. The mandate of the Office of the Quartet is to increase Palestinian economic and institutional development and empowerment, as a support towards achieving a two-state solution.

In 2004 the World Bank Public Financial Reform Trust Fund (WB RTF) facilitated the channelling of approximately $290 million in donor support to Palestine. The main objective of the WB RTF was to facilitate budgetary support to Palestine by enhancing and developing the Public Finance Management systems of Palestine within the broader framework of national reform (The World Bank, 2021).

In December 2007 during the Donor's Conference in Paris, France with the goal of reviewing Palestinian development and institution-building efforts and raising funds to support these, an updated version of the Palestinian Reform and Development Plan (PRDP) was presented. Overall, $7.4bn was pledged by participating countries.

In 2008 the World Bank established the new Palestinian Reform and Development Plan Multi Donor Trust Fund (PRDP-MDTF) to provide reform-linked budget support through a multi-donor budget support mechanism administered by the Bank (The World Bank June, 2021).

As of 2011, the EU and the Member States (MS) have been working on a European Joint Programme that aligns with the Palestinian National Policy agenda to allow development under the unique circumstances of the OPT. The EU Joint Strategy aims to offer untraditional development tools in order to achieve both political objectives and development goals in Palestine.[31] This is taking place as of 2017, with the EU Commission and the Member States combined being the largest aid donor to Palestine.

[31] European Join Strategy in Support of Palestine 2017–2020 Towards a democratic and accountable Palestinian State (EU, 2017); European Join Strategy in Support of Palestine 2021–2024 Towards a democratic and accountable Palestinian State (EU, 2021).

In 2018 the overall aid from the EU together with its Member States amounted to more than €370 million (EU, n.d.).

For years the OPT has been receiving one of the highest levels of per capita official development assistance in the world, with around 40 donor countries, 20 UN bodies and other multilateral agencies giving aid for governance, development, and humanitarian activities (Le More, 2004; Turner, 2014). Between 1993 and the beginning of the twenty-first century alone more than US$7 billion have been disbursed to the OPT, with the EU and MS combined being the largest aid contributors followed by the Arab League states, and the US (Le More, 2005) (Fig. 7.1).

With the peace process taking place during the beginning of the 1990s coming to fruition, a fundamental change in the international community's approach towards assistance to the Palestinian people came into being, aligning assistance with the development of the OPT. The perception of economic development in the OPT as the way leading to peace and prosperity was brought to the fore. Furthermore, with peace seen as being within reach, it was believed that positive progress in the peace process would benefit from Palestine's economic development, as much as advancing the economic development of Palestine would assist in facilitating the peace process from the interim to the permanent agreement.

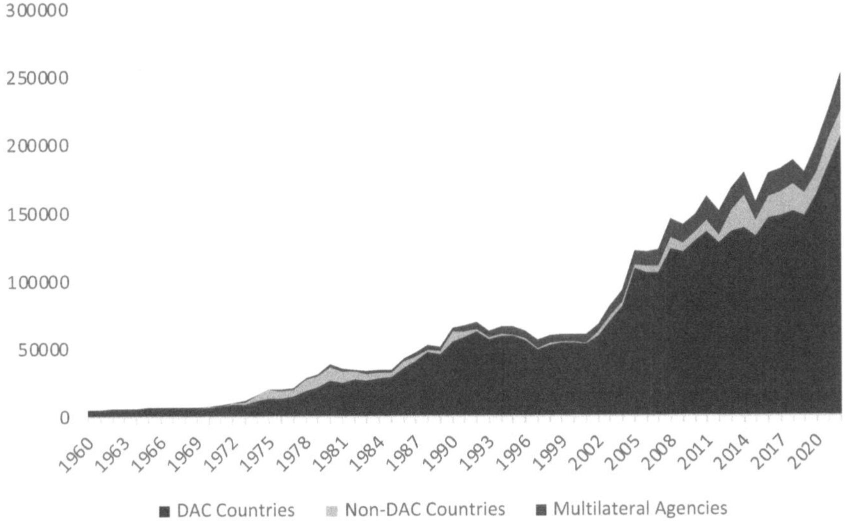

Fig. 7.1 Total bilateral aid to all sectors (West Bank Gaza Strip 1960–2020 Current Prices, USD millions). Source: OECD (n.d.-a)

7.1.1 *Promoting Peace Through Economic Incentives*

With the end of the Cold War, the international community has increasingly become involved in multilateral efforts in support of civil conflict transitions to peace. These efforts, further to traditional tools of diplomacy, and mechanisms of peacekeeping, included a variety of social and economic objectives and instrumentalities, underpinned by substantial commitments of financial support.

The share of foreign aid resources devoted to conflict-related programming throughout the 1990s has significantly grown within a decade. Between 1990 and 1995 the bilateral humanitarian and refugee assistance expenditure increased from $1 billion to over $3 billion, and the amount channelled through the major multilateral agencies increased from $1 billion to over $2 billion. Between 1993 and 1997 the total aid to war-torn and post-conflict countries averaged over $11 billion per year. Considering the parallel decline in total Western aid during this decade meant that an increase of 8 per cent (from 20 per cent to 28 per cent) of all official development assistance (ODA) has been in place (Brynen, 2000: 7).

The Oslo process brought high expectations regarding economic development in Palestine, and for this development process to support further progress in the peace process itself (Cobham, 2001). The agreement was anticipated to provide the scope for the Palestinians to allocate economic resources independently, to engage freely in commerce with both external markets and Israel, and thus to build their own viable economy. The donors would provide the necessary external financing to establish an enabling environment to build or rehabilitate neglected infrastructure and to establish Palestinian capacity to provide social services (The World Bank and The United Nations Office of the Special Coordinator in the Occupied Territories, 1999: 8–9).

Subsequent to the progress in the region following the 1990s peace process, including the Madrid process, the 1993 Oslo accord, and the 1994 Israel-Jordan peace treaty, promotion of regional economic development cooperation took place, with the purpose of creating a strong economic pillar to help achieve and sustain peace in the Middle East. The economic development process in the region carried with it the potential to enhance mutual economic exchange and cooperation, to invigorate the national economy, and to promote the development of the regional economy, leading to vast interests of many of the countries in the MENA region. This came to manifestation in the form of the *Middle East/North Africa Economic Summits and Conferences.*

Held under the leadership of the US government and the Russian Federation as co-chairs of the MEPP, along with the World Economic Forum, four summits took place between the years 1994–1997:

- Casablanca, Morocco, 30 October to 1 November 1994;
- Amman, Jordan, 29 to 31 October 1995;
- Cairo, Egypt, 12 to 14 November 1996; and
- Doha, Qatar, 16 to 18 November 1997.

Emphasizing the role of public-private partnership for economic development, the summits focused on ways to foster the integration of business executive's views and concerns into government economic decisions, project development and presentation, and investment opportunities (US Department of State, 2001).

Moreover, during the 1990s

> European companies started to plan roads and rail tracks to the Middle East (…) The Japanese took on them to plan the tourism, the French and the Germans the communication and transportation, Italians digging the canal from the Red Sea to the Dead Sea, Austrians water and electricity, British the free movement trade zone, Danish agriculture, Americans training personal; and Canadians taking care of refugees. (Peres & Naor, 1993: 19)

The Dutch together with the French invested in both a harbour and airport designed in the Gaza Strip.[32]

The various economic development initiatives and projects at the bilateral and regional level, however, did not yield the fruits of economic development in Palestine following the Oslo I Accord. In the period between 1993 and 2000 a deterioration in the economic situation in Palestine took place. Unemployment and poverty emerged as the main problems alongside a slowdown in private investments, and a collapse in the trade flows

[32] Pronk, Interview, 20 November 2020.

(Diwan & Shaban, 1999; Levine, 1996). Gross national product (GNP) per head (including labour incomes earned in Israel) fell by 4.9 per cent in 1994, by 9.6 per cent in 1995, and by 9 per cent in 1996. Although from 1997 there was some economic recovery, it reached in 1999 a level that was 10 per cent below that of 1993 (Cobham, 2001) (Fig. 7.2).

One of the most prominent examples of aligning assistance and development policy was with the full support of the United Nations, European leaders, the US President Barack Obama administration and the Quartet of the development programme for Palestine of Prime Minister Salam Fayyad—*Ending the Occupation, Establishing the State* (PNA August, 2009), first presented at the AHLC meeting in Paris, 17 December 2007 as the updated version of the Palestinian National Development Plan—Palestinian Reform and Development Plan (PRDP) (PNA, 2007). The US administration alone pledged a total of $200 million for development aid in Palestine, the largest amount of external financial assistance ever to be made available to Palestine in a single deposit, by any donor since 1996 (Simanovsky, 2011).

Despite decades of instituted donor-sponsored peace processes, the Israeli-Palestinian conflict is one of the most protracted conflicts in the world (Turner & Hussein, 2015), evidently not because of a lack of resources or efforts to achieve this goal. Almost three decades after Oslo I,

Fig. 7.2 The share of trade contribution to GDP (per cent) from 1993 to 2022. Source: The World Bank Group (2023)

while Israel has become an OECD Member State,[33] the West Bank economic performance has been rapidly deteriorating, and the economy of the Gaza Strip has experienced the process of de-development.[34]

7.2 The Security-Development Nexus of the Israeli-Palestinian Conflict

> This is my understanding of the main problem of Oslo, it was negotiated by politicians. If you go to the text of the agreement, it looks fine, especially the economic side. But when you go to the implementation a few years later, the implementation is different because it was taken over by the security establishment on both sides, and these are different people with different orientations, different preferences, different priorities, and all that they care for is to make sure that security arrangements are as stringent as possible while disregarding the importance of working together and creating economic interdependence on both sides.[35]

The 1993 Oslo process sought to learn from past mistakes. Unlike the preceding peace accords of Camp David, the Oslo I perception was that there is a need to promote economic development in the West Bank and Gaza Strip, and there is a need to encourage economic cooperation between the Palestinians and Israel (Hirschfeld, 2014: 133).[36] Indeed, the initial negotiations in Oslo during the first few meetings, at a time when the future of this trajectory was far from evident, revolved around economic cooperation and economic aid in the form of a *Marshall plan* for the West Bank and Gaza Strip, and the Middle East region, as well as mutual economic projects between the two sides (Beilin, 1997: 80–81; Hirschfeld, 2000: 111; Pundak, 2013: 117–119; Qurei, 2006: 85; Savir, 1998: 29).

[33] On 29 June 2010 Israel signed the OECD Accession Agreement, and on 7 September 2010 Israel signed the OECD convention (OECD, n.d.-b).

[34] De-Development as coined by Roy (1999; first articulated in 1987) describes a structural relationship between a stronger (dominant) and weaker (subordinate) economy. However, whereas most definitions of underdevelopment allow for structural change and reform within the weaker economy (though that change often is disarticulated because it is oriented to the needs of the dominant economy), de-development not only distorts the development process but undermines it entirely.

[35] Elkurd, Interview, 27 August 2018.

[36] Hirschfeld, Interview, 2 January 2017.

This was in full alignment with that of high-ranking officials from both sides. Peres, appointed in 1992 as the Foreign Minister of Israel, promoted *The New Middle East* vision, envisioning the global reorganization of states into economic clusters spreading to the ME region through economic projects crossing from Casablanca to Amman to Jenin. Abu Ala, a senior official in the Palestinian leadership, and later on head of the Palestinian negotiation delegation to the Oslo track, presented a very similar project vision, much like the vision presented in *The New Middle East*, a regional economic cooperation in the promotion of peace in the ME region.

Following the Oslo Accords, negotiations on the economic agreement between Israel and Palestine took place with a clear perspective of both sides that the only way to overcome conflict is by creating economic interdependency on both sides.[37] The preamble of the Paris Protocol proclaimed an ambitious goal: to lay 'the groundwork for strengthening the economic base of the Palestinian side and for exercising its right of economic decision-making in accordance with its own development plan and priorities'.[38] Indeed, the Oslo perception prioritized the promotion of economic development in the OPT, alongside economic cooperation between Palestine and Israel. Furthermore, these were supported through vast international aid and investments in both Palestine and the ME region.

However, while the political relations between Israel and Palestine improved as a result of the Oslo process, the economic relations deteriorated (Roy, 1998: 13). The aspirations for economic development in Palestine have been far from being fulfilled, with the economic growth of Palestine continuing to deteriorate. The dependency of Palestine on Israel, with the peace process never coming to fruition and the holding agreements being those designed as interim agreements for a period of five years, created a situation of growing dependency between the two nations' economies while one is striving, and the other is on the verge of collapsing. 'The center of gravity of the Palestinian economy is not Ramallah; it is Tel Aviv' (Ya'alon, 2017) (Figs. 7.3–7.5).[39]

[37] Elkurd, Interview, 27 August 2018.

[38] The Protocol on Economic Relations between the Government of the States of Israel and the P.L.O., representing the Palestinian people (29 April 1994), UNGA, UNSC, A/49/180, S/1994/727 (4 May 1994).

[39] Moshe, 'Bogie' Ya'alon, is an Israeli politician and former Chief of Staff of the IDF, who also served as Israel's Defence Minister under Benjamin Netanyahu from 2013 until his resignation on 20 May 2016. The quote is retrieved from an article written following Ya'alon's

Fig. 7.3 Israel trade and financial globalization 1970–2020. Source: KOF Swiss Economic Institute (2023)

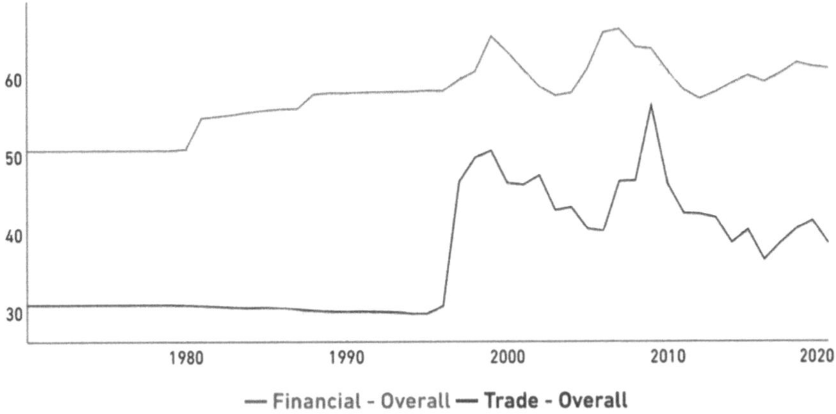

Fig. 7.4 Palestine trade and financial globalization 1970–2020. Source: KOF Swiss Economic Institute (2023)

The fundamental problems of the Palestinian economy in the twenty-first century, are very much like those that existed when the Palestinian Authority was established. The persisting problems include underdevelopment, the lack of adequate physical infrastructure, insufficient social

resignation from the Israeli government and parliament and expresses his perspective, which differed from that of the government at the time, regarding the peace process.

Fig. 7.5 Israel and Palestine political globalization 1970–2020. Source: KOF Swiss Economic Institute (2023)

services in health, education and welfare, and restricted mobility of people and merchandise within the OPTs themselves, and between the OPTs and the rest of the world. All these are on top of a high level of unemployment, a heavy dependence on the Israeli economy and on workers' remittances, a heavy dependence on foreign aid mainly for the spending of public finance and trade deficits, with a high degree of openness to trade when it comes to imports together with a significant aforementioned import surplus (Arnon, 2007; Arnon & Bamya, 2015). The negative effects on Palestine's economic growth are attributed to restrictive Israeli measures, including closures and curfews, internal barriers and others. All have been in place since the beginning of the 1967 occupation and implemented at different levels, being determinative for the Palestinian economy and having disrupted the daily lives of the Palestinian population (UN CEIRPP, 2014). The dependence of the Palestinian economy from its early days on the trade policy in place, particularly vis-à-vis Israel and Israel's major trading partners, and on the nature of the security controls, are the two main factors affecting the results of the Palestinian trade performance and economic outcome (Dessus & Bulmer, 2004).

While foreign aid is often dictated by political and strategic considerations and tends to respond to political incentives, specifically in the form of political liberalization, foreign direct investments are sensitive to economic conditions in receiving countries and respond more to improvement in policy management, trade liberalization, and better protection of property rights (Alesina & Dollar, 2000). In view of the deterioration in the security situation from the first years following Oslo, Israel implemented more restrictive measures through repeated closures that prevented Palestinian workers from working in Israel, and Palestinian goods from being transported to Israel, including all air and seaports for onward export (Cobham, 2001). Thus, the foreign assistance inflow even in times when these were at their highest contribution, has been able only partially to offset these restrictive measures (United Nations CEIRPP, 2014).

The dependence of security upon a successful move towards progress and modernity and vice versa, is at the core of the security-development nexus. The nexus is the mutually reinforcement juncture of the conditions of and for security, and those of development and progress. This is valid whether security and development both occur within the same geographical space, as well as between borders when security and continued development of one state/entity are implicated by the security and development of another (Stern & Öjendal, 2010). With development policy being redefined from economic to human development, the security policy goal accordingly has become that of human security. This type of security, however, does not necessarily lead to national development, international security, or vice versa; though all different layers the nexus entails, are potentially mutually reinforcing goals (Tschirgi, 2006).

Indeed, geographic proximity enhanced the security-development nexus; with the Israeli-Palestinian conflict being no exception. Yet, in this case, the nexus may be even more prominent because of other unique characteristics of the conflict. As it was the military law under the military ruling that defined the Israeli control over all of Palestine, the military was the sovereign in the OPT. Thus, the dependency between security and development until Oslo simply could not have been separated (Grinberg, 2007). From 1967 until the Oslo Accords, the Occupied Palestinian Territories have been under the rule of the Israeli Civil Administration, with economic, political, and institutional affairs including taxation, customs, banking, money and insurance, agriculture, industry and crafts, land and water, labour, and other resources, all under its full authority (Taghdisi-Rad, 2014). Moreover, the DOP recognized Israel's overriding power with the remaining military law in force during the transitional phase. Thus, even though the PA gained control over certain sectors of activity, ultimately the authority over the disposition of the Occupied Territories lay with Israel. As such, although the Protocol presented new economic powers for Palestine, the control over key economic aspects of Palestine, for example, external borders control, water, land, and labour, were maintained by Israel (Roy, 1998: 7–8).

The two other prominent justifications to strengthen this nexus in the case of the Israeli-Palestinians conflict are:

- The joint interests between the Israeli security and economic elite gave rise to a military-economic control pattern. This pattern of ruling expresses the mutual interest of the military and economic elites in Israel: both ask to create economic dependency, that allows the IDF to control the Palestinian population and provide profits to the Israeli manufacturers, employees, and merchants. This pattern creates a 'captive market' for Israeli merchandise and a cheap labour force for Israeli employers. It prevents the development of the Palestinian economy and investments in its territory and blocks the entrance of Palestinian goods to Israel that may compete with Israeli production. The need to define this unique pattern arises from the sheer fact that there is a territorial sequence in this case unlike imperial and colonial regimes (Grinberg, 2007).
- The evident asymmetry in both military and economic power between Israel and Palestine from the time of occupation. While 'Israel boasts one of the best equipped and well-trained military in the world' and has a 'first-world' economy, the Palestinians 'have virtually no coercive power and their ability to inflict costs and casualties on Israel is extremely limited' (L. Ross, 2014: 121).

With the Oslo Accords and defining territories into A, B and C regions,[40] the division of authority had changed according to the competencies agreed upon, to that between the Civil Administration and Palestinian Authority; nonetheless with the Civil Administration maintaining its supremacy.[41]

[40] See also Chap. 6, Figure 6.1 Interim Agreement 1995–1998.

[41] The Defence (Emergency) Regulations are a set of regulations promulgated in 1945 by the British authority in Mandatory Palestine. The purpose of the regulations was to give the Mandatory government and security forces additional authority to act against Jewish and Arab underground organizations, enabling the government to put restrictions on movement and free speech, establish a military court system, expropriate and demolish houses, place suspects under administrative detention and more. The regulations along with most of the existing Mandatory law were incorporated into Israeli domestic law with the establishment of the state of Israel in 1948 and remain in effect in Israel and the Palestinian Territory under

This was clear and discussed already during the initial negotiations of Oslo as was put in the exchange of words between Savir, and Abu-Alaa, back in 1993 saying to each other that without guaranteeing the security needs of Israel there could be no economic development for the Palestinian territories, as much as that without economic development in the Palestinian Territories, Israel's security needs could not be achieved (Savir, 1998: 30–31). This dependency between economic development and security for both sides of the conflict may have received its form most obviously in the fate of the Protocol. While originally planned to be signed as a stand-alone agreement, the *Protocol on Economic Relations* became an annex to the *Agreement on the Gaza Strip and the Jericho Area* (the *Cairo Agreement)*, which was the first follow-up agreement achieved after the Oslo Accords, and was subjected first and foremost to the security considerations of Israel.

> The main parameters that determined the place of the Protocol (in the general scheme of the peace process) have been the political and security ones; indeed, the economic component came third. This was the first blow to the implementation of the agreement (...) It's not just a misconception, but also the marginalization of the economic means from bottom up to top down, with even the economic Minister of Finance in Israel de facto subjected to the approval of the army, and the security-level Shabak,[42] further to the political level that is inevitable.[43]

According to Khan (2005), the Oslo agreement and all sequential negotiations and agreements have been subjected to a unique set of terms under which the withdrawals are made partial, phased, conditional, and reversible until a permanent agreement is reached. This conditioning, termed 'security first' is beyond the dependency between the

Israeli law, apart from several that were repealed over the years, with the application of some dependent on the official existence of a state of emergency, that has been continuously declared since 1948. Following the 1967 occupation the military governor issued orders to the effect that existing domestic law in the territories would be continued, including the Defence (Emergency) Regulations, arguing that they were not revoked during the Jordanian and Egyptian administration of the WSBG, therefore continued to be in effect since 1945 (Tzur, 1989).

[42] The Israel Security Agency known by the abbreviation Shin Bet (Hebrew abbreviation of 'Security Service') or Shabak (Hebrew abbreviation of 'General Security Service')—is the internal security service of Israel.

[43] Hulileh, Interview, 13 December 2018.

renouncement of violence between the two sides and economic development in Palestine, and is what Khan defines as the security-development nexus in this conflict as the impact of the security containment is at the heart of Palestinian poverty and well-being.

7.2.1 The Double Development Trajectory for Peace in the Middle East

'Development policy today is extremely mixed up with the political, not the security'[44]

The negotiations of Oslo I, and especially the Paris Protocol are often perceived as those that were led by the Israeli security interests. Yet it was the political interests all along that determined the course of negotiations (Kleiman, 1994). Security was, is, and always will be a condition, constraint, and consideration, even at times when the peace process moves forward since the security events are those that shape the reality in conflict zones. Nonetheless, security should not be the focus as these events are merely a delay or a setback, as the security sphere is always being subjected to the political interests of those in power.[45]

The approach towards economics and peace in relation to the MEPP taken by the international community was premised upon the assumptions of an intertwined progress between peace, security, and development (Le More, 2008; Makovsky, 2018: 148). Following the signing of the Oslo Accords, aid to the WBGS and its system of management and coordination have been inextricably linked to the Middle East peace process. ODA not only targeted the promotion of *economic development and welfare*, as constituting the principal objective of foreign aid;[46] but it also had an explicit political aim: sustainable peace (Le More, 2004; Le More, 2005).

As Israel maintained control of all borders all the development cooperation initiatives required its involvement. Thus 'development discussions were political in nature' from the start, according to Pronk.[47]

[44] Shaath, Interview, 13 September 2018.

[45] Oz, Interview, 4 August 2021.

[46] Literature on aid sanctions exists, for example, Jeong (2019), Hansen and Borchgrevink (2006), Peksen and Drury (2009).

[47] Pronk, Interview, 20 November 2020.

The dependency between development and politics as claimed by Shaath in the quote above has been motivating both the Israeli interests in regard to Palestine's development, the interests of the international community in regard to the peace process development, and the international community and /or third parties to the conflict bilateral relations with both Palestine and Israel. Indeed, Palestine's development and the MEPP development throughout the years since conflict emergence exist not only alongside but have become heavily interdependent, leading to a double development trajectory in this case.

The Israeli prolonged occupation together with the high fragmentation within the Palestinian leadership in relation to the peace process, resulted in the conflict evoking highly intense intertwined notions between the identity and security for each of the sides to the conflict (Barak, 2005). More than that, Roy (2002: 9) argued for the process for which the Oslo Agreements gave shape to be 'not about peace or reconciliation but about security…' being the manifestation of the common security strategy of both Israel and Palestine, the OPT stability.

However, in the first years following the signing of Oslo I the international assistance failed in its development strategy as these efforts supported capacity building in Palestine, prioritizing the provision of security to Israel in addition to essential services to the Palestinians (Arnon, 2007; Khan, 2014). Even more, it was this support, of the international community through aid in Oslo, in many ways that detached the direct responsibility of Israel in regard to the occupation and enabled its continuation, with only an indirect responsibility of Israel for it (Bouris, 2014: 51–52).

From the conflict emergence during the years of the British Mandate in Palestine, the search for peace has been a part of the Israeli-Palestinian trajectory. Major diplomatic efforts undertaken by the United States, the United Nations, and others, followed each of the 1948, 1956, 1967, 1973, and 1982 Arab-Israeli wars; intervening events in the region following the turning point in the conflict in 1967, including among others the Egyptian-Israeli peace treaty; the Intifada of the late 1980s, and the first Gulf War challenging its intractability (Wanis-St, 2011: 23; Kelman, 2007). Though in the 1978 Camp David peace accord between Egypt and Israel, the Palestinian right to autonomy, based on an interim period of self-rule to be followed by a permanent status agreement, was agreeable for the first time (Lundberg, 1999), it was with the Oslo Accords that the foundation for a two states solution was laid.

The Oslo Accord laid the cornerstone for a comprehensive and lasting peace in the Israeli-Palestinian conflict. The signing of the Declaration of Principles between the government of Israel and the Palestinian Liberation Organization in September 1993, constitutes a historical event, one that hoped to inaugurate a new era between the two nations. Indeed, following the Oslo I Accord the double development trajectory had been framed through the development-security nexus, as that determining the level of development in the region, applying both for international and local road-maps and strategies. However, from the times of Oslo, it was clear to all those engaged in the peace process that a permanent agreement would entail a redistribution of territory that was directly commensurate to the exact amount of territorial area that had been occupied in 1967.[48] Yet, territorial exchange (though necessary for achieving a permanent agreement), has not been considered either as required or as sufficient for developing the Palestinian economy and/or the peace process trajectories, much unlike the 'economic peace'.

If UNSC Resolution 242[49] was the first stepping stone to set the path for peace, the global context and prolonging of the Israeli-Palestinian conflict brought with Oslo I the second stepping stone—economic peace. Thus, even though the framing of Oslo, successes and failures, in regard to bilateral and international policy to follow have been framed through the security-development nexus, for understanding the development trajectory of both the MEPP and Palestine, and even more for their alignment to yield the desired developmental result, it is not only through the security-development nexus, but also the political-development one that the peace process, and especially that of economic peace, should be addressed—the political development security nexus—as this book presents.

7.3 Mind the Liberal Gap

Since 2010 with the peace process stagnation, while Israel has become the '*Start-up Nation*' the West Bank economic performance has been rapidly deteriorating, and the economy of the Gaza Strip experienced the process of de-development, a change of approach towards the MEPP started to

[48] Gabai, Interview, 2 January 2017.

[49] UNSC (1967) *Resolution 242. Situation in the Middle East*, S/RES/242 (22 November 1967).

take shape. The continuation of Israeli expansion in the settlements and further deterioration in the security situation, and the eight-day Gaza Conflict of fighting between Israel and Hamas, during November 2012,[50] alongside the interdependence between Palestine's economic development and progress in the MEPP, brought into force an economic dependence between the bilateral relations of the EU with Israel and the progress of the MEPP.

In July 2013, following the adoption of guidelines by the EC, the European Union made a linkage between all future possible upgrades of EU-Israel economic bilateral relations, as framed in the Association Agreement, the legal framework defining the bilateral relations, and the expected progress in the Middle East peace process (EC, 2013).[51] This linkage resulted, among other measures, in labelling Israeli products that originated in the Occupied Territories, and the withdrawal by Israel from understandings on extending the relations in other fields.[52]

Another step in the dependency of bilateral economic relations with third parties and the MEPP progress was seen with the co-dependent policy adopted by US President Trump during his first term in office. In mid-2018 the Trump Administration announced withdrawing $200 million from the US development agency, USAID for humanitarian projects in OPT.[53] Shortly after, it also declared cutting all US aid funds for UNRWA in order to press Palestinian officials to restart the peace negotiations with Israel and re-engage with the White House in light of the Peace to Prosperity Plan announcement.

During the monthly Foreign Affairs Council meetings throughout 2020 in response to the declaration of Israel regarding future annexation, the EU leaders have considered the implementation of economic sanctions on Israel. Also, in February 2020, a 'blacklist of businesses operating in Israeli settlements affecting Palestinian human rights was published by

[50] 14–21 November 2012; Also known as Operation Pillar of Defence.

[51] Also see: European External Action Service (EEAS) – Statement by EU High Representative Catherine Ashton on the publication of guidelines on Israel and EU funding Instruments (EU and EC, 2013).

[52] Guidelines on the eligibility of Israeli entities and their activities in the territories occupied by Israel since June 1967 for grants, prizes, and financial instruments funded by the EU from 2014 onward (EC, 2013).

[53] UNGA Fourth Committee (2018) *SPD/684*. 'Palestine Refugee Agency Faces Greatest Financial Crisis in Its History Following 2018 Funding Cuts, Commissioner-General Tells Fourth Committee', GA/SPD/684 (9 November 2018).

the United Nations Human Rights Council (UNHRC), following the adoption of UNHRC Resolution 31/36 in March 2016'. [54]

The May 2021 war between Israel and Hamas has led employees in multinational companies, including Apple, Google and Amazon to voice their support for Palestine in public letters asking their employees to show support for the Palestinian people, to sever contracts with the IDF, and to demand the termination of all contracts with institutions that support Israeli violations of Palestinian rights.[55]

These examples are only the tip of the iceberg demonstrating that beyond the bilateral economic dependency between Israel and Palestine, there is a clear dependency between bilateral economic relations and the MEPP progress. Indeed, with the trust between the two sides being broken for more than a decade resorting to linking economic bilateral relations with the progress of the Middle East peace process in order to pressure both conflicting sides is expected. Yet, these calls for economic pressure on Israel to end the occupation are not new and have been seen alongside the conflict from its emergence during the first half of the twentieth century, with little result if any. Furthermore, neither the co-dependency demonstrated in the policy the US President Trump took towards the Palestinians, nor has the EU dependency policy towards Israel led to positive results.

US President Biden, the 46th President from 2021 to 2025, already at the start of his term resumed close ties with the Palestinian administration, as well as acted to reassert US leadership in the region (Lincoln, 2022). The resuming of the security coordination between Israel and the Palestinians following Biden's elections attests on regaining trust between the Palestinian and American administration (Halbfinger & Rasgon, 2021). As for the US position at the regional level, a normalization agreement between Saudi Arabia and Israel has already been reported to be under discussion during the midst of 2023. An agreement with Saudi

[54] UNHCR (2016) *Resolution 31/36. Israeli settlements in the Occupied Palestinian Territory, including East Jerusalem, and in the occupied Syrian Golan*, A/HRC/RES/31/36 (24 March 2016). The Resolution recalls reports of the UN Secretary-General, resolutions of the UN General Assembly and Security Council, an advisory opinion of the International Court of Justice and the opinions of several human rights bodies reaffirming the illegality of the Israeli settlements in the occupied territory, including in East Jerusalem.

[55] Jewish Diaspora in Tech: Letter on Google Communication and Cloud Contracts (Jewish Diaspora in Tech, 2021); Amazon workers' letter to the executive board urging solidarity with Palestinians (Dutton, 2021).

Arabia was declared by Netanyahu in the first government meeting after being elected as Prime Minister in November 2022 as a key objective of the government. Saudi Arabia had been a central proponent of the 2002 Arab Peace Initiative, but more so has officially declared that advancing the relations with Israel is conditioned to the situation regarding the Question of Palestine. If and what this conditioning will yield is for the future to hold (Guzansky, 2023).

The asymmetric nature of the Israeli-Palestinian conflict, with Israel holding the upper hand in each and every aspect, implies that being the stronger side, Israel is to determine the rules of the game. As for the EU linkage between a further upgrade of economic relations with Israel and the MEPP, despite EU guidelines in regard to Israel's territory within the green lines, Israel was not excluded from the Research and Development programme of the EU,[56] as a compromise accepted on both sides was reached (EC, 2014).[57] As for labelling Israeli goods, the enforcement of the legislation was the primary responsibility of Member States, and only following the 2019 ruling of the European Court of Justice did it become compulsory for all Member States (European Parliament (EP), 2019).[58]

Lovatt and Toaldo (2015) refer to this policy implemented by the EU as a de facto *Differentiation* policy between Israel and the settlement's activities in the Occupied Territories. According to the argument this policy has not been sufficiently acknowledged or implemented in a consistent way due to concerns that these measures might affect the on-off peace negotiations, especially as being Israel's largest trading partner the EU may take the lead on potential peace negotiations.

However, it is not only because of the effect that economic sanctions would have on the future of the peace process potential that this policy is addressed,[59] but also because of the comprehensive economic benefits

[56] Horizon 2020 is the financial instrument implementing the Innovation Union, a Europe 2020 flagship initiative aimed at securing Europe's global competitiveness and was the biggest EU Research and Innovation programme ever with nearly €80 billion of funding available over seven years (2014 to 2020), prior to the approval of the current programme, Horizon Europe (EC, 2023).

[57] Agreement between the European Union and the State of Israel on the participation of the State of Israel in the EU programme 'Horizon 2020 — the Framework Programme for Research and Innovation (2014–2020)' L.177/1, 17 June 2014 (EC, 2014).

[58] Ruling of the Court of Justice of the European Union on the labelling of Israeli settlement goods (EP, 2019).

[59] See Demena et al.'s(2021) meta-analysis for an assessment of the effectiveness of sanctions policy.

these economic relations have for both sides. Furthermore, specifically in regard to the US policy in the Middle East this argument is supported by Alesina and Dollar (2000) demonstrating that the pattern of aid-giving is vastly influenced by its interest in the region. The resolution adopted by UNHRC (2021) on the establishment of an international commission of inquiry to investigate violations in the Occupied Palestinian Territories, including East Jerusalem and Israel, with Bahrain and Sudan voting in favour, is providing support in relations to the Arab world's duality.[60] As the Abraham Accords were not conditioned with the end of occupation, voting in support of the resolution, would not have any implications on the economic relations with Israel. Indeed, economic (inter)dependency and negative sanctions do not necessarily guarantee progress towards peace.

Where threats and sanctions damage cannot be enlarged to accomplish compliance, the only instrument that will be able to provide this is positive sanctions (van Bergeijk, 2009: 163–166). This finds support in Nincic (2010, 2011, 2012) who demonstrated the effectiveness of positive incentives and argued that opportunities are missed by not exploring positive incentives to see if they will work when negative inducements do not. Indeed, despite the limited scholarship on the use of positive sanctions, it provides evidence that inducements can also work in adversarial relationships, with positive incentives being used as a means to bring belligerents to the bargaining table, including when the incentives are offered by third parties to the conflict (Barbieri, 2017).

Positive incentive strategies may inadvertently become a form of appeasement (Cortright, 1997), though the risks are lower in the context of arms control or nuclear proliferation (Barbieri, 2017). The moral hazard in cases of asymmetric conflicts is evident. Yet, positive sanctions may be implemented when the threat of sanction damage cannot be enlarged to accomplish compliance according to van Bergeijk (2009: 163–166). It is either because of historical, cultural, or political reasons that sanction's compliance is prevented while the economic aspect clearly holds the potential to be used as a source of power. Economic incentives should be the way forward instead of international powers continuing to hold the stick at both ends.

[60] UNHCR (2021) *Resolution S-30/L.1.Ensuring respect for international humanitarian law and international human rights law*, A/HRC/S-30/L.1 (26 May 2021).

7.4 The Liberal Way Forward—Summary and Conclusions

The liberal global order supports trade interdependence. Yet, it is the future trade level that is expected to determine the interdependency that should be analysed (Levy, 2003). The untapped potential has motivated the peace process in the ME region in the past, with the latest Abraham Accords and their extensions being no exception. Analysis of the trade potential in the MENA region, with a focus on the Israeli-Palestinian conflict for the year 2019 shows that this 'pot of gold' in per cent of intra-MENA trade amounts to 10 per cent to 54 per cent (import based) and 21 per cent to 48 per cent (export based), respectively. Not only is this trade potential still substantial, but furthermore, zooming in on the intra-MENA trade of individual countries in the region, a large trade potential is reported in relation to the bilateral trade between these countries and Israel, including the United Arab Emirates one of the three partners in the Abraham Accords, Morocco which the signing of the Accord paved the way for the revival of this relationship, and Saudi Arabia (Lahar, 2024). Indeed, these accords did not only come as a reaction to the lack of success of the direct peace initiative between Israel and Palestine under the 2019 *Peace to Prosperity* framework, but they also accommodated the Israeli government's strategy for promoting the peace process with Palestine.[61] The Abraham Accords marked the first step towards establishing official economic relations between the two countries Israel and Saudi Arabia (Crowley et al., 2023). However, if the Normalization Agreement with Saudi Arabia comes through, unlike the Abraham Accords, it will be the motivation for initiating the peace process as Saudi Arabia signals concessions towards the Palestinians, if not more (The Times of Israel, 2023).

Economics as the means of pressure for political change in the region has always played a significant role, especially with the Israeli-Palestinian conflict being a part of the Arab-Israeli conflict from its emergence. Furthermore, according to Hever (2010: 188), despite the disputed territory size, this territory is the nexus of three international economic interests. That is, it is where three continents meet, near the Suez Canal, and centrally located in the Middle East through which oil and natural gas flow

[61] PM Netanyahu's Speech at the United Nations General Assembly, 29 September 2014 (Netanyahu, 2014); series of interviews with US President Trump following his first term during April 2021 (Ravid, 2022: 178–179).

to the Mediterranean area. Past attempts either in the form of negative economic pressure and/or aid through international mechanisms, have proven to be ineffective and by one interviewee have even been called a 'useless exercise' in relation to their political influence.

International involvement in conflict management and even more, its resolution, is a must and not an option ('Interview I: Nabil Shaath' December, 2013). However, this involvement should take a different form than only pursuing the liberal peace only through the security-development nexus framework. The framework for achieving the liberal peace should also take into consideration the political-development nexus. Thus, it is through economic incentives, particularly positive ones that the international community should aim to explore the Pot of Gold of the MENA region, with the already established normalization of the relations with Arab countries potentially providing an additional layer of opportunity. Oslo I, however, beyond economic peace also brought another stepping stone in the form of a change in the status of conflict, laying the foundations for Palestinian statehood.

As stated by President Biden, the timing of the 7 October 2023 attack was also intended to prevent the potential normalization agreement between Israel and Saudi Arabia from coming to fruition (Reuters, 2023). While the potential normalization of these relations played a role in the timing of Hamas' surprise attack on Israel on 7 October 2023, and the subsequent Israel-Hamas War, it can also play a significant role in ending the catastrophic ongoing situation in the region. The normalization of relations between Israel and Saudi Arabia, as supported by the 2019 POG prediction analysis, has a substantial economic potential. Far beyond this economic potential, the agreement also holds promise of security and stability for the whole region (Yaari, 2018). Indeed, this agreement entails the potential to change the balance of power at all levels—the Fatah-Hamas domestic Palestinian politics, the Israeli-Palestinian conflict, and the Palestinian cause.

The geopolitical developments in the ME region from the early 2010s onwards, with the Arab Spring altering traditional power relations in the region, led to a new division of the ME countries. This larger division between radicals led by Iran, and pragmatists that are traditionally considered to be led by Egypt and Saudi Arabia, has been part of the internal Palestinian Fatah-Hamas struggle over power. The extent of external involvement in the October 2023 attack and the war to follow is yet to be uncovered and this should not be disregarded in consideration of the potential effects of the normalization agreement. In support, following the attack, leading figures of Hamas were quoted as saying that the attack came as the entire equation needed to be shifted and that the whole region would bear its consequences (Hubbard & Abi-Habib, 2023; Rubin & Warrick, 2023).

With the Oslo I Accords, not only did each side resign itself to parting with territory that until then was regarded as its patrimony and vital to its national identity, but more than that, the Palestinian Government, the PNA, was established (Shlaim, 1994). Following this, between 1993 and 2000, the emerging de facto statehood in Palestine showed positive development. In July 2000, Israeli Prime Minister Barak and Palestinian Chairman Arafat failed to reach an agreement regarding the Permanent Status Agreement, at the Camp David Summit under the auspice of President Clinton, and with the outbreak of the Second Intifada not long after, during October the Oslo process came to an end (Tschirgi, 2004). However, even if an agreement had been reached the policy parameters presented at Camp David were not necessarily sufficient for the new phase of Palestinian sovereignty that Oslo brought with it (Roy, 2002). Indeed, from an asymmetric, identity-based, deep-rooted, intractable conflict, with the establishment of the PA, the de facto statehood of Palestine was officially born. The unanimous adoption of UN Security Council Resolution 1515 (2003b)[62] re-endorsed the Quartet Road Map envisaging a Palestinian State by 2005.

The 1933 Montevideo Convention on the Rights and Duties of States defines the criteria of statehood, that is, the permanent population, defined territory, government, and the capacity to enter into relations with other states.[63] The essence of the sovereignty of the state is internal sovereignty, with the government of the state being considered as the ultimate authority within its borders and jurisdiction. Yet, as the state is not subjected to the legal power of another state or any other higher authority, and in principle stands on equal footing with other states, it also has an external sovereignty (Schrijver, 1999). Considering that in its original meaning sovereignty necessarily came from within, the issue of recognition of other

[62] UNSC (2003b) *Resolution 1515*. S/RES/1515 (19 November 2003).

[63] 'The State as a person of international law should possess the following qualifications: (a) a permanent population; (b) a defined territory; (c) government; and (d) capacity to enter into relations with the other states' (Article I Convention on the Rights and Duties of States, Montevideo, 26 December 1933).

states had no separate place in the law of nations. The issue of recognition came to the fore in the middle of the eighteenth century in regard to the unclarity about whether a revolutionary entity separating from the parent state could be treated as an independent state before its recognition by the parent state itself (Crawford, 2006: 11–12). Ever since, this has been a subject of contestation between the declaratory and constitutive theories within international law (Ker-Lindsay, 2022). Following WWII, the establishment of the new liberal world order especially from the post-colonial era, brought the issue of external sovereignty and its role in the international system to the centre of attention also of the international relations (Jackson, 1991: 40–49; Lake, 2003). Indeed, the external sovereignty, state as sovereign and status of non-state entities, have all been issues of contestation not only within international law but also between international law and international relations from the middle of the twentieth century onwards.

The European State ideal and its key concepts of sovereignty became the cornerstone of the international order (Mikhaikanin, 2004). As such the external borders of the state are those above national, denoting that unilateral changes of these borders are unacceptable (Ker-Lindsay, 2022). This principle was reflected in the Charter of the United Nations, emphasizing the non-interference in the domestic affairs of other states (UN Charter Article 2(7)).[64] [65] In the period following 1945 the decolonization process led to the creation of 96 new states. Out of that, however, 25 per cent of the total former colonial dependencies that were decolonized (32 in number[66]), failed to achieve the status of independent states at the time (Christopher, 2002). While the new states were modelled on the

[64] See Article 2(7) of the UN Charter. Bangladesh is the only country that has unilaterally declared independence since 1945 and achieved full membership in the United Nations. Kosovo, the next most successful case of unilateral secession has no prospect of being a full member of the United Nations and has been recognized by only half of the international community (Ker-Lindsay, 2022). The successful secession of Eritrea from Ethiopia in 1993 involved the UN and the international community in the transition process (UNDPI and SG Boutros-Ghali December 1996 [ST/]DPI/1850).

[65] The UN Charter provided a right to self-determination of peoples in the Preamble and Articles 1 and 55. However, the right to self-determination as defined in the UN General Assembly Resolutions 1514 and 1541 (1960) only applies to colonial peoples (Ker-Lindsay, 2022; Mikhaikanin, 2004).

[66] That is: Alaska, British Cameroon, British Somaliland, British Togoland, Canal Zone, Dodecanese, Eritrea, Fernando Poo, Fezzan, French Guiana 4 Guadeloupe, French India, Hawaii, Hong Kong, Ifni, Macau, Martinique, Newfoundland, North Borneo, Port

European ideal, their territorial basis more often than not retained the colonial borders (Axtmann, 2004), in line with the so-called *Uti possideties* principle. These borders, however, did not align with lines of nationalism (Barkin & Cronin, 1994). Thus, though many of these new states gained external recognition, they lacked the internal power capabilities (that is, negative sovereignty).[67]

On the other hand, the new sovereignty regime also led to the creation of another form of state (Pegg, 2019: 5). Many of the new states' borders were arbitrary, giving rise to entities with power capabilities, and attributes that until then had been only associated with sovereign states, Somaliland being an example, yet no external recognition (Barkin & Cronin, 1994; Clapham, 1998; Pegg & Berg, 2016). It is the sanctification of these territorial borders, together with the role of the international order in the recognition of states, that is, external sovereignty, that led to the creation of a new form of statehood (Mikhaikanin, 2004). These non-state actors operating quasi-independently with appropriate aspects of sovereign statehood, are de facto states (Florea, 2017).

The de facto states[68] are entities that control and govern a territory and its populations, receive popular support, and persist over time, without widespread recognition of their proclaimed sovereignty (Pegg, 2017).[69] The de facto state creates a space of self-rule and fulfils roles that are often considered exclusive to the state, projecting the image of sovereignty

Arthur, Portuguese India, Reunion, Sarawak, Senegal, Sikkim, Singapore, Spanish Morocco, Spanish Sahara, Tangier, Timor, Tripolitania, West New Guinea.

[67] 'Positive' and 'negative' sovereignty have been coined by Jackson (1991). States that enjoy "positive" sovereignty hold both the formal legal rights of non-intervention and other international immunities, as well as the capabilities and the wherewithal to provide political goods for its citizens as the sovereign, while states that hold 'negative' sovereignty have the external legal status of sovereign. The latter results in the creation of 'quasi-states' (that is, fragile states, failed states, least developed states).

[68] That is, unrecognized states, partially recognized states, contested states, informal states, quasi-states, pseudo-states and para-states, separatist states (Ker-Lindsay, 2012; Knotter, 2019).

[69] The definition of de facto states in the literature varies with many subtle differences regarding the time of their existence, exertion of military control and the portion of territory it is applied to, and the level of governance demonstration among others (Berg & Kursani, 2021: 5; Pegg, 2017; Florea, 2014, 2017 among others). Yet there is a consensus that these entities need to meet the essential criteria of statehood in accordance with the four principles that were laid down in the 1933 Montevideo Convention on the Rights and Duties of States: having a defined territory, a settled population, a form of governance, and the ability to enter into relations with other states (Ker-Lindsay, 2022).

(Florea, 2017). These polities represent the realm between rebellion and statecraft, as they attempt to exercise a legitimate yet illegal internal sovereignty in their designated territory (Florea, 2014, 2017). The entities act outside of the legal international framework and pose a challenge to the international system, while the majority of states and international organizations address them as illegal (Berg & Toomla, 2009). Thus, even though de facto state became the common term for these polities, from a legal perspective they do not exist. In legal terms, a state exists when the requirements laid down under the Montevideo Convention are met (Ker-Lindsay, 2022).

Though the phenomenon of the de facto states emerged following World War II, between 1955 and 1975 their number increased slowly from 2 to 13 respectively. Only later, these polities started to gain more dominance with their number reaching a peak by 1995 with a total of 28 de facto states (Florea, 2014). Despite being perceived as marginal actors in the global system (Pegg & Berg, 2016), from the 1990s onwards, largely resulting from the end of the Cold War, the de facto states have become a permanent feature of the contemporary international system (Ker-Lindsay, 2022).

The ongoing prolonged War between Russia and Ukraine, originating back in 2015 with the secessionist movement in the Donetsk and Luhansk regions, demonstrates the need to address the phenomenon of the de facto states at the international level. In regard to the Israeli-Palestinian conflict, the 1993 de facto state of Palestine, was succeeded by the emergence of the de facto state of Hamas, turning Palestine into not only the subject of contestation with the Israeli parent state but also the object of contestation of the Hamas leadership in relations to its ruling of the Gaza Strip from 2008 onwards, with which the scope of this book ends. Indeed, the international system has been nothing but lukewarm or indifferent in regard to the economic development of the OPT, as aforementioned, nor to the question of Palestine and the inalienable rights of the Palestinian people. From the dozens of resolutions adopted by a variety of UN organs and agencies, to the 2012 UNGA majority voting in support of according Palestine a *non-member observer state* (UNGA, 2012b),[70] symbolically on the same date 65

[70] UNGA (2012a) *Resolution 67/19. Status of Palestine in the United Nations* (4 December 2012); UNGA Press Release (2012b) *11317* 'General Assembly Votes overwhelmingly to Accord Palestine "Non-Member Observer State" Status in United Nations', GA/11317 Plenary (29 November 2012).

years prior the UNGA adopted the Plan of Partition (UNGA, 1947)[71] which resulted with the establishment of the State of Israel; and from granting Palestine the status of a full member state or special status in various international organizations,[72] to the 2004 International Court of Justice (ICJ) advisory opinion,[73] and to the 2023 request for an advisory opinion from the ICJ,[74] the scope of this conflict and the determints of its trajectory have never been limited to its domestic level.

Yet, much like the Russian veto paralysing the UN Security Council from taking measures against Russian aggression, the US has exercised its veto right in support of Israel, blocking draft resolutions censuring Israel. Since the adoption of Resolution 465 in 1980 (UNSC, 1980),[75] UNSC Resolution 2334, adopted on 23 December 2016 (UNSC, 2016)[76] was the only time the US abstained, allowing the condemnation of settlements construction by Israel in the OPT and demanding of its ceasing.[77] However, for the Ukraine war and the *Uniting for Peace*[78] procedure, beyond the Security Council which is the 'primus inter pares for the maintenance of peace and security', the other three key main organs of the international system, that is, the General Assembly, the International Court of Justice, and the Secretary-General have the possibility to

[71] UNGA (1947) Resolution *181 (II). Future government of Palestine-Plan of partition with Economic Union*, GA RES/181(II) (29 November 1947).

[72] For example, Palestine becoming a full member of: UNESCO, 31 October 2011 (UN, 2011; UNESCO, 2011); the International Criminal Court (ICC) 1 April 2015 (ICC, 2015) (and Palestinian Declaration Accepting the Jurisdiction of the International Criminal Court 31 December 2014) (Abusada, 2017); and the chair of the group of the 77 developing nations in 2019 following the 2018 Palestinian request for UNCTAD membership (UNGA, 2019, *Resolution 73/L.3. Chair of the Group of 77 for 2019*, A/73/L.5 (10 October 2018)).

[73] ICJ (2004) 'Legal Consequences of the Construction of a Wall in the Occupied Palestinian Territory', *Press Release No.2004/28* (9 July 2004).

[74] ICJ (2023) 'Legal Consequences arising from the Policies and Practices of Israel in the Occupied Palestinian Territory, including East Jerusalem', *Press Release No. 2023/43* (7 August 2023).

[75] UNSC (1980) *Resolution 465*. S/RES/465 (1 March 1980) on the Territories occupied by Israel.

[76] UNSC (2016) *Resolution 2334*. S/RES/2334 (23 December 2016).

[77] There have been multiple UNSC resolutions dealing with the conflict and its implications as have been discussed before as UNSC 1515, as well as many other including for example UNSC Resolutions 1397 (2002). Yet, UNSC Resolutions 465 and 2334 stand out in their affirmative language against Israel's settlements.

[78] UNGA (1950) *Resolution 377 (V) Uniting for Peace*, GA RES/377(V) (3 November 1950).

intervene in meaningful ways, in the event the Security Council fails to exercise its primary responsibility in this field (Schrijver, 2022: 13). But even more than the competencies of these three organs for the implementation of the *Uniting for Peace* procedure, a 're-uniting for peace through international law' should always be enforced. The international law being both the international value system and the concrete regulatory framework, has the potential capacity to maintain or restore international peace and security, despite the lack of adequate performance of the Security Council or the other principal organs of the UN (Schrijver, 2022: 16).

The disastrous ongoing situation in the region is far from close to being resolved. However, it also brings with it a potential opportunity depending on the road to be taken by Israel and Palestine, and perhaps at least if not more by the international community, including leading powers. For the day after to bring a positive paradigm shift in the conflict and for the bloodshed to end there is no other option than a political solution. This solution should take into consideration the economic incentives to the scale of external sovereignty. From positive sanctions to a 're-uniting' for peace through international law, the economic diplomacy toolbox of the political-development nexus should be addressed in paving the way forward in cases of asymmetricity.

Economic incentives were and remain a pivotal instrument in the political trajectory of the Middle East region, and especially that of the Middle East Peace Process, as clearly indicated by this research. Nonetheless, as Trump's 2025 declaration on reconstructing Gaza while relocating the Palestinian people clearly demonstrates that these incentives, in themselves, are not sufficient to overcome other motives and thus should be considered within the bigger political-development-security scheme.

Bibliography

Abusada, M. (2017). Palestinian diplomacy: 'Past and present'. In G. Gürbey, S. Hofmann, & F. I. Seyder (Eds.), *Between state and non-state: Politics and society in Kurdistan-Iraq and Palestine* (pp. 197–212). Palgrave Macmillan.

Alesina, A., & Dollar, D. (2000). Who gives foreign aid to whom and why? *Journal of Economic Growth, 5*, 33–63.

Arnon, A. (2007). Israeli policy towards the occupied Palestinian territories: The economic dimension, 1967–2007. *The Middle East Journal, 61*(4), 573–595.

Arnon, A., & Bamya, S. (Eds.). (2015). *Economics and politics in the Israeli Palestinian conflict*. The Aix Group.

Axtmann, R. (2004). The state of the state: The model of the modern state and its contemporary transformation. *International Political Science Review, 25*(3), 259–279.

Barak, O. (2005). The failure of the Israeli–Palestinian peace process, 1993–2000. *Journal of Peace Research, 42*(6), 719–736.

Barbieri, K. (2017). Economic incentives as weapons of war. *Oxford Research Encyclopedia of Politics.*

Barkin, J. S., & Cronin, B. (1994). The state and the nation: Changing norms and the rules of sovereignty in international relations. *International Organization, 48*(1), 107–130.

Beilin, Y. (1997). *Touching peace: From the Oslo Accord to a final agreement.* Miskal-Yedioth Ahronoth Books and Chemed Books.

Berg, E., & Kursani, S. (2021). *De facto states and land-for-peace agreements: Territory and recognition at odds?* Routledge.

Berg, E., & Toomla, R. (2009). Forms of normalisation in the quest for de facto statehood. *The International Spectator, 44*(4), 27–45.

Bouris, D. (2014). *The European Union and occupied Palestinian territories: State-building without a state.* Routledge.

Brynen, R. (2000). *A very political economy: Peacebuilding and foreign aid in the West Bank and Gaza.* US Institute of Peace Press.

Bush, G.W. (2003, April 30). The Middle East and the roadmap for peace, released by the Office of the White House Press Secretary, Washington, DC.

Christopher, A. (2002). Decolonisation without independence. *GeoJournal, 56*, 213–224.

Clapham, C. (1998). Degrees of statehood. *Review of International Studies, 24*(2), 143–157.

Cobham, D. (2001). Economic aspects of the Israeli-Palestinian conflict: Introduction. *The Economic Journal, 111*(472), 249–253.

Cortright, D. (1997). Incentives and cooperation in international affairs. In D. E. Cortright (Ed.), *The price of peace: Incentives and international conflict prevention* (pp. 3–18). Rowman & Littlefield Publishers, Inc.

Crawford, J. (2006). *The creation of states in international law.* Oxford University Press.

Crowley, M., Nereim, V., & Kingsley, P. (2023, March 9). Saudi Arabia offers its price to normalize relations with Israel. *New York Times.* Retrieved July 23, 2023, from https://www.nytimes.com/2023/03/09/us/politics/saudi-arabia-israel-united-states.html.

Demena, B. A., Reta, A. S., Jativa, G. B., Kimararungu, P. B., & van Bergeijk, P. A. G. (2021). Publication bias of economic sanctions research: A meta-analysis of the impact of trade linkage, duration and prior relations on sanctions success. In P. A. G. van Bergeijk (Ed.), *Research handbook on economic sanctions* (pp. 125–150). US Edward Elgar Publishing Limited; Edward Elgar Publishing, Inc.

Dessus, S., & Bulmer, E. R. (2004). 'The choice of trade regime depends on multiple other factors. In D. Cobham & N. M. Kanafani (Eds.), *The economics of Palestine: Economic policy and institutional reform for a viable Palestine state.* Routledge.

Diwan, I., & Shaban, R. A. (Eds.). (1999). *Development under adversity: The Palestinian economy in transition.* Palestine Economic Policy Research Institute (MAS) and the World Bank.

Dutton, J. (2021, May 26). Read letter Amazon Workers sent to Jeff Bezos urging solidarity with Palestinians. *Newsweek.* Retrieved May 31, 2021, from https://www.newsweek.com/amazon-workers-send-letter-bezos-solidarity-palestinians-1594896.

European Commission (EC). (2013, July 19). Guidelines on the eligibility of Israeli entities and their activities in the territories occupied by Israel since June 1967 for grants, prizes and financial instruments funded by the EU from 2014 onward, *Official Journal of the European Union* 2013/C 205/5.

European Commission (EC). (2014, June 17). Agreement between the European Union and the State of Israel on the participation of the State of Israel in the EU programme 'Horizon 2020—the Framework Programme for Research and Innovation (2014–2020)', *Official Journal of the European Union L.177/1.*

European Commission (EC). (2023). *Horizon 2020.* Retrieved July 10, 2023, from http://wayback.archiveit.org/12090/20220124080448/https://ec.europa.eu/programmes/horizon2020/en/what-horizon-2020.

European Parliament (EP). (2019, December 12). Ruling of the Court of Justice of the European Union on the labelling of Israeli settlement goods. *Parliamentary question - E-004388/2019.*

European Union (EU). (2017). European Join Strategy in Support of Palestine 2017–2020 towards a democratic and accountable Palestinian State.

European Union (EU). (2021). European Join Strategy in Support of Palestine 2021–2024 towards a democratic and accountable Palestinian State.

European Union (EU). (n.d.). *Palestine.* Retrieved August 5, 2020, from https://europa.eu/capacity4dev/joint-programming-tracker/palestine.

European Union (EU) and European Commission (EC). (2013, July 9). Statement by EU High Representative Catherine Ashton on the publication of guidelines on Israel and EU funding instruments, A391/13 Brussels.

Florea, A. (2014). De facto states in international politics (1945–2011): A new data set. *International Interactions, 40*(5), 788–811.

Florea, A. (2017). De facto states: Survival and disappearance (1945–2011). *International Studies Quarterly, 61*(2), 337–351.

Grinberg, L. (2007). Political economy of Kibush; an Economic strangulation envelope: Three turning points in forty years of military-economic ruling. *Teorya Vebikoret, 31*, 233–245.

Guzansky, Y. (2023, July 30). Agreement with Saudi Arabia: The ball is in Israel's court. *News 12.* Retrieved August 7, 2023, from https://www.mako.co.il/news-columns/2023_q3/Article-83a34775cb5a981026.htm.

Halbfinger, D. M., & Rasgon, A. (2021, January 20). Reassured by Biden win, Palestinians will resume cooperation with Israel. *The New York Times*. Retrieved July 7, 2023, from https://www.nytimes.com/2020/11/17/world/middleeast/israel-palestinians-security-annexation.html.

Hansen, K. F., & Borchgrevink, A. (2006). Cutting aid to promote peace and democracy? Intentions and effectiveness of aid sanctions. *The European Journal of Development Research, 18*(4), 622–641.

Hever, S. (2010). *The political economy of Israel's occupation: Repression beyond exploitation*. New York Pluto Press.

Hirschfeld, Y. (2000). *Oslo: A formula for peace*. Am-Oved.

Hirschfeld, Y. (2014). *Track-two diplomacy toward an Israeli-Palestinian solution, 1978–2014*. Woodrow Wilson Center Press.

Hubbard, B., & Abi-Habib, M. (2023, November 8). Behind Hamas bloody Gambit to create a 'Permanent' State of War. *The New York Times*. Retrieved December 20, 2023, from https://www.nytimes.com/2023/11/08/world/middleeast/hamas-israel-gaza-war.html.

International Court of Justice (ICJ). (2004, July 9). Legal consequences of the construction of a wall in the occupied Palestinian territory, *Press Release No.2004/28*. Retrieved August 18, 2023, from https://www.icj-cij.org/sites/default/files/case-related/131/131-20040709-PRE-01-00-EN.pdf.

International Court of Justice (ICJ). (2023, August 7). Legal consequences arising from the policies and practices of Israel in the occupied Palestinian territory, including East Jerusalem, *Press Release No. 2023/43*. Retrieved August 18, 2023, from https://www.icj-cij.org/sites/default/files/case-related/186/186-20230807-pre-01-00-en.pdf.

International Criminal Court (ICC). (2015, January 5). Palestine declares acceptance of ICC jurisdiction since 13 June 2014, *Press Release ICC-CPI-20150105-PR1080*. Retrieved August 18, 2023, from https://www.icc-cpi.int/news/palestine-declares-acceptance-icc-jurisdiction-13-june-2014.

'Interview I: Nabil Shaath' (2013, December). In B. Scheller, R. Wildangel, & J. Paul (Eds.), *20 years since Oslo: Palestinian perspectives. Perspectives political analyses and commentary from the Middle East & North Africa*, Issue 5, 23–29.

Jackson, R. H. (1991). *Quasi-states: Sovereignty, International relations and the Third World*. Cambridge University Press.

Jeong, J. M. (2019). Do sanction types affect the duration of economic sanctions? The case of foreign aid. *International Political Science Review, 40*(2), 231–245.

Jewish Diaspora in Tech. (2021). Jewish diaspora in tech: Letter on Google Communication and Cloud Contracts. *Google Forms*. Retrieved May 31, 2021, from https://docs.google.com/forms/d/e/1FAIpQLSck0yb4OgXJlf5N2Ap21BhW-QNTL0rigFSYsW_o09QkJO-JVbw/viewform.

Kelman, H. C. (2007). The Israeli-Palestinian peace process and its vicissitudes: Insights from attitude theory. *American Psychologist, 62*(4), 287–303.

Ker-Lindsay, J. (2012). *The foreign policy of counter secession: Preventing the recognition of contested states.* Oxford University Press.
Ker-Lindsay, J. (2022). De facto states in the 21st century. In N. Snadal (Ed.), *Oxford research encyclopedia of international studies.*
Khan, M. H. (2005). 'Security first' and its implications for a viable Palestinian state. In M. Keating, A. Le More, & R. Lowe (Eds.), *Aid, diplomacy and facts on the ground: The case of Palestine* (pp. 59–73). Royal Institute of International Affairs, Chatham House.
Khan, M. H. (2014). Learning the lessons of Oslo: State-building and freedoms in Palestine. In M. Turner & O. Shweiki (Eds.), *Decolonizing Palestinian political economy* (pp. 238–256). Palgrave Macmillan UK.
Kleiman, E. (1994). The economic provisions of the agreement between Israel and the PLO. *Israel Law Review, 28*(2–3), 347–373.
Knotter, L. (2019). The de facto Sovereignty of Unrecognised States: Towards a classical realist perspective? *Ethnopolitics, 18*(2), 119–138.
KOF Swiss Economic Institute. (2023). *Globalization index.* Retrieved August 20, 2023, from https://kof.ethz.ch/en/forecasts-and-indicators/indicators/kof-globalisation-index.html.
Lahar, L. (2024). The Political Development Nexus of economic peace in the Middle East: The Paris Protocol to the Oslo Accords, International Institute of Social Studies The Hague, of Erasmus University Rotterdam, The Netherlands.
Lake, D. A. (2003). The new sovereignty in international relations. *International Studies Review, 5*(3), 303–323.
Le More, A. (2004). Foreign aid strategy. In D. Cobham & N. Kanafani (Eds.), *The economics of Palestine: Economic policy and institutional reform for a viable Palestine state* (pp. 206–227). Routledge.
Le More, A. (2005). Killing with kindness: Funding the demise of a Palestinian state. *International Affairs, 81*(5), 981–999.
Le More, A. (2008). *International assistance to the Palestinians after Oslo: Political guilt, wasted money.* Routledge.
League of Arab States (LAS). (2002, March 28). *Summit resolution 14/221. Arab Peace Initiative.* Retrieved July 7, 2023, from https://www.un.org/unispal/document/auto-insert-181223/.
Levine, M. (1996). Palestinian economic progress under the Oslo agreements. *Fordham International Law Journal Fordham, 19*, 1393–1418.
Levy, J. S. (2003). Economic interdependence, opportunity costs, and peace. In E. D. Mansfield & B. M. Pollins (Eds.), *Economic interdependence and international conflict: New perspectives on an enduring debate* (pp. 127–147). University of Michigan Press.
Lincoln, J. B. (2022, August 31). The Middle East Peace: The Biden Administration's approach. *The RAND Blog.* Retrieved July 7, 2023, from https://www.rand.org/pubs/commentary/2022/08/middle-east-peace-the-biden-administrations-approach.html.

Lovatt, H., & Toaldo, M. (2015). EU differentiation and Israeli settlements. European Council on Foreign Relations, London.
Lundberg, K. (1999). *The Oslo channel: Getting to the negotiating table* (p. 1333). John F. Kennedy School of Government Case.
Makovsky, D. (2018). *Making peace with the PLO: The Rabin Government's road to the Oslo Accord*. Routledge.
Mikhaikanin, E. (2004). The Abkhazians A national minority in their own homeland. In T. Bahcheli, B. Bartmann, & H. Srebrnik (Eds.), *De Facto states the quest for sovereignty* (pp. 143–163). Routledge.
Ministère de L'europe et des Affaires Étrangères. (2017). Conference for peace in the Middle East. Retrieved December 26, 2022, from https://www.diplomatie.gouv.fr/en/country-files/israel-palestinian-territories/peace-process/initiative-for-the-middle-east-peace-process/article/conference-for-peace-in-the-middle-east-15-01-17/.
Netanyahu, B. (2009, June 14). Address by PM Netanyahu at Bar-Ilan University. Retrieved July 7, 2023, from https://www.gov.il/en/departments/news/address-by-pm-netanyahu-at-bar-ilan-university-14-jun-2009.
Netanyahu, B. (2014, September 29). PM Netanyahu's Speech at the United Nations General Assembly. Retrieved August 17, 2023, from https://www.gov.il/en/Departments/news/speechun290914.
Nincic, M. (2010). Getting what you want: Positive inducements in international relations. *International Security, 35*(1), 138–183.
Nincic, M. (2011). *The logic of positive engagement*. Cornell University Press.
Nincic, M. (2012). Positive incentives, positive results? Rethinking US counterproliferation policy. In E. Solingen (Ed.), *Sanctions, statecraft, and nuclear proliferation* (pp. 125–153). Cambridge University Press.
OECD. (n.d.-a). *QWIDS—Query Wizard for International Development Statistics*. Retrieved August 20, 2023, from https://stats.oecd.org/qwids.
OECD. (n.d.-b). *Israel's accession to the OECD*. Retrieved August 20, 2023, from https://www.oecd.org/israel/israelsaccessiontotheoecd.htm#.
Palestinian National Authority (PNA). (2007). *Palestinian reform and development plan 2008–2010*.
Palestinian National Authority (PNA). (2009, August). *Palestine ending the occupation, establishing the state*. Program of the Thirteenth Government.
Pegg, S. (2017). Twenty years of de facto state studies: Progress, problems, and prospects. In W. R. Thompson (Ed.), *Oxford research encyclopedia of politics*. https://doi.org/10.1093/acrefore/9780190228637.013.516.
Pegg, S. (2019). *International society and the de facto state*. Routledge.
Pegg, S., & Berg, E. (2016). Lost and found: The WikiLeaks of de facto state–great power relations. *International Studies Perspectives, 17*(3), 267–286.

Peksen, D., & Drury, A. C. (2009). Economic sanctions and political repression: Assessing the impact of coercive diplomacy on political freedoms. *Human Rights Review, 10*, 393–411.

Peres, S., & Naor, A. (1993). *The new Middle East*. Harper Element.

Pundak, R. (2013). *A ruts Hasha'i: Oslo, ha-Sipur ha-Male' [Secret Channel: Oslo, The Full Story*]. Yediot Books.

Qurei, A. (2006). *From Oslo to Jerusalem: The Palestinian story of the secret negotiations*. IB Tauris.

Ravid, B. (2022). *Trump's peace: The Abraham Accords and the reshaping of the Middle East*. Rishon LeZion, Israel, Miskal–Yedioth Ahronoth Books and Chemed Books.

Reuters. (2023, October 21). Hamas attack aimed to disrupt Saudi-Israel normalization Biden says, Washington, DC. Retrieved December 23, 2023, from https://www.reuters.com/world/middle-east/hamas-attack-aimed-disrupt-saudi-israel-normalization-biden-2023-10-20/.

Ross, L. (2014). Barriers to agreement in the asymmetric Israeli–Palestinian conflict. *Dynamics of Asymmetric Conflict, 7*(2–3), 120–136.

Roy, S. (1998). *The Palestinian economy and the Oslo process: Decline and fragmentation*. Emirates Center for Strategic Studies and Research.

Roy, S. (1999). De-development revisited: Palestinian economy and society since Oslo. *Journal of Palestine Studies, 28*(3), 64–82.

Roy, S. (2002). Why peace failed: An Oslo autopsy. *Current History, 101*(651), 8–16.

Rubin, S., & Warrick, J. (2023, November 13). Hams envisioned deeper attacks, aiming to provoke an Israeli war. *The Washington Post*. Retrieved November 30, 2023, from https://www.washingtonpost.com/national-security/2023/11/12/hamas-planning-terror-gaza-israel/.

Savir, U. (1998). *The process: 1,100 days that changed the Middle East*. Vintage.

Schrijver, N. (1999). The changing nature of state sovereignty. *British Year Book of International Law, 70*(1), 65–98.

Schrijver, N. (2022, July 1). Re-uniting for peace through international law. Valedictory Lecture, Leiden University, The Netherlands.

Shlaim, A. (1994). The Oslo Accord. *Journal of Palestine Studies, 23*(3), 24–40.

Simanovsky, N. (2011). The Fayyad Plan: Implications for the State of Israel. *Palestine-Israel Journal of Politics, Economics, and Culture, 17*(12).

Stern, M., & Öjendal, J. (2010). Mapping the security—development nexus: Conflict, complexity, cacophony, convergence? *Security Dialogue, 41*(1), 5–29.

Taghdisi-Rad, S. (2014). The economic strategies of occupation: Confining development and buying-off peace. In M. Turner & O. Shweiki (Eds.), *Decolonizing Palestinian political economy* (pp. 13–31). Springer, Palgrave Macmillan.

The Times of Israel. (2023, September 17). Israel denies report Saudis suspending normalization talks over Palestinian issue. Retrieved September 20, 2023, from https://www.timesofisrael.com/report-saudis-ask-to-suspend-normalization-talks-with-israel-over-palestinian-issue/.

The World Bank. (2021, June). *Palestinian recovery and development plan multi-donor trust fund*. Retrieved June 5, 2022, from https://www.worldbank.org/en/ programs/palestinian-recovery-and-development-program-trust-fund.

The World Bank and the United Nations Office of the Special Coordinator in the Occupied Territories (UNSCO). (1999). *The promise, the challenges, and the achievements donor investment in Palestinian development 1994–1998*. The World Bank West Bank and Gaza Resident Mission Jerusalem; United Nations Office of the Special Coordinator in the Occupied Territories, Government House, Jerusalem.

The World Bank Group. (2023). *Data bank—world development indicators*. Retrieved August 20, 2023, from https://databank.worldbank.org/source/world-development-indicators#.

Trump White House. (2020, January). *Peace to prosperity a vision to improve the lives of the Palestinian and Israeli People*. Retrieved December 5, 2020, from https://trumpwhitehouse.archives.gov/wp-content/uploads/2020/01/Peace-to-Prosperity-0120.pdf.

Tschirgi, D. (2004). Palestine 2003: The perils of de facto statehood. In T. Balicheli, B. Bartmann, & H. Srebnik (Eds.), *De Facto States the quest for sovereignty* (pp. 209–231). Routledge.

Tschirgi, N. (2006). Security and development policies: Untangling the relationship. In S. Klingebiel (Ed.), *New interfaces between security and development* (pp. 39–67). Deutsche Instiitut für Entwicklungspolitik.

Turner, M. (2014). The political economy of western aid in the occupied Palestinian territory since 1993. In M. Turner & O. Shweiki (Eds.), *Decolonizing Palestinian political economy* (pp. 32–52). Palgrave Macmillan UK.

Turner, M., & Hussein, C. (2015). *Israel-Palestine after Oslo: Mapping transformations and alternatives in a time of deepening crisis*. Taylor & Francis.

Tzur, M. (1989). The [Emergency] defence regulations, 1945. Policy Paper No. 16, The Israel Democracy Institute.

United Nations (UN). (1994, June 1). *Press Release 585|SG/SM/5298*. 'Secretary-General appoints Terje Røed Larsen of Norway as Special Coordinator in the Occupied Territories' *Statement by Secretary-General Boutros Boutros-Ghali*, SG/A/585|SG/SM/5298. Retrieved July 7, 2022, from https://www.un.org/unispal/document/auto-insert-212930/.

United Nations (UN). (2011, October 31). The United Nations Educational, Scientific and Cultural Organization (UNESCO) today voted to admit Palestine as a full member of the Paris-based agency. *UN NEWS*. Retrieved August 18, 2023, from https://news.un.org/en/story/2011/10/393562.

United Nations Committee on the Exercise of the Inalienable Rights of the Palestinian People (UN CEIRPP). (2014). *The origin and evolution of the Palestinian problem Part V (1989–2000)*. New York: United Nations, 2014.

United Nations Conference on Trade and Development (UNCTAD). (1981). Resolution *109 (V)*. Assistance to the Palestinian People (7 May–3 June 1979) TD/L.162 in *Proceedings of the United Nations Conference on Trade and Development: 5th session, Manila, 7 May–3 June 1979, Volume I: Report and annexes,* New York: United Nations, TD/269 (vol. 1), p. 210. Retrieved March 14, 2020, from https://unctad.org/system/files/official-document/td269vol1_en.pdf.

United Nations Conference on Trade and Development (UNCTAD). (1984). Resolution*146(VI)*. Assistance to the Palestinian people in *Proceedings of the United Nations Conference on Trade and Development: 6th session, Belgrade, 6 June–2 July 1983, Volume 1: Report and annexes,* TD/326 (vol. 1), p. 34. Retrieved April 16, 2020, from https://unctad.org/en/pages/gds/Assistance%20to%20the%20Palestinian%20People/CONF%2D%2DRES%2D%2D146-(VI).aspx-.

United Nations Conference on Trade and Development (UNCTAD). (2018). *Mandate of UNCTAD's Assistance to the Palestinian People mandates (2000–2018)*. Geneva: United Nations Conference on Trade and Development. Retrieved August 21, 2023, from https://unctad.org/topic/palestinian-people/APPU-Mandate.

United Nations Conference on Trade and Development (UNCTAD). (2020, August 5). *Report on UNCTAD assistance to the Palestinian people: Developments in the economy of the Occupied Palestinian Territory,* TD/B/67/5. Retrieved August 21, 2023, from https://documents-dds-ny.un.org/doc/UNDOC/GEN/G20/201/92/PDF/G2020192.pdf?OpenElement.

United Nations Economic and Social Council (UN ECOSOC). (1989, July 26). *Resolution 1989/96. Assistance to the Palestinian people,* E/RES/1989/96. Retrieved July 7, 2023, from https://documents-dds-ny.un.org/doc/UNDOC/GEN/NL3/593/85/PDF/NL359385.pdf?OpenElement.

United Nations Economic and Social Council (UN ECOSOC). (1990, July 26). *Resolution 1990/56.* Assistance to the Palestinian People, E/RES/1990/56. Retrieved July 7, 2023, from https://documents-dds-ny.un.org/doc/RESOLUTION/GEN/NR0/693/42/IMG/NR069342.pdf?OpenElement.

United Nations Economic and Social Council (UN ECOSOC). (1991, July 26). *Resolution 1991/69. Assistance to the Palestinian people,* E/RES/1991/69. Retrieved July 7, 2023, from https://documents-dds-ny.un.org/doc/RESOLUTION/GEN/NR0/721/38/IMG/NR072138.pdf?OpenElement.

United Nations Economic and Social Council (UN ECOSOC). (1992, July 31). Resolution *1992/58. Assistance to the Palestinian people,* E/RES/1992/58. Retrieved July 7, 2023, from https://documents-dds-ny.un.org/doc/RESOLUTION/GEN/NR0/015/64/IMG/NR001564.pdf?OpenElement.

United Nations Economic and Social Council (UN ECOSOC). (1993, July 30). *Resolution 1993/78. Assistance to the Palestinian people,* E/RES/1993/78. Retrieved July 7, 2023, from https://documents-dds-ny.un.org/doc/RESOLUTION/GEN/NR0/725/56/IMG/NR072556.pdf?OpenElement.

United Nations Economic and Social Council (UN ECOSOC). (1994, July 27). *Resolution 1994/29. Assistance to the Palestinian people,* E/RES/1994/29. Retrieved July 7, 2023, from https://www.un.org/unispal/document/auto-insert-188012/.

United Nations Educational Scientific and Cultural Organization (UNESCO). (2011, October 31). Palestine Admitted to UNESCO. *UNESCO TV AUD-DIT/ISS/ARC/0773.* Retrieved August 18, 2023, from https://www.unesco.org/archives/multimedia/document-2168?TSPD_101_R0=080713870fab20004c565fe65a954244d94167d06b0caa59f4409b80d980985a33da651ea9e5352d08d0ed4e1b1430001814660030d64eccac343caa30ae930ccfbafc45080aa09c9233a94647499e652201865a4637370a7951c07288582ad7.

United Nations General Assembly (UNGA). (1947, November 29). Resolution *181 (II). Future government of Palestine-Plan of partition with Economic Union,* GA RES/181(II). Retrieved April 5, 2020, from https://documents-ddsny.un.org/doc/RESOLUTION/GEN/NR0/038/88/PDF/NR003888.pdf?OpenElement; https://www.un.org/unispal/document/auto-insert-185393/.

United Nations General Assembly (UNGA). (1948, November 27). Resolution *194 (III). Palestine—Progress Report of the Unite Nations Mediator,* GA RES 194 (III). Retrieved April 17, 2020, from https://documents-dds-ny.un.org/doc/RESOLUTION/GEN/NR0/043/65/PDF/NR004365.pdf?OpenElement.

United Nations General Assembly (UNGA). (1949, December 8). Resolution *302(IV). Assistance to Palestine refugees,* GA RES/302(IV). Retrieved April 14, 2020, from https://documents-dds-ny.un.org/doc/RESOLUTION/GEN/NR0/051/39/PDF/NR005139.pdf?OpenElement.

United Nations General Assembly (UNGA). (1950, November 3). *Resolution 377 (V) Uniting for Peace,* GA RES/377(V). Retrieved July 7, 2023, from https://documents-dds-ny.un.org/doc/RESOLUTION/GEN/NR0/059/75/PDF/NR005975.pdf?OpenElement.

United Nations General Assembly (UNGA). (1989, December 22). *Resolution 44/235. Assistance to the Palestinian people,* A/RES/44/235. Retrieved August 7, 2023, from https://documents-dds-ny.un.org/doc/RESOLUTION/GEN/ NR0/549/94/IMG/NR054994.pdf?OpenElement.

United Nations General Assembly (UNGA). (1993, March 10). *Resolution 47/170. Assistance to the Palestinian People* A/RES/47/170. Retrieved August 21, 2023, from https://documents-dds-ny.un.org/doc/UNDOC/GEN / N93/149/05/IMG/N9314905.pdf?OpenElement.

United Nations General Assembly (UNGA). (1994, March 15). *Resolution 48/213. Assistance to the Palestinian people*, A/RES/48/213. Retrieved August 21, 2023, from https://documents-dds-ny.un.org/doc/UNDOC/GEN/N94/ 134/34/PDF/N9413434.pdf?OpenElement.

United Nations General Assembly (UNGA). (1998, June 23). *Report 53/153.* United Nations Economic and Social Council (UN ECOSOC) (1998) *Report 1998/75. Assistance to the Palestinian people Report of the Secretary-General*, A/53/153, E/1998/75. Retrieved June 7, 2023, from https://documents-dds-ny.un.org/doc/UNDOC/GEN/N98/190/03/PDF /N9819003.pdf?OpenElement.

United Nations General Assembly (UNGA). (2000a, January 20). *Resolution 54/39. Committee on the Exercise of the Inalienable Rights of the Palestinian People* A/RES/54/39. Retrieved July 7, 2022, from https://documents-dds-ny.un.org/doc/UNDOC/GEN/N00/236/10/PDF/N0023610.pdf?OpenElement.

United Nations General Assembly (UNGA). (2000b, January 21). *Resolution 54/40. Division of the Palestinian Rights of the Secretariat* A/RES/54/40. Retrieved August 21, 2023, from https://documents-dds-ny.un.org/doc/UNDOC /GEN/N00/236/16/PDF/N0023616.pdf?OpenElement.

United Nations General Assembly (UNGA). (2000c, July 24). *Report 53/153.* United Nations Economic and Social Council (UN ECOSOC) (2000) *Report 1998/75. Assistance to the Palestinian people Report of the Secretary-General*, A/55/137, E/2000/95 para. 10. Retrieved July 7, 2023, from https://documents-dds-ny.un.org/doc/UNDOC/GEN/N00/547/61/PDF / N0054761.pdf?OpenElement.

United Nations General Assembly (UNGA). (2012a, December 4). *Resolution 67/19. Status of Palestine in the United Nations.* Retrieved July 7, 2023, from https://documents-dds-ny.un.org/doc/UNDOC/GEN/N12/479/74/PDF /N1247974.pdf?OpenElement.

United Nations General Assembly (UNGA). (2012b, November 29). *Press Release 11317.* General Assembly Votes overwhelmingly to Accord Palestine 'Non-Member Observer State' Status in United Nations, GA/11317 Plenary. Retrieved July 7, 2023, from https://press.un.org/en/2012/ga11317.doc.htm.

United Nations General Assembly (UNGA). (2014, November 25). *Resolution 69/20. Committee on the Exercise of the Inalienable Rights of the Palestinian People*, A/RES/69/20. Retrieved August 21, 2023, from https://documents-dds-ny.un.org/doc/UNDOC/GEN/N14/652/23/PDF /N1465223.pdf?OpenElement.

United Nations General Assembly (UNGA). (2015, November 24). *Resolution 70/12. Committee on the exercise of the inalienable rights of the Palestinian People*, A/RES/70/12. Retrieved August 21, 2023, from https://documents-dds-ny.un.org/doc/UNDOC/GEN/N15/389/97/PDF /N1538997.pdf?OpenElement.

United Nations General Assembly (UNGA). (2016, November 30). *Resolution 71/20. Committee on the exercise of the inalienable rights of the Palestinian People: Resolution*, A/RES/71/20. Retrieved August 21, 2023, from https://documents-dds-ny.un.org/doc/UNDOC/GEN/N16/408/29/PDF / N1640829.pdf?OpenElement.

United Nations General Assembly (UNGA). (2017, November 30). *Resolution 72/13. Committee on the exercise of the inalienable rights of the Palestinian People: Resolution*, A/RES/72/13. Retrieved August 21, 2023, from https://documents-dds-ny.un.org/doc/UNDOC/GEN/N17/406/38/PDF / N1740638.pdf?OpenElement.

United Nations General Assembly (UNGA). (2018, November 30). *Resolution 73/18. Committee on the exercise of the inalienable rights of the Palestinian people: Resolution*, A/RES/73/18. Retrieved August 21, 2023, from https://documents-dds-ny.un.org/doc/UNDOC/GEN/N18/409/32/PDF / N1840932.pdf?OpenElement.

United Nations General Assembly (UNGA). (2019). *Resolution 73/L.3. Chair of the Group of 77 for 2019*, A/73/L.5 (10 October 2018). Retrieved August 18, 2023, from https://documents-dds-ny.un.org/doc/UNDOC/LTD/N18/316/10/PDF /N1831610.pdf?OpenElement.

United Nations General Assembly (UNGA). (2022, December 12). *Resolution 77/123. Assistance to Palestine refugees*, A/RES/77/123. Retrieved August 7, 2023, from https://documents-dds-ny.un.org/doc/UNDOC/ GEN/N22/748/25/PDF/N2274825.pdf?OpenElement.

United Nations Human Rights Council (UNHCR). (2016, March 24). *Resolution 31/36. Israeli settlements in the occupied Palestinian territory, including East Jerusalem, and in the occupied Syrian Golan*, A/HRC/RES/31/36. Retrieved May 8, 2021, from https://documents-dds-ny.un.org/doc/ UNDOC/GEN/G16/082/57/PDF/G1608257.pdf?OpenElement.

United Nations Human Rights Council (UNHCR). (2021, May 26). *Resolution S-30/L.1.Ensuring respect for international humanitarian law and international human rights law*, A/HRC/S-30/L.1. Retrieved May 31, 2021, from https://documents-dds-ny.un.org/doc/UNDOC/LTD/ G21/112/74/PDF/G2111274.pdf?OpenElement.

United Nations Security Council (UNSC). (1967, November 22). *Resolution 242. Situation in the Middle East*, S/RES/242. Retrieved May 7, 2020, from https://documents-ddsny.un.org/doc/RESOLUTION/GEN/NR0/240/94 /PDF/NR024094.pdf?OpenElement.

United Nations Security Council (UNSC). (1980, March 1). *Resolution 465*. S/RES/465. Retrieved August 18, 2023, from https://documents-dds-ny.un.org/doc/RESOLUTION/GEN/NR0/399/58/PDF/NR039958.pdf?OpenElement.

United Nations Security Council (UNSC). (2002, March 12). *Resolution 1397.* S/RES/1397. Retrieved August 20, 2023, from https://documents-dds-ny.un.org/doc/UNDOC/GEN/N02/283/59/PDF/N0228359.pdf?OpenElement.

United Nations Security Council (UNSC). (2003a, May 7). *Resolution 2003/529. A performance-based road map to a permanent two-state solution to the Israeli-Palestinian conflict*, S/RES/2003/529. Retrieved July 23, 2023, from https://documents-dds-ny.un.org/doc/UNDOC/GEN/N03/348/79/IMG /N0334879.pdf?OpenElement.

United Nations Security Council (UNSC). (2003b, November 19). *Resolution 1515.* S/RES/1515. Retrieved July 7, 2023, from https://documents-dds-ny.un.org/doc/UNDOC/GEN/N03/621/85/PDF/N0362185.pdf?OpenElement.

United Nations Security Council (UNSC). (2016, December 23). *Resolution 2334.* S/RES/2334. Retrieved August 18, 2023, from https://www.un.org/webcast/pdfs/SRES2334-2016.pdf.

United States Department of State. (2001). Archive—*The Middle East/North Africa Economic Summits and Conferences.* Retrieved August 8, 2020, from https://19972001.state.gov/regions/nea/fs_mena_econ_summ_971107.html.

UNSCO. (2023a). *UNSCO Reports.* Retrieved August 5, 2020, from https://unsco.unmissions.org/ahlc-socioeconomic-reports?page=1.

UNSCO. (2023b). *The Office of the United Nations Special Coordinator for the Middle East Peace Process–About.* Retrieved August 5, 2020, from https://unsco.unmissions.org/ahlc-socioeconomic-reports?page=1.

van Bergeijk, P. A. G. (2009). *Economic diplomacy and the geography of international trade.* Edward Elgar Publishing.

Wanis-St, J. A. (2011). *Back channel negotiation: Secrecy in the Middle East peace process.* Syracuse University Press.

Ya'alon, M. (2017). How to build Middle East peace: Why bottom-up is better than top-down. *Foreign Affairs, 96*, 73–84.

Yaari, M. (2018, July). Israel and Saudi Arabia: On the way to normalization. *Israel's relations with Arab countries: The unfulfilled potential.* MITVIM the Israeli institute for Regional Foreign Policies.

Appendices

Appendix A

Declaration of Principles on Interim Self-Government Arrangements[1]

Declaration of Principles on Interim Self-Government Arrangements

The Government of the State of Israel and the PLO team (in the Jordanian-Palestinian delegation to the Middle East Peace Conference) (the "Palestinian Delegation"), representing the Palestinian people, agree that it is time to put an end to decades of confrontation and conflict, recognize their mutual legitimate and political rights, and strive to live in peaceful coexistence and mutual dignity and security and achieve a just, lasting and comprehensive peace settlement and historic reconciliation through the agreed political process.

Accordingly, the two sides agree to the following principles:

[1] Declaration of Principles on Interim Self-Government Arrangements ISR-PA (13 September 1993), UNGA, UNSC, A/48/486, S/26560 (11 October 1993).

L. Lahar, *The Economic Diplomacy of Peace in the Middle East*,
https://doi.org/10.1007/978-3-031-93991-4

Article I: Aim of the Negotiations
The aim of the Israeli-Palestinian negotiations within the current Middle East peace process is, among other things, to establish a Palestinian Interim Self-Government Authority, the elected Council (the "Council"), for the Palestinian people in the West Bank and the Gaza Strip, for a transitional period not exceeding five years, leading to a permanent settlement based on Security Council resolutions 242 (1967) and 338 (1973). It is understood that the interim arrangements are an integral part of the whole peace process and that the negotiations on the permanent status will lead to the implementation of Security Council resolutions 242 (1967) and 338 (1973).

Article II: Framework for the Interim Period
The agreed framework for the interim period is set forth in this Declaration of Principles.

Article III: Elections
1. In order that the Palestinian people in the West Bank and Gaza Strip may govern themselves according to democratic principles, direct, free and general political elections will be held for the Council under agreed supervision and international observation, while the Palestinian police will ensure public order.

2. An agreement will be concluded on the exact mode and conditions of the elections in accordance with the protocol attached as Annex I, with the goal of holding the elections not later than nine months after the entry into force of this Declaration of Principles.

3. These elections will constitute a significant interim preparatory step toward the realization of the legitimate rights of the Palestinian people and their just requirements.

Article IV: Jurisdiction
Jurisdiction of the Council will cover West Bank and Gaza Strip territory, except for issues that will be negotiated in the permanent status negotiations. The two sides view the West Bank and the Gaza Strip as a single territorial unit, whose integrity will be preserved during the interim period.

Article V: Transitional Period and Permanent Status Negotiations

1. The five-year transitional period will begin upon the withdrawal from the Gaza Strip and Jericho area.

2. Permanent status negotiations will commence as soon as possible, but not later than the beginning of the third year of the interim period, between the Government of Israel and the Palestinian people's representatives.

3. It is understood that these negotiations shall cover remaining issues, including: Jerusalem, refugees, settlements, security arrangements, borders, relations and cooperation with other neighbours, and other issues of common interest.

4. The two parties agree that the outcome of the permanent status negotiations should not be prejudiced or preempted by agreements reached for the interim period.

Article VI: Preparatory Transfer of Powers and Responsibilities

1. Upon the entry into force of this Declaration of Principles and the withdrawal from the Gaza Strip and the Jericho area, a transfer of authority from the Israeli military government and its Civil Administration to the authorized Palestinians for this task, as detailed herein, will commence. This transfer of authority will be of a preparatory nature until the inauguration of the Council.

2. Immediately after the entry into force of this Declaration of Principles and the withdrawal from the Gaza Strip and Jericho area, with the view to promoting economic development in the West Bank and Gaza Strip, authority will be transferred to the Palestinians in the following spheres: education and culture, health, social welfare, direct taxation and tourism. The Palestinian side will commence in building the Palestinian police force, as agreed upon.

Pending the inauguration of the Council, the two parties may negotiate the transfer of additional powers and responsibilities, as agreed upon.

Article VII: Interim Agreement

1. The Israeli and Palestinian delegations will negotiate an agreement on the interim period (the "Interim Agreement").

2. The Interim Agreement shall specify, among other things, the structure of the Council, the number of its members, and the transfer of powers and responsibilities from the Israeli military government and its Civil

Administration to the Council. The Interim Agreement shall also specify the Council's executive authority, legislative authority in accordance with Article IX below, and the independent Palestinian judicial organs.

3. The Interim Agreement shall include arrangements, to be implemented upon the inauguration of the Council, for the assumption by the Council of all of the powers and responsibilities transferred previously in accordance with Article VI above.

4. In order to enable the Council to promote economic growth, upon its inauguration, the Council will establish, among other things, a Palestinian Electricity Authority, a Gaza Sea Port Authority, a Palestinian Development Bank, a Palestinian Export Promotion Board, a Palestinian Environmental

Authority, a Palestinian Land Authority and a Palestinian Water Administration Authority and any other Authorities agreed upon, in accordance with the Interim Agreement, that will specify their powers and responsibilities.

5. After the inauguration of the Council, the Civil Administration will be dissolved, and the Israeli military government will be withdrawn.

Article VIII: Public Order and Security

In order to guarantee public order and internal security for the Palestinians of the West Bank and the Gaza Strip, the Council will establish a strong police force, while Israel will continue to carry the responsibility for defending against external threats, as well as the responsibility for overall security of Israelis for the purpose of safeguarding their internal security and public order.

Article IX: Laws and Military Orders

1. The Council will be empowered to legislate, in accordance with the Interim Agreement, within all authorities transferred to it.

2. Both parties will review jointly laws and military orders presently in force in remaining spheres.

Article X: Joint Israeli-Palestinian Liaison Committee

In order to provide for a smooth implementation of this Declaration of Principles and any subsequent agreements pertaining to the interim period, upon the entry into force of this Declaration of Principles, a Joint Israeli-Palestinian Liaison Committee will be established in order to deal with issues requiring coordination, other issues of common interest and disputes.

Article XI: Israeli-Palestinian Cooperation in Economic Fields
Recognizing the mutual benefit of cooperation in promoting the development of the West Bank, the Gaza Strip and Israel, upon the entry into force of this Declaration of Principles, an Israeli-Palestinian Economic Cooperation Committee will be established in order to develop and implement in a cooperative manner the programmes identified in the protocols attached as Annex III and Annex IV.

Article XII: Liaison and Cooperation with Jordan and Egypt
The two parties will invite the Governments of Jordan and Egypt to participate in establishing further liaison and cooperation arrangements between the Government of Israel and the Palestinian representatives, on the one hand, and the Governments of Jordan and Egypt, on the other hand, to promote cooperation between them. These arrangements will include the constitution of a Continuing Committee that will decide by agreement on the modalities of admission of persons displaced from the West Bank and Gaza Strip in 1967, together with necessary measures to prevent disruption and disorder. Other matters of common concern will be dealt with by this Committee.

Article XIII: Redeployment of Israeli Forces
1. After the entry into force of this Declaration of Principles, and not later than the eve of elections for the Council, a redeployment of Israeli military forces in the West Bank and the Gaza Strip will take place, in addition to withdrawal of Israeli forces carried out in accordance with Article XIV.

2. In redeploying its military forces, Israel will be guided by the principle that its military forces should be redeployed outside populated areas.

3. Further redeployments to specified locations will be gradually implemented commensurate with the assumption of responsibility for public order and internal security by the Palestinian police force pursuant to Article VIII above.

Article XIV: Israeli Withdrawal from the Gaza Strip and Jericho Area
Israel will withdraw from the Gaza Strip and Jericho area, as detailed in the protocol attached as Annex II.

Article XV: Resolution of Disputes
1. Disputes arising out of the application or interpretation of this Declaration of Principles, or any subsequent agreements pertaining to the interim period, shall be resolved by negotiations through the Joint Liaison Committee to be established pursuant to Article X above.

2. Disputes which cannot be settled by negotiations may be resolved by a mechanism of conciliation to be agreed upon by the parties.

3. The parties may agree to submit to arbitration disputes relating to the interim period, which cannot be settled through conciliation. To this end, upon the agreement of both parties, the parties will establish an Arbitration Committee.

Article XVI: Israeli-Palestinian Cooperation Concerning Regional Programmes
Both parties view the multilateral working groups as an appropriate instrument for promoting a "Marshall Plan", the regional programmes and other programmes, including special programmes for the West Bank and Gaza Strip, as indicated in the protocol attached as Annex IV.

Article XVII: Miscellaneous Provisions
1. This Declaration of Principles will enter into force one month after its signing.

2. All protocols annexed to this Declaration of Principles and Agreed Minutes pertaining thereto shall be regarded as an integral part hereof.

DONE at Washington, D.C., this thirteenth day of September 1993.

For the Government of Israel:	For the PLO:
(Signed) Shimon PERES	(Signed) Mahmud ABBAS

Witnessed By:

The United States of America	The Russian Federation
(Signed) Warren CHRISTOPHER	(Signed) Andrei V. KOZYRE

Annex I: Protocol on the Mode and Conditions of Elections
1. Palestinians of Jerusalem who live there will have the right to participate in the election process, according to an agreement between the two sides.

2. In addition, the election agreement should cover, among other things, the following issues:

(a) The system of elections;

(b) The mode of the agreed supervision and international observation and their personal composition;
(c) Rules and regulations regarding election campaigns, including agreed arrangements for the organizing of mass media, and the possibility of licensing a broadcasting and television station.

3. The future status of displaced Palestinians who were registered on
4. June 1967 will not be prejudiced because they are unable to participate in the election process owing to practical reasons.

Annex II: Protocol on Withdrawal of Israeli Forces from the Gaza Strip and Jericho Area

1. The two sides will conclude and sign within two months from the date of entry into force of this Declaration of Principles an agreement on the withdrawal of Israeli military forces from the Gaza Strip and Jericho area. This agreement will include comprehensive arrangements to apply in the Gaza Strip and the Jericho area subsequent to the Israeli withdrawal.

2. Israel will implement an accelerated and scheduled withdrawal of Israeli military forces from the Gaza Strip and Jericho area, beginning immediately with the signing of the agreement on the Gaza Strip and Jericho area and to be completed within a period not exceeding four months after the signing of this agreement.

3. The above agreement will include, among other things:
(a) Arrangements for a smooth and peaceful transfer of authority from the Israeli military government and its Civil Administration to the Palestinian representatives;
(b) Structure, powers and responsibilities of the Palestinian authority in these areas, except: external security, settlements, Israelis, foreign relations and other mutually agreed matters;
(c) Arrangements for the assumption of internal security and public order by the Palestinian police force consisting of police officers recruited locally and from abroad (holding Jordanian passports and Palestinian documents issued by Egypt). Those who will participate in the Palestinian police force coming from abroad should be trained as police and police officers;
(d) A temporary international or foreign presence, as agreed upon;
(e) Establishment of a joint Palestinian-Israeli Coordination and Cooperation Committee for mutual security purposes;

(f) An economic development and stabilization programme including the establishment of an Emergency Fund, to encourage foreign investment and financial and economic support. Both sides will coordinate and cooperate jointly and unilaterally with regional and international parties to support these aims;

(g) Arrangements for a safe passage for persons and transportation between the Gaza Strip and Jericho area.

4. The above agreement will include arrangements for coordination between both parties regarding passages:

(a) Gaza–Egypt;

(b) Jericho–Jordan.

5. The offices responsible for carrying out the powers and responsibilities of the Palestinian authority under this Annex II and Article VI of the Declaration of Principles will be located in the Gaza Strip and in the Jericho area pending the inauguration of the Council.

6. Other than these agreed arrangements, the status of the Gaza Strip and Jericho area will continue to be an integral part of the West Bank and Gaza Strip, and will not be changed in the interim period.

Annex III: Protocol on Israeli-Palestinian Cooperation in Economic and Development Programmes

The two sides agree to establish an Israeli-Palestinian Continuing Committee for Economic Cooperation, focusing, among other things, on the following:

1. Cooperation in the field of water, including a Water Development Programme prepared by experts from both sides, which will also specify the mode of cooperation in the management of water resources in the West Bank and Gaza Strip, and will include proposals for studies and plans on water rights of each party, as well as on the equitable utilization of joint water resources for implementation in and beyond the interim period.

2. Cooperation in the field of electricity, including an Electricity Development Programme, which will also specify the mode of cooperation for the production, maintenance, purchase and sale of electricity resources.

3. Cooperation in the field of energy, including an Energy Development Programme, which will provide for the exploitation of oil and gas for industrial purposes, particularly in the Gaza Strip and in the Negev, and will encourage further joint exploitation of other energy resources. This Programme may also provide for the construction of a petrochemical industrial complex in the Gaza Strip and the construction of oil and gas pipelines.

4. Cooperation in the field of finance, including a Financial Development and Action Programme for the encouragement of international investment in the West Bank and the Gaza Strip, and in Israel, as well as the establishment of a Palestinian Development Bank.

5. Cooperation in the field of transport and communications, including a Programme, which will define guidelines for the establishment of a Gaza Sea Port Area, and will provide for the establishing of transport and communications lines to and from the West Bank and the Gaza Strip to Israel and to other countries. In addition, this Programme will provide for carrying out the necessary construction of roads, railways, communications lines, etc.

6. Cooperation in the field of trade, including studies, and Trade Promotion Programmes, which will encourage local, regional and inter-regional trade, as well as a feasibility study of creating free trade zones in the Gaza Strip and in Israel, mutual access to these zones and cooperation in other areas related to trade and commerce.

7. Cooperation in the field of industry, including Industrial Development Programmes, which will provide for the establishment of joint Israeli-Palestinian Industrial Research and Development Centres, will promote Palestinian-Israeli joint ventures, and provide guidelines for cooperation in the textile, food, pharmaceutical, electronics, diamonds, computer and science-based industries.

8. A Programme for cooperation in, and regulation of, labour relations and cooperation in social welfare issues.

9. A Human Resource Development and Cooperation Plan, providing for joint Israeli-Palestinian workshops and seminars, and for the establishment of joint vocational training centres, research institutes and data banks.

10. An Environmental Protection Plan, providing for joint and/or coordinated measures in this sphere.

11. A Programme for developing coordination and cooperation in the field of communications and media.

12. Any other programmes of mutual interest.

Annex IV: Protocol on Israeli-Palestinian Cooperation Concerning Regional Development Programmes

1. The two sides will cooperate in the context of the multilateral peace efforts in promoting a Development Programme for the region, including the West Bank and the Gaza Strip, to be initiated by the Group of Seven. The parties will request the Group of Seven to seek the participation in this Programme of other interested States, such as members of the Organisation for Economic Cooperation and Development, regional Arab States and institutions, as well as members of the private sector.

2. The Development Programme will consist of two elements:
   - (a) An Economic Development Programme for the West Bank and the Gaza Strip;
   - (b) A Regional Economic Development Programme.
     - A. The Economic Development Programme for the West Bank and the Gaza Strip will consist of the following elements:
       - (1) A Social Rehabilitation Programme, including a Housing and Construction Programme;
       - (2) A Small and Medium Business Development Plan;
       - (3) An Infrastructure Development Programme (water, electricity, transportation and communications, etc.);
       - (4) A Human Resources Plan;
       - (5) Other programmes.
     - B. The Regional Economic Development Programme may consist of the following elements:
       - (1) The establishment of a Middle East Development Fund, as a first step, and a Middle East Development Bank, as a second step;
       - (2) The development of a joint Israeli-Palestinian-Jordanian Plan for coordinated exploitation of the Dead Sea area;
       - (3) The Mediterranean Sea (Gaza)–Dead Sea Canal;
       - (4) Regional desalinization and other water development projects;

(5) A regional plan for agricultural development, including a coordinated regional effort for the prevention of desertification;
(6) Interconnection of electricity grids;
(7) Regional cooperation for the transfer, distribution and industrial exploitation of gas, oil and other energy resources;
(8) A Regional Tourism, Transportation and Telecommunications Development Plan;
(9) Regional cooperation in other spheres.

3. The two sides will encourage the multilateral working groups and will coordinate towards their success. The two parties will encourage intersessional activities, as well as pre-feasibility and feasibility studies, within the various multilateral working groups.

Agreed Minutes to the Declaration of Principles on Interim Self-Government Arrangements

A. General Understandings and Agreements

Any powers and responsibilities transferred to the Palestinians pursuant to the Declaration of Principles prior to the inauguration of the Council will be subject to the same principles pertaining to Article IV, as set out in these Agreed Minutes below.

B. Specific Understandings and Agreements

<u>Article IV</u>

It is understood that:

1. Jurisdiction of the Council will cover West Bank and Gaza Strip territory, except for issues that will be negotiated in the permanent status negotiations: Jerusalem, settlements, military locations and Israelis.

2. The Council's jurisdiction will apply with regard to the agreed powers, responsibilities, spheres and authorities transferred to it.

<u>Article VI (2)</u>

It is agreed that the transfer of authority will be as follows:

1. The Palestinian side will inform the Israeli side of the names of the authorized Palestinians who will assume the powers, authorities and responsibilities that will be transferred to the Palestinians according to the

Declaration of Principles in the following fields: education and culture, health, social welfare, direct taxation, tourism and any other authorities agreed upon.

2. It is understood that the rights and obligations of these offices will not be affected.

3. Each of the spheres described above will continue to enjoy existing budgetary allocations in accordance with arrangements to be mutually agreed upon. These arrangements also will provide for the necessary adjustments required in order to take into account the taxes collected by the direct taxation office.

4. Upon the execution of the Declaration of Principles, the Israeli and Palestinian delegations will immediately commence negotiations on a detailed plan for the transfer of authority on the above offices in accordance with the above understandings.

Article VII (2)

The Interim Agreement will also include arrangements for coordination and cooperation.

Article VII (5)

The withdrawal of the military government will not prevent Israel from exercising the powers and responsibilities not transferred to the Council.

Article VIII

It is understood that the Interim Agreement will include arrangements for cooperation and coordination between the two parties in this regard. It is also agreed that the transfer of powers and responsibilities to the Palestinian police will be accomplished in a phased manner, as agreed in the Interim Agreement.

Article X

It is agreed that, upon the entry into force of the Declaration of Principles, the Israeli and Palestinian delegations will exchange the names of the individuals designated by them as members of the Joint Israeli-Palestinian Liaison Committee. It is further agreed that each side will have an equal number of members in the Joint Committee. The Joint Committee will reach decisions by agreement. The Joint Committee may add other technicians and experts, as necessary. The Joint Committee will decide on the frequency and place or places of its meetings.

Annex II

It is understood that, subsequent to the Israeli withdrawal, Israel will continue to be responsible for external security, and for internal security and public order of settlements and Israelis. Israeli military forces and civilians may continue to use roads freely within the Gaza Strip and the Jericho area.

DONE at Washington, D.C., this thirteenth day of September 1993.

For the Government of Israel:	For the PLO:
(Signed) Shimon PERES	(Signed) Mahmud ABBAS

Witnessed By:

The United States of America	The Russian Federation
(Signed) Warren CHRISTOPHER	(Signed) Andrei V. KOZYREV

Appendix B

Paris Protocol[2]

Protocol on Economic Relations
between
the Government of the State of Israel
and
the P.L.O., representing the Palestinian people

Preamble

The two parties view the economic domain as one of the cornerstone in their mutual relations with a view to enhance their interest in the achievement of a just, lasting and comprehensive peace. Both parties shall cooperate in this field in order to establish a sound economic base for these relations, which will be governed in various economic spheres by the principles of mutual respect of each other's economic interests, reciprocity, equity and fairness.

This protocol lays the groundwork for strengthening the economic base of the Palestinian side and for exercising its right of economic decision-making in accordance with its own development plan and priorities. The two parties recognise each other's economic ties with other markets and the need to create a better economic environment for their peoples and individuals.

[2] *The Protocol on Economic Relations between the Government of the States of Israel and the P.L.O., representing the Palestinian people* (29 April 1994), UNGA, UNSC, A/49/180, S/1994/727 (4 May 1994).

Article I: Framework and Scope of this Protocol

1. This protocol establishes the contractual agreement that will govern the economic relations between the two sides and will cover the West Bank and the Gaza Strip during the interim period. The implementation will be according to the stages envisaged in the Declaration of Principles on Interim Self Government Arrangements signed in Washington D.C. on September 13, 1993 and the Agreed Minutes thereto. It will therefore begin in the Gaza Strip and the Jericho Area and at a later stage will also apply to the rest of the West Bank, according to the provisions of the Interim Agreement and to any other agreed arrangements between the two sides.

2. This Protocol, including its Appendixes, will be incorporated into the Agreement on the Gaza Strip and the Jericho Area (in this Protocol—the Agreement), will be an integral part thereof and interpreted accordingly. This paragraph refers solely to the Gaza Strip and the Jericho Area.

3. This Protocol will come into force up on the signing of the Agreement.

4. For the purpose of this Protocol, the term "Areas" means the areas under the jurisdiction of the Palestinian Authority, according to the provisions of the Agreement regarding territorial jurisdiction. The Palestinian Jurisdiction in the subsequent agreements could cover areas, spheres or functions according to the Interim Agreement. Therefore, for the purpose of this Protocol, whenever applied, the term "Areas" shall be interpreted to mean functions and spheres also, as the case may be, with the necessary adjustments.

Article II: The Joint Economic Committee

1. Both parties will establish a Palestinian-Israeli Joint Economic Committee (hereinafter – the JEC) to follow up the implementation of this Protocol and to decide on problems related to it that may arise from time to time. Each side may request the review of any issue related to this Agreement by the JEC.

2. The JEC will serve as the continuing committee for economic cooperation envisaged in Annex III of the Declaration of Principles.

3. The JEC will consist of an equal number of members from each side and may establish sub-committees specified in this Protocol. A sub-committee may include experts as necessary.

4. The JEC and its sub-committees shall reach their decisions by agreement and shall determine their rules of procedure and operation, including the frequency and place or places of their meetings.

Article III: Import Taxes and Import Policy

1. The import and customs policies of both sides will be according to the principles and arrangements detailed in this Article.

2. a. The Palestinian Authority will have all powers and responsibilities in the sphere of import and customs policy and procedures with regard to the following:

(1) Goods on List Al, attached hereto as Appendix I locally-produced in Jordan and in Egypt particularly and in the other Arab countries, which the Palestinians will be able to import in quantities agreed upon by the two sides up to the Palestinian market needs as estimated according to para 3 below.

(2) Goods on List A2, attached hereto as Appendix II, from the Arab, Islamic and other countries, which the Palestinians will be able to import in quantities agreed upon by the two sides up to the Palestinian market needs as estimated according to para 3 below.

b. The import policy of the Palestinian Authority for Lists Al and A2 will include independently determining and changing from time to time the rates of customs, purchase tax, levies, excises and other charges, the regulation of licensing requirements and procedures and of standard requirements. The valuation for custom purposes will be based upon the GATT 1994 agreement as of the date it will be introduced in Israel, and until then—on the Brussels Definition of Valuation (BDV) system. The classification of goods will be based on the principles of "the Harmonized Commodity Description and Coding System". Concerning imports referred to in Article VII of this Protocol (Agriculture), the provisions of that Article will apply.

3. For the purposes of para 2(a) above, the Palestinian market needs for 1994 will be estimated by a sub-committee of experts. These estimates will be based on the best available data regarding past consumption, production, investment and external trade of the Areas. The sub-committee will submit its estimate within three months from the signing of the Agreement. These estimates will be reviewed and updated every six months by the

sub-committee, on the basis of the best data available regarding the latest period for which relevant data are available, taking into consideration all relevant economic and social indicators. Pending an agreement on the Palestinian market needs, the previous period's estimates adjusted for population growth and rise in per-capita GNP in the previous period, will serve as provisional estimate.

4. The Palestinian Authority will have all powers and responsibilities to independently determine and change from time to time the rates of customs, purchase taxes; levies, excises and other charges on the goods on List B, attached hereto as Appendix III, of basic food items and other goods for the Palestinian economic development program, imported by the Palestinians to the Areas.

5. a. With respect to all goods not specified in Lists Al, A2 and B, and with respect to quantities exceeding those determined in accordance with paras 2(a) & 3 above (hereinafter—the Quantities), the Israeli rates of customs, purchase tax, levies, excises and other charges, prevailing at the date of signing of the Agreement, as changed from time to time, shall serve as the minimum basis for the Palestinian Authority. The Palestinian Authority may decide on any upward changes in the rates on these goods and exceeding quantities when imported by the Palestinians to the Areas.

b. With respect to all goods not specified in Lists A1 and A2, and with respect to quantities exceeding the Quantities, Israel and the Palestinian Authority will employ for all imports the same system of importation, as stipulated in para 10 below, including inter alia standards, licensing, country of origin, valuation for customs purposes etc.

6. Each side will notify the other side immediately of changes made in rates and in other matters of import policy, regulations and procedures, determined by it within its respective powers and responsibilities as detailed in this Article. With regard to changes which do not require immediate application upon decision, there will be a process of advance notifications and mutual consultations which will take into consideration all aspects and economic implications.

7. The Palestinian Authority will levy VAT at one rate on both locally produced goods and services and on imports by the Palestinians (whether covered by the three Lists mentioned above or not), and may fix it at the level of 15% to 16%.

8. Goods imported from Jordan, Egypt and other Arab countries according to para 2(a)(1) above (List Al) will comply with rules of origin agreed upon by a joint sub-committee within three months of the date of the signing of the Agreement. Pending an agreement, goods will be considered to have been "locally produced" in any of those countries if they conform with all the following:

(i) They have been wholly grown, produced, or manufactured in that country, or have been substantially transformed there into new or different goods, having a new name, character, or use, distinct from the goods or materials from which they were so transformed;

(ii) They have been imported directly from the said country;

(iii) The value or the costs of the materials produced in that country, plus the direct processing costs in it, do not fall short of 30 percent of the export value of the goods. This rate may be reviewed by the joint committee mentioned in para 16 a year after the signing of the Agreement.

(iv) The goods are accompanied by an internationally recognized certificate of origin;

(v) No goods will be deemed as substantially new or different goods, and no material will be eligible for inclusion as domestic content, by virtue of having merely undergone simple combining or packaging, or dilution with water or other substances, which do not materially alter the characteristics of the said goods.

9. Each side will issue import licences to its own importers, subject to the principles of this Article and will be responsible for the implementation of the licensing requirements and procedures prevailing at the time of the issuance of the licenses. Mutual arrangements will be made for the exchange of information relevant to licensing matters.

10. Except for the goods on Lists Al and A2 and their Quantities—in which the Palestinian Authority has all powers and responsibilities, both sides will maintain the same import policy (except for rates of import taxes and other charges for goods in List B) and regulations including classification, valuation and other customs procedures, which are based on the principles governing international codes, and the same policies of import licensing and of standards for imported goods, all as applied by Israel with respect to its importation. Israel may from time to time introduce changes in any of the above, provided that changes in standard requirements will not constitute a non-tariff-barrier and will be based on considerations of

health, safety and the protection of the environment in conformity with Article 2.2. of the Agreement on Technical Barriers to trade of the Final Act of the Uruguay Round of Trade Negotiations. Israel will give the Palestinian Authority prior notice of any such changes, and the provisions of para 6 above will apply.

11. a. The Palestinian Authority will determine its own rates of customs and Purchase tax on motor vehicles imported as such, to be registered with the Palestinian Authority. The vehicle standards will be those applied at the date of the signing of the Agreement as changed according to para 10 above. However, the Palestinian Authority may request, through the sub-committee on transportation, that in special cases different standards will apply. Used motor vehicles will be imported only if they are passenger cars or dual-purpose passenger cars of a model of no more than three years prior to the importation year. The sub-committee on transportation will determine the procedures for testing and confirming that such used cars comply with the standards' requirements for that model year. The issue of importing commercial vehicles of a model prior to the importation year will be discussed in the joint sub-committee mentioned in para 16 below.

b. Each side may determine the terms and conditions for the transfer of motor vehicles registered in the other side to the ownership or use of a resident of its own side, including the payment of the difference of import taxes, if any, and the vehicle having been tested and found compatible with the standards required at that time by its own registration administration, and may prohibit transfer of vehicles.

12. a. Jordanian standards, as specified in the attached Appendix I, will be acceptable in importing petroleum products into the Areas, once they meet the average of the standards existing in the European Union countries, or the USA standards, which parameters have been set at the values prescribed for the geographical conditions of Israel, the Gaza Strip and the West Bank. Cases of petroleum products which do not meet these specifications will be referred to a joint experts' committee for a suitable solution. The committee may mutually decide to accept different standards for the importation of gasoline which meet the Jordanian standards even though, in some of their parameters, they do not meet the European Community or USA standards. The committee will give its decision within six months. Pending the committee's decision, and for not longer than six months of the signing of the Agreement, the Palestinian Authority may

import to the Areas, gasoline for the Palestinian market in the Areas, according to the needs of this market, provided that:

(1) this gasoline is marked in a distinctive colour to differentiate it from the gasoline marketed in Israel; and

(2) the Palestinian Authority will take all the necessary steps to ensure that this gasoline is not marketed in Israel.

b. The difference in the final price of gasoline to consumers in Israel and to consumers in the Areas, will not exceed 15% of the official final consumer price in Israel. The Palestinian Authority has the right to determine the prices of petroleum products, other than gasoline, for consumption in the Areas.

c. If Egyptian gasoline standards will comply with the conditions of sub-para (a) above, the importation of Egyptian gasoline will also be allowed.

13. In addition to the points of exit and entry designated according to the Article regarding Passages in Annex I of the Agreement for the purpose of export and import of goods, the Palestinian side has the right to use all points of exit and entry in Israel designated for that purpose. The import and export of the Palestinians through the points of exit and entry in Israel will be given equal trade and economic treatment.

14. In the entry points of the Jordan River and the Gaza Strip:

a. Freight shipment

The Palestinian Authority will have full responsibility and powers in the Palestinian customs points (freight-area) for the implementation of the agreed upon customs and importation policy as specified in this protocol, including the inspection and the collection of taxes and other charges, when due.

Israeli customs officials will be present and will receive from the Palestinian customs officials a copy of the necessary relevant documents related to the specific shipment and will be entitled to ask for inspection in their presence of both goods and tax collection.

The Palestinian customs officials will be responsible for the handling of the customs procedure including the inspection and collection of due taxes.

In case of disagreement on the clearance of any shipment according to this Article, the shipment will be delayed for inspection for a maximum period of 48 hours during which a joint sub-committee will resolve the issue on the basis of the relevant provisions of this Article. The shipment will be released only upon the sub-committee's decision.

b. Passengers customs lane

Each side will administer its own passengers customs procedures, including inspection and tax collection. The inspection and collection of taxes due in the Palestinian customs lane will be conducted by customs officials of the Palestinian Authority.

Israeli customs officials will be invisibly present in the Palestinian customs lane and entitled to request inspection of goods and collection of taxes when due. In the case of suspicion, the inspection will be carried out by the Palestinian official in a separate room in the presence of the Israeli customs official.

15. The clearance of revenues from all import taxes and levies, between Israel and the Palestinian Authority, will be based on the principle of the place of final destination. In addition, these tax revenues will be allocated to the Palestinian Authority even if the importation was carried out by Israeli importers when the final destination explicitly stated in the import documentation is a corporation registered by the Palestinian Authority and conducting business activity in the Areas. This revenue clearance will be effected within six working days from the day of collection of the said taxes and levies.

16. The Joint Economic Committee or a sub-committee established by it for the purposes of this Article will deal inter alia with the following:

1. Palestinian proposals for addition of items to Lists Al, A2 and B. Proposals for changes in rates and in import procedures, classification, standards and licensing requirements for all other imports;
2. Estimate the Palestinian market needs, as mentioned in para 3 above;
3. Receive notifications of changes and conduct consultations, as mentioned in para 6 above;
4. Agree upon the rules of origin as mentioned in para 8 above, and review their implementation;
5. Coordinate the exchange of information relevant to licensing matters as mentioned in para 9 above;
6. Discuss and review any other matters concerning the implementation of this Article and resolve problems arising therefrom.

17. The Palestinian Authority will have the right to exempt the Palestinian returnees who will be granted permanent residency in the Areas from import taxes on personal belongings including house appliances and passenger cars as long as they are for personal use.

18. The Palestinian Authority will develop its system for temporary entry of needed machines and vehicles used for the Palestinian Authority and the Palestinian economic development plan.

Concerning other machines and equipment, not included in Lists Al, A2 and B, the temporary entry will be part of the import policy as agreed in para 10 above, until the joint sub-committee mentioned in para 16 decides upon a new system proposed by the Palestinian Authority. The temporary entry will be coordinated through the joint sub-committee.

19. Donations in kind to the Palestinian Authority will be exempted from customs and other import taxes if destined and used for defined development projects or non-commercial humanitarian purposes. The Palestinian Authority will be responsible exclusively for planning and management of the donors' assistance to the Palestinian people. The Joint Economic Committee will discuss issues pertaining to the relations between the provisions in this Article and the implementation of the principles in the above paragraph.

Article IV: Monetary and Financial Issues

1. The Palestinian Authority will establish a Monetary Authority (PMA) in the Areas. The PMA will have the powers and responsibilities for the regulation and implementation of the monetary policies within the functions described in this Article.

2. The PMA will act as the Palestinian Authority's official economic and financial advisor.

3. The PMA will act as the Palestinian Authority's and the public sector entities' sole financial agent, locally and internationally.

4. The foreign currency reserves (including gold) of the Palestinian Authority and all Palestinian public sector entities will be deposited solely with the PMA and managed by it.

5. The PMA will act as the lender of last resort for the banking system in the Areas.

6. The PMA will authorize foreign exchange dealers in the Areas and will exercise control (regulation and supervision) over foreign exchange transactions within the Areas and with the rest of the world.

7. a. The PMA will have a banking supervision department that will be responsible for the proper functioning, stability, solvency and liquidity of the banks operating in the Areas.

b. The banking supervision department will predicate its supervision on the international principles and standards reflected in international conventions and especially on the principles of the "Basle Committee".

c. The supervision department will be charged with the general supervision of every such bank, including: –The regulation of all kinds of banking activities, including their foreign activities; –The licensing of banks formed locally and of branches, subsidiaries, joint ventures and representative offices of foreign banks and the approval of controlling shareholders; –The supervision and inspection of banks.

8. The PMA will relicense each of the five branches of the Israeli banks operating at present in the Gaza Strip and the West Bank, as soon as its location or the authorities regarding it come under the jurisdiction of the Palestinian Authority. These branches will be required to comply with the general rules and regulations of the PMA concerning foreign banks, based on the "Basle Concordat". Para I0 d, e, and f below will apply to these branches.

9. a. Any other Israeli bank wishing to open a branch or a subsidiary in the Areas will apply for a license to the PMA and will be treated equally to other foreign banks, provided that the same will apply to the Palestinian banks wishing to open a branch or a subsidiary in Israel.

b. Granting of a license by both authorities will be subject to the following arrangements based on the "Basle Concordat" valid on the date of signing of the Agreement and to the host authority's prevailing general rules and regulations concerning opening of branches and subsidiaries of foreign banks.

In this para 10 "host authority" and "home authority" apply only to the Bank of Israel (BOI) and the PMA.

c. A bank wishing to open a branch or establish a subsidiary will apply to the host authority, having first obtained the approval of its home authority. The host authority will notify the home authority of the terms of the license, and will give its final approval unless the home authority objects.

d. The home authority will be responsible for the consolidated and comprehensive supervision of banks, inclusive of branches and subsidiaries in the area under the jurisdiction of the host authority. However, the distribution of supervision responsibilities between the home and the host authorities concerning subsidiaries will be according to the "Basle Concordat".

e. The host authority will regularly examine the activities of branches and subsidiaries in the area under its jurisdiction. The home authority will have the right to conduct on site examinations in the branches and subsidiaries in the host area. However, the supervision responsibilities of the home authority concerning subsidiaries will be according to the "Basle Concordat".

Accordingly, each authority will transfer to the other authority copies of its examination reports and any information relevant to the solvency, stability and soundness of the banks, their branches and subsidiaries.

f. The BOI and the PMA will establish a mechanism for cooperation and for the exchange of information on issues of mutual interest.

10. a. The New Israeli Sheqel (NIS) will be one of the circulating currencies in the Areas and will legally serve there as means of payment for all purposes including official transactions. Any circulating currency, including the NIS, will be accepted by the Palestinian Authority and by all its institutions, local authorities and banks, when offered as a means of payment for any transaction.

b. Both sides will continue to discuss, through the JEC, the possibility of introducing mutually agreed Palestinian currency or temporary alternative currency arrangements for the Palestinian Authority.

11. a. The liquidity requirements on all deposits in banks operating in the Areas will be determined and announced by the PMA.

b. Banks in the Areas will accept NIS deposits. The liquidity requirements on the various kinds of NIS deposits (or deposit linked to the NIS) in banks operating in the Areas will not be less than 4% to 8%, according to the type of deposits. Changes of over 1% in the liquidity requirements on NIS deposits (or deposits linked to the NIS) in Israel will call for corresponding changes in the above mentioned rates.

c. The supervision and inspection of the implementation of all liquidity requirements will be carried out by the PMA.

d. The reserves and the liquid assets required according to this paragraph will be deposited at the PMA according to rules and regulations determined by it. Penalties for non compliance with the liquidity requirements will be determined by the PMA.

12. The PMA will regulate and administer a discount window system and the supply of temporary finance for banks operating in the Areas.

13. a. The PMA will establish or license a clearing house in order to clear money orders between the banks operating in the Areas, and with other clearing houses.

b. The clearing of money orders and transactions between banks operating in the Areas and banks operating in Israel will be done between the Israeli and the Palestinian clearing houses on same working day basis, according to agreed arrangements.

14. Both sides will allow correspondential relations between each others' banks.

15. The PMA will have the right to convert at the BOI excess NIS received from banks operating in the Areas into foreign currency, in which the BOI trades in the domestic inter-bank market, up to the amounts determined per period, according to the arrangements detailed in para 16 below.

16. a. The excess amount of NIS, due to balance of payments flows, that the PMA will have the right to convert into foreign currency, will be equal to:

(1) Estimates of all Israeli "imports" of goods and services from the Areas, valued at market prices (inclusive of taxes), which were paid for in NIS, less:
- (i) the taxes collected by the Palestinian Authority on all Israeli "imports" from the Areas and rebated to Israel in NIS, and
- (ii) the taxes collected by Israel on all Israeli "imports" from the Areas and included in their market value, and not rebated to the Palestinian Authority, minus

(2) Estimates of all Israeli "exports" of goods and services to the Areas, valued at market prices (inclusive of taxes), which were paid for in NIS, less:
- (i) the taxes collected by Israel on such "exports" and rebated to the Palestinian Authority, and
- (ii) the taxes collected by the Palestinian Authority on such "exports" and included in their market value, and not rebated to Israel; plus

(3) The accumulated net amounts of foreign currency converted previously into NIS by the PMA, as recorded in the BOI Dealing Room.

b. The said flows and amounts will be calculated as of the date of the signing of the Agreement.

Notes to para 16:

(i) The estimates of the said "exports and imports" of goods and services will include inter alia labor services, NIS expenditure of tourists and Israelis in the Areas and NIS expenditure of Palestinians of the Areas in Israel.

(ii) Taxes and pension contributions on "imports" of labor services, paid to "importing" side and rebated to the "exporting" one, will not be included in the estimates of the sums to be converted, as the "exports" earnings of labor services are recorded in the statistics inclusive of them, although they do not accrue to the individuals supplying them.

17. The PMA and the BOI will meet annually to discuss and determine the annual amount of convertible NIS during the following calendar year and will meet semi-annually to adjust the said amount. The amounts determined annually and adjusted semi-annually will be based on data and estimates regarding the past and on forecasts for the following period, according to the formula mentioned in para 16. The first meeting will be as soon as possible within three months after the date of the signing of the Agreement.

18. a. The exchange of foreign currency for NIS and vice-versa by the PMA will be carried out through the BOI Dealing Room, at the market exchange rates.

b. The BOI will not be obliged to convert in any single month more than 1/5 of the semi-annual amount, as mentioned in para 17.

19. There will be no ceiling on the annual foreign currency conversions by the PMA into NIS. However, in order to avoid undesirable fluctuations in the foreign exchange market, monthly ceilings of such conversions will be agreed upon in the annual and semi-annual meetings referred to in para 17.

20. Banks in the Areas will convert NIS into other circulating currencies and vice-versa.

21. The Palestinian Authority will have the authorities, powers and responsibilities regarding the regulation and supervision of capital activities in the Areas, including the licensing of capital market institutions, finance companies and investment funds.

Article V: Direct Taxation

1.. Israel and the Palestinian Authority will each determine and regulate independently its own tax policy in matters of direct taxation, including income tax on individuals and corporations, property taxes, municipal taxes and fees.

2. Each tax administration will have the right to levy the direct taxes generated by economic activities within its area.

3. Each tax administration may impose additional taxes on residents within its area on (individuals and corporations) who conduct economic activities in the other side's area.

4. Israel will transfer to the Palestinian Authority a sum equal to:

a. 75% of the income taxes collected from Palestinians from the Gaza Strip and the Jericho Area employed in Israel.

b. The full amount of income taxes collected from Palestinians from the Gaza Strip and Jericho Area employed in the settlements.

5. The two sides will agree on a set of procedures that will address all issues concerning double taxation.

Article VI: Indirect Taxes on Local Production

1. The Israel and the Palestinian tax administrations will levy and collect VAT and purchase taxes on local production, as well as any other indirect taxes, in their respective areas.

2. The purchase tax rates within the jurisdiction of each tax administration will be identical as regards locally produced and imported goods.

3. The present Israeli VAT rate is 17%. The Palestinian VAT rate will be 15% to 16%.

4. The Palestinian Authority will decide on the maximum annual turnover for businesses under its jurisdiction to be exempt from VAT, within an upper limit of 12,000 US $.

5. The VAT on purchases by businesses registered for VAT purposes will accrue to the tax administration with which the respective business is registered.

Businesses will register for VAT purposes with the tax administration of the side of their residence, or on the side of their ongoing operation.

There will be clearance of VAT revenues between the Israeli and Palestinian VAT administrations on the following conditions:

a. The VAT clearance will apply to VAT on transactions between businesses registered with the VAT administration of the side in which they reside.
b. The following procedures will apply to clearance of VAT revenues accruing from transactions by businesses registered for VAT purposes:
   (1) To be acceptable for clearance purposes, special invoices, clearly marked for this purpose, will be used for transactions between businesses registered with the different sides.
   (2) The invoices will be worded either in both Hebrew and Arabic or in English and will be filled out in any of these three languages, provided that the figures are written in "Arabic" (not Hindi) numerals.
   (3) For the purpose of tax rebates, such invoices will be valid for six months from their date of issue.
   (4) Representatives of the two sides will meet once a month, on the 20th day of the month, to present each other with a list of invoices submitted to them for tax rebate, for VAT clearance. This list will include the following details regarding each invoice:
      (a) The number of the registered business issuing it;
      (b) The name of the registered business issuing it;
      (c) The number of the invoice;
      (d) The date of issue;
      (e) The amount of the invoice;
      (f) The name of the recipient of the invoice.
   (5) The clearance claims will be settled within 6 days from the meeting, through a payment by the side with the net balance of claims against it, to the other side.
   (6) Each side will provide the other side, upon demand, with invoices for verification purposes. Each tax administration will be responsible for providing invoices for verification purposes for 6 months after receiving them.
   (7) Each side will take the necessary measure to verify the authenticity of the invoices presented to it for clearance by the other side.
   (8) Claims for VAT clearance which will not be found valid will be deducted from the next clearance payment.
   (9) Once an inter-connected computer system for tax rebates to businesses and for VAT clearance between the two sides is

operational, it will replace the clearance procedures specified in sub-paras (4)-(8).

(10) The two tax administrations will exchange lists of the businesses registered with them and will provide each other with the necessary documentation, if required, for the verification of transactions.

(11) The two sides will establish a sub-committee which will deal with the implementation arrangements regarding the clearance of VAT revenues set above.

6. VAT paid by not-for-profit Palestinian organizations and institutions, registered by the Palestinian Authority, on transactions in Israel, will accrue to the Palestinian tax administration. The clearance system set out in para 5 will apply to these organizations and institutions.

Article VII: Labor

1. Both sides will attempt to maintain the normality of movement of labor between them, subject to each side's right to determine from time to time the extent and conditions of the labor movement into its area. If the normal movement is suspended temporarily by either side, it will give the other side immediate notification, and the other side may request that the matter be discussed in the Joint Economic Committee.

The placement and employment of workers from one side in the area of the other side will be through the employment service of the other side and in accordance with the other sides' legislation. The Palestinian side has the right to regulate the employment of Palestinian labor in Israel through the Palestinian employment service, and the Israeli Employment Service will cooperate and coordinate in this regard.

2. a. Palestinians employed in Israel will be insured in the Israeli social insurance system according to the National Insurance Law for employment injuries that occur in Israel, bankruptcy of employers and maternity leave allowance.

b. The National Insurance fees deducted from the wages for maternity insurance will be reduced according to the reduced scope of maternity insurance, and the equalization deductions transferred to the Palestinian Authority, if levied, will be increased accordingly.

c. Implementation procedures relating thereto will be agreed upon between the Israeli National Insurance Institute and the Palestinian Authority or the appropriate Palestinian social insurance institution.

3. a. Israel will transfer to the Palestinian Authority, on a monthly basis, the equalization deductions as defined by Israeli legislation, if imposed and to the extent levied by Israel. The sums so transferred will be used for social benefits and health services, decided upon by the Palestinian Authority, for Palestinians employed in Israel and for their families.

The equalization deductions to be so transferred will be those collected after the date of the signing of the Agreement from wages of Palestinians employed in Israel and from their employers.

These sums will not include

(1) Payments for health services in places of employment.

(2) 2/3 of the actual administrative costs in handling the matters related to the Palestinians employed in Israel by the Payments Section of the Israeli Employment Service.

4. Israel will transfer, on a monthly basis, to a relevant pension insurance institution to be established by the Palestinian Authority, pension insurance deductions collected after the establishment of the above institution and the completion of the documents mentioned in para 6.

These deductions will be collected from wages of Palestinians employed in Israel and their employers, according to the relevant rates set out in the applicable Israeli collective agreements. 2/3 of the actual administrative costs in handling these deductions by the Israeli Employment Service will be deducted from the sums transferred. The sums so transferred will be used for providing pension insurance for these workers. Israel will continue to be liable for pension rights of the Palestinian employees in Israel, to the extent accumulated by Israel before the entry into force of this para 4.

5. Upon the receipt of the deductions, the Palestinian Authority and its relevant social institutions will assume full responsibility in accordance with the Palestinian legislation and arrangements, for pension rights and other social benefits of Palestinians employed in Israel, that accrue from the transferred deductions related to these rights and benefits. Consequently, Israel and its relevant social institutions and the Israeli employers will be released from, and will not be held liable for any obligations and responsibilities concerning personal claims, rights and benefits arising from these transferred deductions, or from the provisions of paras 2–4 above.

6. Prior to the said transfers, the Palestinian Authority or its relevant institutions, as the case may be, will provide Israel with the documents

required to give legal effect to their aforesaid obligations, including mutually agreed implementation procedures of the principles agreed upon in paras 3–5 above.

7. The above arrangements concerning equalization deductions and/or pension deductions may be reviewed and changed by Israel if an authorized court in Israel will determine that the deductions or any part thereof must be paid to individuals, or used for individual social benefits or insurance in Israel, or that it is otherwise unlawful. In such a case the liability of the Palestinian side will not exceed the actual transferred deductions related to the case.

8. Israel will respect any agreement reached between the Palestinian Authority, or an organization or trade-union representing the Palestinians employed in Israel, and a representative organization of employees or employers in Israel, concerning contributions to such organization according to any collective agreement.

9. a. The Palestinian Authority may integrate the existing health insurance scheme for Palestinians employed in Israel and their families in its health insurance services. As long as this scheme continues, whether integrated or separately, Israel will deduct from their wages the health insurance fees ("health stamp") and will transfer them to the Palestinian Authority for this purpose.

b. The Palestinian Authority may integrate the existing health insurance scheme for Palestinians who were employed in Israel and are receiving pension payments through the Israeli Employment Service, in its health insurance services. As long as this scheme continues, whether integrated or separately, Israel will deduct the necessary sum of health insurance fees ("health stamp") from the equalization payments and will transfer them to the Palestinian Authority for this purpose.

10. The JEC will meet upon the request of either side and review the implementation of this Article and other issues concerning labor, social insurance and social rights.

11. Other deductions not mentioned above, if any, will be jointly reviewed by the JEC. Any agreement between the two sides concerning these deductions will be in addition to the above provisions.

12. Palestinians employed in Israel will have the right to bring disputes arising out of employee-employer relationships and other issues before the Israeli Labor Courts, within these courts' jurisdiction.

13. This Article governs the future labor relations between the two sides and will not impair any labor rights prior to the date of signing of the Agreement.

Article VII: Agriculture

1. There will be free movement of agricultural produce, free of customs and import taxes, between the two sides, subject to the following exceptions and arrangements.

2. The official veterinary and plant protection services of each side will be responsible, within the limits of their respective jurisdiction, for controlling animal health, animal products and biological products, and plants and parts thereof, as well as their importation and exportation.

3. The relations between the official veterinary and plant protection services of both sides will be based on mutuality in accordance with the following principles, which will be applied in all the areas under their respective jurisdiction:

a. Israel and the Palestinian Authority will do their utmost to preserve and improve the veterinary standards.

b. Israel and the Palestinian Authority will take all measures to reach equivalent and compatible standards regarding animal disease control, including mass vaccination of animals and avians, quarantines, "stamping out" measures and residue control standards.

c. Mutual arrangements will be made to prevent the introduction and spread of plant pests and diseases, for their eradication and concerning residue control standards in plant products.

d. The official veterinary and plant protection services of Israel and the Palestinian Authority will coordinate and regularly exchange information regarding animal diseases, as well as plant pests and diseases, and will establish a mechanism for immediate notification of the outbreak of such diseases.

4. Trade between the two sides in animals, animal products and biological products will be in keeping with the principles and definitions set out in the current edition of the OIE National Animal Health Code as updated from time to time (hereinafter—I.A.H.C.).

5. Transit of livestock, animal products and biological products from one side through the area under the jurisdiction of the other side, should be conducted in a manner aimed at the prevention of diseases spreading to or from the consignment during its movement. For such a transit to be permitted, it is a prerequisite that the veterinary conditions agreed upon

by both sides will be met in regard to importation of animals, their products and biological products from external markets. Therefore the parties agree to the following arrangements.

6. The official veterinary services of each side have the authority to issue veterinary import permits for import of animals, animal products and biological products to the areas under its jurisdiction. In order to prevent the introduction of animal diseases from third parties, the following procedures will be adopted:

a. The import permits will strictly follow the professional veterinary conditions for similar imports to Israel as prevailing at the time of their issuance. The permits will specify the country of origin and the required conditions to be included in the official veterinary certificates which should be issued by the veterinary authorities in the countries of origin and which should accompany each consignment.

   Each side may propose a change in these conditions. The change will come into force 10 days after notice to the other side, unless the other side requested that the matter be brought before the Veterinary Sub-Committee specified in para 14 (hereinafter—VSC). If it is more stringent than the prevailing conditions—it will come into force 20 days after the request, unless both sides decide otherwise through the VSC, and if more lenient—it will come into force only if agreed upon by both sides through the VSC. However, if the change is urgent and needed for the protection of animal and public health, it will come into force immediately after notice by the other side and will remain in force unless and until both sides agree otherwise through the VSC.

b. The official veterinary certificates will include the provisions regarding OIE

   Lists A & B Diseases as specified in the I.A.H.C. When the I.A.H.C. allows alternative requirements regarding the same disease, the most stringent one will be adopted unless otherwise agreed upon by the VSC.

c. When infectious diseases which are not included in Lists A & B of the I.A.H.C. exist or are suspected, on scientific grounds, to exist in the exporting country, the necessary veterinary import conditions that will be required and included in the official veterinary certificates, will be discussed in the VSC, and in the case of different professional opinions, the most stringent ones will be adopted.

d. The import of live vaccines will be permitted only if so decided by the VSC.
e. Both sides will exchange, through the VSC, information pertaining to import licensing, including the evaluation of the disease situation and zoosanitary capability of exporting countries, which will be based upon official information as well as upon other available data.
f. Consignments which do not conform with the above mentioned requirements will not be permitted to enter the areas under the jurisdiction of either side.

7. Transportation of livestock and poultry and of animal products and biological products between areas under the jurisdiction of one side through areas under the jurisdiction of the other side, will be subject to the following technical rules:

a. The transportation will be by vehicles which will be sealed with a seal of the official veterinary services of the place of origin and marked with a visible sign "Animal Transportation" or "Products of Animal Origin" in Arabic and Hebrew, in coloured and clearly visible letters on white background;
b. Each consignment will be accompanied by a veterinary certificate issued by the official veterinary services of the place of origin, certifying that the animals or their products were examined and are free of infectious diseases and originate from a place which is not under quarantine or under animal movement restrictions.

8. Transportation of livestock and poultry, animal products and biological products destined for Israel from the Areas and vice versa will be subject to veterinary permits issued by the official veterinary services of the recipient side, in keeping with the OIE standards used in international traffic in this field. Each such consignment will be transported by a suitable and marked vehicle, accompanied by a veterinary certificate in the form agreed upon between the official veterinary services of both sides. Such certificates will be issued only if permits of the recipient side are presented.

9. In order to prevent the introduction of plant pests and diseases to the region, the following procedures will be adopted:

a. The transportation between the Areas and Israel, of plants and parts thereof (including fruits and vegetables), the control of pesticide residues in them and the transportation of plant propagation material and of animal feed, may be inspected without delay or damage by the plant protection services of the recipient side.

b. The transportation between the Areas through Israel of plants and parts thereof (including fruits and vegetables) as well as of pesticides, may be required to pass a phytosanitary inspection without delay or damage.

c. The official Palestinian plant protection services have the authority to issue permits for the import of plants and parts thereof as well as of pesticides from external markets. The permits will be based on the prevailing standards and requirements.

The permits will specify the required conditions to be included in the official Phytosanitary Certificates (hence P.C.) based upon the standards and the requirements of the International Plant Protection Convention (I.P.P.C.) and those of the European and Mediterranean Plant Protection Organization (E.P.P.O.) which should accompany each consignment.

The P.C.'s will be issued by the plant protection services in the countries of origin. Dubious or controversial cases will be brought before the sub-committee on plant protection.

10. The agricultural produce of both sides will have free and unrestricted access to each other's markets, with the temporary exception of sales from one side to the other side of the following items only: poultry, eggs, potatoes, cucumbers, tomatoes and melons. The temporary restrictions on these items will be gradually removed on an increasing scale until they are finally eliminated by 1998, as listed below:

Year	Poultry (tons)	Eggs (millions)	Potatoes (tons)	Cucumbers (tons)	Tomatoes (tons)	Melons (tons)
1994	5,000	30	10,000	10,000	13,000	10,000
1995	6,000	40	13,000	13,000	16,000	13,000
1996	7,000	50	15,000	15,000	19,000	15,000
1997	8,000	60	17,000	17,000	22,000	17,000
1998	unlimited	unlimited	unlimited	unlimited	unlimited	unlimited

Note: The above figures refer to the combined quantities marketed from the West Bank and Gaza Strip to Israel and vice-versa. The Palestinian Authority will notify Israel the apportioning of these quantities between these areas concerning the quantities pertaining to the Palestinian produce.

11. The Palestinians will have the right to export their agricultural produce to external markets without restrictions, on the basis of certificates of origin issued by the Palestinian Authority.

12. Without prejudice to obligations arising out of existing international agreements, the two sides will refrain from importing agricultural products from third parties which may adversely affect the interests of each other's farmers.

13. Each side will take the necessary measures in the area under its jurisdiction to prevent damage which may be caused by its agriculture to the environment of the other side.

14. The two sides will establish sub-committees of their respective official veterinary and plant protection services, which will update the information and review issues, policies and procedures in these fields. Any changes in the provisions of this Article will be agreed upon by both sides.

15. The two sides will establish a sub-committee of experts in the dairy sector in order to exchange information, discuss and coordinate their production in this sector so as to protect the interests of both sides. In principle, each side will produce according to its domestic consumption.

Article IX: Industry

1. There will be free movement of industrial goods free of any restrictions including customs and import taxes between the two sides, subject to each side's legislation.

2. a. The Palestinian side has the right to employ various methods in encouraging and promoting the development of the Palestinian industry by way of providing grants, loans, research and development assistance and direct-tax benefits. The Palestinian side has also the right to employ other methods of encouraging industry resorted to in Israel.

b. Both sides will exchange information about the methods employed by them in the encouragement of their respective industries.

c. Indirect tax rebates or benefits and other subsidies to sales shall not be allowed in trade between the two sides.

3. Each side will do its best to avoid damage to the industry of the other side and will take into consideration the concerns of the other side in its industrial policy.

4. Both sides will cooperate in the prevention of deceptive practices, trade in goods which may endanger health, safety and the environment and in goods of expired validity.

5. Each side will take the necessary measures in the area under its jurisdiction to prevent damage which may be caused by its industry to the environment of the other side.

6. The Palestinians will have the right to export their industrial produce to external markets without restrictions, on the basis of certificates of origin issued by the Palestinian Authority.

7. The JEC will meet and review issues pertaining to this Article.

Article X: Tourism

1. The Palestinian Authority will establish a Palestinian Tourism Authority which will exercise, inter alia, the following powers in the Areas.

   a. Regulating, licensing, classifying and supervising tourist services, sites and industries.
   b. Promoting foreign and domestic tourism and developing the Palestinian tourist resources and sites.
   c. Supervising the marketing, promotion and information activities related to foreign and domestic tourism.

2. Each side shall, under its respective jurisdiction, protect, guard and ensure the maintenance and good upkeep of historical, archaeological, cultural and religious sites and all other tourist sites, to fit their status as well as their purpose as a destination for visitors.

3. Each side will determine reasonable visiting hours and days for all tourist sites in order to facilitate visits at a wide variety of days and hours, taking into consideration religious and national holidays. Each side shall publicize such opening times. Meaningful changes in the opening times will take into consideration tourist programs already committed to.

4. Tourist buses or any other form of tourist transport authorized by either side, and operated by companies registered and licensed by it, will be allowed to enter and proceed on their tour within the area under the jurisdiction of the other side, provided that such buses or other vehicles conform with the EEC technical specifications [I. currently adopted.] All such vehicles will be clearly marked as tourist vehicles.

5. Each side will protect the environment and the ecology around the tourist sites under its jurisdiction. In view of the importance of beaches and maritime activities for tourism, each side will do its best efforts to ensure that development and construction on the Mediterranean coast, and especially at ports (such as Ashqelon or Gaza), will be planned and

carried out in a manner that will not adversely affect the ecology, environment or the functions of the coastline and beaches of the other side.

6. Tourism companies and agencies licensed by either side shall enjoy equal access to tourism-related facilities and amenities in border points of exit and entry according to the regulations of the authority operating them.

7. a. Each side will license, according to its own rules and regulations, travel agents, tour companies, tour guides and other tourism businesses (hereinafter—tourism entities) within its jurisdiction.

b. Tourism entities authorized by either side, will be allowed to conduct tours that include the area under the jurisdiction of the other side, provided that their authorization as well as their operation will be in accordance with rules, professional requirements and standards agreed upon by both sides in the sub-committee mentioned in para 9. Pending that agreement, existing tourism entities in the Areas which are currently allowed to conduct tours that include Israel, will be allowed to continue to do so, and Israeli authorized tourism entities will continue to be allowed to conduct tours that include the Areas.

In addition, any tourism entity of one side that the tourism authorities of the other side will certify as fulfilling all its rules, professional requirements and standards, will be allowed to conduct tours that include that other side.

8. Each side will make its own arrangement for compensation of tourists for bodily injury and property damages caused by political violence in the areas under its respective jurisdiction.

9. The JEC or a tourism sub-committee established by it shall meet upon the request of either side in order to discuss the implementation of the provisions of this Article and resolve problems that may arise. The sub-committee will also discuss and consider tourist issues of benefit to both sides, and will promote educational programs for tourism entities of both sides in order to further their professional standards and their ethics. Complaints of one side against the behaviour of tourism entities of the other side will be channelled through the committee.

Note: It is agreed that the final wording in the last sentence in para 4 will be adopted according to the final wording in the relevant provisions of the Agreement.

Article XI: Insurance Issues

1. The authorities, powers and responsibilities in the insurance sphere in the Areas, including inter alia the licensing of insurers, insurance agents and the supervision of their activities, will be transferred to the Palestinian Authority.

2. a. The Palestinian Authority will maintain a compulsory absolute liability system for road accident victims with a ceiling on the amount of compensation based upon the following principles:

(1) Absolute liability for death or bodily injury to road accident victims, it being immaterial whether or not there was fault on the part of the driver and whether or not there was fault or contributory fault on the part of others, each driver being responsible for persons travelling in his vehicle and for pedestrians hit by his vehicle.

(2) Compulsory insurance for all motor vehicles, covering death or bodily injury to all road accident victims, including drivers.

(3) No cause of action in tort for death or bodily injury resulting from road accidents.

(4) The maintenance of a statutory fund (hereinafter—the Fund) for compensation of road accident victims who are unable to claim compensation from an insurer for the following reasons:

(i) the driver liable for compensation is unknown;

(ii) the driver is not insured or his insurance does not cover the liability involved; or

(iii) the insurer is unable to meet his liabilities.

b. Terms in this Article will have the same meaning as in the legislation prevailing at the date of signing of the Agreement concerning compulsory motor vehicle insurance and compensation of road accident victims.

c. Any change by either side in the rules and regulations regarding the implementation of the above mentioned principles will require prior notice to the other side. A change which might substantially affect the other side will require prior notice of at least three months.

3. a. Upon the signing of the Agreement the Palestinian Authority will establish a Fund for the Areas (hereinafter—the Palestinian Fund) for the purposes detailed in para 2(a)(4) above and for the purposes detailed below. The Palestinian Fund will assume the responsibilities of the statutory Road Accident Victims Compensation Fund in the West Bank and the Gaza Strip (hereinafter—the Existing Fund) regarding the Areas, according to the prevailing law at that time. Accordingly, the Existing

Fund will cease to be responsible for any liability regarding accidents occurring in the Areas from the date of signing of the Agreement.

b. The Existing Fund will transfer to the Palestinian Fund, after the assumption of the above mentioned responsibilities by it, the premiums paid to the Existing Fund by the insurers for vehicles registered in the Areas, pro-rata to the unexpired period of each insurance policy.

4. a. Compulsory motor vehicle insurance policies issued by insurers licensed by either side will be valid in the territories of both sides. Accordingly, a vehicle registered in one side covered by such a policy will not be required to have an additional insurance coverage for travel in the areas under the other side's jurisdiction. These insurance policies will cover all the liabilities according to the legislation of the place of the accident.

b. In order to cover part of the liabilities which may incur due to road accidents in Israel by uninsured vehicles registered in the Palestinian Authority, the Palestinian Fund will transfer to the Israeli Fund, on a monthly basis, for each insured vehicle, an amount equal to 30% of the amount paid to the Israeli Fund by an insurer registered in Israel, for the sat-ne type of vehicle, for the same period of insurance (which will not be less than 90 days).

5. In cases where a victim of a road accident wishes to claim compensation from an insurer registered by the other side or from the Fund of the other side or in cases where a driver or an owner of a car is sued by a victim, by an insurer or by the Fund of the other side, he may nominate the Fund of his side as his proxy for this purpose. The Fund so nominated may address any relevant party from the other side directly or through the other sides' Fund.

6. In the case of a road accident in which neither the registration number of the vehicle nor the identity of the driver are known, the Fund of the side which has jurisdiction over the place of the accident will compensate the victim, according to its own legislation.

7. The Fund of each side will be responsible towards the victims of the other side for any liability of the insurers of its side regarding the compulsory insurance and will guarantee their liabilities.

8. Each side will guarantee its Fund's liabilities according to this Article.

9. The two sides will negotiate within three months from the date of the signing of the Agreement a cut-off agreement between the Existing Fund and the Palestinian Fund concerning accidents which occurred in the Areas prior to the date of the signing of the Agreement, whether

claims have been reported or not. The cut-off agreement will not include compensation for Israeli victims involved in accidents which occurred in the Areas prior to the date of the signing of the Agreement.

10. a. The two sides will establish immediately upon the signing of the Agreement, a sub-committee of experts (hereinafter—the Sub-Committee) which will deal with issues regarding the implementation of this Article, including:

(1) Procedures concerning the handling of claims of victims of the one side from insurers or from the Fund of the other side;
(2) Procedures concerning the transfer of the amounts between the Funds of both sides as mentioned in para 4(b) above;
(3) The details of the cut-off agreement between the Existing Fund and the Palestinian Fund, as set out in para 9 above;
(4) Any other relevant issue raised by either side.

b. The Sub-Committee will act as a continuous committee for issues regarding this Article.

c. The two sides will exchange, through the Sub-Committee, the relevant information regarding the implementation of this Article, including police reports, medical information, relevant statistics, premiums, etc. The two sides will provide each other with any other assistance required in this regard.

11. Each side may require the re-examination of the arrangements set out in this Article a year after the date of the signing of the Agreement.

12. Insurers from both sides may apply for a license to the relevant authorities of the other side, according to the rules and regulations regarding foreign insurers in the latter side. The two sides agree not to discriminate against such applicants.

Done in Paris, this twenty ninth day of April, 1994

For the Government of Israel	For the PLO
Finance Minister Avraham Shohat	Abu Ala (Ahmed Korei)

Bibliography

Abbas, M. (1995). *Through secret channels: The road to Oslo; Senior PLO Leader Abu Mazen's revealing story of the negotiations with Israel.* Garnet.

Abed, G. T. (1990). The economic viability of a Palestinian state. *Journal of Palestine Studies, 19*, 3–28.

Abusada, M. (2017). Palestinian diplomacy: 'Past and present'. In G. Gürbey, S. Hofmann, & F. I. Seyder (Eds.), *Between state and non-state: Politics and society in Kurdistan-Iraq and Palestine* (pp. 197–212). Palgrave Macmillan.

Ackermann, A. (2003). The idea and practice of conflict prevention. *Journal of Peace Research, 40*(3), 339–347.

Adler, E. (1997). Seizing the middle ground: Constructivism in world politics. *European Journal of International Relations, 3*(3), 319–363.

Adler, E. (2008). The spread of security communities: Communities of practice, self-restraint, and NATO's post—Cold War transformation. *European Journal of International Relations, 14*(2), 195–230.

Adler, E., & Barnett, M. (Eds.). (1998). *Security communities.* Cambridge University Press.

Aggestam, K. (2002). Quasi-informal mediation in the Oslo Channel: Larsen and Holst as individual mediators. In *Studies in international mediation: Essays in honor of Jeffrey Z. Rubin.* Palgrave Macmillan.

Aggestam, K. (2012). The psychology of peacemaking: Terje Rød-Larsen. In M. Fixdal (Ed.), *Ways out of war: Peacemakers in the Middle East and Balkans* (pp. 71–90). Palgrave Macmillan US.

Agreement on Preparatory Transfer of Powers and Responsibilities. (1994, August 29). Government of the States of Israel, PLO, Erez.

L. Lahar, *The Economic Diplomacy of Peace in the Middle East*,
https://doi.org/10.1007/978-3-031-93991-4

Agreement on Temporary International Presence in the City of Hebron (TIPH). (1996, May 9). Government of the State of Israel, PLO.

Agreement on the Gaza Strip and Jericho Area. (1994, May 4). Cairo, United Nations General Assembly (UNGA) *A/149/180.* United Nations Security Council (UNSC) *S/1994/727.* (20 June 1994). https://documents-dds-ny.un.org/doc/UNDOC/GEN/N94/257/38/IMG/N9425738.pdf?OpenElement.

Aix Group. (2004). *Economic road map: An Israeli-Palestinian perspective on permanent status.* Aix-en-Provence, Jerusalem.

Aix Group. (2005). *Israel and Palestine: Between disengagement and the economic road map.* Centre d'Economie Régionale, de l'Emploi et des Firmes Internationales (CEREFI), Faculté d'Economie Appliquée, Université de Droit, d'Economie et des Sciences d'Aix-Marseille III, France.

Albin, C., & Jarblad, A. (2012). The sustained dialogue approach: Harold H. Saunders. In M. Fixdal (Ed.), *Ways out of war: Peacemakers in the Middle East and Balkans* (pp. 53–70). Palgrave Macmillan US.

Al-Botmeh, S., & Kanafani, N. (2006). The Paris economic protocol and beyond–in search of an optimal trade arrangement. *The Palestine Yearbook of International Law Online, 14*, 75–97.

Alesina, A., & Dollar, D. (2000). Who gives foreign aid to whom and why? *Journal of Economic Growth, 5*, 33–63.

Alexander, K. (2009). *Economic sanctions law and public policy.* Palgrave Macmillan.

Aminoff, N. A. (1991). The United States–Israel free trade area agreement of 1985: In theory and practice. *Journal of World Trade, 25*, 5–42.

Ananyev, B. (2019). Sanctions in IR: Understanding, defining, studying. *International Organisations Research Journal, 14*(3), 136–150.

Annapolis Conference Joint Understanding on Negotiations. (2007, November 27). Government of Israel, PLO, under the auspice of US President Bush of the United States of America, Annapolis, MD.

Arel, D., & Driscoll, J. (2023). *Ukraine's unnamed war: Before the Russian invasion of 2022.* Cambridge University Press.

Arieli, S. (2009). *Israel and Palestine, a brief history of the negotiations. Babylon Nordisk tidsskrift for Midtøstenstudier.*

Arieli, S.. (2021). *Shaul Arieli the Israeli-Palestinian conflict maps.* Retrieved August 3, 2023, from https://www.shaularieli.com/en/maps/political-arrangements.

Arnon, A. (1997). *The Palestinian economy: Between imposed integration and voluntary separation.* Brill.

Arnon, A. (2002). The implications of economic borders between Israel and Palestine. *Palestine-Israel Journal of Politics, Economics, and Culture, 9*(3), 32.

Arnon, A. (2007). Israeli policy towards the occupied Palestinian territories: The economic dimension, 1967–2007. *The Middle East Journal, 61*(4), 573–595.

Arnon, A., & Bamya, S. (Eds.). (2015). *Economics and politics in the Israeli Palestinian conflict*. The Aix Group.

Arnon, A., & Spivak, A. (1995a). Notes on the protocol on economic relations between Israel and the PLO—The Monetary aspect. *The Economic Quarterly, 42*(1), 155–159.

Arnon, A., & Spivak, A. (1995b). A seigniorage perspective on the introduction of a Palestinian currency. *The Economic Quarterly, 42*(1), 180–197.

Arnon, A., & Weinblatt, J. (2001). Sovereignty and economic development: The case of Israel and Palestine. *The Economic Journal, 111*(472), 291–308.

Aronoff, M. J., & Aronoff, Y. S. (1998). Domestic determinants of Israeli foreign policy. In O. R. Freedman (Ed.), *The Middle East and the peace process: The impact of the Oslo Accords*. University Press of Florida.

Arreguín-Toft, I. (2012). Contemporary asymmetric conflict theory in historical perspective. *Terrorism and Political Violence, 24*(4), 635–657.

Ashrawi, H. (1996). *This side of peace: A personal account*. Simon & Schuster.

Astrup, C., & Dessus, S. (2001). Trade options for the Palestinian economy: Some orders of magnitude. World Bank Mid-East and North. Africa Working Paper.

Astrup, C., & Dessus, S. (2005). Exporting goods or exporting labor?: Long-term implications for the Palestinian economy. *Review of Middle East Economics and Finance, 3*(1), 39–61.

Axtmann, R. (2004). The state of the state: The model of the modern state and its contemporary transformation. *International Political Science Review, 25*(3), 259–279.

Bachar, G., & Weiner, A. S. (2014). Governments, publics, and enemies: Intragroup dynamics as barriers to conflict resolution. *Dynamics of Asymmetric Conflict, 7*(2–3), 198–225.

Bamya, S. (2013). The economics of the Oslo Accords. In B. Scheller, R. Wildangel, & J. Paul (Eds.), *20 Years Since Oslo: Palestinian perspectives. Perspectives Political Analyses and Commentary from the Middle East & North Africa*, Issue 5, 61–68.

Bandeira, L. A. M. (2019). *The world disorder: US hegemony, proxy wars, terrorism and humanitarian catastrophes*. Springer.

Bank of Israel Research Department. (2014). *Recent economic developments 137 October 2013–March 2014*. Ayalon Press, Israel: Bank of Israel.

Barak, O. (2005). The failure of the Israeli–Palestinian peace process, 1993–2000. *Journal of Peace Research, 42*(6), 719–736.

Barbieri, K. (2002). *The liberal illusion: Does trade promote peace?* University of Michigan Press.

Barbieri, K. (2017). Economic incentives as weapons of war. *Oxford Research Encyclopedia of Politics*.

Barbieri, K., & Schneider, G. (1999). Globalization and peace: Assessing new directions in the study of trade and conflict. *Journal of Peace Research, 36*(4), 387–404.

Barkin, J. S., & Cronin, B. (1994). The state and the nation: Changing norms and the rules of sovereignty in international relations. *International Organization, 48*(1), 107–130.

Bauck, P. (2016). The Oslo Accords: A common savior for Israel and the PLO in exile? In P. Bauck & M. Omer (Eds.), *The Oslo Accords a critical assessment* (pp. 79–87). The American University Cairo Press.

Bayne, N. (2008). Financial diplomacy and the credit crunch: The rise of central banks. *Journal of International Affairs, 62*, 1–16.

Bayne, N., & Woolcock, S. (2011). *The new economic diplomacy: Decision-making and negotiation in international economic relations.* Ashgate Publishing, Ltd.

Behrendt, S. (2007). *The secret Israeli-Palestinian negotiations in Oslo: Their success and why the process ultimately failed.* Routledge.

Beilin, Y. (1997). *Touching peace: From the Oslo Accord to a final agreement.* Miskal-Yedioth Ahronoth Books and Chemed Books.

Bekaert, G., Harvey, C. R., & Lundblad, C. (2005). Does financial liberalization spur growth? *Journal of Financial Economics, 77*(1), 3–55.

Ben Shahar, H. (1995). The economic consulting team to the political negotiations—1993. *Quarterly for Economics*, 135–154.

Benoit, K. (1996). Democracies really are more Pacific (in general) reexamining regime type and war involvement. *Journal of Conflict Resolution, 40*(4), 636–657.

Bentsur, E. (1997). *The road to peace goes through Madrid.* Yediot Books.

Berg, E., & Kursani, S. (2021). *De facto states and land-for-peace agreements: Territory and recognition at odds?* Routledge.

Berg, E., & Toomla, R. (2009). Forms of normalisation in the quest for de facto statehood. *The International Spectator, 44*(4), 27–45.

Berthelon, M., & Freund, C. (2008). On the conservation of distance in international trade. *Journal of International Economics, 75*(2), 310–320.

Bijaoui, I. (2014). *The economic reconciliation process: Middle Eastern populations in conflict.* Springer.

Bilaterals. (2017). *Negotiations Agadir Agreement.* Retrieved August 12, 2023, from https://www.bilaterals.org/?-agadir-agreement-#:~:text=The%20Agadir%20Agreement%20is%20a,into%20force%20in%20March%202007.

Borchert, I., & Yotov, Y. V. (2017). Distance, globalization, and international trade. *Economics Letters, 153*, 32–38.

Bordo, M. D., Taylor, A. M., & Williamson, J. G. (2007). *Globalization in historical perspective.* University of Chicago Press.

Bouris, D. (2014). *The European Union and occupied Palestinian territories: State-building without a state.* Routledge.

Boutros-Ghali, B. (1995). *An agenda for development 1995: With related UN documents*, [ST/]DPI/1622/DEV, United Nations: New York.
Boutros-Ghali, B. (1996, December 20). United Nations General Assembly (UNGA) Report 51/761 *An agenda for democratization*, New York: UN Department of Public Information [ST/]DPI/1867, A/51/761. Retrieved December 20, 2020, from https://documents-dds-ny.un.org/doc/UNDOC/GEN/N96/371/60/PDF/N9637160.pdf?OpenElement.
Bremer, S. A. (1992). Dangerous dyads: Conditions affecting the likelihood of interstate war, 1816–1965. *Journal of Conflict Resolution, 36*(2), 309–341.
Brynen, R. (2000). *A very political economy: Peacebuilding and foreign aid in the West Bank and Gaza*. US Institute of Peace Press.
Bush, G. H. W. (1991, October 30). Remarks by Mr. George Bush—President of the United States, The Madrid Conference opening speeches October 30–31, 1991. Retrieved April 20, 2020, from https://www.gov.il/en/Departments/General/remarks-by-mr-george-bush-president-of-the-united-states-30-october-91.
Bush, G.W. (2003, April 30). The Middle East and the roadmap for peace, released by the Office of the White House Press Secretary, Washington, DC.
Chan, S. (1997). In search of democratic peace: Problems and promise. *Mershon International Studies Review, 41*(1), 59–91.
Christopher, A. (2002). Decolonisation without independence. *GeoJournal, 56*, 213–224.
Clapham, C. (1998). Degrees of statehood. *Review of International Studies, 24*(2), 143–157.
Cleveland, W. L., & Bunton, M. (2016). *A history of the modern Middle East*. Hachette UK.
Clinton, J. W. (2000, December 23). *The Clinton Parameters*, Clinton proposal on Israeli-Palestinian Peace Meeting minutes, White House.
Cobham, D. (2001). Economic aspects of the Israeli-Palestinian conflict: Introduction. *The Economic Journal, 111*(472), 249–253.
Cobham, D., & Kanafani, N. M. (2004). Introduction. In D. Cobham & N. M. Kanafani (Eds.), *The economics of Palestine: Economic policy and institutional reform for a viable Palestine state*. Routledge.
Cohen-Almagor, R. (2018). The Oslo peace process: Interview with Joel Singer. *Israel Affairs, 24*(5), 733–766.
Coleman, P. T. (2003). Characteristics of protracted, intractable conflict: Toward the development of a metaframework-I. *Peace and Conflict: Journal of Peace Psychology, 9*(1), 1–37.
Coleman, P. T. (2006). Intractable conflict. *The Handbook of Conflict Resolution: Theory and Practice, 2*, 533–559.
Coleman, P. T., Vallacher, R. R., Nowak, A., & Bui-Wrzosinska, L. (2007). Intractable conflict as an attractor: A dynamical systems approach to conflict escalation and intractability. *American Behavioral Scientist, 50*(1), 1454–1475.

Convention on the Rights and Duties of States. (1933, December 26). 165 LNTS 19. p. 47, Article I, Montevideo.

Cortright, D. (1997). Incentives and cooperation in international affairs. In D. E. Cortright (Ed.), *The price of peace: Incentives and international conflict prevention* (pp. 3–18). Rowman & Littlefield Publishers, Inc.

Covell, C. (1998). The definitive articles of perpetual peace. In *Kant and the law of peace: A study in the philosophy of international law and international relations.* Palgrave Macmillan.

Crawford, J. (2006). *The creation of states in international law.* Oxford University Press.

Crocker, C. A., Hampson, F. O., & Aall, P. (2005). Introduction: Mapping the nettle field. Grasping the nettle: Analyzing cases of intractable conflict. In C. A. Crocker, F. O. Hampson, & P. Aall (Eds.), *Grasping the nettle: Analyzing cases of intractable conflict* (pp. 3–30). US Institute of Peace Press.

Crowley, M., Nereim, V., & Kingsley, P. (2023, March 9). Saudi Arabia offers its price to normalize relations with Israel. *New York Times.* Retrieved July 23, 2023, from https://www.nytimes.com/2023/03/09/us/politics/saudi-arabia-israel-united-states.html.

D'Anieri, P. (2022). Conflict studies and the war in Ukraine, 2014–2022. *Journal of Soviet and Post-Soviet Politics and Society, 8*(2), 117–152.

Daigle, C., & Wittes, T. (2012). Peacemaking as interstate diplomacy: Samuel Lewis. In M. Fixdal (Ed.), *Ways out of war: Peacemakers in the Middle East and Balkans.* Palgrave Macmillan US.

Đào, K. T., & van Bergeijk, P. A. G. (2022). Winds from the East: Ancient Asian views on international trade. ISS working papers. General series, no. 705, International Institute of Social Studies (ISS), Den Haag.

Darby, J., & Ginty, R. M. (2000). Introduction: Comparing peace processes. In J. Darby & R. M. Ginty (Eds.), *The management of peace processes.* Palgrave Macmillan UK, United States of America: St. Martin's Press LLC..

Darby, J., & Ginty, R. M. (2008). Introduction: What peace? What process? In J. Darby & R. M. Ginty (Eds.), *Contemporary peacemaking: Conflict, peace processes and post-war reconstruction.* Springer.

de Carvalho, B., & Lie, J. H. S. (2015). A great power performance: Norway, status and the policy of involvement. In B. de Carvalho & I. B. Neumann (Eds.), *Small state status seeking Norway's quest for international standing* (pp. 56–72). Routledge.

De Groot, H. L., Linders, G. J., Rietveld, P., & Subramanian, U. (2004). The institutional determinants of bilateral trade patterns. *Kyklos, 57*(1), 103–123.

De Mesquita, B. B., Morrow, J. D., Siverson, R. M., & Smith, A. (1999). An institutional explanation of the democratic peace. *American Political Science Review, 93*(4), 791–807.

Declaration of Principles on Interim Self-Government Arrangements ISR-PA. (1993, September 13). United Nations General Assembly (UNGA), United Nations Security Council (UNSC), A/48/486, S/26560 (11 October 1993). Retrieved May 14, 2020, from https://www.un.org/unispal/document/auto-insert-180015/.

Demena, B. A., & Afesorgbor, S. K. (2020). The effect of FDI on environmental emissions: Evidence from a meta-analysis. *Energy Policy, 138*, 111192.

Demena, B. A., Reta, A. S., Jativa, G. B., Kimararungu, P. B., & van Bergeijk, P. A. G. (2021). Publication bias of economic sanctions research: A meta-analysis of the impact of trade linkage, duration and prior relations on sanctions success. In P. A. G. van Bergeijk (Ed.), *Research handbook on economic sanctions* (pp. 125–150). US Edward Elgar Publishing Limited; Edward Elgar Publishing, Inc.

Dessus, S. (2004). A Palestinian growth history, 1968–2000. *Journal of Economic Integration, 19*(3), 447–469.

Dessus, S., & Bulmer, E. R. (2004). 'The choice of trade regime depends on multiple other factors. In D. Cobham & N. M. Kanafani (Eds.), *The economics of Palestine: Economic policy and institutional reform for a viable Palestine state*. Routledge.

Deutsch, K. W., Burrell, S. A., Kann, R. A., Lee, M., Lichterman, M., Lindgren, R. E., Loewenheim, F. L., & van Wagenen, R. W. (1957). *Political community and the North Atlantic Area: International organization in the light of historical experience*. Princeton University Press.

Disdier, A. C., & Head, K. (2008). The puzzling persistence of the distance effect on bilateral trade. *The Review of Economics and Statistics, 90*(1), 37–48.

Diwan, I., & Shaban, R. A. (Eds.). (1999). *Development under adversity: The Palestinian economy in transition*. Palestine Economic Policy Research Institute (MAS) and the World Bank.

Doyle, M. W. (1986). Liberalism and world politics. *American Political Science Review, 80*(4), 1151–1169.

Doyle, M. W. (1997). Ways of war and peace: Realism. *Liberalism, and Socialism, 219*, 24–25.

Doyle, M. W. (2005). Three pillars of the liberal peace. *American Political Science Review, 99*(3), 463–466.

Duncombe, C., & Dunne, T. (2018). After liberal world order. *International Affairs, 94*(1), 25–42.

Dutton, J. (2021, May 26). Read letter Amazon Workers sent to Jeff Bezos urging solidarity with Palestinians. *Newsweek*. Retrieved May 31, 2021, from https://www.newsweek.com/amazon-workers-send-letter-bezos-solidarity-palestinians-1594896.

ECF. (2015). *Overview*. Retrieved July 7, 2020, from https://ecf.org.il.

Egeland, J. (1994). Norway's Middle East peace channel: An insider's view. *Security Dialogue, 25*(3), 349–351.

Eisenberg, L. Z., & Caplan, N. (2010). *Negotiating Arab-Israeli peace: Patterns, problems, possibilities*. Indiana University Press.

El-Jafari, M. (1997). Potential merchandise trade of the West Bank and Gaza Strip. *Journal of Economic Cooperation Among Islamic Countries, 18*(4), 23–55.

Elmusa, S. S., & El-Jaafari, M. (1995). Power and trade: The Israeli-Palestinian economic protocol. *Journal of Palestine Studies, 24*, 14–32.

European Commission (EC). (1996). *Communication of April 30 from the commission to the council and the European Parliament on Linking, Relief, Rehabilitation and Development (LRRD)*. Commission of the European Communities.

European Commission (EC). (2013, July 19). Guidelines on the eligibility of Israeli entities and their activities in the territories occupied by Israel since June 1967 for grants, prizes and financial instruments funded by the EU from 2014 onward, *Official Journal of the European Union* 2013/C 205/5.

European Commission (EC). (2014, June 17). Agreement between the European Union and the State of Israel on the participation of the State of Israel in the EU programme 'Horizon 2020—the Framework Programme for Research and Innovation (2014–2020)', *Official Journal of the European Union L.177/1.*

European Commission (EC). (2023a). *Economic partnerships*. Retrieved August 19, 2023, from https://policy.trade.ec.europa.eu/development-and-sustainability/economic-partnerships_en.

European Commission (EC). (2023b). *Horizon 2020*. Retrieved July 10, 2023, from http://wayback.archiveit.org/12090/20220124080448/https://ec.europa.eu/programmes/horizon2020/en/what-horizon-2020.

European Parliament (EP). (2019, December 12). Ruling of the Court of Justice of the European Union on the labelling of Israeli settlement goods. *Parliamentary question - E-004388/2019.*

European Union (EU). (2017). European Join Strategy in Support of Palestine 2017–2020 towards a democratic and accountable Palestinian State.

European Union (EU). (2021). European Join Strategy in Support of Palestine 2021–2024 towards a democratic and accountable Palestinian State.

European Union (EU). (n.d.). *Palestine*. Retrieved August 5, 2020, from https://europa.eu/capacity4dev/joint-programming-tracker/palestine.

European Union (EU) and European Commission (EC). (2013, July 9). Statement by EU High Representative Catherine Ashton on the publication of guidelines on Israel and EU funding instruments, A391/13 Brussels.

Fafo. (n.d.). *Fafo and our history*. Retrieved July 7, 2020, from https://www.fafo.no/en/about-fafo/fafo.

Falk, R. (2016). After Oslo: A legal historical perspective. In P. Bauck & M. Omer (Eds.), *The Oslo Accords a critical assessment* (pp. 67–79). The American University Cairo Press.

Fisher, R. (2000). Sources of conflict and methods of conflict resolution. *International Peace and Conflict Resolution, School of International Service*, The American University, 1–6.

Fixdal, M. (2012). Introduction: Peacemaking in asymmetrical conflicts. In M. Fixdal (Ed.), *Ways out of war: Peacemakers in the Middle East and Balkans* (pp. 1–30). Palgrave Macmillan US.

Fligstein, N. (2005). The political and economic sociology of international economic arrangements. In *Handbook of economic sociology* (pp. 183–204). Princeton University Press.

Florea, A. (2014). De facto states in international politics (1945–2011): A new data set. *International Interactions, 40*(5), 788–811.

Florea, A. (2017). De facto states: Survival and disappearance (1945–2011). *International Studies Quarterly, 61*(2), 337–351.

Freedman, R. O. (1993). *The Middle East after Iraq's invasion of Kuwait.* University Press of Florida.

Friedman, T. L. (2006). *The world is flat [updated and expanded]: A brief history of the twenty-first century.* Macmillan.

Friend, W., & Malhotra, D. (2019). Psychological barriers to resolving intergroup conflict: An extensive review and consolidation of the literature. *Negotiation Journal, 35*(4), 407–442.

Fukuyama, F. (2022, March 4). Putin's war on the liberal order. *Financial Times.*

Gal, Y., & Rock, B. (2018, October 17). *Israeli Palestinian trade: In-depth analysis*, Middle East, Tony Blair Institute for Global Change.

Gartzke, E. (1998). Kant we all just get along? Opportunity, willingness, and the origins of the democratic peace. *American Journal of Political Science, 42*(1), 1–27.

Gartzke, E. (2007). The capitalist peace. *American Journal of Political Science, 51*(1), 166–191.

Gartzke, E., & Hewitt, J. J. (2010). International crises and the capitalist peace. *International Interactions, 36*, 115–145.

Gelvin, J. L. (2005). *The modern Middle East: A history.* Oxford University Press.

Gilpin, R., & Gilpin, J. M. (2001). *Global political economy: Understanding the international economic order.* Princeton University Press.

Gleditsch, N. P. (2008). The liberal moment fifteen years on. *International Studies Quarterly, 52*(4), 691–712.

Golan, G., & Sher, G. (2019). *Spoiling and coping with spoilers: Israeli-Arab negotiations.* Indiana University Press.

Goldman, J. S., & Coleman, P. T. (2022). A theoretical understanding of how emotions fuel intractable conflict: The case of humiliation. New York: Colombia University. http://www.humiliationstudies.org/documents/GoldmanNY05meetingRT2.Pdf.

Grinberg, L. (2007). Political economy of Kibush; an Economic strangulation envelope: Three turning points in forty years of military-economic ruling. *Teorya Vebikoret, 31*, 233–245.

Grossman, M. (2024). As the Israel-Hamas war continues, the Abraham Accords quietly turns four. Atlantic Council. Retrieved January 9, 2024, from https://www.atlanticcouncil.org/blogs/menasource/abraham-accords-anniversary-gaza/.

Guzansky, Y. (2023, July 30). Agreement with Saudi Arabia: The ball is in Israel's court. *News 12*. Retrieved August 7, 2023, from https://www.mako.co.il/news-columns/2023_q3/Article-83a34775cb5a981026.htm.

Habeeb, W. M. (1988). *Power and tactics in international negotiation: How weak nations bargain with strong nations*. Johns Hopkins University Press.

Halbfinger, D. M., & Rasgon, A. (2021, January 20). Reassured by Biden win, Palestinians will resume cooperation with Israel. *The New York Times*. Retrieved July 7, 2023, from https://www.nytimes.com/2020/11/17/world/middleeast/israel-palestinians-security-annexation.html.

Halcoussis, D., Kaempfer, W. H., & Lowenberg, A. D. (2021). The public choice approach to international sanctions: Retrospect and prospect. In P. A. G. van Bergeijk (Ed.), *Research handbook on economic sanctions* (pp. 152–166). US Edward Elgar Publishing Limited; Edward Elgar Publishing, Inc.

Hansen, K. F., & Borchgrevink, A. (2006). Cutting aid to promote peace and democracy? Intentions and effectiveness of aid sanctions. *The European Journal of Development Research, 18*(4), 622–641.

Harris, P., & Reilly, B. (1998). *Democracy and deep-rooted conflict: Options for negotiators*. International Institute for Democracy and Electoral Assistance.

Hashkes, E. (2021). *The economic bridges*. Matar.

Hayes, J. (2012). The democratic peace and the new evolution of an old idea. *European Journal of International Relations, 18*(4), 767–791.

Hegre, H. (2000). Development and the liberal peace: What does it take to be a trading state? *Journal of Peace Research, 37*(1), 5–30.

Held, D., Goldblatt, D., McGrew, A., Perraton, J., & Hampson, F. O. (1999). Global transformations: Politics, economics and culture. In C. Pierson & S. Tormey (Eds.), *Politics at the edge: The PSA yearbook 1999* (pp. 14–28). Palgrave Macmillan UK.

Held, D., & McGrew, A. (2000). *The global transformations reader*. Polity Press.

Helleiner, E. (2014). *Forgotten foundations of Bretton Woods: International development and the making of the postwar order*. Cornell University Press.

Hermann, T., & Newman, D. (2000). A path strewn with thorns: Along the difficult road of Israeli-Palestinian peacemaking. In J. Darby & R. M. Ginty (Eds.), *The management of peace processes* (pp. 107–153). Palgrave Macmillan UK, United States of America: St. Martin's Press LLC Springer.

Hever, S. (2010). *The political economy of Israel's occupation: Repression beyond exploitation*. New York Pluto Press.

Hirschfeld, Y. (2000). *Oslo: A formula for peace*. Am-Oved.
Hirschfeld, Y. (2014). *Track-two diplomacy toward an Israeli-Palestinian solution, 1978–2014*. Woodrow Wilson Center Press.
Holsti, K. J. (1991). *Peace and war: Armed conflicts and international order, 1648–1989*. Cambridge University Press.
Hubbard, B., & Abi-Habib, M. (2023, November 8). Behind Hamas bloody Gambit to create a 'Permanent' State of War. *The New York Times*. Retrieved December 20, 2023, from https://www.nytimes.com/2023/11/08/world/middleeast/hamas-israel-gaza-war.html.
Hufbauer, G. C., Schott, J. J., Elliott, K. A., & Oegg, B. (2009). *Economic sanctions reconsidered* (3rd ed.). Peterson Institute for International Economics.
Hughes, G. (2014). Ukraine: Europe's new proxy war. *Fletcher Security Review, 1*(II), 105–118.
Husseini, H. I., & Khalidi, R. (2013). Fixing the Paris protocol twenty years later: Some lessons for diehard reformers. In B. Scheller, R. Wildangel, & J. Paul (Eds.), *20 years since Oslo: Palestinian perspectives. Perspectives political analyses and commentary from the Middle East & North Africa*, Issue 5, 56–61.
Ikenberry, G. J. (2011). *Liberal leviathan: The origins, crisis, and transformation of the American world order*. Princeton University Press.
Ikenberry, G. J. (2014). The illusion of geopolitics: The enduring power of the liberal order. *Foreign Affairs, 93*, 80–92.
Independent Evaluation Group (IEG) World Bank. (2010). *The World Bank Group in the West Bank and Gaza, 2001–2009*. The World Bank.
International Court of Justice (ICJ). (2004, July 9). Legal consequences of the construction of a wall in the occupied Palestinian territory, *Press Release No.2004/28*. Retrieved August 18, 2023, from https://www.icj-cij.org/sites/default/files/case-related/131/131-20040709-PRE-01-00-EN.pdf.
International Court of Justice (ICJ). (2023, August 7). Legal consequences arising from the policies and practices of Israel in the occupied Palestinian territory, including East Jerusalem, *Press Release No. 2023/43*. Retrieved August 18, 2023, from https://www.icj-cij.org/sites/default/files/case-related/186/186-20230807-pre-01-00-en.pdf.
International Criminal Court (ICC). (2015, January 5). Palestine declares acceptance of ICC jurisdiction since 13 June 2014, *Press Release ICC-CPI-20150105-PR1080*. Retrieved August 18, 2023, from https://www.icc-cpi.int/news/palestine-declares-acceptance-icc-jurisdiction-13-june-2014.
International Monetary Fund (IMF). (2011, June). *Changing Patterns of Global Trade*.
'Interview I: Nabil Shaath' (2013, December). In B. Scheller, R. Wildangel, & J. Paul (Eds.), *20 years since Oslo: Palestinian perspectives. Perspectives political analyses and commentary from the Middle East & North Africa*, Issue 5, 23–29.
Israeli, R. (2017). *The Oslo idea: The euphoria of failure*. Routledge.

Israeli—Palestinian Interim Agreement on the West Bank and the Gaza Strip. (1995, September 28). Washington, United Nations General Assembly (UNGA) *A/51/889*. United Nations Security Council (UNSC) *S/1997/357* (5 May 1997). https://documents-dds-ny.un.org/doc/UNDOC/GEN/N97/119/98/IMG/N9711998.pdf?OpenElement.

Israel-PLO Permanent Status Negotiations-Joint Communique. (1996, May 6). First Session–Taba.

Jackson, R. H. (1991). *Quasi-states: Sovereignty, International relations and the Third World*. Cambridge University Press.

Jayousi, A. (2010). The Oslo II accords in retrospect: Implementation of the water provisions of the Israeli and Palestinian Interim peace agreements. In A. Tal & A. Abed-Rabbo (Eds.), *Water wisdom preparing the ground for cooperative and sustainable water management in the Middle East* (pp. 43–49). Rutgers, The State University.

Jennings, C. (2011). Intra-group competition and inter-group conflict: An application to Northern Ireland. *Defence and Peace Economics, 22*(1), 63–83.

Jeong, J. M. (2019). Do sanction types affect the duration of economic sanctions? The case of foreign aid. *International Political Science Review, 40*(2), 231–245.

Jewish Diaspora in Tech. (2021). Jewish diaspora in tech: Letter on Google Communication and Cloud Contracts. *Google Forms*. Retrieved May 31, 2021, from https://docs.google.com/forms/d/e/1FAIpQLSck0yb4OgXJlf5N2Ap21BhW-QNTL0rigFSYsW_o09QkJO-JVbw/viewform.

Johnsen, I. (2015). Gifts favour the giver: Norway, status and the Nobel Peace Prize. In B. de Carvalho & I. B. Neumann (Eds.), *Small state status seeking Norway's Quest for international standing* (pp. 108–126). Routledge.

Kaempfer, W. H., & Lowenberg, A. D. (2007). The political economy of economic sanctions. In T. Sandler & K. Hartley (Eds.), *Handbook of defense economics Volume 2 Defence in a globalized world* (pp. 867–911). North-Holland.

Kanafani, N. M. (1996). Trade relations between Palestine and Israel: Free trade area or customs union. *Jerusalem and Ramallah: MAS.*

Kanafani, N. M. (2001). Trade—A catalyst for peace? *Economic Journal, 111*(472), 276–290.

Kanafani, N. M., & Taghdisi-Rad, S. (2012). *The Palestinian economy: Macroeconomic and trade policymaking under occupation*. United Nations Conference on Trade and Development.

Kaufmann, J. (1996). *Conference diplomacy: An introductory analysis*. Springer.

Kaufmann, J., Leurdijk, D. A., & Schrijver, N. (1991). *The world in turmoil: Testing the UN's capacity*. Academic Council on the United Nations System.

Kaye, D. D. (1998). *Beyond the handshake: Multilateral cooperation in the Arab-Israeli peace process, 1991–1996*. Columbia University Press.

Kelman, H. C. (1995). Contributions of an unofficial conflict resolution effort to the Israeli-Palestinian breakthrough. *Negotiation Journal, 11*, 19–27.

Kelman, H. C. (1997). Group processes in the resolution of international conflicts: Experiences from the Israeli–Palestinian case. *American Psychologist, 52*(3), 212–2020.

Kelman, H. C. (2005). Building trust among enemies: The central challenge for international conflict resolution. *International Journal of Intercultural Relations, 29*(6), 639–650.

Kelman, H. C. (2007). The Israeli-Palestinian peace process and its vicissitudes: Insights from attitude theory. *American Psychologist, 62*(4), 287–303.

Keohane, R. O., & Nye, J. S. (1973). *Power and interdependence*. Pearson.

Ker-Lindsay, J. (2012). *The foreign policy of counter secession: Preventing the recognition of contested states*. Oxford University Press.

Ker-Lindsay, J. (2022). De facto states in the 21st century. In N. Snadal (Ed.), *Oxford research encyclopedia of international studies*.

Kerry, J. (2016, December 28). *Remarks on Middle East Peace*. John Kerry Secretary of State, The Dean Acheson Auditorium.

Khalidi, R. J., & Taghdisi-Rad, S. (2009). *The economic dimensions of prolonged occupation: Continuity and change in Israeli policy towards the Palestinian economy*. United Nations, UNCTAD.

Khalil, M. H. (2009). Guide to Palestine–Israel economic and trade relations, Czech Representative Office.

Khan, M. H. (2005). 'Security first' and its implications for a viable Palestinian state. In M. Keating, A. Le More, & R. Lowe (Eds.), *Aid, diplomacy and facts on the ground: The case of Palestine* (pp. 59–73). Royal Institute of International Affairs, Chatham House.

Khan, M. H. (2014). Learning the lessons of Oslo: State-building and freedoms in Palestine. In M. Turner & O. Shweiki (Eds.), *Decolonizing Palestinian political economy* (pp. 238–256). Palgrave Macmillan UK.

Kleiman, E. (1994). The economic provisions of the agreement between Israel and the PLO. *Israel Law Review, 28*(2–3), 347–373.

Kleiman, E. (1999). Fiscal separation with economic integration: Israel and the Palestinian authority. In A. Razin & E. Sadka (Eds.), *The economics of globalization policy perspective from public economics*. Cambridge University Press.

Kleiman, E. (2000). Round table discussion. *The Economic Quarterly, 47*(1), 80–92.

Knotter, L. (2019). The de facto Sovereignty of Unrecognised States: Towards a classical realist perspective? *Ethnopolitics, 18*(2), 119–138.

Kock, U., & Qassis, H. (2011). *West Bank and Gaza: Recent developments in clearance revenues*. International Monetary Fund.

KOF Swiss Economic Institute. (2023). *Globalization index*. Retrieved August 20, 2023, from https://kof.ethz.ch/en/forecasts-and-indicators/indicators/kof-globalisation-index.html.

Kriesberg, L. (2001). Mediation and the transformation of the Israeli-Palestinian conflict. *Journal of Peace Research, 38*(3), 373–392.

Kriesberg, L. (2005). Nature, dynamics, and phases of intractability. In C. A. Crocker, F. O. Hampson, & P. R. Aall (Eds.), *Grasping the nettle: Analyzing cases of intractable conflict* (pp. 63–89). Springer.

Krugman, P. R. (1987). Is free trade passé? *The Journal of Economic Perspectives, 1*(2), 131–144.

Lahar, L. (2024). The Political Development Nexus of economic peace in the Middle East: The Paris Protocol to the Oslo Accords, International Institute of Social Studies The Hague, of Erasmus University Rotterdam, The Netherlands.

Lameli, A., Südekum, J., Nitsch, V., & Wolf, N. (2015). Same same but different: Dialects and trade. *German Economic Review, 16*(3), 290–306.

Lavie, E. (2013). The Israeli-Palestinian economic agreement and current consequences. *Middle East Economy, 3*(1), 1–6.

Law Library of Congress. (2019, March). Israel: Law on freezing revenues designated for the Palestinian authority. (LL File No. 2019-017447), The Law Library of Congress, Global Legal Research Directorate.

Le More, A. (2004). Foreign aid strategy. In D. Cobham & N. Kanafani (Eds.), *The economics of Palestine: Economic policy and institutional reform for a viable Palestine state* (pp. 206–227). Routledge.

Le More, A. (2005). Killing with kindness: Funding the demise of a Palestinian state. *International Affairs, 81*(5), 981–999.

Le More, A. (2008). *International assistance to the Palestinians after Oslo: Political guilt, wasted money*. Routledge.

League of Arab States (LAS). (2002, March 28). *Summit resolution 14/221. Arab Peace Initiative*. Retrieved July 7, 2023, from https://www.un.org/unispal/document/auto-insert-181223/.

Leamer, E. E. (2007). A flat world, a level playing field, a small world after all, or none of the above? A review of Thomas L Friedman's the world is flat. *Journal of Economic Literature, 45*(1), 83–126.

Lee, D., & Hudson, D. (2004). The old and new significance of political economy in diplomacy. *Review of International Studies, 30*(3), 343–360.

Levine, M. (1996). Palestinian economic progress under the Oslo agreements. *Fordham International Law Journal Fordham, 19*, 1393–1418.

Levy, J. S. (2003). Economic interdependence, opportunity costs, and peace. In E. D. Mansfield & B. M. Pollins (Eds.), *Economic interdependence and international conflict: New perspectives on an enduring debate* (pp. 127–147). University of Michigan Press.

Lincoln, J. B. (2022, August 31). The Middle East Peace: The Biden Administration's approach. *The RAND Blog*. Retrieved July 7, 2023, from https://www.rand.org/pubs/commentary/2022/08/middle-east-peace-the-biden-administrations-approach.html.

Lombardo, C. E. (2001). The making of an agenda for democratization: A Speechwriter's view. *Chicago Journal of International Law, 2*(1), 253–266.

Lopez, G. A., & Cortright, D. (2018). Economic sanctions in contemporary global relations. In D. Cortright (Ed.), *Economic sanctions panacea or peace-building in a post-cold war world?* (pp. 3–16). Routledge.

Lovatt, H., & Toaldo, M. (2015). EU differentiation and Israeli settlements. European Council on Foreign Relations, London.

Lundberg, K. (1999). *The Oslo channel: Getting to the negotiating table* (p. 1333). John F. Kennedy School of Government Case.

Ma, J., & Lu, Y. (2011). Free trade or protection: A literature review on trade barriers. *Research in World Economy, 2*(1), 69–76.

Makovsky, D. (2018). *Making peace with the PLO: The Rabin Government's road to the Oslo Accord*. Routledge.

Maoz, Z., & Russett, B. (1993). Normative and structural causes of democratic peace, 1946–1986. *American Political Science Review, 87*(3), 624–638.

Massad, J. (1999). Return or permanent exile? Palestinian refugees and the ends of Oslo. *Critique: Journal for Critical Studies of the Middle East, 8*(4), 5–23.

McDonald, P. J. (2007). The purse strings of peace. *American Journal of Political Science, 51*(3), 569–582.

McDonald, P. J. (2009). *The invisible hand of peace: Capitalism, the war machine, and international relations theory*. Cambridge University Press.

McDonald, P. J. (2010). Capitalism, commitment, and peace. *International Interactions, 36*(2), 146–168.

Mearsheimer, J. J. (2014). Why the Ukraine crisis is the West's fault: The liberal delusions that provoked Putin. *Foreign Affairs, 93*, 77–89.

Mikhaikanin, E. (2004). The Abkhazians A national minority in their own homeland. In T. Bahcheli, B. Bartmann, & H. Srebrnik (Eds.), *De Facto states the quest for sovereignty* (pp. 143–163). Routledge.

Milner, H. V. (1999). The political economy of international trade. *Annual Review of Political Science, 2*(1), 91–114.

Milton-Edwards, B. (2007). The ascendance of political Islam: Hamas and consolidation in the Gaza Strip. *Third World Quarterly, 29*(8), 1585–1599.

Ministère de L'europe et des Affaires Étrangères. (2017). Conference for peace in the Middle East. Retrieved December 26, 2022, from https://www.diplomatie.gouv.fr/en/country-files/israel-palestinian-territories/peace-process/initiative-for-the-middle-east-peace-process/article/conference-for-peace-in-the-middle-east-15-01-17/.

Misyef, J. M. (2017). *National policy for Palestine—Analysis of tariff and industrial policy option*. Palestine Economic Policy Research Institute (MAS).

Mitchell, T. G. (2014). *When peace fails: Lessons from Belfast for the Middle East*. McFarland.

Moravcsik, A. (1997). Taking preferences seriously: A liberal theory of international politics. *International Organization, 51*(4), 513–553.

Moravcsik, A. (2010). *Liberal theories of international relations: A primer*. Princeton University.

Mousseau, M. (2013). The democratic peace unraveled: It's the economy. *International Studies Quarterly, 57*(1), 186–197.

Mousseau, M., Hegre, H., & O'neal, J. R. (2003). How the wealth of nations conditions the liberal peace. *European Journal of International Relations, 9*(2), 277–314.

Mousseau, M., & Mousseau, D. Y. (2008). The contracting roots of human rights. *Journal of Peace Research, 45*(3), 327–344.

Müller, H., & Wolff, J. (2004). Dyadic democratic peace strikes back, 5th Pan-European International Relations Conference, The Hague.

Murshed, S. M. (2002). Conflict, civil war and underdevelopment: An introduction. *Journal of Peace Research, 39*(4), 387–393.

Murshed, S. M. (2010). *Explaining civil war: A rational choice approach.* Edward Elgar Publishing.

Murshed, S. M. (2011). Economic dimensions of the liberal peace and its implications for conflict in developing countries. In S. Tadjbakhsh (Ed.), *Rethinking the liberal peace: External models and local alternatives* (pp. 164–179). Taylor & Francis.

Nashashibi, K., Gal, Y., & Rock, B. (2015). *Palestinian–Israeli economic relations: Trade and economic regime.* Palestine International Business Forum, International Council of Swedish Industry (NIR) and Office of the Quartet Representative Tony Blair.

Naz, A. (2023). Continued hostilities between Russia and Ukraine (2015–2022). *Pakistan Review of Social Sciences (PRSS), 4*(1), 70–84.

Netanyahu, B. (2009, June 14). Address by PM Netanyahu at Bar-Ilan University. Retrieved July 7, 2023, from https://www.gov.il/en/departments/news/address-by-pm-netanyahu-at-bar-ilan-university-14-jun-2009.

Netanyahu, B. (2014, September 29). PM Netanyahu's Speech at the United Nations General Assembly. Retrieved August 17, 2023, from https://www.gov.il/en/Departments/news/speechun290914.

Newman, E., & Richmond, O. (2006). *The impact of spoilers on peace processes and peacebuilding.* United Nations University Press.

Nilsson, D., & Söderberg Kovacs, M. (2011). Revisiting an elusive concept: A review of the debate on spoilers in peace processes. *International Studies Review, 13*(4), 606–626.

Nincic, M. (2010). Getting what you want: Positive inducements in international relations. *International Security, 35*(1), 138–183.

Nincic, M. (2011). *The logic of positive engagement.* Cornell University Press.

Nincic, M. (2012). Positive incentives, positive results? Rethinking US counterproliferation policy. In E. Solingen (Ed.), *Sanctions, statecraft, and nuclear proliferation* (pp. 125–153). Cambridge University Press.

Nye, J. S. (1999). *Understanding international conflicts: An introduction to theory and history.* Longman.

OECD. (2002). Development co-operation Report 2001: *Efforts and Policies of the Members of the Development Assistance Committee*, OECD Publishing, Paris.

OECD. (n.d.-a). *QWIDS—Query Wizard for International Development Statistics*. Retrieved August 20, 2023, from https://stats.oecd.org/qwids.

OECD. (n.d.-b). *Israel's accession to the OECD*. Retrieved August 20, 2023, from https://www.oecd.org/israel/israelsaccessiontotheoecd.htm#.

Okano-Heijmans, M. (2011). Conceptualizing economic diplomacy: The crossroads of international relations, economics, IPE and diplomatic studies. *The Hague Journal of Diplomacy, 6*(1–2), 7–36.

Oneal, J. R., & Russet, B. M. (1997). The classical liberals were right: Democracy, interdependence, and conflict, 1950–1985. *International Studies Quarterly, 41*(2), 267–293.

Oren, N., & Bar-Tal, D. (2007). The detrimental dynamics of delegitimization in intractable conflicts: The Israeli–Palestinian case. *International Journal of Intercultural Relations, 31*(1), 111–126.

Owen, J. M. (1994). How liberalism produces democratic peace. *International Security, 19*(2), 87–125.

Palestinian National Authority (PNA). (2007). *Palestinian reform and development plan 2008–2010*.

Palestinian National Authority (PNA). (2009, August). *Palestine ending the occupation, establishing the state*. Program of the Thirteenth Government.

Paris, R. (2002). International peacebuilding and the 'mission civilisatrice'. *Review of International Studies, 28*(4), 637–656.

Parsons, N. (2005). *The politics of the Palestinian Authority: From Oslo to Al-Aqsa*. Routledge.

Pearlman, W. (2009). Spoiling inside and out: Internal political contestation and the Middle East peace process. *International Security, 33*(3), 79–109.

Pegg, S. (2017). Twenty years of de facto state studies: Progress, problems, and prospects. In W. R. Thompson (Ed.), *Oxford research encyclopedia of politics*. https://doi.org/10.1093/acrefore/9780190228637.013.516.

Pegg, S. (2019). *International society and the de facto state*. Routledge.

Pegg, S., & Berg, E. (2016). Lost and found: The WikiLeaks of de facto state–great power relations. *International Studies Perspectives, 17*(3), 267–286.

Peksen, D., & Drury, A. C. (2009). Economic sanctions and political repression: Assessing the impact of coercive diplomacy on political freedoms. *Human Rights Review, 10*, 393–411.

Peres Center for Peace and Paltrade. (2006). *The untapped potential: Palestinian-Israeli economic relations: Policy options and recommendations*.

Peres, S. (1993, September 28). Address by Foreign Minister Peres to the United Nations General Assembly. Retrieved August 4, 2020, from https://embassies.gov.il/MFA/InternatlOrgs/Speeches/Pages/Address%20by%20FM%20Peres%20to%20the%20UN%20General%20Assembly-%2028.aspx.

Peres, S. (1995). *Battling for peace: A memoir*. Random House.

Peres, S., & Naor, A. (1993). *The new Middle East*. Harper Element.

Peters, J. (1999). Can the multilateral Middle East talks be revived? *Middle East Review of International Affairs (MERIA), 3*(4), 90–99.

Peterson, J. W., & Kuck, S. (2014). Civil War in Ukraine: Ethnic conflict, authoritarian leadership, and outside involvement. *Contemporary European Studies, 1*, 23–44.

Polachek, S. W. (1980). Conflict and trade. *Journal of Conflict Resolution, 24*(1), 55–78.

Polachek, S. W., & McDonald, J. (1992). Strategic trade and the incentive for cooperation. In *Disarmament, economic conversion, and management of peace*, 273–284.

Polachek, S. W., & Seiglie, C. (2007). Trade, peace and democracy: An analysis of dyadic dispute. In T. Sandler & K. Hartley (Eds.), *Handbook of defense economics Volume 2 Defence in a globalized world* (pp. 1017–1073). North-Holland.

Press-Barnathan, G. (2009). *The political economy of transitions to peace*. University of Pittsburgh Press.

Protocol Concerning Safe Passage between the West Bank and the Gaza Strip. (1999, October 5). Government of the State of Israel, PLO, Jerusalem.

Protocol Concerning the Redeployment in Hebron. (1997, January 17). Government of the State of Israel, PLO, Jerusalem.

Protocol on Further Transfer of Powers and Responsibilities. (1995, August 27). Government of the States of Israel, PLO, Cairo.

Pruitt, D. (2008). Back-channel communication in the settlement of conflict. *International Negotiations, 13*(1), 37–54.

Pundak, R. (2001). From Oslo to Taba: What went wrong? *Survival, 43*(3), 31–45.

Pundak, R. (2013). *A ruts Hasha'i: Oslo, ha-Sipur ha-Male' [Secret Channel: Oslo, The Full Story*]. Yediot Books.

Quandt, W. B. (2010). *Peace process: American diplomacy and the Arab-Israeli conflict since 1967*. Brookings Institution Press.

Qurei, A. (2006). *From Oslo to Jerusalem: The Palestinian story of the secret negotiations*. IB Tauris.

Ramsbotham, O., Miall, H., & Woodhouse, T. (2011). *Contemporary conflict resolution*. Polity.

Ravid, B. (2022). *Trump's peace: The Abraham Accords and the reshaping of the Middle East*. Rishon LeZion, Israel, Miskal–Yedioth Ahronoth Books and Chemed Books.

Reich, R. B. (2010). *The work of nations: Preparing ourselves for 21st century capitalism*. Vintage.

Reisman, W. M. (2009). Sanctions and international law. *Intercultural Human Rights Law Review, 4*, 9–20.

Report of the Economic Advisory Team for the Political Negotiations submitted to the Government of Israel. (1993, July).

Reuters. (2023, October 21). Hamas attack aimed to disrupt Saudi-Israel normalization Biden says, Washington, DC. Retrieved December 23, 2023, from https://www.reuters.com/world/middle-east/hamas-attack-aimed-disrupt-saudi-israel-normalization-biden-2023-10-20/.

Richmond, O. P. (2006). The problem of peace: Understanding the 'liberal peace'. *Conflict, Security and Development, 6*(3), 291–314.

Richmond, O. P. (2009). A post-liberal peace: Eirenism and the everyday. *Review of International Studies, 35*(3), 557–580.

Risse-Kappen, T. (1995). Democratic peace—warlike democracies? A social constructivist interpretation of the liberal argument. *European Journal of International Relations, 1*(4), 491–517.

Rivlin, P. (1992). *The Israeli economy*. Westview Press.

Rød-Larsen, T., Laiq, N., & Aidan, F. (Eds.). (2014). *The search for peace in the Arab-Israeli conflict: A compendium of documents and analysis*. Oxford University Press, USA.

Rosato, S. (2003). The flawed logic of democratic peace theory. *American Political Science Review, 97*(4), 585–602.

Rosecrance, R. N. (1986). *The rise of the trading state: Commerce and conquest in the modern world*. Basic Books.

Ross, D. (2005). *The missing peace: The inside story of the fight for Middle East peace*. Farrar, Straus and Giroux.

Ross, L. (2014). Barriers to agreement in the asymmetric Israeli–Palestinian conflict. *Dynamics of Asymmetric Conflict, 7*(2–3), 120–136.

Rousseau, D. L., Gelpi, C., Reiter, D., & Huth, P. K. (1996). Assessing the dyadic nature of the democratic peace, 1918–88. *American Political Science Review, 90*(3), 512–533.

Roy, S. (1987). The Gaza Strip: A case of economic de-development. *Journal of Palestine Studies, 17*(1), 56–88.

Roy, S. (1998). *The Palestinian economy and the Oslo process: Decline and fragmentation*. Emirates Center for Strategic Studies and Research.

Roy, S. (1999). De-development revisited: Palestinian economy and society since Oslo. *Journal of Palestine Studies, 28*(3), 64–82.

Roy, S. (2002). Why peace failed: An Oslo autopsy. *Current History, 101*(651), 8–16.

Rubin, S., & Warrick, J. (2023, November 13). Hams envisioned deeper attacks, aiming to provoke an Israeli war. *The Washington Post*. Retrieved November 30, 2023, from https://www.washingtonpost.com/national-security/2023/11/12/hamas-planning-terror-gaza-israel/.

Russett, B. (1994). *Grasping the democratic peace: Principles for a post-Cold War world*. Princeton University Press.

Russett, B. (2011). *Hegemony and democracy*. Taylor & Francis.

Samour, S. (2016). *Review and assessment of Palestinian trade policy options*. Palestine Economic Policy Research Institute (MAS).

Saner, R., & Yiu, L. (2003). International economic diplomacy: Mutations in post-modern times. Discussion Paper in Diplomacy No. 84, SSN 1569-2981, Netherlands Institute of International Relations "Clingendael".

Savir, U. (1998). *The process: 1,100 days that changed the Middle East*. Vintage.

Schenker, H. (2018). Oslo then and now-what's next? *Palestine-Israel Journal of Politics, Economics, and Culture, 23*(2/3), 5–7.

Schiavone, G. (1981). *The institutions of Comecon*. Springer.

Schneider, G., & Gleditsch, N. P. (2010). The capitalist peace: The origins and prospects of a liberal idea. *International Interactions, 36*(2), 107–114.

Schrijver, N. (1993). *The use of economic sanctions by the UN Security Council: An international law perspective*. Centre for Development Studies.

Schrijver, N. (1999). The changing nature of state sovereignty. *British Year Book of International Law, 70*(1), 65–98.

Schrijver, N. (2005). Challenges to the prohibition to use force: Does the strait-jacket of Article 2 (4) UN charter begin to gall too much? In N. M. Blokker & N. Schrijver (Eds.), *The security council and the use of force* (pp. 31–45). Brill Nijhoff.

Schrijver, N. (2006). The future of the charter of the United Nations. In A. V. Bogdandy & R. Wolfrum (Eds.), *Max Planck yearbook of United Nations Law Online* (Vol. 10, pp. 1–34). Brill.

Schrijver, N. (2022, July 1). Re-uniting for peace through international law. Valedictory Lecture, Leiden University, The Netherlands.

Selby, J. (2008). The political economy of peace processes. In M. Pugh, N. Cooper, & M. E. Turner (Eds.), *Whose peace? Critical perspectives on the political economy of peacebuilding* (pp. 11–29). Palgrave Macmillan UK.

Sharm el-Sheikh Memorandum on Implementation Timeline of Outstanding Commitments of Agreements Signed and the Resumption of Permanent Status Negotiations. (1999, September 4). Government of Israel, PLO, Sharm el-Sheikh.

Shlaim, A. (1994). The Oslo Accord. *Journal of Palestine Studies, 23*(3), 24–40.

Shlaim, A. (2005). The rise and fall of the Oslo Peace process. *International Relations of the Middle East, 285*, 241–261.

Simanovsky, N. (2011). The Fayyad Plan: Implications for the State of Israel. *Palestine-Israel Journal of Politics, Economics, and Culture, 17*(12).

Singer, J. (2020). The case of constructive ambiguity in Israel-Arab peace negotiations. In Y. Dinstein (Ed.), *Israel yearbook on human rights, volume 50* (pp. 305–347). Brill Nijhoff.

Stedman, S. J. (1997). Spoiler problems in peace processes. *International Security, 22*(2), 5–53.

Stedman, S. J. (2003). Peace processes and the challenges of violence. In J. Darby (Ed.), *Contemporary peacemaking: Conflict, violence and peace processes* (pp. 103–113). Springer, Palgrave Macmillan.

Stein, A. A. (2003). Trade and conflict: Uncertainty, strategic signaling, and interstate disputes. In E. D. Mansfield & B. Pollins (Eds.), *Economic interdependence and international conflict: New perspectives on an enduring debate* (pp. 111–126). University of Michigan Press.

Stern, M., & Öjendal, J. (2010). Mapping the security—development nexus: Conflict, complexity, cacophony, convergence? *Security Dialogue, 41*(1), 5–29.

Supreme Court of Israel. (1998, March 16). *53/96.* Alony Group Ltd.-Ministry of Industry, Trade and Labor.

Swedberg, R. (2005). Markets in society. In N. J. Smelser & R. Swedberg (Eds.), *The handbook of economic sociology*. Princeton University Press.

Tadesse, B., & White, R. (2010). Does cultural distance hinder trade in goods? A comparative study of nine OECD member nations. *Open Economies Review, 21*, 237–261.

Taghdisi-Rad, S. (2014). The economic strategies of occupation: Confining development and buying-off peace. In M. Turner & O. Shweiki (Eds.), *Decolonizing Palestinian political economy* (pp. 13–31). Springer, Palgrave Macmillan.

The Geneva Accord a Model Israeli-Palestinain Peace Agreement. (2003, December 1).

The Madrid Peace Conference. (1992). *Journal of Palestine Studies, 21*(2), 117–149.

The Office of the Quartet. (2023). *Office of the Quartet about us.* Retrieved July 15, 2023, from http://www.quartetoffice.org/page.php?id=4e3e7y320487Y4e3e7.

The Peres Center for Peace. (2009, July). *Economic peace? Political peace with economic prosperity*, Department of Economic and Business, Res 01-09/A07.

The Protocol on Economic Relations between the Government of the State of Israel and the P.L.O., Representing the Palestinian People. (1994, April 29). United Nations General Assembly (UNGA), United Nations Security Council (UNSC), A/49/180, S/1994/727 (4 May 1994). Retrieved May 14, 2020, from https://www.un.org/unispal/document/auto-insert-185298/.

The Times of Israel. (2023, September 17). Israel denies report Saudis suspending normalization talks over Palestinian issue. Retrieved September 20, 2023, from https://www.timesofisrael.com/report-saudis-ask-to-suspend-normalization-talks-with-israel-over-palestinian-issue/.

The World Bank. (2021, June). *Palestinian recovery and development plan multi-donor trust fund.* Retrieved June 5, 2022, from https://www.worldbank.org/en/ programs/palestinian-recovery-and-development-program-trust-fund.

The World Bank and the United Nations Office of the Special Coordinator in the Occupied Territories (UNSCO). (1999). *The promise, the challenges, and the achievements donor investment in Palestinian development 1994–1998.* The World Bank West Bank and Gaza Resident Mission Jerusalem; United Nations Office of the Special Coordinator in the Occupied Territories, Government House, Jerusalem.

The World Bank Group. (2023). *Data bank—world development indicators*. Retrieved August 20, 2023, from https://databank.worldbank.org/source/world-development-indicators#.

The Wye River Memorandum. (1998, October 23). Government of the State of Israel, PLO, Washington, DC.

Todaro, M. P., & Smith, S. C. (2009). *Economic development*. Pearson Education.

Trilateral Statement on the Middle East Peace Summit at Camp David. (2000, June 25). President William J. Clinton; Prime Minister Ehud Barak; Palestinian Authority Chairman Yasser Arafat.

Trump White House. (2020, January). *Peace to prosperity a vision to improve the lives of the Palestinian and Israeli People*. Retrieved December 5, 2020, from https://trumpwhitehouse.archives.gov/wp-content/uploads/2020/01/Peace-to-Prosperity-0120.pdf.

Tschirgi, D. (2004). Palestine 2003: The perils of de facto statehood. In T. Balicheli, B. Bartmann, & H. Srebnik (Eds.), *De Facto States the quest for sovereignty* (pp. 209–231). Routledge.

Tschirgi, N. (2006). Security and development policies: Untangling the relationship. In S. Klingebiel (Ed.), *New interfaces between security and development* (pp. 39–67). Deutsche Instiitut für Entwicklungspolitik.

Turan, İ. (2023). The Ukraine-Russia crises of 2014 and 2022 on the axis of the perception of the "other". In A. Kara & R. Bazancir (Eds.), *Pioneer and contemporary studies in social, human and administrative sciences* (pp. 207–220). Duvar Publishing.

Turner, M. (2014). The political economy of western aid in the occupied Palestinian territory since 1993. In M. Turner & O. Shweiki (Eds.), *Decolonizing Palestinian political economy* (pp. 32–52). Palgrave Macmillan UK.

Turner, M., & Hussein, C. (2015). *Israel-Palestine after Oslo: Mapping transformations and alternatives in a time of deepening crisis*. Taylor & Francis.

Tzur, M. (1989). The [Emergency] defence regulations, 1945. Policy Paper No. 16, The Israel Democracy Institute.

United Nations (UN). (1945, October 24). Charter of the United Nations and Statute of the International Court of Justice. Retrieved March 17, 2023, from https://www.un.org/en/about-us/un-charter.

United Nations (UN). (1994, June 1). *Press Release 585|SG/SM/5298*. 'Secretary-General appoints Terje Røed Larsen of Norway as Special Coordinator in the Occupied Territories' *Statement by Secretary-General Boutros Boutros-Ghali*, SG/A/585|SG/SM/5298. Retrieved July 7, 2022, from https://www.un.org/unispal/document/auto-insert-212930/.

United Nations (UN). (2011, October 31). The United Nations Educational, Scientific and Cultural Organization (UNESCO) today voted to admit Palestine as a full member of the Paris-based agency. *UN NEWS*. Retrieved August 18, 2023, from https://news.un.org/en/story/2011/10/393562.

United Nations Committee on the Exercise of the Inalienable Rights of the Palestinian People (UN CEIRPP). (2014). *The origin and evolution of the Palestinian problem Part V (1989–2000)*. New York: United Nations, 2014.

United Nations Conference on Trade and Development (UNCTAD). (1981). Resolution *109 (V)*. Assistance to the Palestinian People (7 May–3 June 1979) TD/L.162 in *Proceedings of the United Nations Conference on Trade and Development: 5th session, Manila, 7 May–3 June 1979, Volume I: Report and annexes,* New York: United Nations, TD/269 (vol. 1), p. 210. Retrieved March 14, 2020, from https://unctad.org/system/files/official-document/td269vol1_en.pdf.

United Nations Conference on Trade and Development (UNCTAD). (1984). Resolution*146(VI)*. Assistance to the Palestinian people in *Proceedings of the United Nations Conference on Trade and Development: 6th session, Belgrade, 6 June–2 July 1983, Volume 1: Report and annexes,* TD/326 (vol. 1), p. 34. Retrieved April 16, 2020, from https://unctad.org/en/pages/gds/Assistance%20to%20the%20Palestinian%20People/CONF%2D%2DRES%2D%2D146-(VI).aspx-.

United Nations Conference on Trade and Development (UNCTAD). (2018). *Mandate of UNCTAD's Assistance to the Palestinian People mandates (2000–2018)*. Geneva: United Nations Conference on Trade and Development. Retrieved August 21, 2023, from https://unctad.org/topic/palestinian-people/APPU-Mandate.

United Nations Conference on Trade and Development (UNCTAD). (2020, August 5). *Report on UNCTAD assistance to the Palestinian people: Developments in the economy of the Occupied Palestinian Territory,* TD/B/67/5. Retrieved August 21, 2023, from https://documents-dds-ny.un.org/doc/UNDOC/GEN/G20/201/92/PDF/G2020192.pdf?OpenElement.

United Nations Department of Economic and Social Affairs (UN DESA). (2023). *Statistics Division–National Accounts Main Aggregates Database. UNCTAD secretariat estimates.* Retrieved August 7 and 26, 2023, from https://unstats.un.org/unsd/.

United Nations Department of Public Information (UN DPI) and United Nations Secretary-General Boutros-Ghali, B. (1996, December). *The United Nations and The Independence of Eritrea,* Blue Books Series volume XII [ST/] DPI/1850, United Nations: New York, Department of Public Information.

United Nations Economic and Social Council (UN ECOSOC). (1989, July 26). *Resolution 1989/96. Assistance to the Palestinian people*, E/RES/1989/96. Retrieved July 7, 2023, from https://documents-dds-ny.un.org/doc/UNDOC/GEN/NL3/593/85/PDF/NL359385.pdf?OpenElement.

United Nations Economic and Social Council (UN ECOSOC). (1990, July 26). *Resolution 1990/56.* Assistance to the Palestinian People, E/RES/1990/56. Retrieved July 7, 2023, from https://documents-dds-ny.un.org/doc/RESOLUTION/GEN/NR0/693/42/IMG/NR069342.pdf?OpenElement.

United Nations Economic and Social Council (UN ECOSOC). (1991, July 26). *Resolution 1991/69. Assistance to the Palestinian people*, E/RES/1991/69. Retrieved July 7, 2023, from https://documents-dds-ny.un.org/doc/RESOLUTION/GEN/NR0/721/38/IMG/NR072138.pdf?OpenElement.

United Nations Economic and Social Council (UN ECOSOC). (1992, July 31). Resolution *1992/58. Assistance to the Palestinian people*, E/RES/1992/58. Retrieved July 7, 2023, from https://documents-dds-ny.un.org/doc/RESOLUTION/GEN/NR0/015/64/IMG/NR001564.pdf?OpenElement.

United Nations Economic and Social Council (UN ECOSOC). (1993, July 30). *Resolution 1993/78. Assistance to the Palestinian people,* E/RES/1993/78. Retrieved July 7, 2023, from https://documents-dds-ny.un.org/doc/RESOLUTION/GEN/NR0/725/56/IMG/NR072556.pdf?OpenElement.

United Nations Economic and Social Council (UN ECOSOC). (1994, July 27). *Resolution 1994/29. Assistance to the Palestinian people,* E/RES/1994/29. Retrieved July 7, 2023, from https://www.un.org/unispal/document/auto-insert-188012/.

United Nations Educational Scientific and Cultural Organization (UNESCO). (2011, October 31). Palestine Admitted to UNESCO. *UNESCO TV AUD-DIT/ISS/ARC/0773.* Retrieved August 18, 2023, from https://www.unesco.org/archives/multimedia/document-2168?TSPD_101_R0=080713870fab20004c565fe65a954244d94167d06b0caa59f4409b80d980985a33da651e-a9e5352d08d0ed4e1b143000181466003 0d64eccac343caa30ae930ccfbaf-c45080aa09c9233a94647499e652201865a4637370a7951c07288582ad7.

United Nations General Assembly (UNGA). (1947, November 29). Resolution *181 (II). Future government of Palestine-Plan of partition with Economic Union*, GA RES/181(II). Retrieved April 5, 2020, from https://documents-ddsny.un.org/doc/RESOLUTION/GEN/NR0/038/88/PDF/NR003888.pdf?OpenElement; https://www.un.org/unispal/document/auto-insert-185393/.

United Nations General Assembly (UNGA). (1948, November 27). Resolution *194 (III). Palestine—Progress Report of the Unite Nations Mediator*, GA RES 194 (III). Retrieved April 17, 2020, from https://documents-dds-ny.un.org/doc/RESOLUTION/GEN/NR0/043/65/PDF/NR004365.pdf?OpenElement.

United Nations General Assembly (UNGA). (1949, December 8). Resolution *302(IV). Assistance to Palestine refugees*, GA RES/302(IV). Retrieved April 14, 2020, from https://documents-dds-ny.un.org/doc/RESOLUTION/GEN/NR0/051/39/PDF/NR005139.pdf?OpenElement.

United Nations General Assembly (UNGA). (1950, November 3). *Resolution 377 (V) Uniting for Peace*, GA RES/377(V). Retrieved July 7, 2023, from https://documents-dds-ny.un.org/doc/RESOLUTION/GEN/NR0/059/75/PDF/NR005975.pdf?OpenElement.

United Nations General Assembly (UNGA). (1974a, November 22). *Resolution 3236(XXIX). Question of Palestine,* GA RES/ 3236(XXIX). Retrieved August 19, 2023, from https://documents-ddsny.un.org/doc/RESOLUTION/GEN/NR0/738/38/PDF/NR073838.pdf?OpenElement.

United Nations General Assembly (UNGA). (1974b, November 22). *Resolution 3237(XXIX). Observer status for the Palestine Liberation Organization,* GA RES/3237(XXIX). Retrieved August 19, 2023, from https://documents-dds-ny.un.org/doc/RESOLUTION/GEN/NR0/738/38/PDF/NR073838.p df?OpenElement.

United Nations General Assembly (UNGA). (1975, November 10). *Resolution 3376(XXX). Question of Palestine* (1975), GA RES/3376 (XXX). Retrieved August 19, 2023, from https://documents-dds-ny.un.org/doc/RESOLUTION/GEN/NR0/ 000/89/PDF/NR000089.pdf?OpenElement (Accessed 19 August 2023).

United Nations General Assembly (UNGA). (1977, December 2). *Resolution 32/40(B). Assist in the Establishment of the Special Unit on Palestinian Rights,* A/RES/32/40(B). Retrieved December 3, 2022, from https://www.un.org/documents/ga/res/32/ares32r40.pdf.

United Nations General Assembly (UNGA). (1978, December 7). *Resolution 33/28(A-C). Palestine question/Committee on the Exercise of the Inalienable Rights of the Palestinian People (CEIRPP)/ Special Unit on Palestinian Rights (SUPR),* A/RES/33/28(A-C). Retrieved August 19, 2023, from https://www.un.org/unispal/document/auto-insert-189135/.

United Nations General Assembly (UNGA). (1988, November 18). *A/43/827.* United Nations Security Council (UNSC) *S/20278. Annex II Political Communiqué.* Retrieved August 21, 2023, from https://content.ecf.org.il/files/ M00640_PalestinianDeclarationOfIndependenceOriginalEnglish.pdf.

United Nations General Assembly (UNGA). (1989, December 22). *Resolution 44/235. Assistance to the Palestinian people,* A/RES/44/235. Retrieved August 7, 2023, from https://documents-dds-ny.un.org/doc/RESOLUTION/GEN/ NR0/549/94/IMG/NR054994.pdf?OpenElement.

United Nations General Assembly (UNGA). (1992, January 31). *Report 47/277.* United Nations Security Council (UNSC) *Report 24111. An agenda for peace: Preventive diplomacy, peacemaking and peace-keeping, Report of the Secretary-General pursuant to the statement adopted by the Summit Meeting of the Security Council on 31 January 1992,* A/47/277-S/24111. Retrieved December 20, 2020, from https://documents-ddsny.un.org/doc/UNDOC/GEN/N92/259/61/PDF/N9225961.pdf?OpenElement.

United Nations General Assembly (UNGA). (1993, March 10). *Resolution 47/170. Assistance to the Palestinian People* A/RES/47/170. Retrieved August 21, 2023, from https://documents-dds-ny.un.org/doc/UNDOC/GEN / N93/149/05/IMG/N9314905.pdf?OpenElement.

United Nations General Assembly (UNGA). (1994, March 15). *Resolution 48/213. Assistance to the Palestinian people*, A/RES/48/213. Retrieved August 21, 2023, from https://documents-dds-ny.un.org/doc/UNDOC/GEN/N94/ 134/34/PDF/N9413434.pdf?OpenElement.

United Nations General Assembly (UNGA). (1998, June 23). *Report 53/153.* United Nations Economic and Social Council (UN ECOSOC) (1998) *Report 1998/75. Assistance to the Palestinian people Report of the Secretary-General,* A/53/153, E/1998/75. Retrieved June 7, 2023, from https://documents-dds-ny.un.org/doc/UNDOC/GEN/N98/190/03/PDF /N9819003.pdf?OpenElement.

United Nations General Assembly (UNGA). (2000a, January 20). *Resolution 54/39. Committee on the Exercise of the Inalienable Rights of the Palestinian People* A/RES/54/39. Retrieved July 7, 2022, from https://documents-dds-ny.un.org/doc/UNDOC/GEN/N00/236/10/PDF/N0023610.pdf?OpenElement.

United Nations General Assembly (UNGA). (2000b, January 21). *Resolution 54/40. Division of the Palestinian Rights of the Secretariat* A/RES/54/40. Retrieved August 21, 2023, from https://documents-dds-ny.un.org/doc/UNDOC /GEN/N00/236/16/PDF/N0023616.pdf?OpenElement.

United Nations General Assembly (UNGA). (2000c, July 24). *Report 53/153.* United Nations Economic and Social Council (UN ECOSOC) (2000) *Report 1998/75. Assistance to the Palestinian people Report of the Secretary-General,* A/55/137, E/2000/95 para. 10. Retrieved July 7, 2023, from https://documents-dds-ny.un.org/doc/UNDOC/GEN/N00/547/61/PDF / N0054761.pdf?OpenElement.

United Nations General Assembly (UNGA). (2012a, December 4). *Resolution 67/19. Status of Palestine in the United Nations.* Retrieved July 7, 2023, from https://documents-dds-ny.un.org/doc/UNDOC/GEN/N12/479/74/PDF /N1247974.pdf?OpenElement.

United Nations General Assembly (UNGA). (2012b, November 29). *Press Release 11317.* General Assembly Votes overwhelmingly to Accord Palestine 'Non-Member Observer State' Status in United Nations, GA/11317 Plenary. Retrieved July 7, 2023, from https://press.un.org/en/2012/ ga11317.doc.htm.

United Nations General Assembly (UNGA). (2014, November 25). *Resolution 69/20. Committee on the Exercise of the Inalienable Rights of the Palestinian People*, A/RES/69/20. Retrieved August 21, 2023, from https://documents-dds-ny.un.org/doc/UNDOC/GEN/N14/652/23/PDF /N1465223.pdf?OpenElement.

United Nations General Assembly (UNGA). (2015a, October 21). *Resolution 70/1. Transforming our world: The 2030 agenda for sustainable development*, A/RES/70/1. Retrieved January 11, 2023, from https://documents-dds-ny.un.org/doc/UNDOC/GEN/N15/291/89/PDF/N1529189.pdf?OpenElement.

United Nations General Assembly (UNGA). (2015b, November 24). *Resolution 70/12. Committee on the exercise of the inalienable rights of the Palestinian People*, A/RES/70/12. Retrieved August 21, 2023, from https://documents-dds-ny.un.org/doc/UNDOC/GEN/N15/389/97/PDF /N1538997.pdf?OpenElement.

United Nations General Assembly (UNGA). (2016, November 30). *Resolution 71/20. Committee on the exercise of the inalienable rights of the Palestinian People: Resolution*, A/RES/71/20. Retrieved August 21, 2023, from https://documents-dds-ny.un.org/doc/UNDOC/GEN/N16/408/29/PDF / N1640829.pdf?OpenElement.

United Nations General Assembly (UNGA). (2017, November 30). *Resolution 72/13. Committee on the exercise of the inalienable rights of the Palestinian People: Resolution*, A/RES/72/13. Retrieved August 21, 2023, from https://documents-dds-ny.un.org/doc/UNDOC/GEN/N17/406/38/PDF / N1740638.pdf?OpenElement.

United Nations General Assembly (UNGA). (2018, November 30). *Resolution 73/18. Committee on the exercise of the inalienable rights of the Palestinian people: Resolution*, A/RES/73/18. Retrieved August 21, 2023, from https://documents-dds-ny.un.org/doc/UNDOC/GEN/N18/409/32/PDF / N1840932.pdf?OpenElement.

United Nations General Assembly (UNGA). (2019). *Resolution 73/L.3. Chair of the Group of 77 for 2019*, A/73/L.5 (10 October 2018). Retrieved August 18, 2023, from https://documents-dds-ny.un.org/doc/UNDOC/LTD/N18/316/10/PDF /N1831610.pdf?OpenElement.

United Nations General Assembly (UNGA). (2022, December 12). *Resolution 77/123. Assistance to Palestine refugees*, A/RES/77/123. Retrieved August 7, 2023, from https://documents-dds-ny.un.org/doc/UNDOC/ GEN/N22/748/25/PDF/N2274825.pdf?OpenElement.

United Nations General Assembly (UNGA) FOURTH COMMITTEE. (2018, November 9). *SPD/684.* Palestine Refugee Agency Faces Greatest Financial Crisis in its history following 2018 Funding Cuts, Commissioner-General tells Fourth Committee, GA/SPD/684. Retrieved April 15, 2020, from https://press.un.org/en/2018/gaspd684.doc.htm.

United Nations Human Rights Council (UNHCR). (2016, March 24). *Resolution 31/36. Israeli settlements in the occupied Palestinian territory, including East Jerusalem, and in the occupied Syrian Golan*, A/HRC/RES/31/36. Retrieved May 8, 2021, from https://documents-dds-ny.un.org/doc/ UNDOC/GEN/G16/082/57/PDF/G1608257.pdf?OpenElement.

United Nations Human Rights Council (UNHCR). (2021, May 26). *Resolution S-30/L.1.Ensuring respect for international humanitarian law and international human rights law*, A/HRC/S-30/L.1. Retrieved May 31, 2021, from https://documents-dds-ny.un.org/doc/UNDOC/LTD/ G21/112/74/PDF/G2111274.pdf?OpenElement.

United Nations Security Council (UNSC). (1967, November 22). *Resolution 242. Situation in the Middle East,* S/RES/242. Retrieved May 7, 2020, from https://documents-ddsny.un.org/doc/RESOLUTION/GEN/NR0/240/94 /PDF/NR024094.pdf?OpenElement.

United Nations Security Council (UNSC). (1973, October 22). *Resolution 338. Ceasefire in the Middle East,* S/RES/338. Retrieved May 7, 2020, from https://documents-dds-ny.un.org/doc/RESOLUTION/GEN/NR0/288/65 /PDF/NR028865.pdf?OpenElement.

United Nations Security Council (UNSC). (1980a, August 20). *Resolution 478.* S/RES/478. Retrieved August 19, 2023, from https://documents-dds-ny.un.org/doc/RESOLUTION/GEN/NR0/399/71/PDF/NR039971.pdf?OpenElement.

United Nations Security Council (UNSC). (1980b, March 1). *Resolution 465.* S/RES/465. Retrieved August 18, 2023, from https://documents-dds-ny.un.org/doc/RESOLUTION/GEN/NR0/399/58/PDF/NR039958.pdf?OpenElement.

United Nations Security Council (UNSC). (2002, March 12). *Resolution 1397.* S/RES/1397. Retrieved August 20, 2023, from https://documents-dds-ny.un.org/doc/UNDOC/GEN/N02/283/59/PDF/N0228359.pdf?OpenElement.

United Nations Security Council (UNSC). (2003a, May 7). *Resolution 2003/529. A performance-based road map to a permanent two-state solution to the Israeli-Palestinian conflict,* S/RES/2003/529. Retrieved July 23, 2023, from https://documents-dds-ny.un.org/doc/UNDOC/GEN/N03/348/79/IMG /N0334879.pdf?OpenElement.

United Nations Security Council (UNSC). (2003b, November 19). *Resolution 1515.* S/RES/1515. Retrieved July 7, 2023, from https://documents-dds-ny.un.org/doc/UNDOC/GEN/N03/621/85/PDF/N0362185.pdf?OpenElement.

United Nations Security Council (UNSC). (2016, December 23). *Resolution 2334.* S/RES/2334. Retrieved August 18, 2023, from https://www.un.org/webcast/pdfs/SRES2334-2016.pdf.

United States Department of State. (2001). Archive—*The Middle East/North Africa Economic Summits and Conferences.* Retrieved August 8, 2020, from https://19972001.state.gov/regions/nea/fs_mena_econ_summ_971107.html.

UNSCO. (2023a). *UNSCO Reports.* Retrieved August 5, 2020, from https://unsco.unmissions.org/ahlc-socioeconomic-reports?page=1.

UNSCO. (2023b). *The Office of the United Nations Special Coordinator for the Middle East Peace Process–About.* Retrieved August 5, 2020, from https://unsco.unmissions.org/ahlc-socioeconomic-reports?page=1.

Uvin, P. (2002). The development/peacebuilding nexus: A typology and history of changing paradigms. *Journal of Peacebuilding & Development, 1*(1), 5–24.

Vallacher, R. R., Coleman, P. T., Nowak, A., & Bui-Wrzosinska, L. (2011). Rethinking intractable conflict: The perspective of dynamical systems. In P. T. Coleman (Ed.), *Conflict, interdependence, and justice* (*The intellectual legacy of Morton Deutsch*) (pp. 65–94). Springer.

van Bergeijk, P. A. G. (1994). *Economic diplomacy, trade and commercial policy: Positive and negative sanctions in a new world order*. Edward Elgar Publishing.

van Bergeijk, P. A. G. (2009). *Economic diplomacy and the geography of international trade*. Edward Elgar Publishing.

van Bergeijk, P. A. G. (2015). Visible and invisible walls: World trade patterns and the end of the Cold War. *Acta Oeconomica, 65*(2), 231–247.

van Bergeijk, P. A. G. (2019). *Deglobalization 2.0: Trade and openness during the great depression and the great recession*. Edward Elgar Publishing.

van Bergeijk, P. A. G., & Brakman, S. (2010). Introduction: The comeback of the gravity model. In P. A. G. van Bergeijk & S. Brakman (Eds.), *The gravity model in international trade: Advances and applications* (pp. 1–26). Cambridge University Press.

van Bergeijk, P. A. G., & Oldersma, H. (1990). Détente, market-oriented reform and German Unification: Potential consequences for the World Trade System. *Kyklos, 43*(4), 599–609.

Waage, H. H. (2000). Norwegians? Who needs Norwegians?: Explaining the Oslo back channel: Norway's political past in the Middle East. *Royal Norwegian Ministry of Foreign Affairs, 9*.

Waage, H. H. (2002). Explaining the Oslo backchannel: Norway's political past in the Middle East. *The Middle East Journal, 56*(4), 597–615.

Waage, H. H. (2005). Norway's role in the Middle East peace talks: Between a strong state and a weak belligerent. *Journal of Palestine Studies, 34*(4), 6–24.

Waage, H. H. (2007). The 'Minnow' and the 'Whale': Norway and the United States in the peace process in the Middle East. *British Journal of Middle Eastern Studies, 34*(2), 157–176.

Waage, H. H. (2012). Proactive peace diplomacy: Jan Egeland. In M. Fixdal (Ed.), *Ways out of war* (pp. 91–116). Palgrave Macmillan US.

Waage, H. H. (2016). Champions of peace? Tools in whose hands? Norwegians and peace brokering in the Middle East. In P. Bauck & M. Omer (Eds.), *The Oslo Accords 1993–2013: A critical assessment* (pp. 13–29). The American University in Cairo Press.

Wacziarg, R., & Welch, K. H. (2008). Trade liberalization and growth: New evidence. *The World Bank Economic Review, 22*(2), 187–231.

Wanis-St, J. A. (2006). Back-channel negotiation: International bargaining in the shadows. *Negotiation Journal, 22*(2), 119–144.

Wanis-St, J. A. (2011). *Back channel negotiation: Secrecy in the Middle East peace process*. Syracuse University Press.

Watkins, M., & Lundberg, K. (1998). Getting to the table in Oslo: Driving forces and channel factors. *Negotiation Journal, 14*, 115–135.
Watson, G. R. (2000). *The Oslo Accords: International law and the Israeli-Palestinian peace agreements.* Oxford University Press.
Weede, E. (2005). *Balance of power, globalization and the capitalist peace.* Liberal-Verlag Berlin.
Weede, E. (2011). 14 The capitalist peace. In C. J. Coyne & R. L. Matehrs (Eds.), *The handbook on the political economy of war* (pp. 269–274). Edward Elgar Publishing Limited.
Weinberger, P. E. (2006). *Co-opting the PLO: A critical reconstruction of the Oslo Accords, 1993–1995.* Lexington Books.
Williams, M. C. (2001). The discipline of the democratic peace: Kant, liberalism and the social construction of security communities. *European Journal of International Relations, 7*(4), 525–553.
World Bank Group. (2020, June). *Economic monitoring report to the Ad Hoc Liaison Committee.*
World Bank Group and United Nations. (2018). *Pathways for peace inclusive approaches to preventing violent conflict.* International Bank for Reconstruction and Development.
Ya'alon, M. (2017). How to build Middle East peace: Why bottom-up is better than top-down. *Foreign Affairs, 96*, 73–84.
Yaari, M. (2018, July). Israel and Saudi Arabia: On the way to normalization. *Israel's relations with Arab countries: The unfulfilled potential.* MITVIM the Israeli institute for Regional Foreign Policies.
Zartman, I. W. (1995). *Elusive peace: Negotiating an end to civil wars.* Brookings Institution Press.

Index[1]

[1] Note: Page numbers followed by 'n' refer to notes.

L. Lahar, *The Economic Diplomacy of Peace in the Middle East*, https://doi.org/10.1007/978-3-031-93991-4

Kolibri 360 GmbH
Ferdinand-Jühlke-Straße 7
99095 Erfurt, Deutschland
produktsicherheit@kolibri360.de